Science and Ireland – Value for Society

Science and Irish Culture

Volume 2

Royal Dublin Society
Science and Irish Culture Series

Volume 1
Why the History of Science Matters in Ireland

Edited by David Attis & Charles Mollan
ISBN 0 86027 047 5
2004, pp. xvii + 174

Volume 2
Science and Ireland – Value for Society

A volume to acknowledge the return to Dublin
of the British Association for the Advancement of Science
in September 2005
Edited Charles Mollan
ISBN 0 86027 050 5
2005, pp. xxx + 294

Science and Ireland – Value for Society

Science and Irish Culture
Volume 2

A volume to acknowledge the return to Dublin of the British Association for the Advancement of Science in September 2005

Editor

Charles Mollan

RDS Editorial Sub-Committee
Dr William Davis
Dr Charles Mollan
Dr Christopher Moriarty
Professor Fionn Murtagh
Professor Adrian Phillips

Dedication

This volume is dedicated to the memory of Dr Arthur Hughes (1908–2000), and his son-in-law, Professor Adrian Phillips (1936–2003).

Acknowledgement

The Royal Dublin Society acknowledges, with thanks, the setting up by the family of Dr Hughes of the Arthur Hughes Memorial Fund, which has funded the publication of this volume.

Contact details:

Development Executive
Committee of Science and Technology
Ballsbridge
Dublin 4
Ireland
Telephone +353-1-668-0866
Website: www.rds.ie

2005

ISBN 0 86027 050 5

Contents

Authors

Abbreviations etc.

BA(AS) – British Association (for the Advancement of Science)
CalTech – California Institute of Technology
DMMC – Dublin Molecular Medicine Centre
EMBO – European Molecular Biology Organisation
Forfás – The Statutory National Policy and Advisory Board for Enterprise, Trade, Science, Technology and Innovation
FTCD – Fellow of Trinity College Dublin
HEA – Higher Education Authority
HRB – Health Research Board
ICSTI – Irish Council for Science, Technology and Innovation
IIRS – Institute for Industrial Research and Standards
MIT – Massachusetts Institute of Technology
MRIA – Member of the Royal Irish Academy
NIH – National Institutes of Health (USA)
NUI – National University of Ireland
PRTLI – Programme for Research in Third Level Institutions
RDS – Royal Dublin Society
SCI – Science Foundation Ireland
TCD – Trinity College Dublin
UCC – University College Cork
UCD – University College Dublin

Liam Downey is a graduate of UCC, with a PhD from Reading University in England, and a DSc and honorary LLD from NUI. His former Directorships include: The National Institute for Physical Planning and Construction Research (1979–1982); The National Agricultural Advisory and Training Organisation (1983–1988); and Teagasc, The Agriculture and Food Development Authority (1994–2001). He is Honorary Professor in Agriculture and Food Science at UCD, an Honorary Professor of Science at NUI Maynooth, and a Fellow of the Department of Archaeology, UCD.

Edward P. (Ted) Farrell is Associate Professor of Forest Soils, Head of the Department of Environmental Resource Management and Director of the Forest Ecosystem Research Group, Faculty of Agri-Food and the Environment, UCD. He has wide experience in teaching and research and has been involved in a large number of collaborative research projects and committees in Ireland and abroad. He was, for six years, Editor-in-Chief of *Forest Ecology and Management*, a leading international forestry journal.

John Feehan is a Senior Lecturer in the Department of Environmental Resource Management at UCD. He is well known for his television work on the natural and cultural heritage of the Irish landscape, for which he received a Jacobs Television Award. Dr Feehan has researched and written extensively on many facets of Ireland's environmental heritage and history. His recently-published *Farming in Ireland: History, Heritage and Environment* has been widely acclaimed.

Helen Haste is Chair of the BA Council and has been a BA Executive Vice-President since 2002. She is Professor of Psychology at the University of Bath, and is also a Visiting Professor at Harvard Graduate School of Education. Her research and numerous publications (both academic and popular) include the field of science and society, particularly images and metaphors of science and scientists, and their relationship to cultural values and to young people's beliefs about science. She also researches and writes on moral values and citizenship, and she has an interest in gender issues in all these fields. She is currently working on a book on citizenship education, supported by a Leverhulme Trust fellowship. She is a Fellow of the British Psychological Society, and of the Royal Society of Arts. In 2002, she was President of the International Society of Political Psychology. She lectures extensively to both academic and lay audiences (including at the Royal Society in 1996, and the Royal Institution in 2002) and broadcasts frequently.

Dermot Kelleher is Professor of Medicine at TCD and Scientific Co-Director of the DMMC, a joint programme of research between TCD and UCD funded by the HEA PRTLI. He has been the holder of grants from the NIH, Wellcome Trust, European Union, Enterprise Ireland, HRB, and HEA. He has published over 100 papers in the international literature. His research group is focussed on the role of the immune system in the immuno-pathogenesis of disease, with particular interest in the gastrointestinal tract and liver.

David McConnell, PhD (CalTech), FTCD, MRIA, Member of EMBO, is Professor of Genetics at TCD. He is on the Executive Board of the European Federation of Biotechnology and Co-Vice-Chairman of European Action on Global Life Sciences. He was a member of ICSTI, and made a major contribution to the establishment of SFI. He has been President of the Zoological Society of Ireland, President of the Adelaide Hospital Society, Chairman of Fota Wildlife Park, and Vice-Provost of TCD. He is currently Chairman of The Irish Times Trust.

Henry McLoughlin has been involved in Irish Computing for over 30 years. He is currently lecturing in the Computer Science Department in UCD. He has founded a number of companies, most notably WBT Systems, which was one of the first companies in the world to realize the potential which the World-Wide Web offered for the delivery of education and training. His research interests include e-learning, mathematics education, and the construction of reliable software.

Charles Mollan is a graduate (BA and PhD) in Chemistry from TCD. He carried out post-doctoral research at MIT, the University of Oxford, and UCD. He was a Senior Scientific Officer at the IIRS before joining the RDS in 1976 as Science Officer, becoming Science and Arts Officer in 1987. From 1993–2003 he was editor and publisher of *The Irish Scientist Year Book*. He is author or editor of a variety of books on current Irish science and Irish science history.

Matthew Moran is Director of PharmaChemical Ireland. He graduated in Chemistry and Chemical Engineering in 1981 and also holds an MBA. He worked for over ten years in the pharmaceutical industry where he held a number of management positions both in active ingredient and dosage form manufacture. He is Director of the Irish BioIndustry Association, Member of the Industry Council of the European BioIndustry Association and of the European Chemical Industry Council. PharmaChemical Ireland represents the interests of the pharmachem sector in Ireland.

Christopher Moriarty spent forty years as a scientific officer in the fisheries service of the Irish government. He specialised in the eel, was awarded PhD for a study of the species, and published a book on the eels of the world. In the 1970s, as a senior lecturer in the University of Ibadan, Nigeria, he established the country's first course in fisheries management. Besides his scientific papers, he has published many books and articles on a wide range of heritage topics.

Fionn Murtagh holds degrees (BA, BAI, MSc) from TCD, a PhD from Université P&M Curie, Paris, and an Habilitation from Université L. Pasteur, Strasbourg. He held posts with the European Commission's Joint Research Centre, and with the Space Science Department of the European Space Agency. He is Professor of Computer Science at the University of London and is Editor-in-Chief of *The Computer Journal*. He is a MRIA, and a Fellow of the British Computer Society.

Peter Pearson is an artist and historian, author of several contemporary books about Dublin, including: *The Heart of Dublin, Decorative Dublin,* and *Between the Mountains and the Sea.*

Gordon Purvis is an environmental biologist in the UCD Faculty of Agri-Food and Environment with over twenty years experience in research and teaching. He previously worked in the School of Agriculture, University of Nottingham, and with the Agriculture Development and Advisory Service in the UK Ministry of Agriculture,

Fisheries and Food. Dr Purvis is currently co-ordinator of a major Irish biodiversity project, AG-BIOTA, and has research interests in the evaluation of European agri-environmental schemes and environmentally compatible methods of pest control.

Chris Stillman is an Emeritus Fellow of TCD, having retired as an Associate Professor of Geology in 2001. He took up a lectureship at Trinity in 1965 after working for nine years in Southern and Northern Rhodesia. At Trinity, he taught petrology, mineralogy and geochemistry, researching the Ordovician volcanic rocks of Ireland, the more recent volcanics of the Canaries and Cape Verde Islands, and the ophiolites in Cyprus and Norway. He was also Director of Trinity's Environmental Science Unit for seven years.

Don Thornhill is a graduate of UCD (BSc and PhD, Chemistry) and of TCD (MSc, Economics) and is a MRIA. A former Chairman of the HEA (1998–2005) and Secretary General of the Department of Education and Science (1993–1998), his earlier public service career was in the Revenue Commissioners and in the Departments of Finance and Foreign Affairs. His board memberships include the Digital Hub Development Agency, Forfás and SFI, and he currently chairs the Irish–US Fulbright Commission. In March 2005, Dr Thornhill was appointed Chairman of the National Competitiveness Council.

List of Illustrations

Dedication
Arthur Hughes at Work and at Home: a memoir by his children

Rosamond Phillips, Caroline Roaf, Nick Hughes

Arthur Hughes was born on 27 October 1908 in Barnet just outside London, the youngest in a family of three boys, the first child, a girl, having died as a baby. His father, a Welshman, was a barrister. His mother, who came from Cornwall, was a teacher and later London School Board inspector and author of several books, of which the most well-known is *A London Child of the Seventies*.

Although he was reared in London and lived for most of his life in Ireland, he was extremely proud of his Welsh and Cornish origins, in the slate quarries and in tin mining respectively. His father was a Welsh speaker, passionate about the language, people and countryside of Wales.

When Arthur was ten, his father died, leaving the family with little money. His mother went back to work and Arthur attended Merchant Taylors' School in London. From here, he won a scholarship to Cambridge where he achieved a double first degree in Natural Science. This was followed by a PhD and further research in colloid science in the Cavendish laboratory, made possible by a Beit Memorial Fellowship.

He joined Guinness in Dublin in 1935 as a junior brewer. For seven years during the 1940s he was associated with operations in the United States. He was appointed to the board of Guinness in 1951. Later, he spent twelve years with Guinness in London before returning in 1966 as Managing Director of the Dublin brewery, where he remained until his retirement in 1973. He was responsible for the building of the breweries in Nigeria and Malaysia, and was the first Chairman of Guinness Superlatives, which produced *The Guinness Book of Records* and many other titles.

He relished the challenges of working in a large company which gave him opportunities which, as he himself used to say, he might never have enjoyed had he remained an academic. His move from academic life may also have been motivated by his enduring interest in the link between academic research and its benefits to society. While working for Guinness, he was the honorary secretary of the British Association for the Advancement of Science (from 1965 to 1971) and was chairman of its committee planning the introduction of decimal coinage. In recognition of this work, the University of Wales made him an honorary Doctor of Law in 1971.

He enjoyed a full and active retirement, and remained involved in many of his former interests. For a number of years, he was on the Board of the Institute for Industrial Research and Standards and, from 1972 to 1983, was a member of the board of Governors of St Patrick's Hospital. An enduring interest was the Royal Dublin Society. He served on several different committees between 1977 and 1993: the Science Committee from 1977 to 1986 and again in 1992–3, the Council from 1987 to 1990, and the Library Committee from 1984 to 1990.

Our childhood was coloured by Arthur's love of experimentation. His sense of humour and inquiring mind made being his child a challenge. It was nothing unusual to spend a winter's afternoon melting lead in a ladle in front of the open fire of the living room, preparatory to pouring it into moulds (of his designing), or making fireworks for a winter birthday party – Catherine Wheels were considered his *tour de force*.

To be bored was not a concept he understood: we had been born with brains and should always be able to interest and amuse ourselves. While innocently doing nothing in particular, one could suddenly be asked some testing puzzle or conundrum (such as, 'If a herring and a half cost three ha'pence......etc.'?) However, we soon learnt to be careful about what help we asked for, especially with maths homework: Arthur would tend to glance at the problem and say: it's perfectly simple, just introduce ' x '. As we'd invariably never reached the concept required, this could end in tears. Sometimes, after assembling the huge old family telescope, he would allow us to stay up till it was quite dark, so that he could show us how to recognise the constellations. As small children we soon became familiar with the sonorous names of the stars and planets – Orion and Betelgeuse were particular favourites. He would prepare the ground with demonstrations of the workings of the solar system, using an orange and some ping pong balls, then carefully drawn diagrams on the back of an envelope.

Holiday times were usually spent in the lakes and mountains of Connemara, where he could introduce us children to his own wealth of interests. He was interested in a wide variety of subjects and had that rare capacity to switch off completely from the pressures of work and to relax. Reading aloud was a regular feature of these holiday evenings by a turf fire in various rented houses in the West. He introduced us to many of his favourite books – the classics as well as some lesser known but eccentric and hilarious authors – Lord Dunsany, Lewis Carroll, Dickens, Thurber, Damon Runyon, Sherlock Holmes, Erskine Childers and George Birmingham. He loved reading to us and provided a vivid interpretation of the characters, but could often be overcome with laughter. His reading of Uncle Remus was particularly memorable.

As a child, he had been introduced to fishing by his father. This developed into a passion, and the sight or scent of a piece of water that might contain brown trout would initiate an expedition regardless of weather or discomfort. We knew the fascination of being allowed handle his collection of fishing flies with their brightly coloured feathers, the cruel barb and their curious names: silver butcher, cockabundy, dusty miller, Connemara black. He loved the wild and remote parts of Ireland: climbing the mountains, exploring the rivers and swimming in the cold Atlantic reminded him of Wales and his grandfather's home in the slate mining valleys near Machynlleth. We mastered the art of rowing silently with only one oar so that the water was not disturbed on the side where he was casting. You daren't even slap away the swarms of midges that attacked, particularly at good fishing times. We were secretly proud of our skill as ghillies and, although killing the fish was unpleasant, no restaurant meal has ever surpassed the pleasure of a freshly caught trout cooked outdoors over an open fire.

Equally enticing were ancient monuments, disused sulphur mines, old railway tracks or anything that would bring one off the main road and be an excuse for an adventure. A ration of Crunchy bar or Bourneville chocolate was the only reward for hours of tramping over the bogs. His mother had taught him to sketch and paint with water colours and with oils. He encouraged us to do the same regardless of our lack of talent. The names of the paints in his oil set: cobalt, yellow ochre, ultramarine, crimson lake, and the smell of turpentine, are redolent of peaceful days spent outdoors taking in beautiful scenery and learning to observe. Largely self taught, he was always ready to try a new technique. In his retirement, he experimented with painting on pieces of slate and discovered how the surface of the slate could give the impression of different conditions or driving rain. When, after his death, we assembled these paintings together for the first time, we were able to appreciate him as a remarkably skilled artist.

Gardening was another deeply satisfying activity, and one shared by our mother. Their gardens were never conventional. He experimented endlessly with vegetables, shrubs and flowers: sowing the contents taken from the turn ups of his trousers to see what would emerge; growing sweetcorn before this was commonplace; grafting different varieties of apple onto an old Bramley (fourteen varieties on one tree no less!). We were assured as children that you could cook an egg in the heat generated in the compost heap and he proved it with glee. Rare and exotic plants from his various travels would appear in the greenhouse, the seeds or roots often having been smuggled into the country in his wash bag.

He had enormous charm and graciousness, coupled with that rare capacity to relate to everyone he met, regardless of differences in age or background. We were used to it, but his study was a wonder for any visiting child, crowded as it was with books, tools, seed packets, indoor plants and curiosities of every description. 'Have you seen the smallest tube in the world?' he would ask (this was a present from Guinness Superlatives). 'Do you know what a Klein bottle is?' (a wonder whose outer surface mysteriously became its inner surface as your finger traced around the glass). 'See what happens when you touch my sensitive plant' (the leaves would curl up like magic).

He had a wonderful combination of good humour, energy, intellectual curiosity and sense of fun. Above all, these memories typify his profoundly scientific approach to life: always interested, alert to possibilities, optimistic, positive, looking for the evidence and never making assumptions.

One cannot remember him apart from Hilary, our mother, and his most beloved wife for over sixty years. Theirs was a particularly close and happy relationship, remarked on by all who knew them, and her constant support and encouragement facilitated all his achievements both at work and at home.

He died aged 92, on 24 November 2000, just a few months after our mother.

Dedication
Professor W.E.A. Phillips (Adrian): an appreciation

Chris Stillman

Adrian Phillips had a truly rounded and three-dimensional personality; at various times a scientist, an entrepreneur, an idealist and passionate advocate of local sustainability. But he was at all times thoughtful, caring and compassionate. I and many others have had cause to bless him for his unsparing help in times of difficulty.

Adrian spent his working life as a lecturer and professor in the Geology Department of Trinity College, but he was not simply a remote academic working within the university's ivory towers. In fact he was known to many across the length and breadth of Ireland as a living advertisement for the outreach of academia into the real world; a link between local concerns with promoting sustainable development, with the protection of our natural environment, and with the scholastic scientific world of the Earth Sciences. And this mix was what, in his later years, he saw his life work as heading towards; his devotion to Ireland's natural heritage which was sparked off so many years ago when he undertook the field work for his doctoral thesis on the geology of Clare Island. His career spanned over four decades, and progressively evolved from purely scientific and academic research to a close involvement with regional developmental issues, as he felt more and more drawn to using his expertise for the benefit of the people of Ireland. Throughout all, he was supported and encouraged by his wife, Rosamond, and their household was frequently enlarged by Adrian's impecunious graduate research students whom Rosamond took under her wing and who found a temporary home with the family.

Adrian was born into an extended family whose various branches had 200 years of involvement with Trinity College; the Stokes, Jellett, Fitzgerald, Mahaffy and Crookshank families who contributed to medicine, physics, arts, and the United Irishmen in the eighteenth, and southern unionism in the early twentieth centuries. This was a network of families interconnected across the land, a network which had contributed much to the heritage of modern Ireland, and he believed he should continue that tradition. He paid in the coin which he was best able to offer – giving his time and expertise to the development of natural resources for the use of the people in rural Ireland.

Adrian took his first degree in Geology at Cambridge, then in 1959 came to Trinity College Dublin to undertake postgraduate research on the geology of Clare Island. In 1961, he took up part-time teaching of Geology to Engineers and, in 1963, became a Junior Lecturer in the Geology Department, teaching almost all aspects of geology whilst working towards his PhD, which was completed in 1966. On receiving his doctorate, he was elevated to the rank of a full-time Lecturer. In those days, the Department boasted only one professor and three lecturers, and thus his teaching load was considerable. In 1972, he was awarded a Fellowship and, in 1982, promoted to Associate Professor. Throughout this time, he persisted with his research, and many students will recall with pleasure the field trips he led to the west of Ireland, where he was able to pass on the advances his research was discovering and, even more valuably, his enthusiasm for geology and the countryside. To the last, he retained this enthusiasm, not to mention the ability to walk uphill faster than any of his companions – students or professionals – and to clamber down cliffs which all others believed impassable.

In his early days as a research scientist, he developed an intense interest in the structural geology of Ireland, which led him to the recognition of a "Iapetus Suture" running across the breadth of Ireland and northern Britain, a junction between rocks which were originally located on either side of the Iapetus Ocean, a kind of proto-Atlantic which existed around 500 million years ago. The significance of this discovery is shown by the fact that it remains fundamental to geological interpretation of the Caledonides, to this day. Adrian was, at this time, perhaps at the peak of his achievement as a structural geologist, regarded by many as at the forefront of this science.

However his mind was already turning to other things. As his work progressed, Adrian moved away from the classical approach to geology as he became more and more aware of the value of remote sensing, satellite imagery and multidata (geophysical, geochemical and geological) correlation. He quickly saw its application to the identification and mapping of the Earth's surface features and geological structures, and its potential for mineral exploration. Software for image processing and Geographical Information Systems (GIS) had to be written, as these technologies had scarcely emerged internationally. By 1980, he had involved staff and postgraduates in the Departments of Computer Science and Statistics, together with staff from the

Geology Department at Queen's University Belfast, and succeeded in obtaining European Union funds to develop these ideas.

The Irish Government remained reluctant to provide finance for the research and so, in 1983, he established the first Irish university Campus Company, ERA (Environmental Resources Analysis), to test in the 'real world' the methods his group were developing. The company was to advance the use of remote sensing and multidata correlation methods as an aid to the development of mineral, hydrocarbon and groundwater resources, and also as an aid to environmental management.

For the next nine years, Adrian occupied a significant role in the Company. During these years, the company's expertise was called upon in many memorable projects undertaken around the world, including hydrological support for the development of Ballygowan spring water, groundwater resources in the Sahel, the development of mineral resources in North and Central America and Australia, and hydrocarbon resources in Africa and Japan. In 1985, with the increased expertise in the use of satellite imagery, a second company called Maptec was set up to market consumer products of such imagery and, in 1989, the two companies were merged to form the ERA-Maptec company which flourishes to this day.

As if this were not enough, in 1989 Adrian established within Trinity College the Natural Resources Development Centre (NRDC) as the University's first on-campus research centre; its role – to promote the use of GIS, remote sensing and techniques of innovation and environmental management. The Centre focused on introducing GIS as a research and development tool in Ireland, with an emphasis on assisting the Environmental Protection Agency and research organisations dealing with fisheries, forestry, and rural development.

Whilst Adrian was the driving force in identifying, securing funding, and directing these socially oriented projects, he did not abandon his own geological research. By the 1990s, he had become very interested in the geological evolution of Ireland and its landscape during the last 65 million years. This research opened up new dimensions, which included the potential for the development of local geothermal energy and of deep uncontaminated ground water resources. He even found the time to offer his geological expertise to the archaeologists, in the search for the stone used in the construction of Neolithic passage graves at Bru na Boinne.

Up to and beyond his retirement, despite his health, he was supervising post-graduate students working on these problems, and though his wisdom and boundless energy are sorely missed, his students' continuing work is part of his legacy to the scientific knowledge of this land.

Foreword

Helen Haste

It is a very great pleasure to be in Dublin for the 2005 Festival of Science. It is 48 years since the last visit of the British Association for the Advancement of Science (The BA) to the city in 1957, the only one since Ireland's independence. This is in fact the twelfth occasion that we have been in Ireland, the first was only four years after the BA was founded in 1831. Our return to Dublin is long due and we are delighted to be here.

It is a particularly exciting time also because of Ireland's dramatic economic and cultural resurgence, and the opportunities that this has created for investment in many areas of science and technology. Visiting Ireland in recent years has been an exhilarating experience. Everywhere one goes there are signs not only of individual and corporate affluence, but of vitality and vigour. The well-known romantic air of Ireland is now also permeated with a new energy and purpose.

Ireland is a country that has given the world a huge amount, partly because past economic constraints have led to extensive emigration and the dispersion of Irish talent throughout the world – to the great benefit of those who received it. As Charles Mollan notes in this excellent volume, the resurgence of Ireland's economy has meant that those who leave to train abroad can return and bring back their expertise to a vibrant culture, and those who are trained here in the many excellent educational institutions of very longstanding, can flourish on home territory.

The volume that Charles Mollan and his team have put together, with the very generous support of the family of Arthur Hughes and of the Royal Dublin Society, gives us a vivid picture of science and technology and their place in Irish culture, society and economy today. It is a very positive picture, with great indications for the future. The eminent contributors of chapters in the various fields of science show us how Ireland is very much a major international player in the world of innovation and discovery.

But the picture that this volume gives us is also one of *continuity*. Charles Mollan's own chapter on the history of Irish science and Irish scientists shows us an Ireland with many centuries – indeed millennia – of a powerful and active science community. And the diaspora of Irish scientists has been enormously influential. There have been a striking number of leading scientists working in England and in Scotland from an Irish background, and many have been senior and prominent figures in the institutions of science such as the Royal Society and the Royal Institution in London. The BA has also been blessed with many Irish luminaries. The contribution of Irish thought and intellect to the Anglophone world – of which Britain and Ireland are only a fraction – is incalculably large; Charles Mollan could only address a small part of it even in his comprehensive history.

The agenda of the BA has always been to bring current scientific developments to the wider public. 'Science' in our title includes social science and engineering as well as the natural – physical and biological – sciences. In the early years it was in the nature of scientific development that announcements of new developments could be made first at a BA meeting, and there are notable examples where this happened – the first use of 'dinosaur' for example was by Richard Owen at the 1841 meeting.

Nowadays, the complexity of modern science, and the professional procedures required for communicating new work through peer review, have meant a subtle shift in the BA's role. Our current mission is to be *the* forum which both brings exciting new scientific developments to the public, and provides the opportunity for engagement and dialogue between the public and the science community. Science is not something just to be 'handed down' by experts to a lay audience; it is to be engaged with in a context of policy and implications. The chapters in this stimulating volume frequently demonstrate the interaction between scientific and technological developments, and their impact on the society and environment of Ireland.

The importance of effective communication of science has been recognised by many, but particularly by those who become involved with the BA. Charles Mollan cites two forceful Irish scientists on the subject. The first is John Tyndall, a dramatic character who was one of the first to use the term 'physics' in its modern sense. He spent 34 years (from 1853 on) as Professor of Natural Philosophy at the Royal Institution. He was President of the BA at its meeting in Belfast on 1874. His biographer Burchfield described Tyndall as a brilliant lecturer, 'an evangelist for the cause of science' whose goal was 'not merely to entertain or even instruct his audience, but to awaken them to the beauty and importance of science' (*see page 60*).

A more recent figure is John Synge, who died only ten years ago, and who was a fervent advocate of wider public awareness of science. He contrasted the skill and willingness of artists to communicate their expertise to a lay audience, with the reluctance of scientists to do so. In his writings for the wider public, Mollan tells us (*page 70*), 'Synge sought to lead them "into domains where science and commonsense meet" and suggested that we should "watch the spectacle of science with less of the reverence appropriate to a church and more of the freedom of spirit appropriate to a theatre"'.

While effective communication may not guarantee the kind of dialogue between the public and the science community that today we would advocate, it is most surely a prerequisite for the engagement that underpins dialogue. The traditions of communicating enthusiasm that we find in the writings of these passionate Irish scientists are alive and well in today's Festival, and will be most evident in the Dublin meeting.

I wish you all, scientists and laypersons alike, an enjoyable and stimulating Festival week in the intellectual climate that this volume so richly presents – in 'Dublin's fair city' where we, the BA, have again been made most welcome guests.

Introduction

Charles Mollan

Historic occasions

In their book *Victorian Science*[1], George Basalla and his co-editors highlight two meetings of the British Association for the Advancement of Science (BAAS) which received exceptional public attention.

The first of these was the meeting at Oxford in 1860, in which Thomas Henry Huxley (1825–1895), 'Darwin's bulldog', and Bishop Samuel Wilberforce (1805–1873) debated *The Origin of Species* by Charles Darwin (1809–1882). The book had been published the previous year. In response to a query from the Bishop as to whether Huxley traced his descent from the apes through his mother or father, Huxley replied[2]:

> If I would rather have a miserable ape for a grandfather or a man highly endowed by nature and possessed of great means and influence, and yet who employs those faculties for the mere purpose of introducing ridicule into a grave scientific discussion – I unhesitatingly affirm my preference for the ape.

The second was the meeting at Belfast in 1874. The President in that year was Co. Carlow born John Tyndall (1820–1893), Professor of Natural Philosophy at the Royal Institution in London. In his Presidential address, he stated[3] (*see also page 59*):

> The impregnable position of science may be described in a few words. We claim, and we shall wrest, from theology the entire domain of cosmological theory. All schemes and systems which thus infringe upon the domain of science must, in so far as they do this, submit to its control, and relinquish all thought of controlling it. Acting otherwise proved disastrous in the past, and it is simply fatuous to-day.

---

[1] George Basalla, William Coleman & Robert H. Kargon (Eds), *Victorian Science – A Self-Portrait from the Presidential Addresses to the British Association for the Advancement of Science* (New York: Anchor Books, 1970) pp. 436-437.

[2] Quoted in Janet Browne, *Charles Darwin, The Power of Place* (London: Jonathan Cape, 2002), p. 122. Other writers give slightly different versions, but the key message is the same in all.

[3] John Tyndall, 'Presidential Address' in the *Report of the Forty-Fourth Meeting of the British Association for the Advancement of Science; Held at Belfast in August 1874* (London: John Murray, 1875), p. xcv.

The First 'Handbook'

A less remembered aspect of the 1874 Belfast Meeting was the publication 'by Members of the Belfast Naturalists' Field Club' of a book entitled *Guide to Belfast and the Adjacent Counties*[4]. In its Preface, it was stated:

> The Committee of the Club being desirous to add, as far as in their power, to the interest of the Belfast Meeting of the British Association, resolved to prepare a small volume embracing the result of the labours of the Club's members, and thus to bring together in a condensed form an amount of information not easily attainable under ordinary circumstances, and at the same time likely to be of general interest.

The book was indeed small in its external dimensions (72x46mm) but, with a condensed typeface and 328 pages, not including 24 pages of adverts and a map, it is quite a substantial little volume (*see footnote 12 for the contents*). In the Centenary Volume of the Belfast Natural History and Philosophical Society 1821–1921[5], an organisation which had close ties with the Field Club[6], it is noted that: 'This was the first of the "Handbooks" which are now considered indispensable at Association Meetings'.

Following the Belfast initiative

Belfast started a trend which was to survive for many years. For the meeting in York in 1932 (the first meeting had been held there in 1831), the BAAS Annual Volume – a full account of the proceedings of the annual meeting normally published the year after the event – absorbed the handbook as an Appendix: *A Scientific Survey of York and District*, and such an appendix was added to the subsequent Annual Volumes until the Cambridge meeting in 1938, after which the publication of the Annual Volumes ceased. They were replaced with the journal *The Advancement of Science* the following year – to be published in four numbers per year. In the first of these, referring to the Annual Volumes, it is recorded[7]:

> It might have been imagined that such a series of volumes, if only for the sake of their not unimposing appearance upon the bookshelf, would not have been readily condemned to extinction. But for many years there has been evident a growing tendency to regard them as an incubus in the library, and as a place of premature burial for scientific communications unworthy of such a fate. Time and again it has been found that an inquirer into some special branch of

---

[4] Members of the Belfast Naturalists' Field Club, *Guide to Belfast and the Adjacent Counties* (Belfast: Marcus Ward, 1874), pp. 328.

[5] Arthur Deane (Ed.), *The Belfast Natural History and Philosophical Society Centenary Volume 1821–1921* (Belfast: Belfast Natural History and Philosophical Society, 1924), p. 29.

[6] Ruth Bayles, 'Understanding Local Science: The Belfast Natural History Society in the Mid-Nineteenth Century', pp. 139-169 in David Attis and Charles Mollan (Eds), *Science and Irish Culture Volume I – Why the History of Science Matters in Ireland* (Dublin: Royal Dublin Society, 2004).

[7] British Association for the Advancement of Science, *The Advancement of Science*, **1** (No. 1), 1939, p. 8.

science, desiring to possess a report or discussion thereon running to a few pages, was not unreasonably aggrieved when compelled to acquire a book of several hundred pages in which that particular matter happened to be interned. Quarterly publication should at least in a measure abolish that difficulty.

I suppose it has to be conceded that this was a logical and justified decision, but I must confess that I am a great admirer of the Annual Volumes, which contain a wealth of fascinating information to anyone interested in the history of science over the period 1831 to 1938. I greatly regret their demise.

In spite of the outbreak of war, which resulted in the Dundee meeting of 1939 being thereby disrupted (it started but did not finish), the four issues of the journal were published. The *Scientific Survey of Dundee and District* was split between the first three of these. In Issue 3 (published in 1940), it was noted that[8]: 'no survey will be issued in 1940'. The tradition was not continued in future issues. However, the publication by local committees of surveys relating to their cities or districts continued sporadically.

The most recent of these of which I am aware (and the BAAS office had none later when I visited in February 2004) are *The Resources of Merseyside* (1982)[9], *Province, City & People – Belfast and its Region* (Belfast 1987)[10], and *Loughborough and its Region* (Loughborough 1994)[11].

The Irish keep up the initiative

Belfast adhered to the tradition it had set up 113 years earlier by producing a (very attractive) local volume for the last meeting of the BAAS in Ireland before this one in Dublin. The Belfast meeting was the eleventh held in Ireland. The complete list is:

1835 Dublin
1843 Cork
1852 Belfast
1857 Dublin
1874 Belfast
1878 Dublin
1902 Belfast
1908 Dublin
1952 Belfast
1957 Dublin
1987 Belfast
2005 Dublin

8 R.L. Mackie (Ed.), 'A Scientific Survey of Dundee and District (Chapters IX to XIII)', *The Advancement of Science*, **1** (No. 3), 1940, pp. (second pagination) 74-124.
9 William T.S. Gould & Alan G. Hodgkiss, *The Resources of Merseyside* (Liverpool: Liverpool University Press), pp. xiii + 198.
10 R.H. Buchanan & B.M. Walker (Eds), *Province, City & People – Belfast and its Region* (Antrim: Greystones Books in association with the NI Committee of the BAAS, 1987) pp. viii + 333.
11 Keith Boucher (Ed.), *Loughborough and its Region* (Loughborough: Department of Geography, Loughborough University of Technology, 1994), pp. xiii + 202.

Since the initiative was started in Belfast in 1874, a volume has been published for every meeting of the BAAS in Ireland[12].

There is a great deal of valuable historical information contained in these volumes. They deserve to be better known.

The origin of the present volume

The Royal Dublin Society published a book entitled *A Profit and Loss Account of Science in Ireland* in 1983[13]. Around that time, contact had been made informally with the BAAS to explore the possibility of another Dublin meeting, but it was considered inadvisable. It says much for the development of cordial relations between our neighbouring islands in the intervening years that we can now heartily welcome the return of the Association to which Irish people had contributed so much over its history. Even though the BAAS couldn't visit around 1983, the Society's Committee of Science and its Industrial Applications (as it was then called) decided that the time was ripe for another scientific survey, and so it went ahead with its *Profit and Loss Account*.

---

[12] **1874** Members of the Belfast Naturalists' Field Club, *Guide to Belfast and the Adjacent Counties* (Belfast: Marcus Ward & Co, Belfast, 1874), pp. 327 (plus fold out map). Contents: Physical Geography, Geology, Botany, Zoology, Topography, History, Antiquities, Agriculture, Trade and Commerce, Excursions &c.
1878 Alexander Macalister & William Ramsay M'Nab (Editors), *Guide to the County of Dublin: its Geology, Industries, Flora, and Fauna* (Dublin: Hodges, Foster, and Figgis, 1878), pp. vi + 219 + 100 (plus fold-out map and coloured geological map). Contents: Topographical Notes, Physical Geography, Palæontology, Mineralogy, Textile Industries, Chief Places of Industrial Interest, Historical and Antiquarian Notes, Flora, Fauna, Dublin Corporation Records, St. Bride's Parish Records. (Note: the Flora takes up 107 pages and the Fauna [separately paginated] 91 pages – 'On the whole, we think we can claim that these lists constitute a local Fauna and Flora, than which none more complete has been published in Ireland, and very few elsewhere'.)
1902 Belfast Naturalists' Field Club, Francis Joseph Bigger & R. Lloyd Praeger (General Editors), *A Guide to Belfast and the Counties of Down and Antrim* (Belfast: M'Caw, Stevenson & Orr, 1902), pp. 283 (plus fold out coloured map). Contents: Belfast – History and Description, Trade and Commerce, Geology, Botany, Zoology, Antiquities.
1908 Grenville A.J. Cole & R. Lloyd Praeger (General Editors), *Handbook of the City of Dublin and the Surrounding District* (Dublin University Press, 1908), pp. viii + 441 (plus two coloured maps in rere pocket). Contents: Geology, Meteorology, Botany, Zoology, History and Archaeology, Education and Research, Industries and Commerce.
1952 Emrys Jones (Editor), *Belfast in its Regional Setting – A Scientific Survey* (Belfast: Local Executive Committee of the British Association, 1952), pp. 211 (plus two fold out maps). Contents: The Region and its Parts, Geology, Climate and Soils, Botany, Zoology, Prehistoric, Protohistoric, Historical, Historic Monuments, Economic History, The Peoples of Northern Ireland, Agriculture, Industries, Land Use, Settlement and Population, Education and Social Services, Place Names and Dialects, A Survey of the City.
1957 James Meenan & David A. Webb, *A View of Ireland – Twelve Essays on Different Aspects of Irish Life and the Irish Countryside* (Dublin: Local Executive Committee of the British Association, 1957), pp. xv + 254 (plus two maps – one coloured – in rere pocket). Contents: Physiography and Climate, Geology, Botany, Zoology, Inland Fisheries, Economic Structure, Agriculture, Peat, Archaeology, Local Traditions, The Irish Language, The City of Dublin.
1987 R.H. Buchanan & B.M. Walker, *Province, City & People – Belfast and its Region* (Antrim: Greystone Books in association with the Northern Ireland Committee of the BAAS, 1987), pp. viii + 333. Contents: Province, City and People, Land and Land Use, Mineral Resources, Inland Waters, Conservation, Town and Country Planning, The Physical and Social Dimensions of a Regional City, Housing Policy and Trends, Services, Economy and Employment, Agriculture, Forestry and Fishing, Population, Religion and Employment, Administration, Politics and Parties, Arts in Society.
[13] Phyllis Clinch & Charles Mollan (Eds), *A Profit and Loss Account of Science in Ireland* (Dublin: Royal Dublin Society, 1983), pp. vii + 151.

We saw in footnote 12 that James Meenan was co-editor of the volume published to celebrate the BAAS visit to Dublin in 1957. In 1983, Professor Meenan was President of the RDS and, in his Foreword to the new survey, he commented:

> The distinguished contributors [to this volume] have set out for us paths that lead not simply to greater prosperity but to a fuller and richer life in the community. Our founders, however puzzled they might be by some of the concepts and expressions used in these lectures, would surely recognise and applaud the aim.

The volume dealt with Science Policy, Mineral Resources, Marine Resources, Energy, Demographic Resources, The Environment, Art & Design, Employment Needs, Technology Transfer, Communications, and Education.

A key player in the genesis of this volume was Dr Arthur Hughes, at the time both a Member of the RDS Science Committee and former Managing Director of Guinness Ireland Limited. Always conscious of the importance of science and technology to the economy of society, his guidance in preparing the plans for the book were most helpful, and he demonstrated his practical approach by arranging very welcome sponsorship of the volume by his former Company.

When the Royal Dublin Society became aware that the BAAS was to make a return visit to Dublin in 2005, its Committee of Science and Technology (its new name) discussed how it might best contribute to the visit. I had been collecting BAAS publications (both the Annual Reports and the Irish scientific surveys listed above) and was conscious of the tradition started in Belfast in 1874 which had sadly fallen into abeyance. My suggestion that we should revive this tradition as the Society's contribution to the 2005 meeting received an enthusiastic reception in the Committee. A key supporter of the idea was Professor Adrian Phillips, whose wife is Rosamond, daughter of Dr Arthur Hughes. The next step would normally have been to place this idea before the Management Board of the Society to see if funds could be made available for the purpose. Before we did this, though, fate intervened in both a positive and a negative way.

The family of Arthur Hughes had decided to contribute a generous sum of money to the Society in his memory to be devoted to the promotion of scientific activities. With Adrian Phillips acting as emissary between the Committee and his in-laws, the latter very kindly agreed that a first call on their donation could be the costs of publication of the book. Adrian was very closely involved in deciding the contents of the proposed volume, guided by his knowledge of his father-in-law's emphasis on the 'value' of science. He himself agreed to provide the chapter on 'Ireland's Environment'. It was then that fate took a tragic turn. Adrian died prematurely on 1 November 2003 just three years after the death of his father-in-law. This book is dedicated to their memory. In it, we have included appreciations of Arthur Hughes by his family, and of Adrian Phillips by his friend and colleague, Professor Chris Stillman. We miss them and their wise advice very much.

Acknowledgement

As well as acknowledging the financial support of the Arthur Hughes Memorial Fund, we must express our very great appreciation to Rosamond Phillips, who has, despite her sad bereavement, been enormously supportive in this initiative. She has been particularly helpful in suggesting the names of potential contributors.

And we must express our best thanks to these contributors. We were conscious that the people we would like to invite to contribute articles on the topics we chose for inclusion (reflecting Arthur Hughes' 'value for society' ethos) would be (axiomatically) extremely busy. We are enormously grateful that they have all agreed to devote so much valuable time to preparing their chapters. And we acknowledge the very helpful input by the Society's Development Executive in Science and Industry, Dr Ciaran Byrne.

It is a particular pleasure to acknowledge the gracious Foreword provided by Professor Helen Haste, Chair of the Council of the BAAS.

A revitalised scientific scene

In the historical Chapter, it will be seen that Ireland has a distinguished tradition in contributions to the development of scientific thought. And we must, while not ignoring the Irish origins of some of these scientists, pay tribute to Great Britain for the opportunities she gave to them when such opportunities were not available at home at the time. As we shall see, there were many Irish participants and officers at the BAAS meetings both when the Association met at home and abroad. Ireland had a commendably vibrant scientific presence over the hundred or so years between the end of the eighteenth century and the early days of the twentieth century. This can be assessed, for example, by the remarkable number of Irish born men who achieved the distinction of being elected Fellows of the Royal Society in that period. (Women weren't eligible for this distinction until 1945, and one of the first two women to achieve this status was X-ray crystallographer, Kathleen Lonsdale, who was born in Newbridge, Co. Kildare – *see page 40*)

The early decades of the twentieth century were turbulent times at home and abroad. Irish Science suffered in a depressed economy in a divided country. But things began to improve in the second half of the century. We must pay tribute to those Irish scientists who had opted to stay at home, or, more usually, to return from abroad after a period of study in Europe or the US, and who managed against great odds to carry out research of high quality. As a result of the role models which such researchers represented, and to the vision of key players in other sectors of Irish life and politics, self confidence began to grow. The Republic started to look outwards rather than inwards, Ireland joined the EU and received great support, the economy began to thrive, and the Celtic Tiger was born.

In the period 1994 to 2002, I edited and published *The Irish Scientist Year Book*. While this was not published as an historical review, the dramatic change in the vigour of Irish scientific research in this period can be seen in the pages of the successive *Year*

Books. Given any kind of realistic support, it was evident that Irish scientists could carry out research of high international quality: the potential vigour was there and, with encouragement, was becoming actual.

It is only very recently that we have seen a real revival in support for science. It will be clear from several of the Chapters in this volume that a massive boost has resulted from the Higher Education Authority's Programme for Research in Third Level Institutions (PRTLI), from the setting up of Science Foundation Ireland, and from the increased funding being provided through the Health Research Board. Substantial *Irish* money (as distinct from EU money and from funds like the Wellcome Trust) is now being devoted to science in Ireland.

This is not to say that everything is perfect. The nervousness of the scientific community following a period of (fortunately temporary) curtailment of PRTLI funds in 2002 is clearly evident in some of the accounts. Short sighted political decisions can have major negative effects. While the disciplines of Biotechnology and Information and Communications Technology have been chosen for favoured status in view of their suitability and potential, others have been starved. At the time when infrastructural and research money was significantly increasing, funding for third level colleges was severely restricted. Opportunities provided by the new funding could not be fully exploited. The lack of co-ordination between the different funding organisations, affiliated to different Government Departments, was thereby clearly demonstrated. Hopefully the appointment of the State's first Chief Scientific Adviser, Dr Barry McSweeney, in 2004 can help clarify the importance of a more consolidated programme in driving the scientific potential of the country on to greater things.

Unfortunately, though, the proportion of GNP devoted to research and development, and the allocation of support for higher education, remain extremely low by European and other relevant international standards. Having said that, it is good to note that Irish people do not now have to emigrate in order to display their scientific potential, although a period of training abroad remains of great importance to developing scientific careers. We are now in a reverse situation to that in the mid twentieth century. Some of our emigrant scientists are returning home. A significant aspect of the development of science in Ireland in recent years, as demonstrated in the authorship of articles in *The Irish Scientist Year Books,* is the number of names which are clearly not Irish. As well as giving opportunities to natives at home, we are pleased to welcome talented people from outside the country who now choose to develop their scientific careers here. As the economy picks up again after a period of relative depression (though our growth remained high by European standards), we would hope that additional resources can be devoted to science in Ireland, and thus that the recent progress can be further enhanced.

Science and Ireland – Value for Society describes how selected disciplines in science have progressed in recent years, where they are at this time, and where they should go. We do not pretend that this is a complete picture. But we hope that the information provided in this volume will prove of interest to those taking part in the 2005 meeting of the BAAS in 'Dublin's Fair City' (of which a glimpse is given in Chapter 1). We hope also that this volume may be useful to our legislators, administrators and economists. Support for science is support for a modern Ireland.

Dublin's Fair City

Peter Pearson

The City of Dublin may be defined geographically by the Dublin and Wicklow mountains to the south, Dublin Bay with its sandy shores to the east, with Howth and the plains of Meath to the north. It is a city of north and south; a division created by the River Liffey.

Today, Dublin is a busy European Capital, an administrative city with ever-spreading suburbs, consisting of new housing schemes, apartments, schools, shopping centres and office parks that stretch west beyond Leixlip, Clonsilla and Clondalkin, north beyond Swords and Malahide, and south beyond Bray and Greystones. Large tracts of Dublin's former countryside have disappeared completely and the landscape of 'Greater Dublin' is changing as we speak.

Old and new along the banks of the River Liffey: the Matt Talbot Bridge, Liberty Hall, the Custom House (with the Central Bank behind it), and the Financial Services Centre (courtesy of Dublin Tourism)

At no time in the history of this city has the pace and scale of change been so swift and so dramatic, as it has been during the last fifteen years. Socially, economically, architecturally, every sphere of life has been touched by the new Dublin which is emerging. It is a new Dublin which not everybody is happy about although it may have brought prosperity and great wealth to many, and a whole new urban way of life to others.

There are many different Dublins. The old historic city which remained so intact up until the 1960s is only a shadow of its former self, but much that is elegant still remains to be seen. Many of the old inhabitants and families have been displaced to distant suburbs, while the new influx of city dwellers from all over the world has made Dublin lively and cosmopolitan – but also impersonal.

The old city life of forty years ago, with its native owned businesses, shops and factories, has all but vanished, with chain stores and multi-national brand names taking over the main shopping precincts. For instance, Dublin's last family-owned hat shop closed early in 2004. Many of the old family butchers and grocers have now gone, and bland, overpriced convenience stores have appeared in their place. The new, mostly young, city dwellers now occupy the unbelievable number of apartment buildings which have been erected in Dublin over the past twenty years.

The visitor to Dublin might not understand that the outlook for the city centre was extremely grim in the early 1980s, with vast tracts of derelict land in every part of town, derelict houses, boarded up sites, and little or no building activity.

There was a relatively small population of working class residents in certain, often deprived, areas of the city, and no middle class residents there whatsoever. The huge apartment building boom, spurred on by generous tax incentives, changed that picture. Parts of the city which were written off as dead, sites once only considered for surface car parks were rapidly redeveloped, and cafés, shops and other businesses, such as pharmacies, re-appeared in streets which everybody considered to be permanently dormant. In recent years the quality of many of the new buildings has been good and sometimes outstanding, but not before a lot of mediocre developments made their mark on the city. There was a feeling that any development was better than the derelict sites which had blighted Dublin for so long.

To some, Dublin is not so much represented by its historic city centre as by its new suburban town centres, such as Tallaght, which lies to the south west near the Dublin mountains. Tallaght was a small county Dublin village up until the 1970s. First came the sprawl of housing estates to accommodate those whose dilapidated city centre dwellings had been demolished. Churches, schools and other facilities followed slowly, with a proper shopping centre, a theatre and other administrative buildings coming later still. A new 'state-of-the-art' tramline connecting Tallaght to the city centre was opened in 2004. This pattern could be replicated in Blanchardstown, Lucan, Clondalkin or Swords. To many kids under twenty, these places with their new shopping centres _are_ Dublin, and they are mostly unaware of the rich history in which their own families may have played a part which was acted out on the streets of the historic heart of Dublin. Dublin's past was a lively, colourful one, with its fine buildings and interesting old streets, esteemed noblemen and nameless paupers, heroic deeds and acts of treachery. The mansions, the tenements, the taverns and the brothels – it was all there.

Many of the old industries in which the citizens were employed for centuries, such as tanning, brewing, distilling or biscuit making have gone, but vestiges of the buildings do remain still. Powers and Jamesons distillers, two world-renowned makers of whiskey, ceased production in Dublin over thirty years ago, but their buildings were adapted for use, one as the National College of Art and Design and the other as apartments.

The conservation of Dublin's historic streets and other landmarks has presented an uphill struggle for those who were committed to promoting the city's history and architectural beauty. Much was lost.

In the decades following the second World War, some of the worst of the tenement and slum districts were levelled by bulldozer. Some of Dublin's oldest streets, such as Bride street (near St Patrick's Cathedral), Cuffe street and Jervis street have no old houses remaining. Various streets remained undeveloped for years, with vacant lots growing buddlea and weeds. These have only been fully restored as streets with buildings in recent years.

Back in the 1960s, artists such as Flora Mitchell captured the quaint but dilapidated corners of the city, and published her drawings in a book entitled *Vanishing Dublin*. Apart from the major public buildings which she included, most of her streetscapes have indeed 'vanished'.

Another artist, Robert Ballagh, produced a photographic memoir of the city in about 1980, which depicts Dublin at one of its lowest points, with many landmarks either derelict or abandoned. The city is seen as artistically fascinating, decaying but stagnant, a still-life of truncated buildings and broken-down doorways. The bleak picture was also catalogued by journalist Frank McDonald who, in *The Irish Times*, wrote a long series of articles about the lack of political vision, the ruthless greed of certain developers, the official ignorance and bureaucracy which was hanging over the city, preventing any change. He also hinted at the political corruption in the planning process which has only been publicly revealed by two State Tribunals of Inquiry.

However, by the mid 1990s, Dublin was firmly set on a new course, with Dublin Corporation (now renamed Dublin City Council) determined to revitalise the city.

A number of events all combined to bring about Dublin's renaissance – the tax designation for run-down areas, the pedestrianisation of Grafton street, a new paved mall in O'Connell street, and the beginning of stone paving in the Temple Bar area.

The popular Temple Bar outdoor food market operates every Saturday in the centre of Dublin

The gradual upgrading of business premises, along with Dublin's celebration of its, perhaps spurious, 'millennium' in 1988, and its role as European City of Culture in 1991, all helped to regenerate pride in the city. Though these events were not responsible in themselves for any special move to restore or rebuild the city, they gave the Capital a much-needed boost as a venue for tourists, and they revived Dubliners' sense of pride in their city.

Dublin Castle from the air – this historic complex dating back to the 12th century is to-day intensively used by State offices for formal occasions, and by tourists

At about the same time, the Royal Hospital in Kilmainham was converted into the Irish Museum of Modern Art (IMMA), and Dublin Castle, which had been much neglected, was revamped to incorporate a large conference centre. The Custom House was fully restored and the Government buildings in Merrion street were completely remodelled in a grand manner.

An Taisce, the voluntary heritage protection body, which for years lobbied Government on the demise of the capital and its architectural heritage, successfully prevented the Temple Bar area from being demolished to make a site for a bus Station, and the State established Temple Bar Properties to oversee the regeneration of this district. Other notable restoration projects at this time included the General Post Office in O'Connell street, which was carried out by the Office of Public Works (OPW) for An Post.

Voluntary groups also played a significant role, with An Taisce moving into Taylors' Hall (the City's last surviving Guild Hall), the restoration of Drimnagh Castle on the Long Mile Road, and the rescue of a fine Georgian house in North Great George's street, which would become the James Joyce Cultural Centre. During the 1990s, the Dublin Civic Trust initiated the restoration of several city centre houses of note, including a 1660s dwelling in Aungier street.

Dublin Tourism restored a pair of important 18th century houses on Parnell square, which now serve as the Writers' Museum and Writers' Centre respectively. Many private owners were also restoring run-down Georgian houses for use as their own homes. On the commercial front, Dublin's famous Bewley's cafés were rescued from near extinction by Campbell Catering, who proceeded to refurbish the older premises in Grafton and Westmoreland streets. Sadly, however, these did not thrive and ceased to be cafés in 2004.

All of these projects and events helped to bring about a mood of optimism and a new pride in Dublin. Most of the derelict sites of the 1980s, which were so conspicuous, have now been redeveloped. Many other buildings mentioned by Ballagh in his photographic record have been cleaned and restored, and these include the once grimy Fruit and Vegetable Market in Mary's Abbey, the Memorial Gardens at Islandbridge, Sunlight Chambers, and Pearse street Garda station. Even the dramatic stone breakwater at the South Wall has been repaired, allowing for easier public access.

Dublin is today a city of young people; it is a Mecca for the 17–30 year olds who crowd the city's many cafés by day and flock to its pubs at night. You are as likely to be served in a restaurant by a student from Spain, Russia or Hungary as by one from Ireland. The thousands of recently built apartments are full of such people – come to soak up the music culture of Dublin and perhaps improve their English.

There are also numerous immigrants from the far east, from Arabic countries and from Africa, many of whom are working in service industries like Hotels and Catering, and they bring an international ambience to the city which was unimaginable twenty years ago. African and Oriental foodshops abound in districts of the city where rents are less expensive.

View of the Spire in O'Connell Street (courtesy of Dublin Tourism)

Dublin has also several new monuments which celebrate the revitalisation of the capital. Most conspicuous is the Spire, a silvery needle located in the middle of O'Connell street, which is visible from nearly anywhere in Dublin. It is not a monument to anything in particular, having neither political nor religious significance, and as such is perhaps an appropriate symbol of our time – a symbol of prowess, wealth and optimism.

Other monuments have been created for more practical purposes – new bridges over the Liffey, the conversion of the mighty Storehouse at Guinness to a visitor centre, the re-development of Smithfield, the new architecture in Temple Bar, the construction of LUAS and of the M50 motoring ring road which will ultimately encircle Dublin from Shankill to Dublin Airport, the Port Tunnel which will bring heavy traffic onto this ring road.

Dublin has only recently evolved from its long held position as second city of the British Empire, a Georgian capital with its own personality, to being a fully fledged modern European city with its busy airport and motorway ring. Dublin is now a major tourist destination, with a multitude of new hotels, bars and restaurants. The city is famous for its entertainment and cultural life. A selection of theatres provide year round drama and popular musical events, while the National Concert Hall has an excellent programme of classical music. The Abbey, Ireland's National Theatre, has just celebrated its centenary at a time when plans are afoot to rebuild and provide better facilities. The Gate Theatre, which adjoins the Rotunda hospital at Parnell square, tends towards productions of classic plays by Irish and other dramatists, while the Gaiety

Theatre near St Stephen's Green generally provides a more popular programme, including Christmas pantomimes. The elegant Olympia Theatre in Dame street is noted for its concerts and musical performances. Experimental and *avant-garde* theatre can be seen in many venues, including the above, but the smaller Project Arts Centre in Temple Bar and the Andrews Lane Theatre are probably the leaders in this area. There are now many new suburban Arts centres and Theatres in the surrounding area of Dublin, thanks to an active policy of the Arts Council and Local Government. The Helix in Glasnevin, Dríocht in Blanchardstown, the Pavilion in Dun Laoghaire, are but a few examples.

As well as possessing an excellent National Gallery of Art in Merrion square, Dublin also has a Municipal Gallery of Art whose collections include works from the 19th century to the contemporary. The Municipal Gallery is housed, in part, in a beautiful 18th century stone fronted townhouse, originally built for art connoisseur and collector, Lord Charlemont. There are plans to extend the space of the Gallery into the adjoining Georgian houses. The IMMA, already mentioned, in the former Royal Hospital at Kilmainham, has remained a popular venue for visitors since its inauguration in 1991.

Often in the forefront of controversy, IMMA maintains a programme of both Irish and International contemporary Art exhibitions and installations. The four-sided hospital building, which dates from the 17th century, with its large enclosed courtyard, has been successfully adapted for exhibition use, while the old dining hall and Chapel are frequently used for other cultural events, including concerts, balls, formal dinners and charity events.

The Museum is set in a pleasant park, which includes a formal parterre and an axial driveway or avenue, leading to the Kilmainham gate. Kilmainham, once a small village, is today noted for its old Gaol, an impressive and forbidding structure which houses a museum dedicated to the struggle for Irish Independence, and especially the period of 1916.

Testing the LUAS railcars on the new Dundrum Bridge on the Green Line (courtesy of Connex Ltd)

New developments at Smithfield on the North side of the city (courtesy of Dublin Tourism)

Dublin is fortunate in possessing no less than 100 parks of varying size and shape within the city limits. The greatest of these include the Phoenix park, St Stephen's green and Merrion square, but there are many smaller, lesser known retreats of great beauty and peace. The Blessington basin, which is located close to one of the city's largest hospitals, The Mater, is a beautiful park which has been created around a small artificial lake or reservoir. The reservoir supplied water to the nearby, now closed, Jamesons distillery in Smithfield. This small park, with its delightful Victorian gatelodge, is now much frequented by local residents. The majority of these city parks are maintained by Dublin City Council, the local Authority charged with running the city. Known as Dublin Corporation for the last six hundred years, the name was pointlessly changed to Dublin City Council by some petty bureaucratic decree of Government. This body, with its elected members, takes charge of the planning and development of the city; the supply of housing, water and sewerage; maintenance of roads, paving and lighting; cleaning and rubbish collection; and a host of other equally important functions which many of its citizens take for granted.

For instance, the Council has commissioned a wide variety of public sculpture in many different parts of the city. These pieces range widely in style and quality, bordering on what some see as 'kitsch' 'ye Olde Dubline' images of the legendary shellfish seller, Molly Malone, to what others find offensive – lumps of angular rusting steel. Amidst all of these are many excellent works of art, such as the Emigrant sculpture on the long out-of-service fountain dedicated to Thomas Davis which is rather lost in its present position on the traffic island in College Green. The Spire in O'Connell street could well be considered to be the City Council's most ambitious and expensive public sculpture and, whether you like it or not, it is a monument to the Council's commitment to provide for more than just the city's functional needs.

Characteristic green painted Irish post boxes are beginning to disappear: they are a feature of Dublin's streets

One institution which Dublin sorely lacks is a proper City of Dublin Museum. It is extraordinary that the city has made do with a miserly-run collection in a beautiful small building in South William Street. The city deserves a full-scale museum dedicated to showing the many wonderful and fascinating artefacts which are at present scattered about, some in private hands and much lying in storage. Gathered together, these artefacts would form a collection worthy of a capital with a long and noble history. Such precious items would tell the story of the city: the guilds – the strong box of the Linen Hall Guild is still in existence; shop signs and shop fronts, some of which are in the Civic Museum; the magnificent Molyneux Coat of Arms from the vanished Molyneux house near Bride street; the statues from the original Tholsel, which stood in Skinners' Row; the statue of St Andrew from the old St Andrew's church, which lies forlorn in its surrounding car park; fragments of plasterwork from the city's once great Georgian houses; glass from Dublin glasshouses, pieces of wallpaper from Dublin Castle, tools from the once important Dublin tanneries, printed ephemera from shops; bills, documents and letters; shoemaker's lasts; dance cards from Dublin Castle, swords and scissors made in 18th century Temple Bar, book bindings and scientific instruments from the city's finest craftsmen, theatre programmes from yesteryear. The expansion and development of the city, the politics of Dublin, its Parliament homes, its educational establishments; its archaeological past; the history of shipping and the port, the early Custom house, the street sellers, the nobles, the lives of the poor and the work of Dublin's many charities; all of these stories and many more, along with the great events of history need to be recorded and fully presented in a City of Dublin Museum. In this present impersonal age, such a record of past identity is ever more valuable.

The National Museum of Ireland, located on Kildare street, with an additional facility at Collins Barracks near the Phoenix park, has many wonderful displays, but naturally concentrates on the whole country. A small exhibition focussing on the administrative history of Dublin is housed underneath the City Hall, while a magnificent new city archives building has been provided in Pearse street. Ireland's architectural legacy is excellently recorded in The Irish Architectural Archive in Merrion square, lately accommodated in two carefully refurbished Georgian houses. The extensive holdings of the National Archives of Ireland are housed in Bishop street, while other collections such as Business archives are held in University College Dublin, at its Belfield campus.

The National Library of Ireland is based in a fine 19th century building in Kildare street, and has recently been expanded to create additional storage and conservation facilities. The National Library also incorporates a manuscript reading room and an important display of heraldic artefacts relating to both Ireland and Dublin.

Headquarters of the Royal Dublin Society at Ballsbridge (courtesy of the RDS)

The role of the Royal Dublin Society (the RDS) in establishing the major cultural institutions of this State should not be overlooked. When it was founded in 1731, the RDS gave premiums to encourage the arts and crafts – such as painting, sculpture and drawing and, out of this, today's National College of Art and Design evolved. Indeed, the College's premises were, until quite recently, housed adjacent to Leinster House, which was the headquarters of the RDS for over 100 years – from 1815 to 1922.

Other important activities of the RDS included the promotion of agriculture and all aspects of the sciences. Out of this concern, the Botanic Gardens in Glasnevin were founded, and today's museum devoted to Natural History, now part of the National Museum of Ireland, was built on a site facing Merrion square. The present day National

Museum, National Library and National Gallery, lying adjacent to Leinster House, all owe a debt to the RDS for their original establishment.

As previously suggested, the old historic Dublin city is now only a shadow of what it was. What then remains of the medieval, the Georgian or the Victorian city? As already noted, many of the city's historic landmark buildings have been cleaned and repaired in recent years. Some of the city's cultural institutions have also been described in brief.

Over the last thirty years, the clearance of many streets and sites for road widening and development created an opportunity for archaeologists to excavate different parts of the medieval city. This revealed many finds, including everyday objects, jewellery, pottery, and even a boat from Viking times and after. It also offered more information on our ancestors' way of life, eating habits, dress, trade and style of house. Parts of the old city wall were also unearthed.

Dublin possesses two cathedrals of medieval foundation – Christ Church, which lies within the city walls, and St Patrick's which lies outside the walls. Both were very dilapidated by the early 19th century, and were heavily remodelled during the Victorian era. Apart from the cathedrals, St Mary's Abbey Chapter House, the church of St Audeon and some vestiges of the city wall, Dublin has little to show from the medieval period. For instance, most of Dublin Castle was remodelled in the 18th century and no timber-framed houses have survived to give an idea of what medieval Dublin's streets might have looked like.

Much has been learnt about Dublin's fortifications, which stood between the 13th and 17th centuries, through various archaeological digs. For instance, before the development of new apartments at Usher's Quay in the early 1990s, an excavation took place behind the Brazen Head hotel, revealing some of the most western sections of Dublin's old city wall, a revetment or quay whose timbers were dated to the 12th or 13th century. Elsewhere, fragments of pottery from South-West France are evidence of strong trading links in wine and other goods. The archaeological finds at Wood Quay, now built over by the Civic Offices of Dublin City Council, sparked off much controversy in the mid 1970s, and revealed the extent of Dublin's importance as a Viking settlement. Archaeology has since become a significant business, and many city-centre sites have been investigated before building was started. The recorded finds and historical information gleaned have, in many cases, been published.

One of the most striking relics of medieval Dublin is the tomb of Strongbow, which lies in Christ Church Cathedral, on which his effigy is sculpted. Strongbow, king of Leinster, is shown as an armour-clad knight. The vaulted crypt underneath the Cathedral is an interesting space, and appears to date from the 12th century. While some Romanesque features are in evidence, the overall character of the restored Cathedral is one of early Gothic.

St Patrick's Cathedral, lying to the south, was originally built in the 13th century, and is still one of Dublin's largest public buildings. It was once surrounded by many smaller buildings and houses, which it dominated with its imposing bulk and tall spire. St Patrick's is the National Cathedral of the Church of Ireland (Anglican) community, and is adjoined by the choir school, Ireland's oldest secondary school, dating back to 1431. St Patrick's Close is a short, curved street which links Kevin street and Patrick street, a peaceful backwater which is also home to Marsh's library – one of Dublin's greatest treasures. The remarkable building was erected in 1701 by Archbishop Narcissus Marsh in the grounds of his adjoining Palace – St Sepulchre's. It is distinguished by tall windows, steep roofs and mellow red-brick facades. It is filled with a highly important collection of early printed books, which are housed in attractive oak-panelled bookshelves.

Another impressive Georgian building serves as the headquarters of the Royal Irish Academy, an institution established in 1785 for the promotion of science and learning in Ireland. The Academy houses many rare manuscripts, including the *Book of Ballymote*, the *Leabhar Breac* and the *Annals of the Four Masters*. Its Library and lecture room are themselves monuments of Victorian architecture in cast iron.

It is of course Trinity College which is most famous for its precious *Book of Kells*, a rare illuminated manuscript copy of the four gospels dating from the seventh century. Also of interest are the *Book of Durrow* and the *Book of Armagh*, which are also housed in the most impressive Old Library in Trinity. The *Book of Kells*, which was once on open view in the spectacularly timber vaulted Long Gallery, is now housed in a rather sanitised chamber which meets its special conservation requirements.

West Front of Trinity College, built in the mid 18th century, stands across from The Bank of Ireland, once the seat of the Irish Parliament

The Trinity College campus is a very special environment, with many fine old buildings set amid neatly manicured grounds; all right in the heart of Dublin. Many new buildings have been added to the College in recent years, perhaps the most attractive being the timber-clad Samuel Beckett Theatre, which stands near Pearse street. The College was established by Queen Elizabeth I in 1591 on the site of the old Monastery of All Hallows. The Chapel, Exam Hall, and Dining Hall are among the chief architectural treasures of the College, along with the Provost's house, the West Front, the Printing house and the Rubrics – a much altered residential block dating from the 17th century.

Dublin Castle was described, about a century ago, as 'a non-military and somewhat dismal pile of buildings' – a not altogether unfair judgement, given that it is neither a magnificent palace for a viceroy nor a forbidding fortress. Many visitors ask 'where is the Castle?', and focus their cameras on the decorative battlemented Chapel Royal, which was erected in 1814. In terms of Irish history, Dublin Castle is perhaps the most politically symbolic structure in the State; the scene of many historic events leading up to the formation of the Irish Republic, and afterwards. Most recently, the Castle has hosted the various meetings and formal events associated with Ireland's Presidency of the European Union and the accession of the new member states. It is not a museum, and it now accommodates many different State bodies, such as the Revenue Commissioners and the Gardai, along with other semi-state or voluntary groups. Visitors can take a tour through the State Apartments, which include St Patrick's Hall and the Throne room, and the excavated moat area around the Powder tower. The opening of the Chester Beatty Library's new galleries in Dublin Castle provides added interest for the visitor, with its outstanding collection of Oriental Art. The Library is located beside an attractive park to the rere of the Castle.

Much has been published which celebrates the achievements of the Georgian period – the 18th century, when much of Dublin's finest architecture was erected, the fine arts flourished and Ireland had its own Parliament in Dublin's College Green. The Parliament house, now the Bank of Ireland, was completed in 1739, and is a monumental structure with three imposing facades.

Dublin's Georgian houses are noted for their elegant facades, varied doorways with delicate fanlights, and for the beauty of their plaster decorated interiors. Dublin decorative plasterwork reached a very high standard during the 18th century and there are many examples to be seen in both private houses and public buildings. The houses of Parnell square and Mountjoy square in the north city, and those of St Stephen's Green, Merrion square and Fitzwilliam square on the south side, are among the most noteworthy examples. However, there are many others which are equally important, such as those of Henrietta street, and various large houses such as Powerscourt house, Ely house, Newman house, Marlborough house, Tyrone house, or the Mansion house in Dawson street. The internal fittings of these buildings, including mahogany doors, wrought iron staircase balustrades and their decorative ceilings make them outstanding monuments of architecture.

Fitzwilliam square in Dublin – Dublin is justly famous for its elegant 18th century squares and streets of Georgian houses

Typical Georgian houses in Dame street near Dublin Castle, were once the hallmark of the city – many old streets have disappeared in favour of new office buildings and apartments

In the 19th century, house building continued, but began to spread into the new suburbs. Red brick terraces and squares were erected in new districts like Rathgar, Drumcondra and Glasnevin. The arrival of Ireland's first railway from Dublin to Kingstown, now Dun Laoghaire, in 1834 created a new building boom, and residential development took place rapidly along the shores of Dublin Bay, in Blackrock, Monkstown, Dalkey and Killiney.

The LUAS Red Line to Tallaght passes Heuston Station (courtesy of Connex Ltd)

The railway network soon expanded to cover the whole island of Ireland, and several very impressive railway stations were erected, especially in Dublin, to act as terminals. Heuston, Connolly and Westland Row, along with the now disused Broadstone and Harcourt street stations, are fine examples of Victorian architecture. The 19th century saw many new public buildings in Dublin, in the form of markets, hospitals and churches. Dublin also possesses an eclectic group of interesting commercial premises from this period, such as Sunlight Chambers on Parliament street or the Hodges Figgis bookshop building (originally built for Drummond's seeds) in Dawson street.

As Dublin advances into the 21st century, there seems to be no slowing down in the pace of urban development. The hunger for new apartments and office space appears to be insatiable, with large projects planned for the Spencer Dock area, Smithfield and Euston station. A whole new 'town' is planned for an area called Adamstown in west Dublin, while another ambitious scheme is also mooted for the Ringsend/Poolbeg area.

Once noted as a low-rise city with few buildings above four storeys, there is now increasing pressure for high rise developments. Whether this is justified or whether it is purely a manifestation of greed is a point of debate, but the long term social implications of such dwellings, and indeed the visual impact of tall buildings on their surroundings, are issues which must be addressed.

In the past, several 'sky scraper' type projects have been turned down in Dublin, but there is increasing pressure to now maximise every available building site in the city and in the surrounding area. Dublin's Fair City is still 'Fair' in parts, but in much of the more recently developed quarters, it would be impossible to distinguish it from any other city in the western world.

The planning Acts which govern all development in Ireland lay much emphasis on 'the common good', but in an era where financial success is seen by most as the principal goal or only measure of achievement, the search for that which is beautiful or 'Fair' may easily be forgotten.

CHAPTER 2

Elements of Irish Science: an historical sketch

Charles Mollan

'Irish' science

First of all we need some definitions. What is 'Irish' science? Does it matter that Galileo was Italian, that Darwin was English, that Einstein was German? Their discoveries have international, nay, universal application. While recognising the arguments in favour of the universality of so-called scientific 'truth', this essay will take the position that locality **does** matter. Detailed arguments in favour of this position (a topical matter for debate) have been made elsewhere[1], and I'll consider this matter only briefly here.

In passing, it might be noted that scientific truth needs to be assessed critically: our interpretation of the laws of nature and our universe (are there other universes?) must always remain just a best guess: this is what gives science its zing – a dramatic discovery may lie just around the corner. But already I digress.

This essay will stress the Irish dimension of the science which it discusses. Perversely, it will focus chiefly on the physical sciences (astronomy, chemistry, mathematics and physics, plus a glance at technology), which can be considered much more universal than the natural sciences (botany, geology and zoology), in spite of the fact that these latter disciplines could, with much more credibility, be considered to have an Irish dimension clearly distinct from any other nationality[2]. This selectivity is due to a combination of space constraints and to the particular relevance of the physical sciences in the economic development of Ireland in recent years. Thus it will cover (necessarily selected) historical aspects of the physical sciences as carried out in Ireland, by people born in Ireland and by people born elsewhere who carried out their work here. But more, it will claim as Irish some of those people who were born here

---

[1] See, for example, Peter Bowler & Nicholas Whyte (Eds), *Science and Society in Ireland – the Social Context of Science and Technology in Ireland 1800–1950* (Belfast: The Institute of Irish Studies, The Queen's University of Belfast, 1997); David Attis & Charles Mollan (Eds), *Science and Irish Culture* (Dublin: Royal Dublin Society, 2004).

[2] See, for example, John Wilson Foster (Ed), *Nature in Ireland – A Scientific and Cultural History* (Dublin: The Lilliput Press, 1997).

but who did not, and usually could not, have achieved what they did if they had tried to pursue their studies at home.

One of these, Robert Boyle (1627–1691), born in Lismore, Co. Waterford, famously stated in 1654[3]:

> I live here in a barbarous country, where chemical spirits are so misunderstood, and chemical instruments so unprocurable, that it is hard to have any hermetical thoughts in it, and impossible to bring them to experiment.

Nevertheless it was the massive amount money accumulated (by both fair and foul means) in Ireland by his father – the 'upstart'[4] Great Earl of Cork – which gave him the freedom to devote his life to the study of chemistry and other topics.

The Dublin-born 'Iron' Duke of Wellington, Arthur Wellesley (1769–1852 – not known for his scientific accomplishments) is famous, among other things, for his statement that if you are born in a stable you don't have to be a horse. Nevertheless one of the most recent of his many biographers records[5]:

> Wellington was a child of eighteenth-century Ireland, deeply marked by the time and place of his birth. Throughout his long life there was the lonely quality of the outsider about him, and this isolation has clear origins in his childhood as a member of a besieged Protestant minority in a Catholic land. He would have resented George Bernard Shaw's assertion that he was 'an intensely Irish Irishman'.

At the very beginning of the most authoritative of the biographies of Belfast-born William Thomson (1824–1907), later Lord Kelvin, Crosbie Smith and M. Norton Wise write[6]:

> Lord Kelvin, revered and respected statesman of science in the golden age of late nineteenth-century British Imperialism, began life not in Great Britain, but in Ireland. Addressing a Birmingham audience in 1883, he spoke humorously of the Irishman's seventh sense as common sense, believing 'that the possession of that virtue by my countrymen – I speak as an Irishman –....will do more to alleviate the woes of Ireland, than even the removal of the "melancholy ocean" which surrounds its shores'[7]. Less than a decade later, Sir William Thomson's

---

[3]   Letter from Robert Boyle to Frederick Clodius quoted in R.E.W Maddison, *The Life of the Honourable Robert Boyle F.R.S.* (London: Taylor & Francis, 1969), p. 84.

[3]   Nicholas Canny, *The Upstart Earl – A Study of the Social and Mental World of Richard Boyle, First Earl of Cork, 1566-1643* (Cambridge: Cambridge University Press, 1982).

[5]   Richard Holmes, *Wellington the Iron Duke* (London: HarperCollins, 2002), p. 3.

[6]   Crosbie Smith & M. Norton Wise, *Energy & Empire – A Biographical Study of Lord Kelvin* (Cambridge: Cambridge University Press, 1989), p. 3.

[7]   The quoted address, entitled 'The Six Gateways of Knowledge' was his Presidential address to the Birmingham and Midland Institute on October 3, 1883, and is reproduced in William Thomson, *Popular Lectures and Addresses*, Volume 1 (London: Macmillan & Co., 1889), pp. 253-299: the missing bit of the quote is '– I say the large possession of the seventh sense which I believe Irishmen have, and the exercise of it'.

elevation to the peerage as Baron Kelvin of Largs symbolised the social summit of a remarkable life lived in the context of Victorian Britain. Yet that ultimate acclaim did not flow from scientific and technical achievement alone, but also from his direct involvement in the political cause of Liberal Unionism during the 1880s. That involvement derived from the Irish context into which he had been born, a context of cultural and social liberalism upon which his enduring personal values were founded.

So, are Irish-born Robert Boyle, Arthur Wellesley and William Thomson Irish or not? Here we will consider them to be Irish, while, of course, accepting that Great Britain – more precisely England and Scotland – have arguably the greater claim to their main achievements, since the opportunities presented by the larger island and its then Empire allowed their talents to flourish.

'Irish' or 'British'

Which leads to another related definition. It may come as a surprise to visitors that including Ireland in the term 'British' (e.g. 'the British Isles') causes great offence to many Irish people. (It must be conceded, however, that a small minority is offended by NOT being called British!). The island of Ireland is not now, and never has been, part of Great Britain. It has been united to it to a greater or lesser extent, willingly or unwillingly, over several centuries, and part of it remains so to this day. But most of us like to retain the distinction between the two islands in a spirit of friendship, mutual respect, and geographical reality. The decreasing numbers of those who wish to use force of arms, or terrorism, to achieve this end are happily becoming ever more irrelevant, though a great volume of our historical studies still deals with this conflict to the neglect of other aspects of our historic culture – aspects like our contributions to science and technology.

While in this essay I am overstressing the 'Irish' tag (look at benefits this has given to the Republic of Ireland soccer team!), please take note of our sensibilities on this point. Rugby has long since got the point – calling a combined team the 'British & Irish Lions' – the Irish in this case, as in this essay, referring to the whole island.

And I would (wouldn't I?) echo the comment of the distinguished historian of Chemistry, Professor David Knight[8]: 'Historians of science should never forget Ireland with its unique experiences'.

As will become clear, there were substantial Irish (following my definition) contributions to the British Association for the Advancement of Science, but I won't be trying to re-write history by calling for a retrospective change of title to the 'British and Irish Association for the Advancement of Science'! Which is not to say that the future

---

8 David Knight, 'Review of *Science and Engineering in Ireland in 1798: a Time of Revolution*', Patrick Wyse Jackson (Ed), (Dublin: Royal Irish Academy, 2000), in *Ambix*, **48**, 2001, p. 46. David Knight is Professor of the History and Philosophy of Science at Durham University, and former Editor of *The British Journal for the History of Science* (1982–1988).

could not hold developments in this direction. We don't yet have an 'Irish Association for the Advancement of Science'. Should we have one? Or should we start talking to the BAAS? In any event, we are delighted to welcome the BAAS back to the Republic of Ireland after too long a gap.

The first Dublin BAAS Meeting

In a letter addressed to the Rev. Vernon Harcourt (1789-1871), dated 28 July 1834, Thomas Romney Robinson (1793–1882), Director of Armagh Observatory, wrote[9]:

> As the founder of the British Association, you will I hope excuse the liberty which I take in writing to you and requesting you to consider the propriety of having Dublin as the place of meeting for next year.
>
> Notwithstanding what was said last year of the necessity of conciliating the manufacturing class to our objects, and of the danger of connecting ourselves with universities, I submit that on the simple ground of superior accommodation Dublin should be preferred to any of the English towns which are likely to come forward....
>
> I need, I suppose, scarcely add that there is not the slightest cause for apprehension on the part of any member of the British Association from the disturbed state of Ireland. *That* threatens *us* only; *you* will be perfectly safe and treated with kindness even in its wildest parts, and in the metropolis there is as little chance of any annoyance as in London itself. But, on the other hand, if there be a spot in the British dominions where an impulse to the cultivation of science is peculiarly wanted, it is here, and I know of no ground where the presence of our Association would produce a more abundant harvest. At present our scientific bodies are in a state of asphyxia; you I hope will be their *Humane Society.*

So it was that the BAAS met in Dublin in 1835; and it was generally agreed that the meeting was a great success, with a larger attendance of paid (male!) members than had been the case in earlier years (1831 York 353; 1832 Oxford c.600; 1833 Cambridge 852; 1834 Edinburgh 1298; 1835 Dublin 1333[10]). The London weekly journal, *Athenaeum*, recorded[11]:

> In Dublin, notwithstanding the unusual quantity and quality of the scientific communications, business has been positively perplexed by the joyousness and festivities of the occasion....every practicable accommodation has been afforded for the lodging, feeding, feasting and amusing of the stranger....Déjeuners,

---

[9] Jack Morrell & Arnold Thackray, *Gentlemen of Science – Early Correspondence of the British Association for the Advancement of Science* (London: Royal Historical Society, 1984), p. 189.

[10] Morrell & Thackray, *Gentlemen of Science – Early Years of the British Association for the Advancement of Science* (Oxford: Oxford University Press, 1982), p. 548.

[11] Morrell & Thackray 1982, p. 147.

dinners, rural excursions, public entertainments by the learned bodies, and private parties by individuals of distinction, have exhausted all their combinations, to scatter the flowers of sociality over the path of scientific labour.

The Dublin meeting even came to terms with the problem of women and the 'troubles and ill-will generated by the scramble for ladies' tickets'[12]! Female tickets had been available before, but attempts to limit women's attendance at the scientific sessions had not been successful and this, it was suggested, 'limited the range of subjects, and greatly checked discussion'. There was also the problem that 'many persons applied for admission with no other view than to obtain a cheap week's amusement for the females of the family', and there was concern that the females would eat 'more in refreshments than the price of their ticket would have purchased'!

The ingenious Dublin solution was the requirement that, while allowing unrestricted admission to women who had travelled from abroad[13]:

An Irish philosopher had....to pay £2 for either his wife's or his daughter's pleasure; for the entertainment of both, he had to find £10. The size of the female audience was effectively controlled, to the advantage of the Association's income. The Dublin Meeting showed how the coffers of the local subscription fund could be well filled, while the Meeting was not inconveniently overwhelmed by women.

At the final dinner in Trinity College Examination Hall, the Lord Lieutenant knighted William Rowan Hamilton (1805–1865) – one of the local Secretaries of the BAAS for that year. A spectator observed that the 'magnificent entertainment resembled the coronation festival of George IV'[14].

Astronomy

Above we have referred to the Rev. Thomas Romney Robinson (1793–1882), director of Armagh Observatory from 1823 until his death. We have also mentioned William Rowan Hamilton (1805–1865) who was appointed Andrews Professor of Astronomy and Royal Astronomer of Ireland (the English equivalent was called the Astronomer Royal), and thus the Director of Dunsink Observatory, while still an undergraduate at Trinity College Dublin in 1827, a post which he also held until his death. Both of them were key players in the early success of the BAAS. Robinson was President of the BAAS when it met in Birmingham in 1849.

The famous passage grave at Newgrange, in Co. Meath, built around 3200BC, predates both the great Egyptian Pyramids (around 2500BC) and Stonehenge in England (about 2300BC), and is astronomically orientated so as to receive direct

---

[12] Morrell & Thackray 1982, p. 153.
[13] Morrell & Thackray 1982, p. 154.
[14] Morrell & Thackray 1982, p. 184.

sunlight in its inner chamber at winter solstice. Other sites are even more sophisticated, for example one at Loughcrew, Co. Meath, which defines the time of the equinoxes to within a day[15]. Thus, astronomy might be a good place to start this brief summary of the history of Irish physical science. Between the building of Newgrange and the founding of Dunsink, there is evidence of sophisticated astronomical reasoning by Irish monks in monasteries both within and outside Ireland. McCarthy & Breen in their 'An Evaluation of Astronomical Observations in the Irish Annals'[16] have identified:

> a body of records from 442 to 1133 documenting eclipses, comets, aurorae, volcanic dust clouds and possibly a supernova; from 627 to 1133 all of these records are of observations made in or near Ireland, and most of them are accurate in their chronological and descriptive details. Analysis of the details of these records implies that, at least from the seventh to the eleventh centuries, careful and sustained observation and recording of astronomical phenomena were conducted in some Irish monasteries....Critical examination of this [sic] data allows us to throw new light on the circumstances of the Synod of Whitby in 664, to identify the date of the eruption of the volcano Eldgjá in Iceland as the springtime of 939, and to identify a possible Western observation of the supernova of 1054 in the Crab Nebula.

Jim Bennett[17] writes:

> Irish-trained monks on Iona, for instance, worked on the dating of Easter, and Bede's thoroughgoing reform of the same subject, together with accounts of time measurement, chronology and astronomy, relied heavily on Irish sources.

In this essay, though, I won't go back further than the seventeenth century AD and, in the case of astronomy, I'll start in the eighteenth century. Jonathan Swift (1667–1745), the famous Dean of St Patrick's Cathedral in Dublin, is credited with the first mention of the Martian moons[18], for, in his *A Voyage to Laputa* (Part III of *Gulliver's Travels*), first published in 1726, he writes of the Laputans[19]:

> They have made a Catalogue of ten Thousand fixed Stars, whereas the largest of ours do not contain above one third Part of that Number. They have likewise discovered two lesser Stars, or *Satellites*, which revolve about *Mars*; whereof the

---

[15] Ian Elliott, Letter to *The Irish Times*, 25-27 December 2003.
[16] D. McCarthy & A. Breen, 'An Evaluation of Astronomical Observations in the Irish Annals', *Vistas in Astronomy*, **41**, 1971, pp. 117-138. I am grateful to Dr Ian Elliott for drawing this study to my attention.
[17] Jim Bennett, 'Why the History of Science Matters in Ireland', in David Attis & Charles Mollan (Eds), *Science and Irish Culture* (Dublin: Royal Dublin Society, 2004), p. 2.
[18] Patrick Moore, in *The Guinness Book of Astronomy Facts and Feats*, second edition (Middlesex, Guinness Superlatives, 1983), p. 82, gives this credit. Owen Gingerich, in his *The Great Copernicus Chase* (Sky Publishing, Cambridge, 1992), p. 178, reckons that Swift had 'some professional help' in his predictions – my thanks to Dr Ian Elliott for drawing this to my attention.
[19] Jonathan Swift, *Swift – Gulliver's Travels and Selected Writings in Prose and Verse*, Edited by John Hayward (London: Nonesuch Press, 1946), p. 166.

innermost is distant from the Centre of the primary Planet exactly three of his Diameters, and the outermost five; the former revolves in the Space of ten Hours, and the latter in Twenty-one and an Half; so that the Squares of their periodical Times, are very near in the same proportion with the Cubes of their Distance from the Center of *Mars*; which evidently shews them to be governed by the same Law of Gravitation, that influences the other heavenly Bodies.

Since the diameter of Mars is 6787 kilometres, the mean distances of the moons from Mars are 9270 km (Phobos) and 23,400 km (Deimos), and the mean periods 7 hours 39 minutes and 30 hours 21 minutes[20], his figures aren't too accurate, so Swift's description seems to be a good example of science fiction, though he did get the number of moons right. For the record, the moons were not actually discovered until 1877[21]. In passing, I often think it is a great pity that the Earth has only one moon; wouldn't it be fun to have half a dozen or so!

Resuming with scientific fact, Dunsink Observatory, about five miles from the centre of Dublin, was founded by Trinity College in 1783, and Armagh Observatory was founded by Archbishop Richard Robinson in 1790. While both have chequered histories[22,23], they are still going strong.

In terms of nineteenth century astronomy, the most impressive contribution of these Observatories was the publication of Thomas Romney Robinson's *Places of 5,345 Stars Observed from 1828 to 1854 at the Armagh Observatory*[24]. This was printed in 1859 'at the expense of Her Majesty's Government, on the recommendation of the Royal Society'. The 'Armagh catalogue' won for Robinson the Royal Medal of the Royal Society, of which he had become a Fellow in 1856. However, the contributions of these Observatories to science, and not just astronomy, in Great Britain and Ireland has been considerable, taking inspiration from the energy and accomplishments of the two great and long-serving early Directors, Robinson and Hamilton.

It was Robinson who played an important role in getting the Dublin firm of telescope makers, the Grubbs, 'off the ground' (appropriate term that!) by commissioning in 1833 from Thomas Grubb (1800–1878) a reflecting telescope with a 15 inch (38 cm) diameter mirror. The telescope supplied to Armagh in 1835 introduced important design features of great significance to the future development of the telescope[25]. These included the viewing position of the user who could observe the image at the back of the instrument through a small hole in the centre of the main

---

[20] Moore 1983, pp. 66 & 81.

[21] Moore 1983, p. 82 – the discoverer was the US astronomer Asaph Hall (1829–1907) at the US Naval Observatory at Washington.

[22] Patrick Wayman, *Dunsink Observatory 1785–1985 – A Bicentennial History* (Dublin: Dublin Institute for Advanced Studies & Royal Dublin Society, 1987).

[23] Jim Bennett, *Church, State and Astronomy in Ireland, 200 Years of Armagh Observatory* (Armagh/Belfast: Armagh Observatory & The Institute of Irish Studies, the Queen's University of Belfast, 1990).

[24] Rev. T.R. Robinson, *Places of 5,345 Stars Observed from 1828 to 1854 at the Armagh Observatory* (Dublin: Alex. Thom & Sons, 1859) pp. lxvii + 847.

[25] John Butler, *Seeing Stars – Two Hundred Years of Astronomy in Armagh* (Armagh: Armagh Observatory, 1990), p. 54.

mirror. (This arrangement had actually been invented in France as long ago as 1672 by an M. Cassegrain[26], but seemingly was not used in large telescopes before 1835). The more usual Newtonian arrangement (named after Isaac Newton) viewed images from the top of the telescope, which could be both cold and uncomfortable. Grubb also mounted the telescope so that it could revolve around an axis pointing to the North Pole, and this made it easier to keep stars in sight as the earth revolved. And he used a system of 'equilibrated levers' to support the mirror in such a way that the weight was distributed evenly over the back surface, thus minimising distortion of the image due to flexure. This system was later used to support the giant 72 inch (183 cm) diameter mirror of the *Leviathan of Parsonstown* (*see below*).

With this successful start, Thomas, joined later by his son Howard (afterwards Sir Howard) Grubb (1844–1931), built large telescopes in Dublin which were exported all over the world, to Madras, Madrid, Mecca, and Mississippi – to list just a few places beginning with the letter 'M'[27]. Particularly large and important telescopes were built for Melbourne in Australia in 1869 (a reflecting telescope with a 48 inch [122 cm] diameter mirror) and for Vienna in Austria in 1881 (a refracting telescope with a 27 inch [69 cm] diameter lens). Later the firm started to make periscopes and range finders, and their factory removed to England after the First World War in recognition of the vulnerability to enemy attack of the export passage between Ireland and England.

Robinson has made a lasting contribution to meteorology as the inventor of the four cup anemometer, of which he published details in 1850[28]. Now normally reduced to three rotating cups, this little device is still in universal use for measuring wind speed in weather stations, and also to draw attention to road hazards on the top of road warning bollards.

Another Director of Armagh Observatory (between 1882 and 1916) was the Copenhagen born John Louis Emil Dreyer (1852–1926), who is remembered for his revision, while at Armagh, of John Herschel's catalogue of galaxies, nebulae and star clusters. His *New General Catalogue*[29] is still used to day, and accounts for the abbreviation NGC when such objects are referred to. Dreyer contributed also to the history of astronomy, and is remembered particularly for his studies of his countryman, Tycho Brahe (1546–1601).

Estonia born Ernst Öpik (1893–1985) worked at Armagh Observatory from 1948 until 1981. He had predicted the existence of cometary bodies encircling the solar system – the Öpik–Oort cloud – in 1932, and is remembered for his work on dwarf stars, comets, asteroids, the cratering of Mars, and the origin of the Ice Ages[30].

---

[26] Henry C. King, *The History of the Telescope* (New York: Dover Publications, 1979 – republication of the 1955 edition), p. 75.

[27] Charles Mollan, *Irish National Inventory of Historic Scientific Instruments*, (Dublin: Samton Limited 1995), pp. 381-389.

[28] T.R. Robinson, 'Description of an Improved Anemometer for Registering the Direction of the Wind and the Space which it Traverses in Given Intervals of Time', *Transactions of the Royal Irish Academy*, 1855 (Paper read 10 June 1850), **22**, pp. 155-178.

[29] J.L.E. Dreyer, 'A New General Catalogue of Nebulae and Clusters of Stars, Being the Catalogue of the Late Sir John F.W. Herschel, Bart., Revised, Corrected, and Enlarged', *Memoirs of the Royal Astronomical Society*, 1888, **49**, pp. 1-237. Supplements were published in 1895 and 1908.

[30] John Butler, 'Ernst Julius Öpik – Astrophysicist', p. 225 in Charles Mollan, William Davis & Brendan Finucane (Eds), *Irish Innovators in Science & Technology* (Dublin: Royal Irish Academy and Enterprise Ireland, 2002).

While Sir William Rowan Hamilton was a Professor of Astronomy and Royal Astronomer of Ireland, his claim to lasting fame is not in astronomy but in mathematics, so we will deal with him later. Of the other Royal Astronomers at Dunsink, we can mention Sir Robert Stawell Ball (1840–1913) who served between 1874 and 1892, and Sir William Taylor Whittaker (1873–1956), who served between 1906 and 1912.

While Robert Ball, who was born in Dublin, is remembered in mathematics for his work on the theory of screws[31], he was most prominent as a lecturer and author of popular astronomical books, with titles such as *The Story of the Heavens* (1885), *In Starry Realms* (1892), *The Story of the Sun* (1893), and *In the High Heavens* (1893). *The Story of the Heavens*, written while he was at Dunsink (he became Lowndean Professor of Astronomy and Geometry at Cambridge University in 1892), was his masterpiece in this genre: Wayman[32] lists editions in 1886, 1889, 1890, and 1900, but I also have editions dated 1905 and 1910, and I have come across publication dates 1888, 1892, 1893, 1897, 1901, 1908 and 1913. Other titles too achieved multiple editions or reprints.

William Taylor Whittaker, born in Birkdale, Lancashire, wrote the first edition of his most famous work *History of the Theories of the Aether and Electricity, from the Age of Descartes to the Close of the Nineteenth Century* while at Dunsink, and he went on to become Professor of Mathematics at Edinburgh University. Indeed interest in science history studies seems to be a recurring characteristic of the Directors of Dunsink, and it was the late Patrick Wayman (1927–1998), Director from 1964 to 1992, who wrote the bicentennial history of the Observatory[32], in addition to many other historical articles.

Another person who worked briefly at Dunsink as a youngster was Francis Beaufort (1774–1867), born in Navan, Co. Meath, the famous Hydrographer of the Royal Navy, who rose to the rank of Rear Admiral, and who is remembered particularly to-day for his Beaufort scale of wind force at sea[33].

An Irish-born medical doctor, who qualified as a member of the Royal College of Surgeons (in London) in 1815, became interested in astronomy, and ended up as Director of the Royal Observatory at the Cape of Good Hope, a post he held from 1834 to 1869[34]. He was Thomas Maclear (1794–1879), from Newtownstewart in Co. Tyrone. While establishing the Cape Observatory as a leading astronomical observatory, he is particularly remembered for his work in the years 1837 to 1847 in re-measuring and extending the meridian arc (as a basis for the survey of the Colony), originally measured by Nicholas Louis de la Caille in 1751–1753. His observations of Mars during the opposition of 1862 were used in determining the sun's distance. Among other honours, he was elected to Fellowship of the Royal Society in 1831, knighted in 1860, and won the Royal Medal of the Royal Society in 1869. Michael Hoskin in Maclear's *DSB* entry[35] depicts a man of wide interests:

31 Robert Ball, *A Treatise of the Theory of Screws* (Cambridge: Cambridge University Press, 1900).
32 Patrick Wayman, *Dunsink Observatory 1785–1985 – A Bicentennial History* (Dublin: Dublin Institute for Advanced Studies & Royal Dublin Society, 1987), p. 123.
33 Nicholas Courtney, *Gale Force 10 – the Life and Legacy of Admiral Beaufort* (London: Review, 2003).
34 I am grateful to Dr Ian Elliott for drawing the achievements of Maclear to my attention.
35 Michael Hoskin, *Dictionary of Scientific Biography* (New York: Scribner's Sons, 1981), Volume 8, p. 613.

He assembled meteorological, magnetic, and tidal data, and in 1860 established time signals for Port Elizabeth and Simonstown. He sponsored the construction of lighthouses, promoted sanitary improvements, and took part on a commission of weights and measures. He was keenly interested in African exploration and was a friend of Livingstone and Stanley.

Ireland also had its share of private observatories. Edward Cooper (1798–1863) was an early customer of Thomas Grubb, and he set up an observatory at Markree Castle in Co. Sligo. Its most important work was the four-volume *Catalogue of Stars near the Ecliptic, Observed at Markree*, published between 1851 and 1856 by the Government at the recommendation of the Royal Society (as was the Armagh catalogue). It recorded 60,066 stars, only 8,965 of which were previously known[36]. Another of Grubb's customers was William E. Wilson (1851–1908), who made pioneering measurements of the surface temperature of the sun at his observatory at Daramona, Streete, Co. Westmeath – his results agreeing well with modern estimates. He also took part in the first photoelectric measurements of stars, and is remembered too for his superb photographs of celestial objects using his 24-inch Grubb reflector[37].

William H.S. Monck (1839–1915) from Skeirke, near Borris-in-Ossory in Co. Laois, was an able amateur astronomer who was the first to realise the existence of dwarf and giant stars. With Stephen Mitchell Dixon (1866–1940), he made the first photoelectric measurements of the brightness of planets[37]. His *Introduction to Stellar Astronomy* was published in 1899. He was a lawyer, and later Professor of Moral Philosophy at Trinity College Dublin. His nephew, Kenneth Edgeworth (1880–1972), a military engineer and author of books on economics, was another amateur astronomer who correctly predicted a cometary ring beyond the orbit of Neptune in 1943, eight years before Dutch-American astronomer Gerard Kuiper (1905–1973) made a similar prediction. A friend of Monck, John Ellard Gore (1845–1910), from Athlone in Co. Westmeath, was among the first to attempt to estimate the size of white dwarf and red giant stars. He published about ten books on popular astronomy – with titles such as *Planetary and Stellar Studies* (1888), *The Visible Heavens* (1893), *The Stellar Heavens* (1903) and *Astronomical Curiosities* (1909)[38]. We might note in passing that Thomas Maclear, Francis Beaufort, William Monck and John Gore were all sons of clergymen: there are different ways of looking to the heavens.

The most famous of Irish private observatories was that set up at Birr Castle in Co. Offaly by William Parsons, third Earl of Rosse (1800–1867). There he built, first a 36 inch (91.5cm) diameter reflecting telescope, and then an almighty 72 inch (183cm) diameter reflector, nicknamed *The Leviathan of Parsonstown* (Parsonstown being the former name of Birr) which came into operation in 1845. It was the biggest telescope in the world for over 70 years and with it Rosse discovered the spiral shape of some of

---

[36] Susan McKenna, 'Astronomy in Ireland from 1780', *Vistas in Astronomy*, 1968, 9, p. 290.
[37] Personal communication from Dr Ian Elliott.
[38] Personal communication from Dr Ian Elliott.

what are now known to be galaxies. This engineering feat of building such an enormous telescope, involving, among other things, the successful casting of the massive metal mirror, and achieved using local labour, brought such fame to Rosse that he rose to the height of scientific eminence, becoming President of the Royal Society between 1848 and 1854. Some years earlier he had been President of BAAS when it met in Cork in 1843.

Among Rosse's assistants at Birr Observatory were George Johnstone Stoney (1826–1911), whom we shall meet later at the christening of the 'electron', and Robert Ball and J.L.E. Dreyer whom we have already met. His son Laurence, the fourth Earl (1840–1908), continued the work at Birr, being remembered for his work on the surface temperature of the moon. Indeed, he was the first to make infrared measurements of any astronomical body other than the sun, though, to his chagrin, his achievements were ignored by his contemporaries: his estimate of the surface temperature is now recognised as excellent[38]. In recent years, the *Leviathan* has been restored, and remains a remarkably impressive object at the 'Historic Science Centre' at Birr Castle, the initiative of the current (seventh) Earl of Rosse. The youngest son of the third Earl, Charles Parsons (1854–1931), inherited his father's engineering genes and went on to invent the steam turbine engine, which made such a contribution to both marine transport and to electrical generation. Charles later bought the remnants of the Grubb firm in England, and Grubb Parsons continued to make large telescopes – their last being the 1984 4.2 metre William Herschel Telescope at La Palma in the Canary Islands[39]. The flourishing of the inventive mechanical genius in this family has been ascribed, at least in part, to the fact that both the third Earl and his sons were educated at home, and not sent to boarding school in England as would have been normal for aristocratic children[40]:

> The childhood experiences of the Parsons children were quite unusual. The fact that none of them attended a public school had one great advantage: they avoided contamination with the all pervasive contempt for active involvement in industry that characterised wealthy members of the establishment in Britain.

The astronomical assistants at Birr double jobbed as tutors to the third Earl's children.

So far our stars have been male. But two Irish born women made significant contributions to astronomy at a time when it was generally supposed that females were incapable of contributing to such esoteric studies. Agnes Clerke (1842–1907), born in Skibbereen, Co. Cork, amazed the astronomical fraternity by writing influential books – the most famous being her *A Popular History of Astronomy During the Nineteenth Century* (1885 – it went to four editions, and the last edition was re-published in facsimile by Sattre Press in 2003), and *Problems in Astrophysics* (1903). In the latter she had the audacity to suggest to contemporary astronomers how they might proceed! She also

---

[39] Ian Elliott, 'An Irish Galaxy', *Irish Studies Review*, Autumn 1993, 4. p. 22
[40] W. Garrett Scaife, *From Galaxies to Turbines – Science, Technology and the Parsons Family* (Bristol: Institute of Physics, 2000), p. 91.

contributed articles for the *Encyclopaedia Britannica* and the *Dictionary of National Biography*. Sir David Gill (1843–1914) had apparently commented[41]: 'no woman could do justice to this noble science', but he was to change his mind – and he even invited her out to the Cape Observatory in South Africa so that she could have some actual observing experience. Clerke's *Problems in Astrophysics* stated: 'This work is dedicated by permission to Sir David Gill, K.C.B. whose suggestion and encouragement prompted its composition and animated its progress'. Gill was President of the BAAS when it met in Leicester in 1907.

Margaret Huggins (née Murray 1848–1915) was born in Dublin, and married William Huggins (1824–1910) in 1875. She became not only his devoted wife, but also his astronomical collaborator, and between them they carried out pioneering studies in astronomical spectroscopy at their private observatory at Tulse Hill, London. Sir William was President of the Royal Society from 1900 to 1905, and had been President of the BAAS when it met in Cardiff in 1891. Both Lady Huggins and Miss Clerke had the notable distinction of being awarded honorary membership of the Royal Astronomical Society in 1903, a very rare honour for women. The two of them became close friends and, on the death of Agnes, Margaret wrote an appreciation of both Agnes and her also talented sister Ellen[42].

Finally we should mention a couple of more-recent contributors to the development of astronomy. William McCrea (1904–1999) was born in Dublin (though his family moved to England when he was only two years old!). A graduate of Cambridge University (1926), he became Professor of Mathematics in Queen's University Belfast (1936–1944) and followed this with academic appointments in the Royal Holloway College of the University of London and the University of Sussex. At different times he served as Foreign Correspondent, Treasurer, Secretary and President of the Royal Astronomical Society, and he became a Fellow of the Royal Society in 1952. Elliott summarises his chief work[43]:

> McCrea made many fundamental contributions to mathematics, quantum mechanics, stellar astronomy and cosmology....He collaborated with G.C. McVittie in applying relativity to cosmology. With E.A. Milne, he explored the use of Newtonian methods in cosmology to provide simple derivations of relativistic results. Other investigations included the evolution of galaxies, mechanisms for forming planets and satellites, the formation of molecules in the interstellar medium, and the emission of neutrinos from the Sun.

---

[41] Mary Brück, *Agnes Mary Clerke & the Rise of Astrophysics* (Cambridge: Cambridge University Press, 2002) p. 64.

[42] Margaret Huggins, *Agnes Mary Clerke and Ellen Mary Clerke, an Appreciation*, printed for private circulation. 1907, pp. xi + 54.

[43] Ian Elliott, 'William Hunter McCrea, Theoretical Astronomer', p. 242 in Charles Mollan, William Davis & Brendan Finucane (Eds), *Irish Innovators in Science & Technology* (Dublin: Royal Irish Academy and Enterprise Ireland, 2002).

It must be the ultimate dream of many human scientists to discover the little green men (women?) who inhabit our universe, but have yet to reveal themselves to us. An Irish-born woman scientist nearly got there. Jocelyn Bell Burnell (neé Bell – born 1943) was working at the Cavendish Laboratory at Cambridge in 1967 with an extensive radio telescope which she had helped to build. When studying the charts produced from this telescope, she noticed a regular pattern of pulses coming from the skies. It was established that these didn't come from man-made radio interference, so she and her supervisor, Anthony Hewish, christened their project LGM 1 (little green men 1!). It transpired, though, that they didn't come from intelligent life out there – friendly or otherwise. Jocelyn Bell had discovered 'pulsars'. A neutron star is a very compact, dense star composed almost entirely of neutrons, the result of a 'supernova' explosion of a massive star. Rapidly rotating neutron stars which emit pulsating radio waves are known as pulsars[44]. Many more have been discovered since, but it was Bell Burnell who discovered the first four. In 1974, Anthony Hewish was awarded the Nobel Prize in Physics for the pulsar work, and many have felt that Bell Burnell should have been a joint-winner.

Susan Jocelyn Bell was born in Lurgan, Co. Armagh, and graduated from Glasgow University (1965) with a PhD from Cambridge University (1968). She later worked at the University of Southampton, the Mullard Space Science Laboratory London, and the Royal Observatory Edinburgh. Her studies included gamma ray, X-ray, and infra-red astronomy. In 1991 she was appointed Professor of Physics in the largest University in the UK, the Open University. Her interests include the astrophysics of neutron stars, the physics of synchrotron nebulae around pulsars, and the surface temperature of pulsars[45].

Chemistry

If the study of astronomy goes back a long way in human development, so also does the development and use of chemistry, or what today might be called materials science. Some expertise in chemistry is needed to produce metals for use in war, decoration and religious observance. The earliest bronze age artefacts found in Ireland date to around 2000 BC[46]. The beauty of Irish craftsmanship in bronze, silver and gold, particularly from the eighth to twelfth centuries AD is widely recognised, and can be confirmed by a visit to the National Museum in Kildare Street, Dublin[47].

Early Irish chemistry had close associations with medicine, and some of the Irish clans had hereditary physicians[48]:

---

[44] Dr Ian Elliott provided this definition of pulsars.
[45] Charles Mollan, 'Irish Nobel Women – the Sky's the Limit!', *The Irish Scientist 1996 Year Book* (Dublin: Samton Limited, 1996), p. 9.
[46] Michael J. O'Kelly, *Early Ireland – An Introduction to Irish Prehistory* (Cambridge: Cambridge University Press, 1989), p. 148.
[47] Patrick F. Wallace & Raghnall Ó Floinn (Eds), *Treasures of the National Museum of Ireland – Irish Antiquities* (Dublin: Gill & Macmillan, 2002).
[48] Deasmumhan Ó Raghallaigh, *Three Centuries of Irish Chemists* (Cork: Cork University Press, 1941) p. 1.

The O'Hickeys were hereditary physicians to the O'Briens of Thomond, and the O'Shiels to the Mahoneys of Oriel. O'Callenans migrated from Galway to Cork, and their fame became a proverb, so that, down to the middle of the eighteenth century, it was said of an incurable patient: 'Not even an O'Callenan could save him'. Halley [Edmond Halley, 1656–1742], the celebrated astronomer, was descended from an Irish family of hereditary physicians.

Brock[49] writes:

> Chemistry presented the early natural philosopher with particularly difficult problems…There was no universally agreed chemical language, no convenient compartmentilization of substances into organic and inorganic, into solids, liquids and gases, or into acids, bases and salts, and no concept of purity.

The burning of wood had been given as evidence of the four elements – fire, air, water, and earth – of which matter was believed to be composed[50]:

> If You but consider a piece of green-Wood burning in a Chimney, You will readily discern in the disbanded parts of it the four Elements, of which we teach It and other mixt bodies to be compos'd. The fire discovers it self [sic] in the flame by its own light; the smoke by ascending to the top of the chimney, and there readily vanishing into air, like a River losing it self in the Sea, sufficiently manifests to what Element it belongs and gladly returns. The water in its own form boyling and hissing at the ends of the burning wood betrays it self to more then [sic] one of our senses; and the ashes by their weight, their firiness [sic], and their dryness, put it past doubt that they belong to the Element of Earth.

It is the author of this last passage, Robert Boyle (1627–1691), who made such an important contribution to the progress from alchemy (in which he also took an interest) to more rigorous and reproducible experimental chemistry. And he raised doubts about the adequacy of the 'peripatetick elements', fire, air, water, and earth, and even more about their alternatives, the 'hypostatical principles', salt, sulphur and mercury. It is claimed that one reason for his interest in chemistry was his mistrust of the administrations of medical men. Another was perhaps the fact that his father, Richard Boyle (1566–1643), was one of the pioneers of mining in Ireland. Gerard Boate, writing in 1652[51], records:

---

[49] William H. Brock, *The Fontana History of Chemistry* (London: Fontana Press, 1992) p. 42.
[50] Robert Boyle, *The Sceptical Chymist* (London: J. Cadwell for J. Crooke, 1661), pp. 21-22.
[51] Gerard Boate, Thomas Molyneux and Others, *A Natural History of Ireland in Three Parts* (Dublin, Geo. and Alex. Ewing, 1755), p. 76. Boate's *Irelands Naturall History* (reprinted as the first part of this later edition) was originally published in London in 1652.

The Earl of Cork whose iron-works being seated in Munster, afforded unto him very good opportunity of sending his iron out of the land by shipping, did in this particular surpass all others, so as he hath gained great treasures thereby: and knowing persons, who have had a particular insight into his affairs, do assure me, that he hath profited above one hundred thousand pounds clear gain by his said iron-works.

Another person who made good money from iron mining in Ireland was Sir William Petty (1623–1687), whom we shall meet later.

Richard Boyle was born in Canterbury, England, 'the second son of a younger brother' and therefore strapped for money. He grasped opportunities in Ireland to make a vast fortune, eventually enjoying rents far greater than any other subject of King Charles I[52]. It was this success which allowed his youngest son Robert to devote his life to the study of alchemy, chemistry, natural philosophy, and theology. Robert's mother, Catherine Fenton, was born in Ireland, the daughter of Sir Geoffrey Fenton, Principal Secretary of State in Ireland from 1580. Robert didn't spend much time in Ireland, as he was sent at an early age to Eton College, and then went on a grand tour of Europe, before taking up residence in England. On one visit back to Ireland in 1654 he comments[53]:

For my part, that I may not live wholly useless, or altogether a stranger in the study of nature, since I want glasses and furnaces to make a chemical analysis of inanimate bodies, I am exercising myself in making anatomical dissections of living animals: wherein (being assisted by....Dr. Petty, our general's physician) I have satisfied myself of the circulation of the blood.

It was this experimental approach to his studies which made Boyle stand out in the history of science (whether claimed by Ireland or England!), and he was a prolific author, publishing details of his experiments, so that they could be reproduced and confirmed by others. He has been described as 'the son of the Earl of Cork and the father of chemistry'. His chemical work included studies on chemical assay, combustion, indicators, specific gravity, clinical chemistry, and luminescence[54]. In physics, he is best remembered for Boyle's Law which relates the volume of gas to pressure.

Another scientist, from an Ulster Scots family, who has achieved lasting renown in the history of chemistry, is Joseph Black (1728–1799). His father was born in Belfast and his mother in Scotland, but his parents were in Bordeaux (in the wine trade) when he was born. He was sent to school in Belfast from the age of 12 to 16[55]. In 1744 he

---

[52] Nicholas Canny, *The Upstart Earl – A Study of the Social and Mental World of Richard Boyle, First Earl of Cork, 1566–1643* (Cambridge: Cambridge University Press, 1982), p. 6.

[53] Letter from Robert Boyle to Frederick Clodius quoted in R.E.W Maddison, *The Life of the Honourable Robert Boyle F.R.S.* (London: Taylor & Francis, 1969), p. 84.

[54] Duncan Thorburn Burns, 'Robert Boyle', p. 21 in Charles Mollan, William Davis & Brendan Finucane (Eds), *Irish Innovators in Science & Technology* (Dublin: Royal Irish Academy and Enterprise Ireland, 2002).

[55] Duncan Thorburn Burns, 'Joseph Black', p. 33 in Charles Mollan, William Davis & Brendan Finucane (Eds), *Irish Innovators in Science & Technology* (Dublin: Royal Irish Academy and Enterprise Ireland, 2002).

entered the University of Glasgow to study medicine, and his future professional life was divided between that University and the University of Edinburgh. Taking a special interest in chemistry, he was characterised by the carefulness of his quantitative work, using the chemical balance to great effect. He was the first to appreciate the difference between 'fixed air' (carbon dioxide) and atmospheric air, and is credited as the father of pneumatic chemistry. He was also the first to develop the concepts of latent heat and specific heat. He was a close friend and collaborator of James Watt (1736–1819)[56], famous for his development of the separate condenser steam engine. In the year that William Thomson was President of the BAAS (Edinburgh 1871), and Thomas Andrews (see below) was President of the Chemical Sciences Section, letters dating from the years 1789 and 1790 from Antoine Lavoisier (1743–1794) to Joseph Black were published in the BAAS Annual Report (pp. 189-192). The first, dated 19 Septembre 1789 (only a couple of months after the storming of the Bastille on July 14) begins[57]:

> MONSIEUR, – C'est un member de l'académie Royale des Sciences de Paris qui vous écrit à titre de Confrère: c'est un des plus zélés admirateurs de la profondeur de votre génie et des importantes révolutions que vos découvertes ont occasionnées dans les Sciences....

Unfortunately, Lavoisier's more celebrated contributions to chemistry were brought to an end with the help of the guillotine on 8 May 1794.

Another chemist, this time with much closer Irish connections than Boyle and Black, who was also in close touch with his French colleagues, was Richard Kirwan (1733–1812). For example, he had extensive correspondence with the French chemist Guyton de Morveau (1737–1816) between the years 1782 to 1802 (the letters were published by the University of California in 1994[58]). Kirwan was born in Cloughballymore in Co. Galway. After his early education in Ireland, he entered the University of Poitiers in France, and then joined the Jesuits in Paris, intending to enter the priesthood. Due to the untimely death of his older brother, he inherited the family fortune, gave up his holy aspirations, and returned to Galway, where he soon fitted up a laboratory and amassed a library. He lived in London between 1769 and 1772, and again from 1777 to 1787, and received the Copley Medal of the Royal Society in 1782 for his work on chemical affinity. He then lived in Dublin until his death, serving as President of the Royal Irish Academy from 1799 until 1812. He was a man of many parts, and made notable contributions to mineralogy and meteorology as well as to chemistry. He published his *Elements of Mineralogy* in 1784, the first systematic work on the subject in English, which was translated and published in Paris the following year. A second

---

[56] Eric Robinson & Douglas McKie, *Partners in Science – Letters of James Watt and Joseph Black* (London: Constable, 1970).

[57] SIR, – It is a member of the Royal Academy of Sciences of Paris who writes to you under the title Colleague: I am one of the most zealous admirers of your profound genius and of the important revolutions which your discoveries have occasioned in the Sciences....

[58] Emmanuel Grison, Michelle Goupil & Patrice Bret (Eds), *A Scientific Correspondence During the Chemical Revolution* (Berkeley: University of California, 1994).

English edition was published in two volumes in 1794 and 1796, and it was also translated into German and Russian. He noted in his preface that 'Chymistry, the parent of mineralogy, is cultivated by the most enlightened nations in Europe and particularly in France, with a degree of ardour that approaches to enthusiasm'[59] – something which he considered was not the case at that time in Great Britain and Ireland.

He was somewhat unfortunate in that his major chemical work, *An Essay on Phlogiston and the Constitution of Acids*, first published in 1787, supported the then accepted concept of a mysterious phlogiston, which it was believed was lost when something burned. The work was translated into French by Lavoisier's wife, Marie Anne Pierette Paulze, and it was Lavoisier (while he still had his head) who demonstrated that the concept of phlogiston was not necessary. Guyton de Morveau came to support Lavoisier before Kirwan did, and he wrote to him in December 1787 with consummate tact[60]:

> Your system, my dear confrere, is without doubt both the most scientific and the most ingenious that has been proposed, but I hope that you will see with us that one can do without this system and it will be your work that will have brought forward the time when sound eyes will see this as well.

Lavoisier published his classic *Traité Élementaire de Chimie* in 1789. In the same year another Irish chemist, William Higgins (1763–1825), published his major work *A Comparitive View of the Phlogistic and Anti-Phlogistic Theories*, which sided with Lavoisier against Kirwan. Higgins was born in Collooney, Co. Sligo. We don't know much about his early life, but he went to London around 1782 to work with his uncle, the chemist Bryan Higgins (1737–1820), who also was born in Collooney, and then spent a couple of years in Oxford. He became one of a new breed of professional scientists on his appointment as chemist at the Apothecaries' Hall in Dublin in 1792, and then became Professor of Chemistry and Mineralogy in the Dublin Society (later – in 1820 – the Royal Dublin Society) in 1795. He carried out useful work of a practical nature making 'experiments on dyeing materials and other articles, wherein chymistry may assist the arts, as may occur'[61] and, for example, published his *Essay on Bleaching* in 1799. Higgins was convinced that, in his *Comparative View*, he had anticipated John Dalton (1766–1874) in introducing the chemical atomic theory. It does appear that there was some justice in his claim, but few would disagree that Dalton deserves the credit which he has received.

The end of the eighteenth century was a stirring time in world history, and this had dramatic repercussions in Ireland. Inspired by the outcome of the American war of independence (1775–1783), and the French revolution (the Bastille was stormed in 1789 and Louis XIV guillotined in 1793), there was an upswelling of the long felt

[59] Quoted in Eva Philbin, 'Chemistry', in T. Ó Raifeartaigh (Ed), *The Royal Irish Academy – a Bicentennial History 1785–1985* (Dublin: Royal Irish Academy, 1985), p. 278.

[60] Grison 1994, p. 33.

[61] Henry F. Berry, *A History of the Royal Dublin Society* (London: Longmans, Green & Co., 1915), p. 355.

desire among many in Ireland for freedom from what was considered the tyranny of the English occupation. This wasn't confined to the Catholic population, many of the leaders being Protestants. However the hoped for assistance from France did not work out, and risings in 1798 (leading to the death of, among others, Lord Edward FitzGerald and Wolfe Tone) and 1803 (leading to the execution of Robert Emmet) were dramatic failures. Among the results of these failures was the exile of some of the leaders (others had been killed or executed), who subsequently made notable contributions to their adopted countries.

One of these was William James MacNeven (1763–1841), born near Aughram, Co. Galway, who ended up in America (he landed there on 4 July 1805). A medical doctor by training, his interests turned towards practical chemistry, and in New York, where he became 'Professor of Chemistry and Materia Medica in the College of Physicians and Surgeons of the University of the State of New-York'. He published books such as *Exposition of the Atomic Theory of Chymistry and the Doctrine of Definite Proportions* (1819), *Chymical Exercises in the Laboratory of the College of Physicians and Surgeons* (also 1819), and an emended version of William Thomas Brande's *A Manual of Chemistry* (1829)[62]. He has been credited as 'the Father of American Chemistry'[63] and has a 40 foot (12 metre) pillar monument in St Paul's churchyard in Lower Broadway, New York.

Another of these talented exiles was Thomas Addis Emmet (1764–1827), brother of executed Robert. In passing it might be mentioned that Robert Emmet (1778–1803) apparently showed great promise, notably in chemistry and mathematics, while a student at Trinity College Dublin, before he abandoned his studies to escape arrest for his subversive activities[64]. Indeed his interest in chemistry and mathematics preceded his entry into Trinity, and it might have had tragic results when he was aged 14, for the French author and friend of the family, The Countess d'Haussonville, records[65]:

> He was accustomed to make chemical experiments in his father's house. After one of these experiments, he applied himself to study a book of algebra, and endeavoured to solve the problem which, by the author's admission, was of extreme difficulty. Absorbed in his study, he imprudently raised his hand to his mouth, and poisoned himself with some corrosive sublimate, which he had been handling a few moments before.

Fortunately he survived (and hopefully learned the hard way that washing hands is prudent after chemical experiments). Perhaps had he not lost his head he (as had

[62] William Davis, 'William James MacNeven: Chemist and United Irishman', in Patrick Wyse Jackson (Ed), *Science and Engineering in Ireland in 1798: a Time of Revolution* (Dublin: Royal Irish Academy, 2000) p. 7-24.
[63] J.P. Murray, 'W.J. MacNeven: Father of American Chemistry', *Irish Medical Journal* (1986), **79**, pp. 260-263.
[64] Ruán O'Donnell, *Remember Emmet – Images of the Life and Legacy of Robert Emmet* (Bray: Wordwell in association with The National Library of Ireland, 2003), p. 16
[65] Thomas Addis Emmet, *Memoir of Thomas Addis and 'Robert Emmet', with their Ancestors and Immediate Family* (Kilcock: The Warfield Press, 2003 reprint of 1915 original), Volume 2, p. 6.

Lavoisier not so long before), Robert Emmet might now be remembered for his contributions to chemistry.

A nephew of Robert Emmet, one of Thomas Addis Emmet's sons, John Patten Emmet (1796–1842), was born in Dublin, and joined his father in America in 1805. He became a pupil of MacNeven, graduating in medicine, and his talents were recognised in his appointment as Professor of Chemistry and Materia Medica at the University of Virginia in 1827. A noted lecturer, he did not have good health and died at the early age of 46[66].

A later emigrant, after yet another unsuccessful rising, that of 1848, was Thomas Antisell (1817–1893). Also a medical doctor, he became examiner to the US Patent Office in 1856, served in the American Civil-War, rising to the rank of Lieutenant-Colonel, and was chemist to the US Department of Agriculture from 1866 to 1870. His books included: *Agricultural Chemistry* (1847), *Cyclopaedia of the Useful Arts* (1852) and *Manufacture of Photogenic or Hydrocarbon Oils from Coal and Other Bituminous Substances Capable of Supplying Burning Fluids* (1859)[67] – the latter, according to the author, 'the first published monograph on the art of distilling oils from minerals containing Bitumen'.

In passing, we might mention Limerick born Peter Wolfe (1727–1803) who invented the famous Wolfe bottle used ever since in virtually all chemical laboratories; Dublin (or maybe Calais) born Aeneas Coffey (1780–1852) who invented the patent still, the first to incorporate a heat exchanger, which became the standard method for the production of industrial spirit[68]; Edmund Davy (1785–1857), cousin of the more famous Humphrey (1778–1829), who first synthesised what we now call acetylene in the laboratory of the Royal Dublin Society, a success which he communicated to the BAAS in 1836[69]; Culnady, Co. Derry, born James Murray (1788–1871), who patented 'Milk of Magnesia'; and Maxwell Simpson (1815–1902), born in Beech Hill, Co. Armagh, who carried out important early work on aliphatic organic compounds, being, for example, the first to prepare succinic acid from ethylene cyanide (published in 1860), other di- and tri-basic organic acids, and who clarified the picture of the structure of the oxalic acid series[70]. Simpson was President of the Chemical Science Section at the BAAS meeting held in Dublin in 1878, and his address was directed 'to bring before you the claims of this science to a place in general education, and the claims of original research to a place in the curriculum for higher degrees in our Universities'[71].

---

[66] Duncan Thorburn Burns, 'John Patten Emmet (1796–1842): Foundation Professor of Chemistry in the University of Virginia', in Patrick Wyse Jackson (Ed), *Science and Engineering in Ireland in 1798: A Time of Revolution* (Dublin: Royal Irish Academy, 2000), p. 25-33.

[67] Deasmumhan Ó Raghallaigh, *Three Centuries of Irish Chemists* (Cork: Cork University Press, 1941), p. 12.

[68] William Davis, 'Aeneas Coffey', p. 54 in Charles Mollan, William Davis & Brendan Finucane (Eds), *Irish Innovators in Science and Technology* (Dublin: Royal Irish Academy and Enterprise Ireland, 2002).

[69] Edmund Davy, 'Notice of a New Gaseous Bicarburet of Hydrogen', *Notices and Abstracts of Communications to the British Association for the Advancement of Science at the Bristol Meeting, August 1836* (bound into the Annual Report of that year), p. 62.

[70] Desmond Reilly, 'Contributions of Maxwell Simpson (1815–1902) to Aliphatic Chemical Synthesis', *Chymia*, 1953, 4, pp. 159-170.

[71] Maxwell Simpson, *Report of the British Association for the Advancement of Science held at Dublin in August 1878* (London: John Murray, 1879), p. 501.

Among practical chemists who emigrated to England were Josias Gamble (1776–1848) and James Muspratt (1793–1886). After beginning their careers as manufacturing chemists in Ireland, they moved to Liverpool (Muspratt in 1822 and Gamble in 1828), and for a while were in business together. They enjoyed considerable commercial success, and have been hailed as among the founders of chemical industry in England[72], Muspratt indeed being dubbed the 'father of the alkali industry'. These two Irishmen can be credited with cleaning up the English, since they produced vast quantities of soda – and cheaper soda meant cheaper soap! They did, though, get into trouble for polluting the English atmosphere, so perhaps their presence there was a mixed blessing. Several of James Muspratt's sons became chemists. The best known is Dublin born James Sheridan Muspratt (1821–1871), whose massive 1186 page, two-volume *Chemistry, Theoretical, Practical, and Analytical, as Applied to the Arts and Manufactures*, first published between 1854 and 1860 enjoyed great success, as it achieved several English, American and German editions, and was translated into Russian. It earned him an honorary doctorate from Harvard University. Brock[73] records:

> Each fascicule of 32 pages craftily ended in the middle of an entry, so that the subscriber had the incentive to purchase the next monthly part….Muspratt's Chemistry was perhaps distinctive in its uncompromising emphasis on the practice of chemical technology.

Another 1798 exile, John Kean, fled to Paris to escape the attentions of Major Henry Charles Sirr (1764–1841), head of the Dublin Police. Sirr had arrested most of the Leinster Committee of the United Irishmen in advance of the planned rising in '98; later in the same year he shot Lord Edward FitzGerald – who soon after died of his wounds; and, in 1803, he arrested Robert Emmet – who was subsequently hanged and beheaded[74], so John Kean's exit seems to have shown good sense. In Paris, Kean took the opportunity to study chemistry. He later returned to set up a chemical business in Dublin, taking the precaution of changing his name to Kane. He is reputed to have been the first manufacturer in Great Britain and Ireland to set up a Gay-Lussac Tower for producing sulphuric acid[75].

John's second son, Robert Kane (1809–1890), born in Dublin, qualified to practice medicine, but seems to have been influenced by his father's trade, and applied himself to chemistry, being appointed in 1831, at the early age of 21, to the chair of chemistry in the Apothecaries' Hall in Dublin. In the same year he published his *Elements of Practical Pharmacy*, and founded the *Dublin Journal of Medical and Chemical Science*. The

---

[72] J. Fenwick Allen, *Some Founders of the Chemical Industry* (London & Manchester: Sherratt & Hughes, 1906), Gamble is featured on pp. 37-66, and Muspratt on pp. 67-100.
[73] William H. Brock, *The Fontana History of Chemistry* (London: Fontana Press, 1992) p. 275.
[74] Pat Marshall, 'Town Major Sirr, the Arresting Officer', *History Ireland* (2003), **11** (No. 3), p. 13.
[75] T.S. Wheeler, *et al*, *The Natural Resources of Ireland – a Series of Discourses Delivered before the Royal Dublin Society in Commemoration of the Centenary of the Publication by the Society of Sir Robert Kane's 'The Industrial Resources of Ireland'* (Dublin: Royal Dublin Society, 1944), p. 6.

latter became the *Irish Journal of Medical Science* in 1922, and is still being published. Kane was the first to propose what came to be known as the ethyl radical (C_2H_5-), he devised a method of purifying methanol by combining it with calcium chloride, and he synthesised cyclic trimethylbenzene (mesitylene) from acetone in 1837[76]. When he won the Cunningham medal of the Royal Irish Academy in 1843, the then President, William Rowan Hamilton, referred to[77]:

> that combination of genius and industry which has already caused the researches of Kane to influence in no slight degree the progress of chemical science and has won for him a European reputation.

However, Kane is best remembered in Ireland for publication of his seminal *The Industrial Resources of Ireland* (1844, second edition 1845) while employed as Professor of Natural Philosophy at the Royal Dublin Society. His call for the development of Irish resources was inspirational, though the actual reaction of the nation was sluggish. He became Director of the Museum of Irish Industry in 1847, by which time he had also been appointed the (non-resident) President of the newly founded Queen's College Cork, and had received a knighthood. This was the time of the Irish potato famine, but Kane's attempted scientific and social contributions to ameliorating the consequences had little positive result.

A chemist who attained the distinction of being appointed President of the BAAS – for its meeting in Glasgow in 1876 – was Thomas Andrews (1813–1885). In his Presidential address he said[78]:

> Whatever view be taken of the actual condition of scientific research there can be no doubt that it is both the duty and the interest of the country to encourage a pursuit so ennobling in itself, and fraught with such important consequences to the wellbeing of the community.

Born in Belfast, and after a varied education in Ireland, Scotland and France, he graduated in medicine at the University of Edinburgh in 1835, then returned home and set up in practice in Belfast. He was appointed to the Chair of Chemistry in the newly formed Medical School at the Belfast Academical Institution, also in 1835[79]. He was an original member of the Chemical Society in 1841, and became Vice President of Queen's College Belfast when it was founded in 1845, and Professor of Chemistry when students were first admitted in 1849.

76 J.R. Partington, *A History of Chemistry, Volume 4* (Reprinted Edition, New York: Martino Publishing, 1964), pp. 347, 355.
77 Wheeler 1944, p. 11.
78 P.G. Tait & A. Crum Brown (Eds), *The Scientific Papers of the Late Thomas Andrews, M.D., F.R.S.* (London: Macmillan & Co.,, 1889), p. 409.
79 John Jamieson, *The History of the Royal Belfast Academical Institution 1810–1960* (Belfast: William Mullan & Son, 1959), pp. 69-70.

Andrews carried out accurate experiments on heats of neutralisation, heats of formation of metallic halides, heats of reaction of salt solutions, heats of formation of oxides and chlorides, and of water, and latent heats of evaporation[80]. He was the first to use a 'bomb-calorimeter' – a closed metal vessel in which a mixture of gases could be electrically exploded. He demonstrated that ozone was a form of oxygen.

But his major contribution to the history of chemistry was his identification, in 1861, of a critical temperature for gases, above which they could not be liquefied by pressure alone. His work was, in a sense, a continuation of that of Robert Boyle, since he demonstrated that Boyle's Law does not describe the behaviour of gases under extreme conditions. His results could be represented by a three dimensional surface, which added a temperature co-ordinate to those of pressure and volume. He wrote in 1871[81]:

> We may yet live to see, or at least we may feel with some confidence that those who come after us will see, such bodies as oxygen and hydrogen in the liquid, perhaps even in the solid state.

How true this was. What had previously been called 'permanent gases', because they apparently could not be liquefied, were in due course obtained in liquid and solid forms – with dramatic impacts on subsequent scientific and technological development.

Andrews received honorary degrees from the University of Edinburgh (1871), Trinity College Dublin (1873), and the University of Glasgow (1877), and was offered a knighthood in 1880 – but refused it[82].

Two Irish-born scientists made important contributions to the early development of x-ray crystallography. These were John Desmond Bernal (1901–1971) and Kathleen Lonsdale (1903–1971).

Bernal was born in Nenagh, Co. Tipperary, into a family of Jewish origins which had arrived in Ireland in 1840 and had converted to Catholicism. He went to school first in Ireland and then in England, before entering Cambridge University in 1919. It was at Cambridge that he lost his faith[83]:

> I saw my whole life of vanity. My universe was broken into bits!…I lost my faith by a gradual process. First God, then Jesus, then the Virgin Mary, and lastly the rites of the Church disappeared, regretfully, inevitably….I had a quarrel with the Church because I could not help seeing it as an active agent of political reaction throughout the world.

[80] J.R. Partington, *A History of Chemistry, Volume 4* (Reprinted Edition, New York: Martino Publishing, 1964), p. 609.

[81] *Dictionary of Scientific Biography*, Vol. I, p. 161.

[82] T.W. Moody & J.C. Beckett, *Queen's, Belfast 1845–1949 – The History of a University* (London, Faber & Faber, 1959 in two volumes), p. 582.

[83] Ann Synge, 'Early Years and Influences', pp. 1-16 in Brenda Swann & Francis Aprahamian, *J.D. Bernal, a Life in Science and Politics* (London: Verso 1999), pp. 11-13.

He joined the Communist Party and became a left-wing agitator and stridently anti-war. But when the Second World War actually broke out, he became a scientific advisor to Lord Mountbatten, Chief of Combined Operations to the British War effort. He played a key part in planning the successful landings of British troops on the Normandy beaches on D-day (6 June 1944), and indeed himself landed on the beaches on D-day + 1 to confirm that his predictions of the conditions had been accurate – they had. Following the War, he was again a key player internationally in the anti-war movement, rising to be President of the World Peace Council in 1958, having won the Lenin Peace Prize in 1953. A prolific thinker and author, he wrote seminal books on such topics as *The Social Function of Science, Science in History*, and *World without War*. A proponent of free love, one of his lovers was Dorothy Hodgkin, who was the sole winner of the Chemistry Nobel Prize in 1964 – though she felt that the Prize should have been a joint award to Bernal and herself[84].

After graduating in 1923, he worked on X-ray crystallography with Nobel Prize winner, Sir William Bragg, then at the Royal Institution in London. It was in this area that Bernal made his scientific reputation. He used x-ray crystallography on molecules of biological importance, and is credited as the founder of the discipline of molecular biology. He was appointed professor of Physics (1938) and then of Crystallography (1963 – at his wish) at Birkbeck College of the University of London. He became a Fellow of the Royal Society in 1937 and won its Royal Medal in 1945. He was a Foreign Member of academies of science in seven countries; and won a variety of other awards and honorary degrees. On the distaff side, he has the distinction of having been suspended from the Council of the BAAS in 1949 for making the following comment in a speech given in Moscow[85]:

> In the United States it will soon be the case that no one who is not and has not always been an open enemy of the Soviet Union will be allowed to teach or research in science – and Britain will obediently follow suit.

One of the people who, while she did not agree with Bernal, objected to this action of the BAAS was Kathleen Lonsdale. She wrote to the BAAS Secretary[86]:

> I am convinced that it is much more important that the British Association should set its face against witch-hunting and purges of all kinds, than that they should register public disapproval of a particular speech, which would soon have sunk into oblivion if so much attention had not been called to it in the first place.

---

84 Hilary Rose & Steven Rose, 'Red Scientist, two Strands from a Life in Three Colours', pp. 132-159 in Brenda Swann & Francis Aprahamian, *J.D. Bernal, a Life in Science and Politics* (London: Verso, 1999), p. 156.

85 Maurice Goldsmith, *Sage – a Life of J.D. Bernal* (London: Hutchinson, 1980), p. 183-189.

86 Letter dated 5 April 1950, quoted in Goldsmith 1980, p. 188.

Although originally trained in physics and claiming to know very little chemistry, Lonsdale became Professor of Chemistry in University College London in 1949 – the first woman professor there.

She was born in Newbridge, Co. Kildare, the tenth child of Harry Yardley, the postmaster, and his wife, Jessie Cameron. Of her father, Kathleen said, 'I think that it was from him that I inherited my passion for facts'[87]. She also commented, 'Perhaps, for my sake, it was well that there was no testimony against a high birth rate in those days'. It was probably from Jessie, though, that she inherited her character, for her mother was described as 'a considerable character, a Baptist, with an independent mind'.

Hers was a very poor and not a very happy family. Four of her six brothers died in infancy. One of the two who did survive was the eldest, Fred, who became a wireless operator, and had the unhappy distinction of receiving the final signals from the *Titanic* when it sank in 1912. Jessie and the surviving children moved to Essex in 1908, and Kathleen attended classes in physics, chemistry and higher mathematics at the County High School for Boys in Ilford, the only girl from the girls' school to do so. Anxious to progress, she opted not to try for entrance to Cambridge University and entered Bedford College for Women in the University of London at the age of sixteen. She started out studying mathematics, but changed to physics as she felt it offered her more career options. She took first place in the whole University of London in the honours BSc exam in 1922 with the highest marks in ten years.

On graduation, she, like Bernal, worked with Sir William Bragg on X-ray diffraction. In 1927 she moved with her husband, Thomas Lonsdale, to Leeds, and it was there that she made her most memorable contribution to chemical history, for she showed, by her analysis of hexamethyl benzene, in 1929, that the benzene ring was flat, a result of immense importance in organic chemistry. On her return to London, she worked at the Royal Institution for fifteen years. Using a large electromagnet, she studied diamagnetic anisotrophy, and she was able to provide experimental verification of the postulated delocalisation of electrons and the existence of molecular orbitals – results of considerable importance to theoreticians. After the war, in 1946, she was appointed reader in crystallography at University College London, publishing her University extension lectures as *Crystals and X-rays* (1948). She held the post of Professor of Chemistry in UCL from 1949 until 1968, developing her own research school, which dealt with a wide variety of topics, including solid state reactions, pharmacological compounds, and the constitution of bladder and kidney stones. She worked also on synthetic diamonds, and an hexagonal diamond found in meteorites is called *lonsdaleite* in her honour. While at UCL, she edited three volumes of *International tables for X-ray crystallography* (1952,1959,1962), the standard work in the field. Indeed it was said of her that 'there is a sense in which she appeared to own the whole of crystallography in her time'.

Meanwhile, she had become a Quaker and thus a pacifist, and this led to her imprisonment in 1943 for refusing to register for civil defence duties, and then refusing

---

[87] Dorothy Hodgkin, 'Kathleen Lonsdale', *Biographical Memoirs of Fellows of the Royal Society*, **21**, 1975, p. 447.

to pay the £2 fine – 'Do the police come for one or do I just have to go to prison myself?' Following her internment, she wrote to the Governor suggesting how conditions for the prisoners could be improved, and she later became a prison visitor. She got out of prison in time to attend a 1943 scientific meeting at The Dublin Institute for Advanced Studies. This was chaired by Nobel Prizewinner Erwin Schrödinger (1887–1961) – who worked at the Institute from 1940–1956, and became an Irish citizen in 1948 – and the meeting was attended by Taoiseach Eamon de Valera. While in Ireland she visited her birthplace at Newbridge.

In 1945, she broke new ground for women, by being one of the first two of her sex to be admitted Fellow of the 285-year-old Royal Society. She was created a Dame Commander of the Most Excellent Order of the British Empire in 1956 – her pacifism presumably forgiven, though it could hardly be forgotten as she was author of the Penguin Special *Is peace possible?* in 1957. She was the first woman President of the BAAS in 1968, and she received many other awards. She died in London, of cancer. In Ireland, her memory was honoured in 1998 by the University of Limerick when it called a new College of Science building the 'Kathleen Lonsdale Building'.

Mathematics and Physics

Mathematics is considered (by mathematicians anyway) as the queen of the sciences, and there is no doubt that we would not have progressed very far in the understanding of our world without them. A knowledge of mathematics is evident from very early times – for example, the builders of the passage graves in the Boyne Valley in Ireland over 5,000 years ago must have had considerable expertise. Basically what Physics does is measure things, which of course involves both mathematics and the invention of instruments. While we can identify different strands of mathematics and physics, the point at which one stops and the other starts is not easy to define, so we'll consider both together. Dublin-born William Molyneux (1656–1698) put it elegantly: 'there is no part of philosophy wherein the mathematicks are not deeply ingredient'[88] (physics used to be called natural philosophy).

We'll start with a very practical application of mathematics, and with someone whom we have mentioned before – William Petty (1623–1687). Although he wasn't born in Ireland, his time in Ireland was important to him, to Ireland, and to the history of science on a broader front. In a recent book, published by the Royal Dublin Society, David Attis entitled his contribution: 'Sir William Petty and the Mathematical Conquest of Ireland'[89]. He demonstrates Petty's use of mathematics (often quite simple arithmetic) in what Petty hoped would be the subjugation and transformation of Ireland and the Irish into a civilised country and community – like his native Protestant England. Attis comments[90]:

---

[88] K. Theodore Hoppen, *The Common Scientist in the Seventeenth Century – A Study of the Dublin Philosophical Society 1683–1708* (London: Routledge & Kegan Paul, 1970), p. 120.

[89] David Attis, 'Sir William Petty and the Mathematical Conquest of Ireland', pp. 51-76 in David Attis & Charles Mollan (Eds), *Science & Irish Culture* (Dublin: Royal Dublin Society, 2004).

[90] Attis 2004, pp. 59 & 76.

Science....came to Ireland in the hands of the English colonizer....however this was not simply a case of English science imported into Ireland. The Irish context played a key role in shaping English attitudes. Ireland offered an unprecedented opportunity to demonstrate the power and the profitability of the new scientific approach to areas like agriculture, mining and warfare....Petty developed new tools – in surveying and political economy – in response to specific Irish problems. In this sense, the new science made modern Ireland just as Ireland made modern science.

Petty was a medical graduate, but his major claims to fame lie in surveying, cartography, economics and political science, and he is credited as the inventor of the science of statistics[91]. Referring to Ireland, and ignoring the value of any native culture, he stated in the Author's Preface to his book, *The Political Anatomy of Ireland*, written about 1673[92]:

As students in Medicine practice their enquiries upon cheap and common Animals, and such whose actions they are best acquainted with, and where there is least confusion and perplexure of Parts; I have chosen Ireland as such a Political Animal, who is scarce Twenty years old.

Petty was born at Romney in Hampshire. After a varied career, he arrived in Ireland in 1652 as 'physician to the army of the Commonwealth'. The Commonwealth army had laid waste much of the countryside, famously removing large numbers of the native Irish 'to hell or Connaught'. Indeed Petty himself, in his *Political Anatomy*, calculated that, out of a total population of 1,466,000 in 1641, 'about 504,000 of the Irish perished, and were wasted by the Sword, Plague, Famine, Hardship and Banishment' between 1641 and 1652[93]. This raised the practical problem of resettling the land, which in turn demanded an accurate survey. Demonstrating remarkable initiative and self confidence, indeed bravado, Petty in September 1654 offered by October 1655[94]:

To admeasure all the forfeited lands within the three provinces, according to the naturall, artificiall, and civill bounds thereof, and whereby the said land is distinguished into wood, bog, mountaine, arable, meadow, and pasture; moreover to add and sett out such auxiliary lines and lymits as may facilitate and ascertaine the intended finall subdivision without any readmeasurement.

Employing in the process over 1,000 people, he was as good as his word. The result was the famous 'Down Survey', so called because it was written down. Attis comments[95]:

---

[91] *Nature*, 4 February 1993, p. 389.
[92] William Petty, *Political Anatomy of Ireland* (London: D. Brown & W. Rogers, 1691 [Facsimile – Shannon: Irish University Press, 1970]), Author's Preface.
[93] Petty 1691, p. 18.
[94] T.A. Larcom (ed), *A History of the Survey of Ireland Commonly Called the Down Survey by Doctor William Petty, A.D. 1655–6* (Dublin: Irish Archaeological Society, 1967 – reprint of the 1851 edition), p. 9.
[95] Attis 2004, p. 71.

Petty's men reduced an Irish landscape saturated with local memories and traditions to a series of lengths and angles. With his political arithmetic, he reduced the complexities of Irish society to a set of economic measures.

On his return to London in 1659, Petty was one of the key players, along with Robert Boyle and others, in the foundation of the Royal Society in London. This august organisation, which traces some at least of its origins to what was called the 'Invisible College', and to a group who met in Gresham College, London, had a distinctly Irish flavour at its inception. The Invisible College refers to the informal co-operation of a geographically separated group of like minded people interested in 'the utilitarian aspects of natural philosophy'[96] – but details are hazy; its importance in this context derives from the fact that 'it provided the occasion for Boyle's first serious excursion into science'[97], and because it had a very distinct Anglo-Irish composition. Webster[98] writes: 'The Invisible College was intimately linked with Anglo-Irish Independents associated with Lady Ranelagh, whose policies were dictated by their dedication to the reconquest, settlement and exploitation of Ireland'. Katherine, Lady Ranelagh (1615–1691), was an older sister of Robert Boyle, whose influence on her young brother was enormous: she has been dubbed 'the most renowned female intellectual of her generation'[99].

More formal meetings of people interested in experimental philosophy had been held in Gresham College, and it was after a meeting there in 1860 that a group of twelve like-minded people, including Lord Brouncker, Robert Boyle and William Petty, inaugurated the Royal Society[100]. William Brouncker (1620–1684) was the grandson of Sir Henry Brouncker, president of Munster (died 1607) and the son of Sir William Brouncker (1585–1646), who became the first Viscount Brouncker of Castle Lyons (in Co. Cork) in 1645[101]. William junior had a distinguished career, with some mathematical distinction, but is best remembered as first President (nominated by Charles II, and unopposed) of the Royal Society, a post which he held from 1662–1677. Boyle himself was invited to be President in 1680, but declined due to scruples about taking oaths. Since then, several Irish-born people have attained this distinction: Robert Southwell was President from 1690 to 1695; Hans Sloane from 1727 to 1741; William Parsons (actually not born in Ireland, as his mother went to her home in Yorkshire for his birth) from 1849 to 1854; George Gabriel Stokes from 1885 to 1890, and William Thomson from 1890 to 1895. Stokes was Secretary for 31 years, from 1854 to 1885, and Joseph Larmor Secretary from 1901 to 1912. There were many

[96] R.E.W Maddison, *The Life of the Honourable Robert Boyle F.R.S.* (London: Taylor & Francis, 1969), p. 69.
[97] Charles Webster, *The Great Instauration – Science, Medicine and Reform 1626–1660* (London: Duckworth, 1975), p. 57.
[98] Charles Webster, 'New Light on the Invisible College', *Transactions of the Royal Historical Society*, **24**, 1974, p. 41 – this quote is reproduced in Attis 2004, p. 56.
[99] Nicholas Canny, *The Upstart Earl – A Study of the Social and Mental World of Richard Boyle, First Earl of Cork, 1566–1643* (Cambridge: Cambridge University Press, 1982), p. 78.
[100] Maddison 1969, p. 99.
[101] *Dictionary of National Biography*.

Irish Fellows of the Royal Society, particularly in the Nineteenth Century but, although Irish people remained eligible for election, the number who obtained this distinction after Irish independence became tiny. We have mentioned one who did – and the first woman to do so (in 1945) – Kathleen Lonsdale (*see above*), although, of course, she was no longer resident in Ireland at the time. There are signs of a modest reversal of this situation in recent years: Denis Weaire (Trinity College Dublin) became FRS in 1999, John Canny (Queen's University Belfast) in 2002 and Michael Coey (Trinity College Dublin) in 2003.

Returning to the main narrative, we have already featured Robert Boyle 'the father of chemistry' under the chemistry heading above. William Molyneux (1656–1698), born in Dublin, followed the example of the London Royal Society by setting up the 'Dublin Society for the Improving of Naturall Knowledge, Mathematics, and Mechanics', better known as the 'Dublin Philosophical Society' in 1684. It had a rather chequered history until it was abandoned in 1708[102], but it was important in encouraging an interest in science in Ireland. Molyneux himself published *Dioptrica Nova* in 1692, the first optical treatise to be published in English:

> a treatise of dioptricks in two parts, wherein the various effects and appearances of spherick glasses, both convex and concave, single and combined, in telescopes and microscopes, together with their usefulness in many concerns of human life, are explained.

He is, however, best remembered for his (often reprinted) 1698 book *The Case of Ireland's Being Bound by Acts of Parliament in England Stated*. This outspoken book denied the claims of the English Parliament to legislate for Ireland, and of the English House of Lords to be the final Court of Appeal in Irish cases. One of the incentives for his book was a bill of 1697, introduced in the English House of Commons, for a ban on the export to foreign and colonial markets of Irish woollen cloth, which was regarded as a dangerous competitor of the English trade: 'England most certainly will never let us thrive by the woollen trade; this is their darling mistress and they are jealous of any rival'. The Act was duly passed, with the House of Commons resolving that Molyneux' book was[103]:

> of dangerous consequence to the crown and people of England by denying the authority of the king and parliament of England to bind the kingdom and people of Ireland, and the subordination and dependence that Ireland hath and ought to have upon England as united and annexed to the imperial crown of the realm.

---

[102] K. Theodore Hoppen, *The Common Scientist in the Seventeenth Century – A Study of the Dublin Philosophical Society 1683–1708* (London, Routledge & Kegan Paul, 1970).

[103] J.G. Simms, *William Molyneux of Dublin – A Life of the Seventeenth-Century Political Writer and Scientist*, Edited by P.H. Kelly (Dublin: Irish Academic Press, 1982), p. 10.

It was claimed that the book was burned by the common hangman.

Molyneux is also remembered for proposing a 'jocose problem' to his friend, the English philosopher John Locke (1632–1704)[104]. A man, who was born blind, has learned to distinguish by touch a globe from a cube. Suppose that he suddenly regains his sight, and is shown a globe and a cube. Could he tell which was which without touching them? Molyneux' view was that he couldn't, and Locke agreed, as did George Berkeley (1685–1753), the Kilkenny born author of *A New Theory of Vision* (1709). However, since no entirely satisfactory experiment appears to have been carried out, the problem continues to exercise the minds of philosophers three hundred years later.

Berkeley is, of course, best remembered as a philosopher, but the point where philosophy ends and science begins is uncertain. In any event, Berkeley is the first person to be featured in a very select list in William Ewald's important two-volume work, *From Kant to Hilbert – A Source Book in the Foundations of Mathematics*[105] (in spite of the title, Kant is the fourth entry!). Ewald comments:

> Of all the treatises written on the subject in the eighteenth century, Berkeley's *Analyst* was the most sustained and penetrating critique of the methodology of the infinitesimal calculus. Despite its early date (1734) and the fact that it was largely ignored by mathematicians, this work foreshadows the foundational research of the nineteenth century, and provides a link between the mathematical preoccupations of the seventeenth and eighteenth centuries and those of the nineteenth.

Berkeley was only one of several famous students at Kilkenny College and, since my lovely granddaughters are entered there too, the school is sure to have a distinguished future as well! Another student at Kilkenny College was Dublin born Jonathan Swift (1667–1745), the famous Dean of St Patrick's Cathedral, whom we have already met as the person credited as the first to record the Martian moons.

It seems that every Irishman (or woman) wants to write a book, and very many have done so. While our literary heroes are better known, many Irish scientists wrote books too, some of them also having considerable literary merit. One of the most prolific of our authors was Dionysius Lardner (1793–1859). He was born in Dublin but, after a distinguished record in Trinity College Dublin, failed to get elected a Fellow of TCD, and instead went to London in 1827 as the Professor of Natural Philosophy and Astronomy in the newly founded London University (now University College London)[106]. He had also been an applicant for the position of Andrews Professor of Astronomy in TCD in 1827, but was defeated by the undergraduate, William Rowan Hamilton[107] (*see below*). Indeed Lardner's earliest book, *System of Algebraic Geometry* (1823), was prescribed

---

[104] Simms 1982, pp. 125-134.
[105] William Ewald, *From Kant to Hilbert – A Source Book in the Foundations of Mathematics*, Two Volumes (Oxford: Clarendon Press, 1996, paperback edition 1999), Volume I, pp. 11-92.
[106] *Dictionary of National Biography.*
[107] Thomas Hankins, *Sir William Rowan Hamilton* (Baltimore & London: The Johns Hopkins University Press, 1980), p. 45.

reading for mathematics students, including Hamilton, in Trinity[108]. Lardner published many more text books on mathematics and natural philosophy (physics), as well as practical subjects like the steam engine, railways and animal physiology. But his major claim to fame was as the publisher of his *Cabinet Cyclopaedia* which extended to around 133 volumes (some published in several editions) between 1829 and 1849. He was author or joint author of several of these – including *Mechanics; Hydrostatics & Pneumatics; Heat; Arithmetic; Geometry; Electricity, Magnetism & Meteorology* – and recruited eminent contributors for many of the others, people like David Brewster (Optics) and John Herschel (Astronomy). Indeed Brewster's Optics had a life after the *Cabinet Cyclopaedia*, since I have a copy of a 'New Edition' dated 1853 which does not include the *Cabinet Cyclopaedia* attribution. The majority of the books in the *Cyclopaedia* were historical, with, for example, ten volumes on the *History of England*, four on the *History of Ireland*, and three on the *Lives of Eminent Literary and Scientific Men of Great Britain and Ireland*. Although Lardner wasn't married to his mother, it is generally considered that the famous Irish playwright, Dion Boucicault (1820–1890) was a son of Lardner. Boucicault has been called 'the most eminent man in the theatre of England, America, and Ireland in the mid-nineteenth century'[109].

Many of those who made contributions to mathematics and physics while resident in Ireland were protestants and were affiliated to Trinity College Dublin: indeed they were often Church of Ireland clergymen, as it used to be required of the TCD Fellows that they became ordained (*see below*). An exception to this was Nicholas Callan (1799–1864) since he was a Catholic priest, and a Professor at St Patrick's College Maynooth, the chief seminary in Ireland. He was born near Ardee in Co. Louth, and was Professor of Natural Philosophy at Maynooth from 1826 until his death.

Callan was the inventor in 1836 of the induction coil. This was the essential fore-runner of to-day's step-up and step-down transformers without which we wouldn't have limitless electricity at our fingertips (and if you own a petrol driven car, you have one in there as well). He sent an example of his coil to William Sturgeon (1783–1850) in London in 1837, where it was exhibited to members of the Electrical Society to their great amazement. Callan also invented new kinds of batteries, and he produced almighty voltages using his experimental coils.

What better way was there to test the intensity of his electricity than to pass it through a 'voluntary' seminarian or two? And he did. One of his best known 'voltmeters' was William Walsh, later to be the famous Archbishop of Dublin. The unfortunate young Walsh was rendered unconscious by Callan. Another seminarian who received similar treatment was Charles Russell, who, like William Walsh, became President of Maynooth. Russell apparently wasn't knocked out like Walsh, but he had to 'spend time on the infirmary after doses of Callan's high-tension electricity'[110]. A third (this time

---

[108] Hankins 1980, p. 23.

[109] Sven Eric Molin, biography of Boucicault, pp. 169-173 in Robert Hogan (Editor-in-chief), *Dictionary of Irish Literature*, second edition (London: Aldwych Press, 1996)

[110] P.J. McLaughlin, *Nicholas Callan Priest-Scientist 1799–1864* (Dublin: Clonmore & Reynolds, 1965), p. 35.

fatal) casualty of Callan's electricity was an unfortunate turkey, a novel way of preparing for Christmas in a seminary.

But it was not Callan who cashed in on his discovery. This distinction went to his contemporary, Heinrich Ruhmkorff (1803–1877), who was born in Hannover, but set up his own instrument making business in Paris in 1839. He improved the induction coil in the 1850s, and it became one of the most important of electrical instruments, so much so that examples are still usually called 'Ruhmkorff coils'.

What is now the National University of Ireland, Maynooth, still maintains an impressive scientific tradition, and St Patrick's College (the name is now confined to the 'Pontifical University') has a wonderful collection of old scientific instruments displayed in its recently-renovated 'National Science Museum'[111]: well worth a visit!

Two Trinity dons who will for ever be connected in science history are Humphrey Lloyd (1800–1881) and William Rowan Hamilton (1805–1865). We have met Hamilton before, as the undergraduate who was appointed Professor of Astronomy at TCD (in 1827), and who was knighted at the first meeting of the BAAS in Ireland (1835). He really hit the academic headlines by predicting theoretically a special kind of refraction – 'conical refraction' – which he deduced mathematically would take place in a correctly cut and oriented 'biaxial' crystal of 'iceland spar' – a form of calcite (calcium carbonate). You put light into the crystal at one point and it comes out as a cone at another. It was Humphrey Lloyd who confirmed this experimentally in 1832 and Hamilton's prediction was considered to be an amazing achievement. Lloyd, who was Professor of Natural and Experimental Philosophy at Trinity at the time, went on to become Provost in 1867, but in the meantime had furthered his scientific reputation particularly through his involvement in studies on terrestrial magnetism. Together with another Irishman, Edward Sabine (1788–1883), and helped by the substantial involvement of the BAAS, they were largely responsible for the development of this area of investigation, and even invented relevant instruments. Lloyd was President of the BAAS when it met in Dublin in 1857 (his father, Bartholomew Lloyd, had been President at the first meeting in Dublin of the BAAS in 1835). Humphrey Lloyd's magnetical observatory in TCD, set up in 1838, in what used to be the Provost's garden, could be seen there until 1974, when it was removed to the Belfield campus of University College Dublin. It was recently converted to a 38 seat screening room for students of film.

In a letter from Cambridge, Massachusetts, addressed to Sir W.R. Hamilton, and dated 17 May 1865, B.A. Gould (*pro tem* Foreign Secretary) wrote[112]:

> The agreeable duty devolves upon me of announcing to you that the National
> Academy of Sciences, established by the United States on the 3rd of March,

---

[111] Charles Mollan & John Upton, *The Scientific Apparatus of Nicholas Callan an Other Historic Scientific Instruments* (Maynooth & Dublin: St Patrick's College & Samton Ltd, 1994).

[112] Quoted in: Robert Perceval Graves, *Life of Sir William Rowan Hamilton* (Dublin: Hodges Figgis & Co, three volumes, 1882–1891, Vol. 1, p. 205.

1863, elected you, on the 9th of January following, first on the list of its Foreign Associates, now fifteen in number.

An Irishman was considered by the fledgling Academy to be the greatest of living scientists. And Hamilton is still generally regarded as Ireland's top mathematician of all time.

He claimed to have been born in Dominick Street, Dublin, on the stroke of midnight on 3-4 August 1805. Such precision may perhaps be expected in the mind of a mathematical genius, but one wonders whether his mother, Sarah Hutton, acknowledged such an instant birth? It certainly doesn't allow for the labour which, we can assume, preceded it. Whatever about that, young Hamilton was a prodigy, and had a very distinguished career in Trinity College before his appointment as Professor of Astronomy in 1827.

He considered his endeavours in mathematics to be a service to Ireland. When he was writing to his friend Aubrey De Vere, at the height of the Irish famine in 1847, he commented[113]:

> It is the opinion of some judicious friends....that my peculiar path, and best hope of being useful to Ireland, are to be found in the pursuit of those abstract and seemingly unpractical contemplations to which my nature has a strong bent. If the fame of our country shall be in any degree raised thereby, and if the industry of a particular kind thus shown shall tend to remove the prejudice which supposes Irishmen to be incapable of perseverance, some step, however slight, may be thereby made towards the establishment of an intellectual confidence which cannot be, in the long run, unproductive of temporal and material benefits.

Hamilton introduced the familiar mathematical terms vector and scalar, and devised the method of quaternions, involving the square root of minus one. Mathematicians call an entity like this an 'imaginary number'. A combination of real and imaginary numbers is said to be 'complex'. In devising his method of quaternions, he founded a new algebra, and his quaternions are in regular use to-day – for example in computer graphics and in the guidance systems of spacecraft. He actually expected them to be even more useful, and devoted an inordinate amount of time to their development, but some of his other work has proved even more productive. Ewald records[114]:

> Hamilton is today best remembered for his work as a mathematical physicist, and in particular for his contributions to geometrical optics and to

---

[113] Quoted in David Attis, 'The Social Contexts of W.R. Hamilton's Prediction of Conical Refraction', pp. 19-35, in Peter J. Bowler & Nicholas Whyte, *Science and Society in Ireland – The Social Context of Science and Technology in Ireland 1800–1950* (Belfast: The Institute of Irish Studies, 1997), p. 29.

[114] William Ewald, *From Kant to Hilbert – A Source Book in the Foundations of Mathematics*, Two Volumes (Oxford: Clarendon Press, 1996, paperback edition 1999), Volume I, pp. 363-364.

dynamics....Hamilton's work in other areas [i.e. other than quaternions] turned out to have unanticipated physical applications. His explorations of the analogy between optics and dynamics influenced Schrödinger and De Broglie in their formulation of wave mechanics; his work on linear algebra supplied Heisenberg with some of the fundamental mathematical tools for matrix mechanics; his ideas about quaternions inspired others – Sylvester, Cayley, Clifford, Benjamin Peirce, Gibbs, Heaviside – to study matrices, vectors, and their physical applications.

Erwin Schrödinger (1887–1961) was recruited by Eamon de Valera for the newly formed Dublin Institute for Advanced Studies in 1939, and he lived and worked in Ireland from that date until 1956, becoming an Irish citizen in 1948. He had already been awarded the Nobel Prize for Physics in 1933 (with Paul Dirac 1902–1984) 'for the discovery of new forms of atomic theory and applications of them'. Referring to what became known as the 'Schrödinger Equation', McConnell writes[115]:

He wrote a set of papers on wave mechanics which revolutionised scientific thought and had a profound effect on physics, chemistry and biology, as well as on the philosophy of science....Schrödinger applied his equation to the hydrogen atom and obtained discrete, that is discontinuous, energy levels....which agreed with experimental results. This success more than anything else established the position of Schrödinger in the history of physics, and his equation soon became the basis for the quantum-mechanical treatment of problems in atomic and molecular physics and in chemistry.

While in Ireland he published seven books and about 75 papers. When the Irish Post Office brought out two postage stamps in 1943 to commemorate Hamilton, Schrödinger commented[116]:

I daresay not a day passes – and seldom an hour -- without somebody somewhere on this globe, pronouncing or reading or writing Hamilton's name. That is due to his fundamental discoveries in general dynamics. The Hamiltonian Principle has become the cornerstone of modern physics, the thing with which a physicist expects every physical phenomenon to be in conformity....His famous analogy between optics and mechanics virtually anticipated wave mechanics, which did not have much to add to his ideas and had only to take them more seriously.

Praise indeed. And we might note that it was Schrödinger's 1944 book, written in Ireland, *What is Life?*, which had a determining influence on James Watson (born

---

[115] James McConnell, 'Erwin Schrödinger (1887–1961) – Austro-Irish Nobel Laureate', *Occasional Papers in Science & Technology*, No 5 (Dublin: Royal Dublin Society, 1988), pp. 2-3.

[116] Quoted in Ewald 1999, Vol. I, p. 364 – with the source given in Vol. II, p. 1322; the latter gives the date 1945 for the quote, but the stamps themselves are dated 1943.

1928) in leading him into research in which he, with Francis Crick (born 1916), elucidated the double helix structure of DNA *(see also page 264)*.

While blossoming as a mathematician, Hamilton wrote poetry *(see below)*, and was a friend of William Wordsworth and Samuel Taylor Coleridge. It is Wordsworth who is credited with encouraging him to stick to the day job, judging his poetry to be less creative than his sums. The poetess 'Speranza', later Lady Wilde, invited him to become godfather to her 'little pagan' son Oscar, but he refused[117].

Not everything went perfectly for the calculating young genius. At the age of 20 he fell deeply in love with Catherine Disney, the sister of one of his College friends. Her parents didn't approve, and she turned him down, but he retained this unrequited love for the rest of his life. Meanwhile, in 1833, he married Helen Bayly, and they had three children. His wife was sickly (though she outlived him) and this upset their lives. Hamilton in time succumbed to drink and died at Dunsink Observatory in 1865.

On each side of the entrance to what is now the Government Building in Merrion Row, Dublin, but was built in 1911 as the Royal College of Science, there stand two statues – one of Robert Boyle and the other of William Rowan Hamilton – which one hopes will inspire our legislators to give adequate support to our current scientific achievers.

A slightly younger contemporary of Hamilton was James MacCullagh (1809–1847), born in Landahussy, Co. Tyrone, who also had a distinguished career in Trinity College before becoming Professor of Mathematics (1835–1843), and then of Natural and Experimental Philosophy (1843–1847) there. As Brendan Scaife comments[118]: 'Rivalry between MacCullagh and Hamilton is hardly a matter for surprise. Both were brilliant and ambitious and, given MacCullagh's impetuosity, a flare-up was bound to occur sooner or later'. And indeed it did. Most of MacCullagh's work was devoted to the theory of light, and he was of the opinion that Hamilton's famous discovery of conical refraction was 'an obvious and immediate consequence of his own published work', of which Hamilton was aware though he did not see fit to acknowledge it, and he resented the glory which Hamilton received. Hankins does record something of an admission to this effect from Hamilton[119] – '[MacCullagh] seems to have been very near finding the theory [of conical refraction] for himself'.

MacCullagh is particularly remembered for his work on the ether (or aether), the medium thought to be necessary for the propagation of light and other electromagnetic waves – work which was further progressed to great effect by other Irish mathematicians and physicists *(see below)*. Scaife[120] records :

> The outstanding accomplishment of MacCullagh in his work on light seems to
> be his extraordinarily deep analysis of the properties of light and his

---

[117] Thomas Hankins, *Sir William Rowan Hamilton* (Baltimore & London: The Johns Hopkins University Press, 1980), p. 355.

[118] Brendan Scaife, 'James MacCullagh, M.R.I.A., F.R.S.', *Proceedings of the Royal Irish Academy, Section C*, 90(3), 1990, p.71.

[119] Hankins 1980, p. 94.

[120] Scaife 1990, p. 86.

appreciation that the nature of the ether would involve concepts and ideas that were quite new. He was, in fact, extremely modern in his outlook, and had little faith in the possibility of building a mechanical model of the ether. He would have found it much easier to accept the developments of the twentieth century than many of his contemporaries and successors.

The fact that we now know that the aether doesn't exist has not helped to perpetuate MacCullagh's fame, but his influence on a generation of Trinity students was profound.

He was unfortunately a sufferer from periodic bouts of depression. Not long after his failure to be elected to one of the two Dublin University seats at Westminster, he took his own life in his rooms in Trinity in 1847. Hamilton waxed poetic[121]:

Wrapped as we are in an o'erwhelming cloud
Of grief and horror, shake we off awhile
That horror, and that grief with words beguile;
And from our full hearts breathe, although not aloud.
Our minds to God's mysterious dealings bowed,
And mourning with the Genius of the land,
Take we awhile our reverential stand,
In the dread presence of MacCullagh's shroud.
Great, good, unhappy! For his country's fame
Too hard he toiled; from too unresting brain
His arachnaean web of thought he wove.
The planet-form he loved, the crystals frame
Through which he taught to trace light's tremulous train,
Shall be his symbols in the cypress grove.

We might now see why Wordsworth counselled Hamilton to stick to his mathematics!

One of the treasures of the National Museum in Dublin is the Cross of Cong, a magnificent example of Irish craftsmanship in metal dating from the early twelfth century. It is not widely known that it was presented to the Royal Irish Academy (and subsequently transferred by the Academy to the Museum) by MacCullagh. It cost him 100 guineas – no mean sum for an academic at the time.

While all this was going on at Trinity, a Dublin born graduate (he received a rather undistinguished BA in 1830) was making waves elsewhere – notably on a beach to the south of Dublin city. Dean writes[122]:

Though the name of Robert Mallet was once inevitably associated with the scientific study of earthquakes, it is less well known to-day. As part of an overdue reappraisal, this essay examines Mallet's major seismological projects

---

121 Reproduced in Scaife 1990, p. 103.
122 Dennis R. Dean, 'Robert Mallet and the Founding of Seismology', *Annals of Science*, 1991, **48**, p. 39.

and publications, emphasizing his theoretical contributions. Mallet's own claim to be a founder of modern seismology is upheld. Beyond that, however, he is also seen to be an important precursor of plate tectonics.

The *Oxford English Dictionary*, acknowledges Mallet (1810–1881) as the instigator of no less than nine words starting with 'seism' – seismic, seismograph, seismological, seismologist, seismologue, seismology, seismometric, seismometry and seismoscope, and he carried out some of his major experiments using explosives on Killiney beach. He was well qualified to do so, since he ran an important iron works in Dublin, and among other things made monster mortars for the Crimean War. In 1852 he patented the buckled plate, used to strengthen flooring, combining the maximum of strength with the minimum of weight, and this was used, for example, in Westminster Bridge in London. With his son, John W. Mallet (1832–1912), he compiled an extensive two-volume earthquake catalogue of the world (1850–1858), and was the first to measure an earthquake's focus or epicentre – in Naples in 1858[123].

Trinity however didn't attract all the mathematical talent of the time. Queen's College Cork (now University College Cork), founded in 1845, was fortunate to be able to recruit George Boole (1815–1864), born in Lincoln, England, as its first Professor of Mathematics in 1849. From a poor family, he had no degree, and was self taught. MacHale writes[124]:

> Boole was a pioneer in mathematics whom Bertrand Russell described as the 'founder of pure mathematics'. He invented a new branch of mathematics – invariant theory – and made important contributions to operator theory, differential equations and probability. However, his most significant discoveries were in mathematical logic....He invented a new type of algebra, called Boolean algebra, which to-day's engineers and scientists have found to be ideal for the design and operation of electronic computers....Much of the 'new mathematics' now taught in schools can be traced back to Boole's work – for example, set theory, binary numbers and probability.

A devoted teacher, Boole died in Cork after walking in the pouring rain to give a lecture, and is buried at St Michael's Church of Ireland church in Blackrock, Cork city.

Perhaps the most famous Irish born physicist of all time is Belfast-born William Thomson (1824–1907), later (1892) Lord Kelvin. Not far distant in eminence in the pantheon of physics is his slightly older friend George Gabriel Stokes (1819–1903), born in Skreen, Co. Sligo. Both were buried in Westminster Abbey. At the funeral of Stokes, Kelvin – for convenience we'll call him Kelvin from here on – stated[125]: 'for sixty

---

[123] Ronald Cox, 'Robert Mallet – Materials Engineer and Seismologist' p. 106 in Charles Mollan, William David and Brendan Finucane (Eds), *Irish Innovators in Science and Technology* (Dublin, Royal Irish Academy, 2002).

[124] Desmond MacHale, *'George Boole – Mathematician and Logician*, p. 118 in Mollan et al., 2002.

[125] Quoted in Joseph Larmor, *Memoir and Scientific Correspondence of the Late Sir George Gabriel Stokes*, two volumes (Cambridge: University Press, 1907), Vol. I, p. 318.

years of my own life, from 1843 to 1903, I looked up to Stokes as my teacher, guide, and friend. His death was for me truly a bereavement'. A book length study of their scientific relationship was published in 1987[126]. We have already discussed whether or not such people should be referred to as Irish or British. Kelvin actually came from a Scottish family and essentially all his important work was carried out while Professor of Natural Philosophy in Glasgow, a post he held from 1846 until 1899. Similarly, Stokes was Lucasian Professor of Mathematics in Cambridge University from 1849 until 1903. (They both celebrated Jubilees in 1899, the year Thomson retired, and the year Stokes reached fifty years in the job.) So clearly Scotland and England respectively can claim them. So too can Ireland – let's both do it! Wood[127] writes:

> There is no doubt that George Gabriel was greatly inspired by his upbringing in the West of Ireland, and he returned regularly for the summer vacation, a non-trivial exercise in the pre-railway era, while a student in England. Even after the death of his parents he continued to visit his brother John Whitley, then a clergyman in Tyrone, and his sister, Elizabeth Mary, to whom he was greatly attached, in Malahide [Co. Dublin], almost annually until his death.

His wife, whom he married in 1859, was Irish – Mary Susannah Robinson, daughter of Thomas Romney Robinson of Armagh Observatory, and they were regular visitors to her home in Armagh.

Stokes, after schooling in Skreen, Dublin and Bristol, entered Cambridge University in 1837, graduating as 'Senior Wrangler' (first in the Mathematics Tripos) in 1841. We can let his friend Kelvin summarise his contribution to physics and mathematics[128]:

> In his scientific work and thought Stokes ranged over the whole domain of natural knowledge. Hydrodynamics, elasticity of solids and fluids, wave-motion in elastic solids and fluids, were all exhaustively treated by his powerful and unerring mathematics. Even in pure mathematics, he was recognised as a fruitful worker by the whole scientific world. But with him mathematics was the servant and assistant, not the master. His guiding star in science was Natural Philosophy. Sound, light, radiant heat, chemistry, were fields of labour which he cultivated by studying properties of matter, with the aid of experimental and mathematical investigation....He laid the foundation for the whole modern science of elasticity....Stokes greatest province was light and optics...He discovered fluorescence....He gave generously and freely of his treasures to all who were fortunate enough to have opportunity of receiving from him.

126 David B. Wilson, *Kelvin and Stokes: A Comparative Study in Victorian Physics* (Bristol: Adam Hilger, 1987), pp. xvi + 253.
127 Alastair Wood, 'George Gabriel Stokes 1819–1903, and Irish Mathematical Physicist', *Bulletin of the Irish Mathematical Society*, No. 35, Christmas 1995, p. 52.
128 Quoted in Larmor 1907, 317-318.

His long service to the Royal Society, mentioned earlier, is an example of his giving. Indeed several people have voiced regret about the time he allocated to his work with the Royal Society and other pursuits, thinking it would have been better spent in developing further his original scientific and mathematical endeavours. He was an enthusiastic contributor to the BAAS, serving as President at Exeter in 1869. For example, he was one of a committee (which included also William Thomson and John Tyndall) which reported the following conclusions to the Exeter meeting in terms not unfamiliar to us today[129]:

I.   That the provision now existing in the United Kingdom of Great Britain and Ireland is far from sufficient for the vigorous prosecution of Physical Research.

II. It is universally admitted that scientific investigation is productive of enormous advantages to the community at large; but these advantages cannot be duly reaped without largely extending and systematizing Physical research....

Stokes gave important help to his Irish colleagues, for example advising the Grubb telescope enterprise in Dublin and that of Lord Rosse in Birr. He died at Cambridge.

Like his colleague Stokes, Kelvin wasn't an ivory tower theorist, but one who had a particular interest in the practical usefulness of his studies. This attitude would certainly have been helped by his associations with Belfast which was at the time a thriving industrial city: his brother James Thomson (1822–1892) was Professor of Civil Engineering at Queen's College Belfast (now Queen's University) from 1857 until 1872. In his Presidential address to the BAAS at Edinburgh in 1871, Kelvin commented[130]:

Accurate and minute measurement seems to the non-scientific imagination a less lofty and dignified work than looking for something new. But nearly all the grandest discoveries of science have been but the rewards of accurate measurement and patient long-continued labour in the minute sifting of numerical results. The popular idea of Newton's grandest discovery is that the theory of gravitation flashed into his mind, and so the discovery was made....he commenced his calculations...then (and not when, sitting in a garden, he saw an apple fall) did he ascertain that gravitation keeps the Moon in her orbit....

In the same address, he gave special praise to Thomas Andrews (1813–1885), the Professor of Chemistry at Queen's College, Belfast, whom we met under the Chemistry heading above:

---

[129] BAAS, *Report of the Thirty-Ninth Meeting of the British Association for the Advancement of Science Held at Exeter in August 1869* (London: John Murray, 1870), pp. 213-214.

[130] BAAS, *Report of the Forty-First Meeting of the British Association for the Advancement of Science Held at Edinburgh in August 1871* (London: John Murray, 1872), pp. lxxxviii & xci-xcii.

The whole of Andrews' splendid work in Queen's College, Belfast, has been done under great difficulties and disadvantages, and at great personal sacrifices; and up to the present time there is not a student's physical laboratory in any one of the Queen's Colleges in Ireland....Andrews' discovery of the continuity between the gaseous and liquid states was worked out by many years of laborious and minute measurement of phenomena scarcely sensible to the naked eye.

It was an Irish friend and colleague, George Francis FitzGerald (1851–1901) who was called upon to contribute a report on Kelvin's scientific work, which was published in the account of the celebrations 'on the occasion of Lord Kelvin's Jubilee as a Professor' at the University of Glasgow in 1899[131]:

In reading over the articles published in various journals....the characteristic of his genius that is most frequently, indeed universally, noticed is his ability to combine science with practice....He has published most important papers on a great variety of branches of mathematical physics, and he has made a large number of practical inventions, by which the work of the world is lightened and mankind thereby benefited. It is by no means to be imagined that these two directions of his activity are independent of one another. His inventions are the direct outcome of the most advanced theory....without Lord Kelvin's theory as to how signals were transmitted in telegraph cables, it would have taken many years of chance experimenting to evolve the mirror galvanometer.

The latter comment refers to the fact that, of his numerous contributions to science and industry, he is particularly remembered as being the brains behind the successful transatlantic telegraph cable of 1866. The first transatlantic cable, laid in 1858, did not work for long, largely due to poor insulation and to the high voltages which were used. Kelvin's mirror galvanometer could detect extremely feeble signals, and this was an essential element in the successful cable of 1866, which ran from Valentia Island off Co. Kerry to Trinity Bay, Newfoundland, in Canada. He received his knighthood (in 1867) for this work.

A keen sailor himself, Kelvin was actually aboard the *Great Eastern*, the ship which laid the cable. The first officer and key navigator was another Irishman, Robert Halpin (1836–1894) from Wicklow Town. Halpin was appointed captain of the ship in 1869, and went on to earn further distinction for cable laying, being responsible for connecting Portugal and Brazil, Suez and Aden, Aden and India, India and Singapore, Singapore and Australia[132]. He earned the nickname 'Mr Cable'.

131 George Francis FitzGerald, 'Biographical Sketch of Lord Kelvin', pp. 1-29 in *Lord Kelvin Professor of Natural Philosophy in the University of Glasgow 1846–1899* (Glasgow: James MacLehose & Sons, 1899).
132 Jim Rees, 'Captain Robert Halpin, Cable King', *Technology Ireland*, March 1994, pp. 34-37. See also, Jim Rees, *The Life of Captain Robert Halpin* (Arklow: Dee-Jay Publications, 1992), pp. 169.

William Thomson was born in Belfast, where his father, James Thomson (1786–1849) was Professor of Mathematics at the Academical Institution. When his father was appointed Professor of Mathematics at Glasgow University, the family moved there in 1832. He and his older brother James were at first educated by their father and mother at home. He attended classes in Glasgow University before going up to St Peter's College Cambridge, where he graduated Second Wrangler in 1845. After a brief period in Paris, he was appointed Professor of Natural Philosophy at the University of Glasgow in 1846 at the early age of 22. In due course he attained the distinction of becoming President of the Royal Society (from 1890 to 1895). Although married twice – to Margaret Crum in 1852 (she died in 1870) and to Frances Blandy in 1874 – he had no children.

It is recorded that, before his marriage, he had fallen deeply in love with one of the seven daughters – Sabina Smith – of a Glasgow resident. He proposed to her on no less than three occasions between 1850 and 1852, and she refused him each time, but subsequently regretted it. She even travelled to the Belfast meeting of the BAAS in September 1852 'in the vague hope that I might yet win him back'. It was too late – he married Margaret Crum that same month[133].

In Glasgow, Kelvin was the first person in Great Britain to introduce laboratory work for students – 'the greatest advance that has been made in the methods of education for centuries'[134]. His work covered many important areas – including general dynamics, hydrodynamics, thermodynamics, elasticity and electromagnetism. He studied gyroscopes and their vibrations, the stability of equilibrium, vortex motion, the tides (inventing a tide calculating machine), atmospheric electricity, and the age of the Earth. He improved compasses for navigation, and his new compass was adopted by all British Navy vessels. He formed a working relationship, and later a company, with the Glasgow instrument maker James White, and together they produced and sold his new patented instruments[135]. He accumulated great wealth through these patents and his other business interests. He is perhaps best remembered to-day because the 'absolute' scale of temperature is named after him, the freezing point of water on this scale being 273.15 Kelvin.

Joseph Larmor (1857–1942) who was also born in the Belfast area (and who was another Irish Senior Wrangler at Cambridge) collected and edited Thomson's papers, which were published in five volumes between 1882 and 1911. Using a dose of scientific licence, Larmor is reputed to have stated in 1907[136]:

> Conceive a perfectly level line drawn from the summit of Newton's genius across all the intervening generations; probably the only man who reached it in these two centuries has been Kelvin.

---

[133] Crosbie Smith & M. Norton Wise, *Energy & Empire – A Biographical Study of Lord Kelvin* (Cambridge: Cambridge University Press, 1989), pp. 141-142.
[134] FitzGerald 1899, p.3.
[135] See, for example, Charles Mollan, *Irish National Inventory of Historic Scientific Instruments* (Dublin: Samton Ltd, 1995), p. 496.
[136] Quoted in Joe Burchfield, *Lord Kelvin and the Age of the Earth* (Chicago: University of Chicago Press, 1990), p. 56.

Kelvin died in Glasgow and is buried in Westminster Abbey. A commemorative statue in the Botanic Gardens, Belfast, is inscribed 'He elucidated the laws of nature for the service of man'.

Trinity College has for centuries been the training ground for the majority of the clergy of the Church of Ireland (which was the 'Established Church' from the days of Henry VIII until disestablishment in 1871). In passing, I might mention that, in my schooldays, it was claimed that the word 'antidistablishmentarianism' was the longest word in the English language! Whatever about that, several of the TCD educated people we have featured in this essay were ordained: the Rev. Thomas Romney Robinson, the Rev. Dionysius Lardner, and the Rev. Humphrey Lloyd. In 1637, it had been decreed that all except two of those elected to Fellowship in Trinity should proceed to ordination – the exceptions being a Fellow in Law and one in Medicine[137]. (James MacCullagh was elected the 'Jurist' Fellow in 1832, and thus was not required to be ordained.) There remained few exceptions to this rule until the requirement was removed by an act in 1873, which provided that no religious test or declaration of faith was to be required for any post – the Divinity School excepted[138]. Under regulations of 1911 it became possible to elect someone to a Trinity Fellowship without an examination. Before this, a very rigorous examination, much of it carried out *viva voce* in public, was required. Candidates had to be versed in Pure and Applied Mathematics and Experimental Physics in addition to Philosophy, Latin, Greek, and Hebrew[139]. My maternal grandfather, Charles Smith (1864–1930), who took first place in both Mathematics and Experimental Science in the 1889 Moderatorship (honours) exams in TCD, tried on no less than five occasions to get elected to Fellowship but, in spite of achieving third place in 1892 and second place in 1893, he failed (only one Fellow was elected each year at that time) – and this gives an indication of how tough it was; and many others tried repeatedly without success.

Perhaps it is a manifestation of this cynical age, but an obvious query would be whether the TCD Fellows became clerics because of their convictions or because they had to. Some of them certainly had strong religious beliefs. One of these was the Rev. George Salmon (1819–1904), who was born in Cork and who was elected to Fellowship in 1841. He is remembered in mathematics for his textbooks, the most famous of which was *Conic Sections*. First published in 1847, it reached its sixth edition in 1879, and this edition was reprinted many times – the most recent reprint being in 1954. His other famous textbooks were *Higher Plane Curves* (1852), *Modern Higher Algebra* (1859) and *Analytical Geometry of Three Dimensions* (1862). Gow comments[140]:

---

137 R.B. McDowell & D.A. Webb, *Trinity College Dublin 1592–1952 – an Academic History* (Cambridge: Cambridge University Press, 1982), p. 13.
138 McDowell & Webb 1982, p. 256.
139 M.W.J. Fry (Ed), *The Dublin University Calendar Vol. III – being a Special Supplemental Volume for the Year 1912–1923* (Dublin: Hodges, Figgis & Co., 1913), p. 568.
140 Roderick Gow, 'Salmon's *Conic Sections* – the First 150 Years of a Mathematical Best-Seller', in Charles Mollan (Ed), *The Irish Scientist Year Book 1998* (Dublin: Samton Limited, 1998), p. 26.

Historians of mathematics all attest to the important role that these textbooks played in disseminating knowledge of new developments in geometry and algebra in the second half of the nineteenth century.

Salmon became Regius Professor of Divinity in 1866 (and Provost in 1888), and he subsequently published extensively in (Protestant) theology, notably volumes of his lectures and sermons on such topics as *Non-Miraculous Christianity* (1880), *Gnosticism and Agnosticism* (1887), and *The Infallibility of the Church* (1888).

Another Rev. TCD Fellow (1844), who was the Carlow-born author of many books, was Samuel Haughton (1821–1897). He started off in mathematics but subsequently became interested in mineralogy and geology, being appointed Professor of Geology in 1851. Combining disciplines, he made calculations of the age of the earth based on the cooling of its internal heat. But his results did not always agree with those of Lord Kelvin. Smith records[141]:

> [Haughton] at first considered Thomson's one hundred million years as sufficient. Subsequently, his own estimates of geological time took him to over 2000 million years. By 1878, however, he had settled for 153 million years, apparently by compelling his results to yield a figure within Thomson's range.

The earth is now reckoned to be 4,500 million years old, so we can see the dangers of being too much influenced by supposed contemporary wisdom.

While a professor, Haughton studied medicine in Trinity, graduating MD in 1862. Using his mathematical and medical skills, he published his *Principles of Animal Mechanics* in 1873, and he was a key figure in the administration (and indeed the survival at a critical time) of the Dublin Zoo. He was an outspoken opponent of Darwin's theory of evolution[142]:

> If the present state of the solar system be the result, according to fixed laws, of some pre-existing state, it may be said, in the language of Naturalists, to have been evolved out of its former state, but in such an Evolution there was nothing left to chance. It was all foreseen and the evolution itself presided over by the Divine Mind that planned the whole….every step and every result was foreseen and planned beforehand.

Haughton is remembered in 'Haughton's Drop' – the distance a criminal being hanged needs to fall to ensure immediate death. He also made practical contributions to pre-university education by writing 'elementary manuals' in mathematical and scientific subjects, in some of which he collaborated with his colleague the Rev. Joseph

---

[141] Crosbie Smith and M. Norton Wise, *Energy and Empire – a Biographical Study of Lord Kelvin* (Cambridge: Cambridge University Press, 1989), p. 596.
[142] Samuel Haughton, *The Principles of Animal Mechanics* (London: Longmans, 1873), p. vi.

Galbraith, Trinity Professor of Natural and Experimental Philosophy. Haughton also took over editorship of Robert Sullivan's *Geography Generalised*. The 57th edition, dated 1877, reproduces Haughton's Preface to the 47th edition, which he dates 1874 (which means there were 10 editions in three years – presumably because they were produced for different countries[143]), and he continued his editorship until at least the 79th edition in 1895, two years before his death. Dr Robert Sullivan (1800–1868) was a TCD educated barrister, who graduated in 1829, and who played a key role in Irish education, publishing books on etymology and English grammar as well as Geography. His *Introduction to Geography* realised its 92nd edition in 1869[144].

An eminent Irish-born scientist who earned particular fame, indeed notoriety, because of his anti-religious views was John Tyndall (1820–1893), who was born in Leighlinbridge, Co. Carlow. In contrast to the kind of position taken by his Co. Carlow contemporary, Samuel Haughton, Tyndall is remembered particularly for a robust comment he made in his Presidential Address to the BAAS, which was meeting in Belfast in 1874[145]:

> The impregnable position of science may be described in a few words. We claim, and we shall wrest, from theology the entire domain of cosmological theory. All schemes and systems which thus infringe upon the domain of science must, in so far as they do this, submit to its control, and relinquish all thought of controlling it. Acting otherwise proved disastrous in the past, and it is simply fatuous to-day.

Scottish physicist James Clerk Maxwell (1831–1879) waxed poetic[146]:

> From nothing comes nothing they told us,
> Naught happens by chance but by fate;
> There is nothing but atoms and void,
> All else is mere whims out of date;
> Then why should a man curry favour
> With beings who cannot exist
> To compass some petty promotion
> In nebulous kingdoms of mist?

This wasn't the first time that Tyndall had challenged religious belief. Basalla et al. write[147]:

143 Personal communication from Professor Gordon Herries Davies.
144 *Dictionary of National Biography*.
145 John Tyndall, 'Presidential Address' in the *Report of the Forth-Fourth Meeting of the British Association for the Advancement of Science; held at Belfast in August 1874* (London: John Murray, 1875), p. xcv.
146 Quoted in George Basalla, William Coleman & Robert H. Kargon (Eds), *Victorian Science – a Self-Portrait from the Presidential Addresses to the British Association for the Advancement of Science* (New York, Anchor Books, 1970), p. 437.
147 Basalla 1970, p. 439.

Shortly prior to the Belfast meeting Tyndall again became involved in a dispute, this one concerning the efficacy of prayer....Since prayer was invoked to control rainfall and alter the course of windstorms, and since it was believed to affect the growth of crops and the health of men and cattle, Tyndall argued that it might be some form of physical energy. Being a good experimentalist, he suggested that an experimental situation be devised whereby the actual physical effect of prayer could be accurately determined. For example, all of England could be asked to pray for the health of patients in a selected hospital ward. Physicians gathering statistical data on these patients, and on a number of control groups, could then learn if the prayers of a nation did indeed appreciably influence the recovery rate of those in the chosen ward.

It appears that his challenge was not taken up at the time, though apparently it was tried as recently as 2003, and found to be ineffective.

Following local schooling in Carlow, work with the Ordnance Survey in Ireland and England, with the railways, and a teaching job in the famous Queenwood College in Hampshire, England, Tyndall studied for a PhD in Germany. On his return, he was unsuccessful in applications for academic posts in universities in Toronto, Sydney, Cork and Galway, though he was elected Fellow of the Royal Society in 1852. He got his break in 1853, when he was appointed Professor of Natural Philosophy at the Royal Institution in London. He was a brilliant lecturer. Burchfield records[148]:

> Almost from the moment he arrived in London, Tyndall became an evangelist for the cause of science. His experience in Germany had convinced him that traditional British education, with its emphasis on the classics and rote mathematics was hopelessly outdated and detrimental to the good of the country. Thus, his lectures at the Royal Institution were not merely to entertain or even to instruct his audience, but to awaken them to the beauty and importance of science.

Tyndall was to remain at the RI for a further 34 years, refusing tempting academic offers which would have paid better, and he eventually succeeded Faraday as Superintendent in 1867. He retired due to his ill health in 1886.

In addition to his lectures and researches (it was he who explained why the sky is blue – due to light scattering, and he debunked the notion of spontaneous generation by showing it didn't happen if bugs were kept away from various broths – including his own urine), he was a prolific writer of popular science books on topics such as heat, light, sound, electricity and magnetism. His books went through many editions at home and abroad – especially in America, where his lectures were rapturously received.

---

[148] Joe Burchfield, 'John Tyndall – a Biographical Sketch', in William H. Brock, Norman D. McMillan & Charles Mollan (Eds), *John Tyndall – Essays on a Natural Philosopher* (Dublin: Royal Dublin Society, 1981), p. 6.

He was a keen mountaineer in the Alps, being the first to climb the Weisshorn in 1861, and he wrote on glaciers and forms of water, as well as mountaineering. He even owned a house at Bel Alp in view of the Weisshorn, and he and his wife – he had married Louisa Hamilton in 1872 when he was at the advanced age of 56 – spent three months there each summer.

He was one of the first scientists to use the word 'physics' in its modern sense, defining the discipline in 1854 as 'that portion of natural science which lies midway between astronomy and chemistry'[149], and he was one of the founders of the journal *Nature* in 1869.

Tyndall's life ended in 1893, when his wife mistakenly administered to him a lethal dose of chloral.

It was in a publication of the Royal Dublin Society in 1891 that the word 'electron' was introduced into the English language[150]. The author of the paper was Co. Offaly born George Johnstone Stoney (1826–1911). He was studying the theoretical framework which gave rise to spectral lines. While his use of the term didn't refer to what we now know as an electron, but rather to a quantum of electrical charge associated with each chemical bond, it was subsequently used to replace the term 'corpuscle', after the charge to mass ratio of this 'sub-atomic particle' was determined by J.J. Thomson (1856–1940) in 1897. While Thomson is almost always credited as the 'discoverer' of the electron, James O'Hara[151] has argued that:

> The conceptual and experimental discovery of the electron was a process that extended over a period of nearly seventy years from the first formulation of the laws of electrolysis by Michael Faraday, in 1833, until Thomson's establishment of the particulate nature of cathode rays and his conception of the famous corpuscle hypothesis….Among several scientists who contributed to this process, the Irish physicist George Johnstone Stoney deserves particular recognition.

Stoney was born at Oakley Park, near Birr, in Co. Offaly. After graduating in mathematics in Trinity College Dublin in 1847, he worked as astronomical assistant to the Third Earl of Rosse at Birr, and as tutor to the Earl's children, while he studied for TCD Fellowship. Like my grandfather some years later, he reached third place in 1851 and second place in 1852, but didn't obtain fellowship. Disappointed, he returned to Birr, and then, in 1853, was appointed Professor of Natural Philosophy at Queen's College, Galway, a post he held until 1857, when he became Secretary of the Queen's University. This was the administrative body for the colleges at Belfast, Cork and Galway.

---

[149] John Tyndall, 'On the Importance of the Study of Physics', in *The Culture Demanded by Modern Life – a Series of Addresses and Arguments on the Claims of Scientific Education* (New York: International Science Library, A.L. Fowle, 1867), p. 62.

[150] George Johnstone Stoney, 'On the Cause of Double Lines and Equidistant Satellites in the Spectra of Gases', *Transactions of the Royal Dublin Society*, 4, 1891, p. 583.

[151] James G. O'Hara, 'George Johnstone Stoney and the Conceptual Discovery of the Electron', *Occasional Papers in Irish Science and Technology* (Dublin: Royal Dublin Society, 1993), p. 5. See also Charles Mollan, 'Who Discovered the Electron', *Technology Ireland*, October 1992, pp. 56-58.

He thus had to carry out much of his scientific work on an out-of-hours basis, and he made use of the facilities of the Royal Dublin Society for this purpose. The volume and quality of his scientific work were impressive in spite of his difficult circumstances, which were compounded by the untimely death of his wife in 1872, and two severe illnesses – small-pox in 1875 and typhoid in 1877[152]. In astronomy, Stoney deduced, from the kinetic theory of gases, the conditions necessary for the retention of an atmosphere by a planet; he suggested a system of natural units of mass, length and time, similar to those used in modern cosmology[153]; and, with a colleague, A.M.W. Dowling, he showed in principle how meteor storms could be predicted[154]. Stoney was elected to Fellowship of the Royal Society in 1861, and served as Vice-President between 1898 and 1899. In 1893 he left Dublin for London so that his daughters could have the opportunity of a university education, something not possible at the time in Dublin. He was one of the first recipients of the Royal Dublin Society's Boyle Medal in 1899 after it was instituted to reward research of exceptional merit carried out in Ireland. Thomas Preston (*see below*) also received one in that year. Stoney died in London, though his ashes were brought back home to Dublin for burial.

Stoney's sister, Ann Frances, married a Church of Ireland priest, William FitzGerald, who later became a bishop, and their second son, born in Dublin, was George Francis FitzGerald (1851–1901). He had the good fortune to be tutored by Mary Ann, the sister of mathematician George Boole (*see above*) before entering Trinity College, where he graduated with top place in mathematics and experimental science in 1871. He was elected to Fellowship in 1877 on his second attempt (his first attempt was in 1873, but there was no Fellowship contest in the intervening years): thus he was not required to be ordained. He spent the rest of his working life in Trinity, holding the Erasmus Smith Professorship of Natural and Experimental Philosophy there from 1881 until his early death. He became a Fellow of the Royal Society in 1883 and received its Royal Medal in 1899 for his contributions to theoretical physics.

His major work was in the development of the theory of electromagnetic radiation, which had been introduced by James Clerk Maxwell (whose poetic effort following Tyndall's Belfast Address we featured earlier). FitzGerald reported to the BAAS at Southport in 1883 'On a method of producing electro-magnetic disturbances of comparatively short wave-lengths' using alternating currents[155]. German physicist, Heinrich Hertz (1857–1894) in 1887 demonstrated that these waves could be transmitted and received across short distances. It was FitzGerald, in his role as President in 1888 of the Mathematical and Physical Section of the BAAS, who enthusiastically endorsed Hertz' work and ensured that its importance was realised[156].

---

[152] *Dictionary of National Biography.*
[153] John D. Barrow, *The Constants of Nature, from Alpha to Omega* (London: Jonathan Cape, 2002), pp. 16-31. I am grateful to Dr Ian Elliott for drawing this reference to my attention.
[154] Personal communication from Dr Ian Elliott.
[155] George Francis FitzGerald, *Report of the Fifty-Third Meeting of the British Association for the Advancement of Science Held at Southport in September 1883* (London: John Murray, 1884), p. 405.
[156] George Francis FitzGerald, 'Presidential Address to Section A', *Report of the Fifty-Eighth Meeting of the British Association for the Advancement of Science Held at Bath in September 1888* (London: John Murray, 1889), pp. 557-562.

It was only a few years later that Guglielmo Marconi (1874–1937) – whose mother was Annie Jameson (of the whiskey distilling family), from Enniscorthy in Co. Wexford – began the experiments which led to the development of 'wireless' communication using these 'radio waves'. Marconi was able to send and receive signals over progressively increasing distances. In 1898 his equipment was used to report details of the results of the Kingstown (later Dun Laoghaire, Co. Dublin) regatta to the shore – the first time this had been achieved. He himself described the situation[157]:

In July [1898] we were requested by a Dublin paper, the *Daily Express*, to report from the high seas the results and incidents of the Kingstown Regatta. In order to do this we erected a land station, by kind permission of the harbour master at Kingstown, in his grounds, where a pole 110 ft high was placed. A steamer, the *Flying Huntress*, was chartered to follow the racing yachts, the instruments being placed in the cabin. The height of the vertical wire attainable by the mast was 75 ft. A telephone was fixed from our land station at Kingstown to the Express office in Dublin, and as the messages came from the ship they were telephoned to Dublin, and published in succeeding editions of the evening papers.

A reporter with Marconi in the *Flying Huntress* could not resist making further use of this new possibility[158]:

No sooner were we alive to the extraordinary fact that it was possible, without connecting wires, to communicate with a station which was miles away and quite invisible to us, than we began to send silly messages, such as a request to the man in charge of the Kingston [sic] station to be sure to keep sober and not to take too many 'whiskey-and-sodas'.

Marconi carried out a good deal of his experimental work in Ireland, his stations including those at Crookhaven, Co. Cork, Clifden, Co. Galway, and Ballybunion, Co. Kerry. And in 1905 he married an Irish wife, the Hon. Beatrice O'Brien, daughter of Lord and Lady Inchiquin of Dromoland Castle in Co. Clare.

Returning to FitzGerald, he was a firm believer in the existence of the ether (or aether) – the all pervading medium which was thought to be necessary for the propagation of light. German–American Albert Michelson (1852–1931) and American Edward Morley (1838–1923) had tried to prove the existence of the ether by a light interference experiment, but failed (because the ether doesn't exist not because their experiments were faulty). Watson writes[159]:

---

[157] Guglielmo Marconi, 'Wireless Telegraphy', *Journal of the Institution of Electrical Engineers*, **28**, 1899, 273-318. I am grateful to Prof. Michael Sexton for drawing this quote to my attention.

[158] Quoted in: Gavin Weightman, *Signor Marconi's Magic Box – How an Amateur Inventor Defied Scientists and Began the Radio Revolution* (London: Harper Collins, 2003), p. 41.

[159] C. Watson, 'William Thomson, Lord Kelvin (1824–1907)', in R. Harré (Ed), *Some Nineteenth Century British Scientists* (Oxford: Pergamon Press, 1969), p. 150-151.

In 1881 Michelson performed the first of a series of experiments from which he and Morley hoped to settle what had by then become a very vexed question, the motion, if any, of the ether with respect to a moving body such as the earth. A number of theories had been proposed on this subject....It began to appear that the ether, at all points in space, happened to be stationary with respect to the earth. Such a conclusion might have been acceptable had it been reached in the age of Copernicus, but by 1892 it was far too geocentric to be credible, so FitzGerald proposed a new theory of the interaction of ponderable matter and ether that could explain the negative results. This was that all material bodies contracted in length when moving with respect to the ether.

FitzGerald, who usually published in the journals of the Royal Dublin Society, had a falling out with the Society[160], so his contraction idea was actually first published in what was then a rather obscure American journal, *Science*, in 1889. Independently, Dutch physicist, Hendrik Lorentz (1853–1928) had hit upon the same idea in 1892, unaware of FitzGerald's earlier communication, and Lorenz developed it mathematically. FitzGerald's name is preserved in the FitzGerald-Lorentz contraction[161]. Watson continues:

> It was by pondering on this...., and in particular by asking how in principle one could set about verifying such a hypothesis, that Einstein was led to his discovery that the hypothesis so formulated was in principle unverifiable and so to his theory of the relativity of space and time which is now regarded as the true explanation of the Michelson–Morley experiment.

FitzGerald does not receive the recognition he deserves because his name is not remembered by other laws and theories. In a letter to English physicist and engineer, Oliver Heaviside (1850–1925), dated 1889, he writes[162]:

> I admire from a distance those who contain themselves till they worked to the bottom of their results, but as I am not in the very least sensitive to having made mistakes, I rush out with all sorts of crude notions in hope that they may set others thinking and lead to some advance.

He is being unfair to himself here, particularly in the word 'crude' because, as is evident from a fine collection of letters (now in the possession of the Royal Dublin Society) written to him from many eminent scientists of the time, his ideas could be extremely useful. 'He possessed extraordinary versatility....throwing out luminous suggestions

---

[160] Charles Mollan. 'Science and its Industrial Applications', in James Meenan & Desmond Clarke (Eds), *RDS – The Royal Dublin Society 1731–1981* (Dublin: Gill & Macmillan, 1981), pp. 210-211.
[161] Bruce J. Hunt, The Maxwellians (Ithica: Cornell University Press, 1991), p. 193-195.
[162] Quoted in the FitzGerald entry in the *Dictionary of National Biography*.

with splendid prodigality and rejoicing if they were absorbed and utilised by others'[163]. Garratt has endorsed this view[164]:

> The most persistent and influential advocate of Maxwell's view was unquestionably Professor George Francis FitzGerald of Trinity College, Dublin, one of the outstanding physicists of his time and one who, by common consent, had attained a unique position as a judge and critic of the work of others.

FitzGerald inspired a generation of Irish students, including one of his star pupils, my grandfather!

He took a great interest in technical education and he played an important role in the foundation by Dublin Corporation of Kevin Street Technical School (now part of the Dublin Institute of Technology) in 1887. He is remembered in Trinity for building and trying to fly an aeroplane in College Park – not very successfully though – leading to his nickname 'flightless Fitzgerald'! He died in Dublin at the early age of 49.

The post of Lucasian Professor of Mathematics in Cambridge University is a very distinguished one. The most famous appointee was Isaac Newton (1642–1727, who held the post from 1668 until his death), and the current holder, Stephen Hawking (b. 1942, appointed in 1979), is one of the best known scientists of today. Both of these were English. But in between, for a period of no less than 83 years, this prestige position was held by Irish-born mathematicians/physicists. George Gabriel Stokes (*see above*) held the post from 1849 until 1903, while Joseph Larmor (1857–1942) was incumbent from 1903 until 1932. Larmor was born in Magheragall, Co. Antrim, and attended Queen's College Belfast before proceeding to Cambridge University. Students from the Belfast area achieved well in the Cambridge Mathematical Tripos: William Thomson (Lord Kelvin) achieved second place in 1845, Andrew Allen won top place ('Senior Wrangler') in 1879 (he became a vicar in England), and Joseph Larmor took top place in 1880. Between his graduation and his return to Cambridge, Larmor was Professor of Natural Philosophy at Queen's College Galway, a post he held from 1880 to 1885.

We have already noted George Francis FitzGerald's contributions to electromagnetic theory, and Larmor was also closely involved in its development[165]:

> Seen in its place in the history of physics, Larmor's work marks the end of the attempt to express everything in terms of the Newtonian mechanics of matter and the beginning of the electromagnetic theory of matter. But it led on immediately to the more revolutionary theory of relativity. For one of the main problems which Larmor attacked was the failure to find definite evidence of motion of the earth through the aether. Of this he was able to give a partial and

---

163 *Dictionary of National Biography.*
164 G.R.M. Garratt, *The Early History of Radio from Faraday to Marconi* (Stevenage: Institution of Electrical Engineers, 1994), p. 30.
165 *Dictionary of National Biography.*

approximate explanation....This explanation led up directly to the more radical outlook of Einstein which, while completing the discussion, shook the rigid framework of Newtonian conceptions of absolute time and space.

Away from his scientific pursuits, Larmor was of a conservative disposition and, for example, he questioned the need for the installation of baths in his Cambridge College (St John's) – 'We have done without them for 400 years, why begin now'[166]? When they were installed, however, he became a regular user.

Larmor crowned his distinguished contributions in his famous book *Aether and Matter* (1900). He had been elected Fellow of the Royal Society in 1892, and served as one of its Secretaries from 1901 to 1912, continuing the Irish tradition of service to that Society. He received the Royal Society Royal Medal in 1915, and its Copley Medal in 1921. He was knighted in 1909, and from 1911 to 1922 (following the footsteps of G.G. Stokes) he represented Cambridge University in Westminster. He edited the collected works of fellow Irishmen, Stokes, Kelvin and FitzGerald. After his retirement in 1932, he returned to Ireland, and he died at Holywood, Co. Down.

There are some scientists who gain fame for one major discovery, and never reach the same heights of achievement again. There are others who keep on making important and useful discoveries. One of the most fertile of Irish scientific minds was surely that of John Joly (1857–1933). He was born in Hollywood House – the Church of Ireland Rectory – at Bracknagh in Co. Offaly, the third son of the Rev. John Plunket Joly and his wife Julia. He entered Trinity College Dublin in 1876 and graduated in engineering in 1882. He worked in the Engineering and Physics departments before becoming Professor of Geology and Mineralogy, a post he held for 36 years, from 1897 to 1933. He spent all his working life in Trinity and did not marry. He was elected to Fellowship of the Royal Society in 1892, and was awarded its Royal Medal in 1910. He received the third Boyle Medal of the Royal Dublin Society in 1911. He was the first person to be elected to Fellowship of TCD (in 1919) without examination, following the change of rules to allow this.

Joly had a wide range of interests and made many contributions to science, writing about 270 scientific papers and several books. He invented quite a few scientific instruments, the best known being his meldometer for measuring the melting points of minerals, his photometer for measuring light intensity, and his steam calorimeter for measuring specific heats[167]. He was the first to show how to measure the specific heats of gases at constant volume.

One of his claims to fame was his important contributions to the estimation of the age of the earth. Several incumbents of the Trinity chair of Geology were involved in this question over the years: John Phillips (1800–1874), the first Professor of Geology and Mineralogy (from 1843 to 1845), gave an estimate of 96 million years, based on the rate

---

[166] *Dictionary of National Biography.*
[167] Charles Mollan, *The Mind and the Hand – Instruments of Science 1685–1932* (Dublin: Samton Limited, 1995), pp. 33-36.

of sedimentation in the oceans. As we have already seen, Samuel Haughton, Trinity's third Professor of Geology, made several calculations, with widely different estimates ranging from 2,298 million down to 153 million years. William Sollas (1849–1936), the fifth Professor of Geology (from 1883 to 1897), made more estimates, with results between 17 and 80 million years. Few people were prepared to question the limit set by Lord Kelvin of 100 million years, although this was based on assumptions which were much less than rigorous, and which could not be directly measured. Kelvin had subsequently lowered his limit towards 20 million years or even less, and the climate of uncritical acceptance began to change, as more commentators realised that, even if the 100 million year estimate might be acceptable (some thought it OK, others didn't), the lower estimates were not. Such a time scale was insufficient to explain the geological record and the theory of natural selection. Burchfield writes[168]:

> If conventional methods could occasionally lead to radical results, novel methods could give conventional results. In the spring of 1899 [Joly]....announced the first entirely new approach to the earth's age to appear in several decades, a calculation of the age of the oceans based upon their sodium content.

Joly came up with 97.6 million years. But what finally led to the overthrow of Kelvin's limitations placed on the possible age of the earth, was the discovery at the turn of the century of radioactivity. As we now know only too well from our images of atomic and, later, nuclear weapons, enormous stores of latent energy are tied up in atoms. A scientist who came to the fore at this time was the New Zealander, Ernest Rutherford (1871-1937), then at McGill University in Montreal. He realised that this new form of potential heat would have profound implications for Kelvin's estimates of the age of the earth.

In the meantime, Joly was the first to recognise that so-called 'pleiochroic haloes' – spherical colourations around certain minerals – were due to radioactivity. 'By 1907 he was able to show that they were caused by ionisation induced by alpha particles emitted from minute isolated quantities of uranium or thorium'[169]. But Joly resisted accepting the much longer times for the age of the minerals which began to appear likely – including those obtained from his important joint work with Ernest Rutherford (by now in Manchester) which was published in 1913[170]. The age of the earth is now estimated as around 4,500 million years.

Another practical achievement – also connected with radioactivity – was Joly's successful collaboration with Dr Walter Stevenson of Dr Steeven's Hospital in Dublin – of which Joly was a Governor – in the use of radiation for the treatment of cancer.

---

[168] Joe Burchfield, *Lord Kelvin and the Age of the Earth* (Chicago: University of Chicago Press, 1990 – reprint of the 1975 Edition with an new afterword), p. 149.
[169] Burchfield 1990, p. 188.
[170] John Joly & Ernest Rutherford, 'The Age of Pleochroic Haloes', *Philosophical Magazine*, **25**, 1913, pp. 644-657.

With his encouragement, the Royal Dublin Society accumulated a supply of Radium Bromide, and the 'Dublin Method' for treating tumours was developed using radon gas given off from this source, sealed in glass needles in the RDS laboratory, which were inserted into the tumour. In 1952 the Society's stock of radium was transferred to the Cancer Association of Ireland – now St Luke's Hospital, still a key centre for cancer treatment in the country.

In 1894, Joly patented his method for colour photography (Patent 14161), the first successful method of producing colour photographs from a single plate. What he did was effectively to place three filters on the one glass screen by ruling fine lines – about 200 per inch – successively in red/orange, yellow/green, and blue/violet. The resulting transparency, when viewed through a similar screen, 'appears in vivid colour and with all the realism and relief conferred by colour and colour perspective'. Modern methods of colour photography derive from this concept.

Joly collaborated with his close friend and Trinity colleague, Henry Horatio Dixon (1869-1953), in explaining how sap rises in plants[171], due to a combination of the transpiration of leaves and the tensile stress of water, the first time this had been done. They weren't believed at first, but they were right.

Joly remained active to the end of his life, lecturing just days before he died in Dublin.

Some other Trinity educated physicists/mathematicians also achieved distinction in the years leading up to the end of the nineteenth century and the early days of the twentieth. These include Thomas Preston (1860–1900), born in Ballyhagan, Co. Armagh, who graduated in 1885, and who is remembered in spectroscopy for what is called the 'anomolous Zeeman effect' – a phenomenon which relates to unexpected splitting patterns in spectral lines. Although the true explanation of this splitting was not understood until the development of quantum mechanics, Preston's work was of considerable significance. He was also renowned for his important textbooks *The Theory of Light* (1890) and *The Theory of Heat* (1894), each of which extended to several editions, most edited by others after his death. Unfortunately, he died at the early age of 40, otherwise he would surely have achieved even more[172].

Thomas Rankin Lyle (1860–1944), from Coleraine, Co. Derry, who graduated in 1883, and who had the distinction of playing rugby for Ireland while at Trinity, emigrated to Australia as Professor of Natural Philosophy at Melbourne University in 1889, a post which he held until 1915. He is considered 'the father-figure of Australian physics'[173]. He was another who tried but failed to attain Fellowship of TCD, coming third in 1886 and 1887 and second in 1888; but he later (1912) became a Fellow of

---

[171] Francis Darwin, 'On the Ascent of Water in Trees', *Report of the British Association for the Advancement of Science Held at Liverpool in September 1896* (London: John Murray, 1896), pp. 674-683. Darwin's Report and the subsequent discussion at the BAAS Meeting were published in *Annals of Botany*, **10**, 1896, pp. 630-661.

[172] D. Weaire & S. O'Connor, 'Unfulfilled Renown: Thomas Preston (1860–1900) and the Anomalous Zeeman Effect', *Annals of Science*, **44**, 1897, pp. 617-644.

[173] Denis Weaire, 'Thomas Rankin Lyle, Physicist', p. 190 in Charles Mollan, William Davis and Brendan Finucane (Eds), *Irish Innovators in Science and Technology* (Dublin, Royal Irish Academy, 2002).

the Royal Society and was knighted in 1922. His best work was in the analysis of circuits by complex functions, and in electrical technology.

Frederick Trouton (1863–1922) was born in Dublin and, after graduation in 1884, he became assistant to George Francis FitzGerald. He followed FitzGerald's interest in electromagnetism and the ether. When, on his superior's untimely death in 1901, he failed to get his job, he took up the position of Quain Professorship of Physics in University College London. He became a Fellow of the Royal Society in 1897, and is remembered in 'Trouton's Rule' relating latent heat and molecular weight[174].

John Townsend (1868–1957), from Galway, who graduated in 1890, was one of my grandfather's rivals in the TCD Fellowship examination in 1892, 1893, 1894 and 1895. Although Charles Smith did better than him in all but one of these years, neither succeeded. In contrast to my grandfather, who gave up science and became a country vicar in Co. Donegal, Townsend kept up his science. He achieved Fellowship of the Royal Society in 1903 and was knighted in 1941 (there but for the grace of God!). Townsend was fortunate to be one of the first outside research students in the Cavendish Laboratory at Cambridge University, whose director at the time was J.J. Thomson, whom we have met at the 'discovery' of the electron. Townsend's research interests focused chiefly on the electrical properties of gases, and he is credited with introducing the teaching of electricity and magnetism at the rival Oxford University when he was appointed to the Wykeman Professorship of Experimental Physics on the foundation of that chair in 1900[175], a post he held until his retirement in 1941. He worked on radio communication during the first World War, and carried out pioneering work in the development of radar.

John Synge (1897–1995), from Dublin, who graduated in 1919, became a Fellow of TCD (without examination) in 1925, the year he was appointed Professor of Natural Philosophy – a post he held until 1930. His career then took him to Canada and to the United States, before his return to Ireland as Senior Professor at the Dublin Institute for Advanced Studies in 1948. He had in the meantime become a Fellow of the Royal Society in 1943. He is considered 'the most talented and distinguished Irish mathematician of his generation'[176], and he was joint editor in 1931 of the first two volumes (of four) of the papers of the most distinguished mathematician of a previous generation, William Rowan Hamilton. He is remembered particularly for his contributions to relativity, and his books on this topic, *Relativity, the Special Theory* (1956), and *Relativity, the General Theory* (1960) 'profoundly influenced and shaped a whole generation of students of relativity and cosmology'. He was awarded the Boyle Medal of the Royal Dublin Society in 1972.

Synge had a practical approach to his mathematics, and published *Science: Sense & Nonsense* in 1951. In the latter he commented[177]:

---

174 Eric Finch, 'Frederick Thomas Trouton, Physicist', p. 192 in Mollan 2002.
175 David Attis, 'John Sealy Edward Townsend, Physicist', pp. 202-203 in Mollan 2002.
176 David Spearman, 'John Lighton Synge, Mathematician', pp. 232-233 in Mollan 2002.
177 J.L. Synge, *Science: Sense and Nonsense* (London: Jonathan Cape, 1951), pp. 151-153.

The artist is in a peculiar position. A highly skilled craftsman, he communicates to those who lack that skill and who have probably made no effort to acquire it. Apparently he succeeds, for otherwise he would have been starved out of existence long ago.

The scientist on the other hand does not feel this obligation to any great extent. Sympathetic as he may be and anxious to tell what he knows, he feels himself inhibited from the beginning by the fact that his audience is untrained. His real exposition is reserved for the small group of fellow-scientists qualified to understand him by long training in science, and all he can hope to offer the public is a drink so well watered that nearly all its taste is gone. It is as if the paintings of great artists were concealed in locked galleries with admission granted exclusively to those who had studied at an art school for at least four years, and only crude cheap posters reminiscent of the paintings exhibited to the public at large.

In spite of this rather pessimistic assessment, he sought, in his book, to lead the non-scientific reader 'into domains where science and commonsense meet' and suggested that we should 'watch the spectacle of science with less of the reverence appropriate to a church and more of the freedom of spirit appropriate to a theatre'.

The last of this batch of Trinity graduates in mathematics/physics we will feature in this essay (but by no means the last to have achieved distinction) is Ernest Walton (1903–1995). He still has the honour of being the only Irish-born person to have won a scientific Nobel Prize, an award he achieved with John Cockcroft (1897–1967) in 1952 for their 'pioneering work on the transmutation of atomic nuclei by artificially accelerated atomic particles'. In popular parlance, they 'split the atom', and were thus the first successful alchemists, transmuting one element to another by artificial means, though they converted lithium to helium rather than lead into gold. In the process, they confirmed Einstein's famous $E = mc^2$ equation (energy equals mass times the speed of light squared).

Walton was born in Dungarvan, Co. Waterford, but his family moved around a lot, since his father was a Methodist minister. He graduated in 1926, and subsequently was fortunate to secure a place in the Cavendish Laboratory in Cambridge, where Ernest Rutherford was Director. We can recall that John Joly and Rutherford had co-operated in work on pleiochroic haloes (*see above*), and Joly's endorsement of Walton's abilities was a key element in his securing this position. It was in Cambridge that Walton and Cockcroft built their 'linear accelerator' which they used to bombard a lithium target with protons (hydrogen nuclei) in 1932, the beginning of accelerator-based experimental nuclear physics, which continues to teach us so much about the nature of matter. With minimal equipment, due to a very parsimonious approach to expenditure by Rutherford, it was Walton's manual dexterity which made the successful operation of the accelerator possible[178].

---

[178] Charles Mollan, *The Mind and the Hand – Instruments of Science 1685–1932* (Dublin: Samton Limited, 1995), pp. 6 & 40.

Walton soon returned to Trinity College, being elected to Fellowship in 1934, and he became Erasmus Smith's Professor of Natural and Experimental Philosophy in 1946. There, he established a lasting reputation as a devoted teacher who inspired generations of Trinity physicists.

He left his home in Dublin in 1992 and died in Belfast in 1995. I was in the fortunate position of being asked to check over his house in St Kevin's Park, Dublin 6, after he left for Belfast and after the removal of his personal effects and the dispersion of his more important remaining property to family and institutions, to see if anything significant remained. The most dramatic result was the discovery in an old tin box of the spectacles he wore on that day (14 April 1932) when he first observed scintillations on a screen (due to alpha particles – helium nuclei) which confirmed the splitting of the lithium target. These were presented to the National Museum. I had the opportunity also to purchase his copy of the ninth and tenth editions of the *Encyclopaedia Britannica* (35 large leather bound volumes) which he had bought second hand from a neighbour, and had transported by wheelbarrow to his house years earlier. They have been a mine of useful information since.

The final physicist/mathematician whom we shall feature was another son of that city which has produced so many achievers in science and technology. John Bell (1928–1990 – *see also page 270*) was born in Belfast, but his parents did not have the means to send him to University as a student, so he got a job as a technician in the Physics Department of Queen's University Belfast. There his abilities were recognised and he was enabled to complete a first class honours degree in Experimental Physics in 1948 and another in Mathematical Physics in 1949. According to his wife Mary (Ross), he was influenced by Irish Nobel Prize winner, George Bernard Shaw, and became a vegetarian: and he also became, and remained, a 'Protestant Atheist'[179]!

John Gribbin headed an article on Bell in the *New Scientist*[180]: 'The man who proved Einstein was wrong'. He wrote:

Albert Einstein never accepted the indeterminism of quantum mechanics. But a quiet Irishman, John Bell, devised a test that revealed the alarming truth behind quantum reality.

On graduation, Bell had moved to the Atomic Energy Research Establishment at Harwell in England, and after 1951 he there worked on the design of CERN's first accelerator, the Proton Synchroton (a further extension of the pioneering work of Cockcroft and Walton). In 1953 he obtained paid leave to study at the University of Birmingham, and it was while he was there that he married Mary, another physicist, in 1954. It was after his return to Harwell that he obtained his PhD from Birmingham in 1956. He transferred to CERN in Geneva in 1960 and remained there (apart from one year in Stanford) until his premature death in 1990[181].

---

179 Mary Bell, 'Biographical Notes on John Bell', p. xi in John Ellis & Daniele Amati (Eds), *Quantum Reflections* (Cambridge: Cambridge University Press, 2000).
180 John Gribben, ''The Man who Proved Einstein was Wrong', *New Scientist*, 24 November 1990, pp. 43-45.
181 Philip Burke & Ian Percival, 'John Stewart Bell', *Biographical Memoirs of Fellows of the Royal Society London*, **45**, 1999, 1-17.

In 1964 Bell published what has been described as 'the single most important theoretical paper in physics to appear since 1945'[182] – 'On the Einstein Podolsky Rosen paradox'. In essence, he anticipated a test which would establish whether or not there was such a thing as what Einstein dubbed 'spooky action at a distance':

> a communication that operates instantaneously between two particles even when they are far apart, so that particle A can be disturbed by the measurement made on particle B – a communication that Einstein, the originator of relativity theory, could never accept, since it seemed to travel faster than light....To Einstein it was 'obvious' that there could be no action at a distance, and therefore that quantum uncertainty was an illusion.

Bell's paper made the conceptual breakthrough which led to a practical experiment to measure this bizarre effect. The actual experiments, involving the measurement of the polarisation of photons leaving an atom, were carried out by Alain Aspect working at the Institute of Optics at the University of Paris in the 1980s. They established that the quantum theory 'including the spooky action at a distance which Einstein hated so much' is correct.

This has profound implications as, according to the big bang theory, all particles originate from a common set of interactions at the birth of the universe. 'It implies that there is a cosmic web linking all particles in the Universe'. It may imply that absolutely everything is predetermined – and where does that leave our assumption of free will? 'For me', said Bell, 'it's a dilemma. I think it's a deep dilemma, and the resolution of it will not be trivial; it will require a substantial change in the way we look at things'[180].

A colleague wrote of him[183]:

> Many enter our field not only for the opportunity of exploring Nature in its most fundamental workings, but also for what we perceive as the purity and honesty of the profession. These qualities sometimes get submerged by pressure of personal ambition, struggling for achievement and recognition, but John Bell never lost them, and in this way he reminded us of the other reason for becoming a physicist.

And Greenberger wrote[184]:

> He was a colossal figure. Had he not died prematurely, he would almost certainly have won a Nobel Prize. After all, how many physicists have actually started a new field of research?

---

[182] John Daintith, Sarah Mitchell, Elizabeth Tootill & Derek Gjertsen, *Biographical Encyclopedia of Scientists*, Second Edition (Bristol: Institute of Physics, 1994), p. 67.

[183] Roman Jackiw, 'Remembering John Bell, p.198 in John Ellis & Daniele Amati (Eds), *Quantum Reflections* (Cambridge: Cambridge University Press, 2000).

[184] Daniel Greenberger, 'Review of *Quantum Reflections*', *Nature*, 7 December 2000, p. 644.

He did live long enough to receive honorary doctorates of science both from his *alma mater*, Queen's University Belfast, and from Trinity College Dublin, both conferred in 1988. He died in Geneva.

Finally, a little technology

Ireland's recent development has been led by technology. It is fortunately being at last recognised that advances in technology need to be preceded by scientific investigation. While I do not have space in this essay to consider Irish contributions to technology in any detail, it would be a pity not to mention briefly a few highlights. We have already met people like the third Earl of Rosse, builder of the *Leviathan of Parsonstown*, whose real interest was in engineering and not astronomy. Indeed Henry King, the historian of the telescope, has commented[185]: 'The Rosse telescope would have been more effectively used had its maker been as interested in observing as he was in instrument-making'. Northern Ireland and Scotland have had very close historical links, and we have featured Joseph Black who collaborated with James Watt, and Lord Kelvin who was the brains behind the successful transatlantic cable. Scotsman John Dunlop (1840–1921) developed the pneumatic tyre in Belfast and Dublin[186]. We have mentioned Thomas and Howard Grubb who built telescopes of increasingly sophisticated design for the world market, and George Gabriel Stokes who advised both Rosse and the Grubbs in their efforts. Recognising that advances in science cannot be made without instruments – 'you cannot measure, unless you have something to measure with'[187], we can mention in passing that Ireland produced a number of other scientific instrument makers who achieved success[188] – people like the Yeates family who produced instruments in Dublin during a period of over 200 years; Edward Marmaduke Clarke (1791–1859) from Dublin who emigrated to London and became a prolific maker and supplier of the instruments increasingly needed for the development of the physical sciences; and James Joseph Hicks (1837–1916) from Cork who also emigrated to England, and eventually employed over 300 in his factories, making, among many other things, some 13 million clinical thermometers[189].

But I'll finish by a very brief mention of three Irish men who really made a difference due to their engineering and technological abilities.

John Philip Holland (1841–1914), from Liscannor, Co. Clare, played a massive part in the development of the submarine[190]. The youngest son of the third Earl of Rosse, Charles Parsons (1854–1931), from Birr, Co. Offaly, invented the steam turbine

---

185 Henry C. King, *The History of the Telescope* (New York: Dover Publications, 1979 – republication of the 1955 edition of Griffin & Company, Buckinghamshire), p. 216.

186 J.B. Dunlop, *The History of the Pneumatic Tyre* (Dublin: Alex. Thom & Co, undated c. 1925).

187 Charles Mollan, *The Mind and the Hand – Instruments of Science 1685–1932* (Dublin: Samton Limited, 1995), p. 6.

188 John Burnett & Alison Morrison-Low, *'Vulgar and Mechanic' – The Scientific Instrument Trade in Ireland 1650–1921* (Edinburgh & Dublin: National Museums of Scotland & the Royal Dublin Society, 1989).

189 Anita McConnell, *King of the Clinicals – the Life and Times of J.J. Hicks (1837–1916)* (York, William Sessions Limited, 1998).

190 Richard K. Morris, *John P. Holland 1841–1914 – Inventor of the Modern Submarine* (Annapolis: United States Naval Institute, 1966).

engine which transformed not only marine transport, but also the generation of electricity[191]. Harry Ferguson (1884–1960), from Growell, Co. Down, improved the tractor, and his impact on agriculture can be assessed from the fact that 517,649 of his lightweight, inexpensive, and highly manoeuvrable tractors were build in a single decade, from 1946–1956[192].

Conclusion

Thus we welcome the return to Ireland of the BAAS with what is hoped is an indication that Ireland has played its part in the Advancement of Science.

Acknowledgement

I am most grateful to Dr Ian Elliott for reading an earlier draft of this Chapter, for pointing out errors and for suggesting additions. Remaining mistakes and omissions are, of course, my responsibility.

---

[191] Rollo Appleyard, *Charles Parsons – His Life and Work* (London: Constable & Co., 1933).
[192] Massey Ferguson, *Harry Ferguson – a Brief History of his Life and Tractors* (Coventry: Massey Ferguson Tractors Limited, 1993), p. 43.

CHAPTER 3

Developing a Research Culture

Don Thornhill

Introduction

In 2002, the Higher Education Authority (HEA) argued[1] that economy and society in Ireland needed to make a fundamental paradigm shift to what it described as an *Innovation Society*. The Authority used the term *Innovation Society* to describe an economy which *innovates in at least some sectors of the global technological frontier*[2]. This argument was not a new one and the HEA was not unique in expressing this viewpoint. The desirability, or indeed need, to increase the value added in production has been a recurring theme in policy analysis and development for quite some time – and has been confirmed most recently in the report of the Enterprise Strategy Group[3]. However, the HEA saw the challenge as wider than the economic domain:

> the overarching importance of innovation includes, but transcends, the economic and industrial domains and includes every facet of scholarship and knowledge[4].

The HEA argued that:

> innovation is important not just for the economic domain of Irish life but also has overarching significance for societal development and the quality of life, extending, for example into areas of social gain and sustainable development, environmental quality and health care, as well as into the personal domain, i.e., the private lives of citizens and their role as members of communities[5].

---

[1] Higher Education Authority, *Creating and Sustaining the Innovation Society* (Dublin: Higher Education Authority, 2002), p. 10.

[2] John McArthur & Jeffrey I. Sachs, 'The Growth Competitiveness Index: Measuring Technological Advancement and the Stages of Development', in *The Global Competitiveness Report 2001-2002, World Economic Forum* (Oxford University Press, 2001), pp. 28-50.

[3] Forfás, *Ahead of the Curve: Ireland's Place in the Global Economy – Report of the Enterprise Strategy Group* (Dublin: Forfás, 2004).

[4] Higher Education Authority, *Creating and Sustaining the Innovation Society*, p. 28

[5] Higher Education Authority, *Creating and Sustaining the Innovation Society*, p. 29

In this Chapter I will attempt, in a rather unscholarly and incomplete way, to chart the development of Irish public policy during the last fifty years in this critically important area. The story is of a journey – to a point where one hopes that investment in research, development and innovation has become a public policy priority. Some features of the story are not unique to Ireland, particularly the current policy emphasis on increasing the value-added in economic activity. Others are – because they are influenced by aspects of Irish political, social and economic history and circumstances which are specifically Irish or, more correctly, relate to the Republic. The Northern Ireland story is different in a number of significant respects – reflecting the different economic, political and institutional circumstances and histories of the two jurisdictions on the island. Interestingly, the challenges now faced by policy makers in the two parts of the island have perhaps more in common now than was the case during the second half of the twentieth century. This, unsurprisingly, reflects the increasingly pervasive influences of globalization. The overarching imperative facing policy makers in both parts of Ireland, and one which is shared in the European Union (EU), is the commitment to bring about economic, social and environmental renewal through investment in a knowledge society. The so-called 'Lisbon Strategy', to make the EU the world's most dynamic and competitive economy, was agreed in 2000[6]. Two years later at the Barcelona European Council, the EU agreed that research and technological development investment in the EU should be increased, with the aim of approaching 3% of GDP by 2010[7].

The story is, of course, incomplete. It provides only a snapshot. There is no steady state destination. Knowledge develops and opens up new perspectives. Internal circumstance will change, as will external competitive pressures. Policy perspectives and priorities will also evolve and change. I will try to identify the policy challenges, differences and dilemmas which policy makers have to confront – and there are several.

Knowledge and Innovation

Knowledge is at the centre of an innovation society. The capacity of a society to avail of knowledge for economic and social development depends on its human capital. This term was originally understood to mean the stock of accumulated skills, expertise and knowledge of individuals in the labour force. The concept was popularised by the Nobel prize winning economist Gary Becker. According to Becker, just as organisations make investments in physical production-related resources like plant or equipment, expenditure in such areas as training and education are investments in human capital which contribute to improvements in productivity and earnings[8]. This view of the economic and social development role of education is now broadly accepted. For Irish policy makers, the creation and enhancement of human capital is seen as the primary

---

[6] Communication from the European Commission to the Spring Council in Lisbon, *An Agenda of Economic and Social Renewal for Europe,* COM (2000)7, 28.02.2000.
[7] Communication from the European Commission to the Spring European Council in Barcelona, *The Lisbon Strategy – Making Change Happen,* COM (2002)14, 15.01.2002.
[8] Gary S. Becker, *Human Capital* (New York: Columbia University Press, 1964).

purpose of increasing investment in research, technology and innovation. Human capital is the foundation on which the new competitive advantages of the Irish economy will be built – education and research are the cornerstones of the national innovation system, and embedded knowledge in human capital is the most important contribution[9].

Against this perspective, it is interesting that education and research do not appear to have been central to the earlier stages of economic policy in the Republic. Education was seen as having largely a social and cultural purpose. The State, in its earlier years, seems to have seen it as a shared enterprise with the churches – particularly the Roman Catholic Church. Aside from the religious dimension, the main interest of the State in the education system was to use the schools and the teachers as instruments to advance the policy objective of reviving the Irish language. One of the curricular innovations of the early Irish State was to remove science education from the primary school curriculum in order to allow more time for teaching Irish[10]. According to Walsh 'Science was sidelined'[11]. Neither does it appear that attention was given to what would today be seen as important policy issues such as increasing progression to higher levels of education. However, an activist stance by the State in education policy can be seen to emerge in the policy developments initiated during the terms of the late George Colley and the late Donagh O'Malley and (President) Patrick Hillery as Ministers for Education in the 1960s. O'Malley's decision to provide for free access to second level education was, of course, a turning point, and was followed by rapid increases in participation levels in both second and third level education. Prior to O'Malley's decision, Ireland was lagging significantly behind many of the Organisation for Economic Cooperation and Development (OECD) counties in terms of participation and investment in education. The move to enhance education progression can be seen as consistent with the economic policy decisions taken a decade earlier.

Emergence from protection

The repeal of the Control of Manufacturing Act in 1958 represents the end of the post-independence period of protectionism and attempts at economic self-sufficiency. It marks the early stage in the opening up of the economy to foreign investment and the promotion of exports. Formal economic planning can also be dated to the end of the 1950s with the production of the first government *Programme for Economic Expansion* in 1958[12].

Although the Irish application for membership of what is now the EU failed in 1961, the policy emphasis on free trade continued with the negotiation of the Anglo Irish Free Trade Agreement in 1965, which provided tariff-free access to UK markets for

---

[9] Higher Education Authority, *Creating and Sustaining the Innovation Society* (Dublin: Higher Education Authority, 2002), p. 28.

[10] Edward M. Walsh, 'Science for All', *The Irish Journal of Education*, 1999, pp. 3-21.

[11] E. Walsh, 'Science for All', p. 3.

[12] Irish Government, *Programme for Economic Expansion* (Dublin: Government Sales Publications Office, 1958).

Irish exports. The opening up of the Irish economy, and particularly the targeting of foreign direct investment, created pressures for a more activist approach to education policy through the demands which newer sophisticated industries created for higher level skills.

Policy – an overview

Explicit policies for research began to emerge in the early 1960s – the establishment of the Medical Research Council in 1937, the Emergency Research Bureau in 1943, and the Dublin Institute for Advanced Studies in 1940, were significant but can hardly be seen as placing knowledge creation and application at the centre of economic and social development. The Agricultural Research Institute was set up in 1958. It had a strong influence on policy formulation for science and technology for agriculture and food, the dominant research interest at the time. The Institute for Industrial Research and Standards (IIRS) for industry and The Institute for Physical Planning and Construction Research for physical planning, later to become An Foras Forbartha (AFF), were also established. The Agricultural Institute has subsequently been transformed into Teagasc, some of the IIRS activities are undertaken by Enterprise Ireland (EI), and aspects of the work of AFF are now undertaken by the Environmental Protection Agency (EPA). Later developments see the research arena and the emergence of the universities as the dominant research institutions.

The first formal analysis of science and technology policy was in 1966, with the publication of *Science and Irish Economic Development* (SIED)[13] chaired by the late Professor Patrick Lynch, who had also chaired the seminal OECD report *Investment in Education*[14] which provided the intellectual foundation for the significant changes in education policy which took place in the 1960s and later. The SIED analysis found a relatively well-developed agricultural research capability, but industrial research was almost non-existent. The report made proposals to strengthen business investment in R&D and industrial innovation. SIED marks the earliest formal acknowledgement of the importance of science and technology for economic and industrial development policies in Ireland.

The incorporation of this thinking into policy development was slow. The scientific and technological community in Ireland had been promoting these ideas, but it was not apparent that this view was shared by policy makers, at that time. The latter seemed to have considered industrial research as a costly luxury, and favoured a buy-in policy to meet Ireland's industrial research needs. Such attitudes explain, in part, the emphasis on direct foreign investment (FDI) policies – which, in addition to providing jobs, were seen as satisfying most of the technology transfer needs of the economy.

That was more than 30 years ago. Today, science, technology, and education occupy a very active policy arena. The basis for this change was set through a succession of

---

[13] Department of Industry and Commerce in association with the OECD, *Science and Irish Economic Development* (Dublin: Government Sales Publications Office, 1966), Volumes 1 and 2.
[14] Minister for Education in association with OECD, *Investment in Education – Report of the Survey Team* (Dublin: Stationery Office, 1966).

reports from the mid 1970s onwards evaluating and reviewing industrial and technology policies. These included Cooper-Whelan[15], Telesis[16], OECD[17,18], Culliton[19], Science, Technology and Innovation Advisory Council (STIAC)[20] and others.

At the time, some of these reports seemed to have had only modest impacts on policy. In retrospect, it is apparent that incremental actions were taken in respect of both policies and institutional arrangements. Over time, these amount to significant changes in policy orientation. New arrangements include the appointment of a Chief Science Adviser for policy advice and co-ordination. New funding mechanisms and agencies include the HEA-managed Programme for Research in Third Level institutions (PRTLI), Science Foundation Ireland (SFI), and two new research councils, the Irish Research Council for the Humanities and the Social Sciences (IRCHSS) and the Irish Research Council for Science, Engineering and Technology (IRCSET). These developments have been supported by significant increases in the Exchequer allocations for research, development and innovation – reflected in the allocation of €2.5 billion in the National Development Plan for 2000–2006.

By the end of the 1990s, there is evidence of significant shifts in attitude towards basic research. The emergence of severe skill shortages in a rapidly expanding economy appeared to threaten the capacity to attract high quality multinational investment. There was also a growing recognition of the need for a shift from what the *Global Competitiveness Report*[21] described as *Investment-Driven* economy, where economic growth is increasingly achieved by harnessing global technologies to local production, to a position where the economy moves: 'to a technology-generating economy, one which innovates in at least some sectors of the global technology frontier'. The Report states that:

> perhaps the hardest transition is from technology importing, efficiency based development to innovation-based development. This requires a direct government role in fostering a high rate of innovation, through public as well as private investments in research and development, higher education, and improved capital markets and regulatory systems that support the start-up of high technology enterprises.

Significant advances have been made, but there are also significant challenges to address. Our understanding of these may perhaps be enhanced by a closer look at developments during the last forty years.

---

[15] C. Cooper & N. Whelan, *Science, Technology and Industry in Ireland* (Dublin: National Science Council 1972).

[16] Telesis Consulting Group, *A Review of Industrial Policy* (Dublin: National Economic and Social Council, 1982).

[17] OECD, *Review of National Science Policy* (Paris: OECD, 1974).

[18] OECD, *Review of Innovation Policy Ireland* (Paris: OECD, 1985).

[19] J. Culliton, *Report of the Industrial Policy Review Group: A Time for Change: Industrial Policy for the 1990s*, The 'Culliton Report' (Dublin: Stationery Office, 1992).

[20] Forfás, *Making Knowledge Work for Us*, Report of the Science, Technology and Innovation Advisory Council, The 'STIAC Report' (Dublin: Forfás, 1995).

[21] J. McArthur & J.I. Sachs, 'The Growth Competitiveness Index: Measuring Technological Advancement and the Stages of Development' in *The Global Competitiveness Report 2001–2002, World Economic Forum* (Oxford University Press, 2001).

The 1960s

1966 is an appropriate starting point with the publication of SIED[22] – the first formal review of science and technology policies in Ireland. However, the key events occurred towards the end of this period. Having failed with its initial application for membership of the European Communities (now Union), Ireland became a full member in 1973, thus exposing all public policies to an entirely new external dynamic. Also, towards the end of the period, significant new developments occurred in the higher education sector with the establishment of nine Regional Technical Colleges (RTCs, later to be renamed Institutes of Technology) and two National Institutes of Higher Education (NIHEs, later to become the University of Limerick and Dublin City University). This emphasis on technological education set the basis for the important contribution which educational policy was to make to industrial development. The remarkable performance of the Irish economy during the 1990s in Ireland owes a great deal to educational policy as well as to fiscal and industrial policies.

The emergence of the influential and effective Industrial Development Authority (IDA) and the development of a modern industrial sector in Ireland with fast-growing firms, mostly of US origin, in chemicals and pharmaceuticals, electronics and instruments, characterise industrial developments during this period. The IDA was provided with a wide range of financial incentives to attract foreign direct investment. The roots of a modern industrial sector were put in place during this period. However, criticism of the new industrial policies and developments also developed. The main criticisms were that the new industries induced high imports, had low domestic purchasing and poor linkages with the rest of the economy, and did little R&D. In effect, many of the new industries were characterized as low value-added branch plants. Towards the end of this period, science and technology policy was still having little impact on the industrial sector and on policy.

The National Science Council (NSC) was established in 1967, in response to the SIED report, with a (non-statutory) mandate for co-ordination and for bringing science and technology policy closer to industrial and economic policies. The NSC reported to the Minister for Finance whose Department, particularly under Dr T.K. Whitaker as Secretary, had played critically important roles in the opening up and modernisation of the Irish economy through the preparation and publication of Programmes for Economic Expansion, and negotiating Irish membership of the General Agreement on Tariffs and Trade (GATT) and of the European Communities. However, by the early 1970s, the Department of Finance had begun to focus more on its traditional functions in regard to fiscal and monetary management, which did not provide a suitable milieu for the developmental role envisaged for the NSC. The Council had limited financial resources and exerted only modest influence on industrial policies and incentives.

---

[22] Department of Industry and Commerce in association with OECD, *Science and Irish Economic Development (SIED)* (Dublin: Stationery Office, 1966).

The 1970s

The largely autonomous research institutes were still the backbone of the research system, while university research activity was still at a relatively low level. This was to soon change as access to EU research funding and the emergence of initiatives such as the EU Framework Programme were to have significant influences on the growth of the universities as major players in Irish R&D. Agricultural research (mainly production research) still dominated the research scene, during this period.

A few tentative steps were taken to bring science and technology policy centre stage with industrial policy. Two new schemes were introduced (1973) to encourage R&D in industry – the R&D grants scheme for industrial R&D and the Scheme for Scientific and Technological Awards administered by the Department of Industry and Commerce. In addition, the National Science Council (NSC) managed a modest scheme of grants to universities and third level educational institutions, which included the promotion of university/industry co-operation.

Important developments occurred in education. These included the establishment of the HEA, with responsibility for developing higher education including research in the sector and, as mentioned earlier, the setting up of the nine RTCs and two NIHEs. These, together with the universities, greatly increased the supply of trained technicians and graduates and began to forge constructive relationships between third level education and research and industry.

In 1972, the NSC published a report, *Science, Technology and Industry in Ireland*, by Charles Cooper and Noel Whelan[23]. Cooper and Whelan considered the period 1958–1969 from a broad economic perspective and analysed the links between industrial and social development and science and technology. The report questioned the industrial development policies of the time, concluding that the benefit to Ireland of all the foreign industry, attracted in by large grants and tax concessions, was little more than the salaries of employees. There were weak linkages with indigenous Irish firms. Furthermore, the amount of research carried out by Irish scientists was minimal by international standards and, as the new foreign 'high-tech' industries were not involved in any R&D, they employed few scientists and engineers.

Cooper and Whelan argued for the building up of a far more specialised industrial structure with the objective of creating genuine competitive advantage, while maintaining high industrial growth. A case was made for re-examining the role of foreign enterprise in Ireland, and developing new ways for bringing foreign technology into Ireland. In addition, new criteria for state support to industry were proposed.

Even though the Cooper-Whelan report was not well received at the time, it perhaps stimulated major changes over the long term. It can be regarded as signalling changes in policy emphasis which were to occur in the 1980s and 1990s.

The OECD in a 1974 report[24] bluntly criticised Ireland's lack of a centralised science policy, and the ineffective powers of the NSC. The Report made many

---

[23] C. Cooper & N. Whelan, *Science, Technology and Industry in Ireland* (Dublin: National Science Council, 1972).
[24] OECD, *Review of National Science Policy* (Paris: OECD, 1974).

recommendations, and stressed the need for more financial support for R&D, the training of entrepreneurs, and the setting up of a new science and technology body with responsibility and real powers, to replace the NSC. This led to the establishment in 1978 of the statutory National Board for Science and Technology (NBST) as the successor to the NSC.

At the macro economic level, the decision to join the European Monetary System (EMS) in 1979 was a critically important development.

The 1980s

By the beginning of the 1980s, it appeared as if Ireland had failed to capitalise on the benefits and opportunities from its membership of the European Communities/ Union. Unemployment was running at historically high levels, annual Exchequer borrowing in 1981 was 20% of GNP, the national debt had trebled over the previous five years. Inflation was 20% and the balance of payments deficit was an alarming 15% of GNP. However, following tough budgetary and fiscal measures in the late 1980s, the current balance of payments deficit was eliminated, inflation and the Exchequer borrowing requirement were reduced. This improvement in the fiscal balances was to continue in the 1990s.

In 1982, a review of industrial policy, commissioned from the Telesis Group[25], resulted in important changes in the direction of industrial policies.

The Government White Paper on Industrial Policy[26], published in 1984, following Telesis, announced a shift in financial incentives for industry away from fixed asset support towards technology acquisition and export marketing, and a more selective approach towards financial incentives for foreign industry. Foreign industry with desired characteristics would be targeted, especially industry willing to locate key business functions in Ireland, such as R&D, technical design and marketing. These were significant policy shifts, setting industrial policy on the track of high technology investment.

The new science and technology policies of the EU were to have a significant impact on policy and planning, and more specifically on the availability of funding for industry and technology. The new policy instruments included the Framework Programmes and, towards the end of this period, the introduction of Community Support Frameworks (CSFs), with significant support for science and technology.

The NBST focused on strengthening the university sector and used access to international funding, especially the Framework Programmes of the EU, for this purpose. The NBST also attempted to bring a new impetus to innovation policies, and to place innovation prominently on the policy agenda for the first time.

In 1987, the NBST, which had lacked significant implementation powers, was incorporated into the IIRS to form a new agency, EOLAS. The merger was partially a result of the tough fiscal policy stance in the late 1980s and was one of a number of

---

[25] Telesis Consulting Group, *A Review of Industrial Policy* (Dublin: National Economic and Social Council, 1982).

[26] Irish Government, *White Paper on Industrial Policy* (Dublin: Stationery Office, 1984).

'rationalisations' which took place in the public service. Another was the abolition of AFF and the transfer of some of its functions to its parent Department. However, by this time the interconnection between science and technology policy and industry was more widely appreciated and this period also saw the establishment within the Department of Industry and Commerce of the Office of Science and Technology (OST), which now had the responsibility for advising on policy in this sector.

New structures for technology transfer from universities to industry were also launched in the 1980s with the establishment of the Programmes in Advanced Technology (PATs). The PATs were established as working partnerships between the universities, government departments and agencies, and industry, with the aim of assisting in the development of a strategic research base in key industries to support industry, attract investment and to encourage entrepreneurship.

Other developments included the establishment of the Health Research Board (HRB) in 1986 and the development of the Basic Research Grants Scheme. The latter was operated by EI during the 1980s and early 1990s at a time when Exchequer funding for research was seriously constrained. From 2001, the scheme was jointly operated by EI and IRCSET and, since 2004, is administered jointly by SFI and IRCSET. The Basic Research Scheme Budget for 2004 was €8.5million.

From the 1990s to the present

The 1990s were a decade of dramatic change – economically and socially. For the first time, research and development expenditures and policy began to emerge as priorities for Government. Economic recovery began, slowly at the start of the decade, and more dramatically as the decade progressed. The economy became the fastest-growing in Europe and increased its share of US foreign direct investment. Two programmes of EU Structural Funds, 1989 to 1993 and 1994 to 1999, stimulated significant investments in education, technology and training. Unemployment and emigration, which had seemed to be persistent and chronic, were replaced by virtually full employment and sustained inward migration.

Economic circumstances at the beginning of the decade, though much improved on those of the mid-1980s, were still difficult. The Culliton Report[27] included recommendations for an expansion of vocational and technical training, increased investment in R&D and for developing technological competencies.

A greater emphasis on training and the quality of human resources for industrial policy were later expressed in the allocation of Structural Funds for human resource development.

New industrial support structures followed the Culliton Group's recommendations for a restructuring of industrial support agencies, with the establishment of three new development agencies under the Industrial Development Act 1993 – Forbairt (later to become Enterprise Ireland with the addition of the Irish Trade Board) for indigenous

---

[27] J. Culliton, *Report of the Industrial Policy Review Group: A Time for Change: Industrial Policy for the 1990s.* The 'Culliton Report' (Dublin: Stationery Office, 1992).

industry, IDA Ireland exclusively for the attraction of foreign direct investment, and Forfás, an overarching body for industrial, scientific and technological policy. The legislation establishing the new structures assigned the science and technology coordinating functions, which had originally been exercised by the NBST, to Forfás.

At EU level, the reform of Structural Funds in 1988 introduced a stronger emphasis on medium term programme planning, especially for industrial policy and for science and technology policy, into the development of national plans for the CSFs for the periods 1989/93 and 1994/1999.

Policy development and structures

A reappraisal of science and technology policies also took place during this period, driven initially from within what is now the Department of Enterprise, Trade and Employment, where the OST had been established. It is evident (even with limited hindsight) that major and far reaching policy directions began to take shape during this period. The publication of the 1995 STIAC Report[28] was a significant milestone. This was followed by a Government White Paper[29], the first on science and technology, and the establishment of new proposals for the management and co-ordination of science and technology.

The White Paper proposed that Government should adopt an integrated process for prioritising science and technology expenditure through coordinated mechanisms involving an interdepartmental committee on science and technology and a Cabinet Sub-Committee. The White Paper also proposed an independent science policy advisory function to be carried out through the Irish Council for Science, Technology and Innovation (ICSTI).

ICSTI was established in 1997, but the other coordinating arrangements were not fully implemented[30]. The Cabinet Sub-Committee never met and the interdepartmental committee relatively infrequently. Notwithstanding this, the momentum and pace of change quickened.

From 'Higher Education' to 'Higher Education and Research'

Throughout the 1980s and in the first half of the 1990s, most of the developments in research policy and funding activity occurred within the remit of what is now the Department of Enterprise, Trade and Employment and its agencies – particularly Forbairt/Enterprise Ireland and Forfás. However, by the mid-1990s the Department of Education and its Ministers began to pay more attention to research funding and policy. Significantly, in 1997, the legal title of the Ministry and Department was changed from 'Education' to 'Education and Science' following the formation of a new government.

---

28 Forfás, *Making Knowledge Work for Us*, Report of the Science, Technology and Innovation Advisory Council – The 'STIAC Report' (Dublin: Forfás, 1995).

29 Irish Government, *White Paper Science, Technology and Innovation* (Dublin: Stationery Office, 1996).

30 Higher Education Authority, *Creating and Sustaining the Innovation Society* (Dublin: Higher Education Authority, 2002), pp. 88-90.

In 1996, the HEA published a review, carried out by the CIRCA consulting group, of the funding and management of research in the universities. The CIRCA report[31] found that, at the beginning of the 1990s, research in the higher education sector was seriously underfunded – as a % of GDP it was among the lowest of a group of OECD countries surveyed. Surprisingly, the report also found that the number of researchers in Irish higher education institutions was proportionately high – reflecting the low earnings of research workers, particularly research students. The report also commented on institutional and strategic shortcomings in the universities – which were largely a result of underfunding. Institutional strategies for research and development were weak. Activities tended to be dominated by the search for funding and were described as opportunistic rather than strategic. The report recommended increased funding for research and the establishment of new research councils (for science and technology and for humanities and social sciences).

The CIRCA Report also called for a more strategic approach, at the institutional level, to the funding of institutional strengths and core competencies in research, for more explicit institutional planning and prioritisation, and the promotion of greater inter-institutional cooperation and inter-disciplinarity within the third-level system. It also developed some hitherto little noticed provisions in a 1995 Government White Paper on Education[32], which included a number of principles for informing research policy for the third level sector. These included statements that:

– The unified teaching and research budget which forms the basis of the (HEA) block grant would be continued and would provide a basic level of research funding.
– The role of research and course development and the advancement of knowledge in all disciplines would be recognized.
– Additional funding for research would be provided as a separate budget for which competitive bidding would be the norm with an independent assessment by international peers on research proposals.

The emphasis on competitive bidding and internationally benchmarked evaluation and review were to be significant features of subsequent developments.

The establishment in 1997 of the Scientific and Technological Education Fund was the next significant event. This was a statutory fund which provided for multi-annual spending allocations for the Exchequer. It was established on the proposal of the then Minister for Education and Science, Micheál Martin, against opposition from some government departments. It provided statutorily assured medium term funding for a range of measures aimed at raising the technological capacity of the economy through investment in the further and higher education sectors. The total allocation was IR£250m

---

[31] CIRCA Group Europe, *Organisation, Management and Funding of University Research in Ireland and Europe* (Dublin: CIRCA Group, 1996).
[32] Irish Government, *White Paper on Education, 'Charting our Education Future'* (Dublin: Stationery Office, 1995), pp. 106-107.

(€317m), which included an IR£15m (€19m) capital expenditure provision for research and development and technology transfer accompanied by IR£5m (€6m) provision for recurrent expenditure on research and development. A significant feature of this fund was that funding was provided on a guaranteed medium term basis for the first time.

Programme for Research in Third Level Institutions (PRTLI)

The recurrent provision provided the funding for the Programme for Research in Science and Technology at Third Level, which was launched in 1998. This programme was significant in the sense that it was the first time that third level institutions (universities, institutes of technology and other colleges) competed for funding on the basis of research programmes which were accompanied by statements of institutional research strategies. This was followed by the launch in late 1998 of the Programme for Research in Third Level Institutions (PRTLI) with a funding provision of IR£162m (€206m). The launch of PRTLI, and particularly the scale of funding, took the higher education and research communities by surprise. The groundwork for the announcement had been prepared through confidential discussions between officials and advisers in the Department of Education and Science and the HEA with representatives of what is now the Atlantic Philanthropies organisation. This organisation, established by the international philanthropist, Chuck Feeney, had already spent very substantial funds in supporting capital developments in the Irish universities. It continued to support PRTLI through three cycles of the Programme and has committed a total of IR£146.5m (€186m) to the Programme. This has been critical in leveraging and sustaining Government support for the PRTLI. Provision for the PRTLI was significantly enhanced under the National Development Plan (NDP) 2000–2006 with a total Exchequer provision of around €535m of the €700m allocated to Research, Technological Development and Innovation (RTDI) in education.

The PRTLI, which is managed by the HEA on behalf of the Minister for Education and Science, provides integrated financial support for institutional research strategies, programmes and infrastructure. The programme is competitive. Calls for proposals are issued to all publicly funded third level institutions. The proposals are evaluated by international panels of distinguished researchers, scholars and institutional leaders on the basis of excellence under three criteria – strategic planning (including inter-institutional collaboration), research quality, and the impact of research strategy and programmes in improving the quality of the teaching in the proposing institution. One of the requirements of the competition is that the institutions prepare and submit strategies for research and identify institutional priorities.

An unprecedented €600m has been allocated to third level institutions under this programme of research, which has involved three cycles or calls for proposals.

The PRTLI is having a transforming effect on research in the third level system. The scale of the investment has created new capacity and critical mass and has provided funding for the recruitment of over 1,500 new researchers. It has created a new dynamic in the institutions.

Significant collaborations between institutions include the Dublin Molecular Medicine Centre (DMMC), a collaboration between Trinity College Dublin, University College Dublin and the Royal College of Surgeons in Ireland. There are collaborations between universities and Institutes of Technology including, for example, the National Centre for Cellular Biotechnology (NICB), involving Dublin City University and its partners, Institute of Technology, Tallaght, and National University of Ireland (NUI), Maynooth. The Dublin Institute of Advanced Studies (DIAS) is leading 'Cosmogrid', an ICT programme that is enabling scientists from eight institutions and organisations to research and model new emerging 'grid' technologies.

PRTLI has been critical in developing inter-institutional co-operation on a new and unprecedented scale. In doing so, it has directly addressed critical mass shortcomings in the Irish research system. It has also accelerated cross-disciplinary co-operation.

The response of the higher education sector to the strategic, organisational and management challenges posed by the PRTLI has been remarkable. Strategic planning processes for research are now in place in all institutions which have successfully competed for funding under the programme. This has ensured effective prioritisation and selection of research areas, the formation of inter-disciplinary research teams and programmes, as well as very significant levels of inter-institutional co-operation. All of this required institutional leadership, flexibility and capacity of a high order.

Notwithstanding the fact that it represented a step-change in research funding, the launch of the PRTLI was accompanied by controversy. Concern was expressed by some researchers about the strategic and institutional emphasis of the programme (funding was provided for institutional research programmes rather than for individual researchers and their projects). This group was also concerned that the funding allocations were made on the basis of reviews of institutional proposals by panels of international researchers, scholars and institutional leaders rather than through the evaluation of individual research proposals by peers.

The HEA decided in 2003 to establish an independent international assessment committee chaired by Professor Enric Banda, former Secretary General of the European Science Foundation, to conduct an impact assessment of the PRTLI. The in-depth and comprehensive report, published in mid-2004, calls the PRTLI 'the beginning of a major and most beneficial transformation of the research landscape of Ireland that will help to install an innovation-driven economy'[33].

In the period under review (1999–2003), twenty three out of a total of thirty five eligible institutions received funding from the PRTLI; a total of sixty two research programmes covering science and engineering, social sciences, humanities and library services have been supported; 97,000 sq metres of new research space was provided, and over 1,500 postgraduate and postdoctoral researchers funded. As mentioned, there were also several major collaborative initiatives between institutions.

PRTLI was described as a 'remarkable endeavour' and international peer reviewers described the quality of research output as 'high to very high'. However, the report

---

[33] Higher Education Authority, *PRTLI Impact Assessment Volume I* (Dublin: Higher Education Authority, 2004).

identified funding uncertainties as a key problem. It strongly recommended consistent and sustained investment in the programme by Government over the period of the NDP 2000–2006 and its continuation for at least ten years.

The report also anticipated a possible funding crisis for centres based on the unrealistically low levels of overhead funding. It felt that the PRTLI needed to provide about 45% of a laboratory's running costs. Universities were found to be subsidising their PRTLI centres to make up for this shortfall, a practice the report found to be unsustainable in the long term.

Another recommendation included the formation of a high level supervisory body rooted in the Taoiseach's (Prime Minister's) Department to co-ordinate funding policies and programmes. Further recommendations are that colleges put greater emphasis on developing systems to commercialise research and on management strategies that set out how the new centres would co-exist with traditional college structures.

Within the Education and Science 'policy domain' there were other significant policy developments. In 1997, the then Minister, Micheál Martin, commissioned a report which recommended the establishment of a research council for the humanities and the social sciences[34]. The establishment of the Irish Research Council for the Humanities and the Social Sciences (IRCHSS) in 2000 was followed in 2001 by the establishment of the Irish Research Council for Science, Engineering and Technology (IRCSET). The Exchequer allocation for the two councils amounted to €18.5million in 2003.

Under the NDP 2000–2006, the Technological Sector Research sub-measure was established to support and strengthen the research capability of the Institutes of Technology. A total budget of €38 million was allocated.

Health Research, Technology Foresight and Science Foundation Ireland

Substantial developments were also taking place in other Government Departments. In June 2001, the Department of Health and Children published *Making Knowledge Work for Health*, which outlined a strategy for health research. Increased allocations were provided for the HRB, which had a budget of €23m in 2003.

The most significant development was the publication in 1999 by ICSTI of the outcome of a national technology foresight exercise which involved experts and leadership figures from the research, academic, business and public sector communities. ICSTI recommended an investment of IR£500m (€635m) in basic research in the economically important areas of biotechnology and information and communications technology (ICT) in order to develop and sustain competitive economic advantage in these key industries. This recommendation was taken up by Tánaiste (Deputy Prime Minister) and Minister for Enterprise, Trade and Employment, Mary Harney, and her Department, and approved by Government.

---

[34] Maurice J. Bric, *The Humanities and the Social Sciences: A Case for a Research Council* – A report to the Minister for Education and Science (Dublin: Higher Education Authority, 1999).

As was the case with the launch of the PRTLI, the Technology Foresight programme, as it was initially known, was accompanied by controversy. This centred on an initial impression that funding for the programme would be used mainly to fund new 'stand-alone' research institutions on green field sites. The *raison d'être* behind this proposal was that these new institutions would attract leading researchers who, unlike their university colleagues, would not have substantial teaching loads and would be free to devote their energies to research and technology transfer. This view elicited strong negative reactions from leadership figures in the higher education sector, who argued that an exclusive emphasis on funding through dedicated new institutes was an inefficient and high-risk strategy. Concerns were expressed about the risks of poor synergies with the universities, including the substantial investments being made under the PRTLI programme. There were, also, it was argued, risks that over time the new institutions would, through an accumulation of explicit and implicit commitments, have effectively a first call on technology foresight funding which would undermine the competitive dynamic necessary for ensuring quality.

Other concerns included the risk that stand-alone institutes would over time become less dynamic and susceptible to staffing rigidities. A further concern was that, by not being part of the higher education system, the proposed institutes would not benefit from the interaction between research and teaching – a link which it has been argued is central to the capacity of the innovation system[35].

Following a vigorous debate in the research and academic communities, the Government agreed to establish a new organisation, Science Foundation Ireland (SFI) with a mandate to build and strengthen scientific and engineering research and its infrastructure in the areas of greatest strategic value to Ireland's long term competitiveness and development. SFI was originally established as a sub-board of Forfás in 2000 and, in 2003, was established on a statutory basis as a separate legal entity. With a budget allocation of €646m under the NDP 2000–2006, SFI had by the end of 2003 invested €320m through a suite of funding programmes, which include SFI Fellow Awards which support senior distinguished researchers, Research Professorships which aim to attract senior scientists to Ireland from overseas, SFI Investigator Grants, E.T.S. Walton Visitor Awards, Basic Research Grants Programme, and SFI Centres for Science, Engineering, and Technology – Campus-Industry Partnerships (CSET) which fund researchers in building collaborative efforts to develop internationally competitive research clusters allied to industry. The CSET grants normally range from €1m to €5m per year for up to ten years, and a total of five CSETs have been funded to date.

Most of this funding has been allocated to the universities, with a smaller amount going to the institutes of technology. The earlier vexed issue of the so-called stand alone institutes has been dealt with in a provision in the SFI legislation which leaves the option open and provides for a consultative process involving Government, the

---

[35] Higher Education Authority, *Creating and Sustaining the Innovation Society* (Dublin: Higher Education Authority, 2002), pp. 24-26.

Minister for Enterprise, Trade and Employment, and the Foundation. This is perhaps the ideal outcome. The competitive dynamic for funding has been retained, and SFI's activities are firmly embedded in the third level sector. The Foundation can avail of the infrastructure (human and physical) of the third level sector but, if future needs require stand-alone facilities, these can be put in place.

Coherence of the research system

The institutional centre of gravity for publicly funded research in Ireland in now located in the higher education system, particularly in the universities. There are now more than twenty third level institutions with involvement in research. The volume of research performed in the government sector is smaller than in the third level sector. The main organisations in the government sector are Teagasc, the Marine Institute (MI), the Economic and Social Research Institute (ESRI) and the HRB. Most of these organisations also fund research in the third level sector. A summary outline of the activities of public sector organisations involved in the funding of research in higher education institutions is shown in Table 1.

Table 1: Summary of Research Funding Provided to HE Institutions in 2001

Organisation	Funding Activities
Higher Education Authority (HEA)	'Institutional bedrock' funding – block grant Funding of institutional strategies (PRTLI) Collaborative projects between third level institutions and MediaLab Europe (MLE) Transport research (on behalf of Department of Transport) North-South Programme for Collaborative Research (on behalf of the Department of Education & Science – DES) The Cross Border Programme for Research and Education contributing to Peace and Reconciliation (on behalf of DES and the Department of Education & Learning, Northern Ireland)
Irish Research Council for the Humanities and Social Sciences (IRCHSS)	Scholarships, fellowships and research projects in response to applications from researchers and in areas selected by the investigators/scholars
Irish Research Council for Science, Engineering and Technology (IRCSET)	Scholarships, fellowships and research projects in response to applications from researchers and in areas selected by the investigators/scholars
Department of Education and Science (DES)	Technological Sector Research Fund; support of research capabilities in Institutes of Technology; funding provided to researchers and their teams.

Organisation	Funding Activities
Science Foundation Ireland (SFI)	Fellowships and research programmes in response to applications from scientists and technologists in selected areas of economic importance – currently biotechnology and information and communications technologies (including joint funding with industry)
Health Research Board (HRB)	Fellowships and research programmes in response to applications from clinicians, biomedical scientists and technologists in areas of health and social gain
Enterprise Ireland (EI)	Funding support for R&D activities in higher education institutions in the cases of basic and strategic research as well as funding support for scholarships Funding support for co-operation between higher education institutions and firms in the short to medium term exploitation of research, development of an industry agenda to direct these networks, and creation of scale in research groups of strategic importance to firms in Ireland
Department of Agriculture, Food & Rural Development (DAFRD)	Support for projects in agriculture areas where rural development gaps are identified, and support for innovation and project development in the food industry
Marine Institute (MI)	Funding support to enhance and consolidate the performance of the marine sector in Ireland and to provide RTDI capacity and infrastructure.
Environmental Protection Agency (EPA)	A number of programmes to support research in the environmental area and environmental policy

Exchequer funding of research in higher education

Figure 1 provides a schematic illustration of the system and arrangements for state funding for research in the higher education system. The system has the organisational diversity which, as described by An Taoiseach[36], Mr Bertie Ahern, ensures: 'funding schemes providing for individuals, institutions and national strategic priorities'.

---

[36] An Taoiseach, Mr Bertie Ahern, T.D., speech at the Conway Institute of Biomolecular and Biomedical Research, University College Dublin, 6 March 2002.

Figure 1

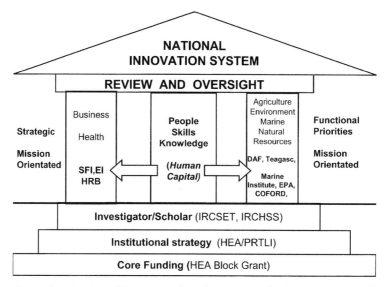

The rationale underpinning this system has been described as persuasive[37]. Provided that it is relatively stable, the funding available from the HEA block grant should contribute core funding for the continuation and development of research activities across disciplines in the universities. The multi-annual funding provided under the PRTLI allows the institutions to focus funding and resources on strategically selected priorities. These areas are selected by the institutions following strategic planning exercises which have regard to the existing and developing strengths of the institutions as well as the external environment (including public policy priorities). The PRTLI funding should also enhance the ability of institutions to compete for funding from other funders, including SFI and HRB. The funding activities of the research councils provide individual scholars and investigators with funding to pursue research in areas selected by themselves. Funding from SFI, EI and HRB are focused on supporting strategic public policy objectives in the areas of industrial policy and the promotion of social gain respectively. Finally, organisations such as the Department of Agriculture and Food, the EPA, and the MI support research directly related to their own sectoral missions (which is described in Figure 1 as the functional dimension).

These institutional arrangements provide the potential for securing an optimum balance between different streams of funding as described by the OECD[38]. A balance needs to be struck between providing the long term security of funding required for institutional capacity building maintenance and renewal on the one hand and, on the other, ensuring that the research system is incentivised to respond to changing public policy priorities, economic and social developments, and new developments in knowledge.

Competition between institutions and researchers plays an important part. This is a stimulus for excellence. Policy challenges include ensuring that the inevitable tensions between academic freedom, institutional autonomy and public policy priorities are

---

[37] Higher Education Authority, *Creating and Sustaining the Innovation Society* (Dublin: Higher Education Authority, 2002), p. 85.
[38] OECD, *The Management of Science Systems* (Paris: OECD, 1999).

resolved constructively and in a way which promotes positive outcomes. A particular concern of public policy should be to ensure that the knowledge and skills base of the system is sufficiently broad so it has the capacity to respond quickly and effectively to unexpected developments in research and in the wider economic and social domains. The architecture of the system is in principle capable of meeting these challenges.

Review and oversight

In the early years of the new millennium, the lack of a satisfactory mechanism for ensuring overarching policy co-ordination was identified as an important and urgent policy problem. Previous attempts and proposals (including the establishment of the NBST in the 1970s and the 1996 White Paper) had not produced workable outcomes. In 2002, ICSTI was requested by Government, following a proposal from the Tánaiste and Minister for Enterprise, Trade and Employment, Mary Harney, to establish a commission to bring forward proposals on developing an appropriate framework for an overarching national policy for research and technological development. The commission was chaired by ICSTI Chairman, Professor Edward Walsh, former President of the University of Limerick, and included Irish and international members[39]. It produced its report at the end of 2002. In June 2004, the government agreed to put in place new co-ordination and governance systems for science, technology and innovation which included a Cabinet Committee and inter-departmental committee on science, technology and innovation. These structures reflected the proposals of the Walsh Commission. A key development in the new structures was the appointment of a Chief Science Adviser with a substantial range of duties – See Box 1

Box 1 : The duties of the Chief Science Adviser to Government[40]

> – Provision of independent expert advice on any aspect of science, technology and innovation as requested by government; provision of analysis and opinion on all major policy proposals being submitted to government in the areas of science, technology and innovation;
> – Advising on all science, technology and innovation issues arising in the context of the EU and internationally;
> – Advising the government periodically on the scale and balance of overall State investment in science, technology and innovation, having consulted with all major stakeholders;
> – Overseeing a system of independent evaluation of STI policy and programmes with particular reference to cost cutting issues;
> – Management of the process of gathering data and intelligence, particularly in relation to R&D performance and spending.

The first appointee to the post was Dr Barry McSweeney who, until his appointment, was Director General of the European Union Joint Research Centre.

---

[39] The Author was a member.
[40] Address by Chief Science Advisor, Dr Barry McSweeney, Dublin, 13 July 2004.

The creation of this new post completes what until then had been a major shortcoming in the structure for a research system. The absence of a review and oversight mechanism and structures had been a source of considerable dissatisfaction accompanied, not surprisingly, by some controversy – particularly in regard to their location within the government system[41]. The government decision underlined the independence of the position of the Chief Science Adviser. The Adviser is to receive management and administrative support from Forfás, but the work programme of the Adviser is to be approved by the Cabinet Committee. Another guarantee of independence is that the Adviser would be fully independent and not accountable to the Board or Chief Executive Officer of Forfás in respect of his advice and activities.

Challenges for future development

The story until the middle 1990s conveys an impression of incremental development and of apparently faltering effort. Expenditure on research and development (both government and private) remained low by international standards. To the extent that government and its agencies were concerned with research, the prevailing belief was that for a small country such as Ireland, the focus of government expenditure should be on or near to market and applied research. Research spending should have a utilitarian bias.

This policy position began to evolve, and there were significant changes during the late 1990s – most notably with the launch of PRTLI and the establishment of SFI. Influences behind these decisions included a recognition that Ireland's economic progress in the 1990s and an increasingly globalised competitive environment posed new challenges and required new strategic directions. A considerably more buoyant Exchequer position and a growing appreciation that all public expenditure on R&D need not have, or perhaps should not have, an immediately utilitarian purpose were also important. There was a growing understanding among policy makers of the complexity of the research and development and innovation processes. The decision to establish a research council for the humanities and social sciences (IRCHSS) is perhaps an interesting example of this more enlightened and holistic view.

However, the journey is far from ended. A number of considerable challenges remain to be addressed. These include funding levels, policy consistency (the pause in capital funding for Cycle 3 of the PRLTI seriously damaged confidence in the research communities), the development of effective mechanisms for commercialisation and technology transfer, and the reform and development of higher education and striking the optimum balance between prioritisation and flexibility.

Funding

Figure 2 shows the levels of gross expenditure on R&D (GERD) in Ireland from 1993 to 2001. Interestingly, the ratio remained broadly unchanged between 1993 and 2001 because significant increases in expenditure on research were offset by rapid increases in the value of GNP. The latest available figures for GERD at 1.17% of GDP (2001

---

[41] See for example the comprehensive list of the submissions received by the ICSTI commission which are available on http://www.forfas.ie/icsti/framework.html.

figures) are significantly below OECD and EU averages and fall far short of the target of 3% set by the EU at Barcelona in 2002 as part of the 'Lisbon strategy'. The report of the international assessment committee on the PRTLI shows that the research intensity of the three Irish universities with the highest proportion of research income falls significantly behind leading European institutions (Table 2).

Figure 2: Gross Expenditure on R&D (GERD) – Ireland 1993 to 2001

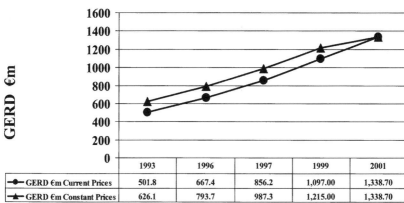

	1993	1996	1997	1999	2001
GERD €m Current Prices	501.8	667.4	856.2	1,097.00	1,338.70
GERD €m Constant Prices	626.1	793.7	987.3	1,215.00	1,338.70

GERD €m Current Prices — GERD €m Constant Prices

Source: Derived from survey of R&D in the Business Sector, 2001 (Forfás); Survey of R&D in the Higher Education Sector, 2000 (Forfás); State Expenditure on Science & Technology, 2001 (Forfás).

Table 2 International Case Study Benchmarking – A Comparison between Irish and European Research Institutions – 2002*

Indicator/Institution	TCD	UCD	UCC	University of Edinburgh[1]	University College London	University of Uppsala[2]	University of Helsinki	University of Leiden	University of Utrecht
Estimated Total Research Grants and Contract Income – € Million	38.6	27.0	33.8	139.6	235.3	257	165.0	68.0	126.6
Estimated Total Academic and Research Staff	1,721	2,367	1,382	2,500	3,833	3,800	3,507	2,025	2,700
Total student population[3]	15,201	19,607	13,227	24,070	17,805	41,500	37,685	16,614	23,716
Total Research Income per Academic and Research Staff Member – €	22,440	11,390	24,463	55,856	61,401	67,521	47,049	33,580	46,889
Total Research Income per Student – €	2,541	1,375	2,556	5,801	13,218	6,183	4,378	4,093	5,338

Source: Indecon analysis of figures from Irish and overseas institutions indicated. Data in relation to estimated total research grants and contract income for Irish institutions are sourced from individual institutions' financial statements.

* Figures presented are for 2002, except where otherwise stated

1 Staff figures pertain to 2003

2 All figures pertain to 2003

3 Includes full-time and part-time undergraduate and postgraduate students

Commercialisation and technology transfer

This area is critically important. If structures and processes work effectively, Irish society will reap significant dividends from increased levels of Exchequer expenditure on research. According to the Enterprise Strategy Group[42]: 'supports should be designed to build a capacity of enterprise to absorb the results of publicly funded research and to employ the highly skilled people it produces and apply them to the development of new products and services'. The Group also said that: 'mechanisms need to be developed to ensure that Irish enterprises – and particularly smaller firms – have timely access to relevant knowledge wherever it may reside'. The Group recommended the establishment, within Enterprise Ireland, of a dedicated structure 'Technology Ireland', with its own budget and strong leadership to develop a cohesive, strategic and focused approach to market led applied research and to technological development, and to leverage increased enterprise investment. Other recommendations made by the Group in this area included the establishment of a consultative process to identify technology platforms, and a recommendation that the Government establish a competitive innovation fund for higher education institutions to encourage them to further exploit knowledge and deliver innovative services to enterprise. A proportion of that fund should be ring-fenced to support the institutes of technology in fulfilling that role. The Group also recommended that public funding for applied research and in-company R&D should be progressively increased to match investments in basic research.

Challenges facing the higher education sector

The higher education institutions have now become the centrepiece of the government funded research system. The central role played by the higher education systems is regarded by observers as a critical factor in explaining the success of the innovation system in the United States. This reflects the centrality of the link between research and teaching and learning (see Box 2).

Box 2:

'... Scientific knowledge is not freely available to all, but only to those with appropriate educational backgrounds and to members of the scientific and technological networks. Information itself is abundant; it is the capacity to absorb it which is scarce. Hence, investment in research has a large human resources element, involving the training of skilled researchers able to link into global knowledge networks and absorb global developments.'

Source: Measuring and Evaluating Research – Report of the ICSTI Task Force, 2002

---

[42] Forfás, *Ahead of the Curve: Ireland's Place in the Global Economy – Report of the Enterprise Strategy Group* (Dublin: Forfás, 2004), p. 93.

Public policy has now essentially begun to appreciate that the return from expenditure on research is to a very considerable extent realized through the enhancement of human capital and that, particularly for a small country, the impact of research spending on enhancing human capital may be as important or more important than the generation of new knowledge. The role of the higher education sector has never been more important.

The higher education sector needs to position itself, and to be positioned, to successfully embrace this increasingly important role. It faces a number of challenges in regard to its relationship with government and other stakeholders, in regard to governance, leadership and management, personnel and remuneration policies, financial and strategic management, access, intellectual property management, quality assurance and improvement, and accountability and transparency. It has to do all this while continuing to protect and enhance the core missions of scholarship, the pursuit of knowledge and academic freedom. These challenges, as described by Skilbeck[43], constitute a formidable agenda.

Other stakeholders also face challenges in their relationships with higher education. Not surprisingly, these are most significant for Government, which needs to assure funding consistency. Government and public agencies also need to focus more on their strategic expectations from higher education, rather than on micro controls, so as to stimulate an evolutionary capacity within the system that will enable the higher education institutions to successfully address the challenges of change[44].

Against this background, the decision of the then Minister for Education and Science, Mr Noel Dempsey TD, to commission a report on higher education from the OECD in late 2003 was timely. The OECD Review Team (September 2004[45]) reported that much progress had been made in developing higher education and research in the past – but that further development was urgent in order to continue the development of the sector, and as a critical means of addressing national economic social and cultural needs.

The review identified the need for change in a number of strategic areas:

- clarity and consistency in national strategy
- greater institutional autonomy for all higher education institutions
- the development of a new funding mechanism for higher education, to support institutional development and to provide appropriate incentives for the institutions to meet national needs
- internal institutional reform, particularly in governance and strategic management
- measures to widen participation in higher education

---

[43] Malcolm Skilbeck, *The University Challenged: A Review of International Trends and Issues with Particular Reference to Ireland* (Dublin: Higher Education Authority, 2001).

[44] Submission of the Higher Education Authority to the OECD Review, *Creating Ireland's Knowledge Society: Proposals for Higher Education Reform* (Dublin: Higher Education Authority, 2004).

[45] *Review of National Policies for Education: Review of Higher Education in Ireland, Examiners' Report*, OECD, September 2004.

– enhanced investment in and new structures to manage research and development.

The Review Team argued that the differentiation between the universities and the institutes of technology be preserved. Policy towards third level education which was fragmented, with universities funded through the HEA and institutes of technology through the Department of Education and Science, needed to be unified under a new Tertiary Education Authority (TEA), a successor body to the HEA, which would have policy and funding responsibility for all higher education institutions.

The report recognised that there is a need for far greater investment in the sector and that the higher education institutions require significantly increased funding if strategic aspirations for the sector and for national development are to be met. Recommendations are made regarding possible options to achieve this goal – including the reintroduction of third level undergraduate fees and improved systems of student support and loan arrangements. Significantly, the report recommended that, if tuition fees for undergraduate study are reintroduced, it should be automatic that the additional income is not offset against reductions in state income and should therefore represent a real and tangible increase in the resources of higher education institutions.

The report recommended significant structural reforms for research funding. It recommended that SFI should become the major national research funding body with a broader remit than is currently provided for in legislation and which would include taking on the roles of the two research councils, i.e. IRCHSS and IRCSET. Under this model, SFI, in the view of the OECD team, would need to move from the top down approach needed to support research in technologies considered to be the key to the country's innovation potential to also supporting bottom up initiatives and providing machinery for research training and research career promotion. It would also need a new board structure with stakeholder representation from research, industry, partner agencies, and tertiary education, and should include some international membership. The OECD report also recommended that a decision needs to be taken on the future of the PRTLI programme, and that there needed to be close links between the new SFI and new TEA to ensure that their programmes are developed concurrently in respect of investment in research infrastructure and capital expenditure.

At the time of writing, the report was under consideration by the newly appointed Minister for Education and Science, Ms Mary Hanafin, TD, prior to making proposals to Government.

In a speech in November 2004[46] the Minister for Enterprise, Trade and Employment, Mr Micheál Martin, TD, set out policy positions which were relevant to the OECD recommendations in respect to the organisational arrangements for research funding. He began by assessing the dramatic growth in dedicated research funding over the past eight years and noting the major achievements that have taken place in the development of the research funding infrastructure foundations, e.g. the PRTLI, the

---

[46] *The Research Agenda: Making Knowledge Work for Ireland*, Conway Institute, UCD, 4 November 2004.

establishment of SFI and the research councils. Significantly, the Minister reiterated the view expressed in the Programme for Government that a 'one size fits all' or a 'one stop shop' approach to designing and delivering research funding was not desirable or under consideration, and he strongly encouraged the growing co-operation between research funders at all levels. He also asked that a Funder's Group[47], comprising the principal research funding agencies, be convened. An important role for this group would be the preparation within a short time scale of a consensus response to the targets identified in *The Irish Action Plan for Promoting Investment in R&D to 2010*[48]. Arising from this and other work, the Minister indicated that he would consult with his colleagues in Government, and particularly with the Minister for Education and Science, in drawing up recommendations for Cabinet on the funding and delivery of research activity up to 2010.

Prioritisation and flexibility

The issues of prioritisation began to emerge very strongly in the late 1990s in both the PRTLI and Technology Foresight/SFI programmes. Under PRTLI, institutions were required to prepare institutional research strategies, and these strategies required the identification of priority areas and a commitment of resources to these. In its Technology Foresight proposals to Government, ICSTI recommended that investments in research and development should be focused on two priority areas – biotechnology and information and communications technology. The concept of prioritisation does not rest easily with the notion of unconstrained academic inquiry. Nonetheless there is clearly the real question that a small society, even if it is an increasingly wealthy one, cannot, if it intends that its research effort should achieve leading edge positions at some points in the technological and knowledge frontier, afford to spread expenditure evenly across a wide range of areas. On the other hand, prioritisation also carries risks. In a narrowly concentrated research system, unexpected developments, either economic, social or in respect of knowledge development, can have major consequences – positive and negative. A small entity like Ireland needs to focus the application of resources in order to have impact, but this comes at a cost of increased vulnerability. However, small size can also be an advantage in terms of flexibility and capacity for speed of response. The challenge for Irish policy makers and research leaders is to establish an optimum balance between achieving a critical mass and presence in key research areas, while retaining the capacity for a flexible response. This point was made very strongly in the report of the international assessment committee on the PRTLI:

> Institutions are of the view which we fully support that it is important to be able
> to respond to new developments in the external environment, which demand
> flexibility and which may motivate adjustments of focus within broad areas of
> expertise. Building a strong research backbone, with a flexible response capability,

---

[47] Recommended in the Walsh Commission Report (December 2002).
[48] *Building Ireland's Knowledge Economy, The Irish Action Plan for Promoting Investment in R&D to 2010; A report to the InterDepartmental Committee on Science, Technology and Innovation*, Forfás, Dublin, July 2004.

is seen as a key objective of PRTLI. We believe the Irish Government should avoid any narrowing of focus or overspecialisation in research carried out in third level institutions. We recommend that the Government continue to support a flexible and diverse funding system for third level institutions in Ireland; a system that underpins the highest quality teaching and learning in the institutions and that motivates and enables multiple research opportunities and potentials[49].

Conclusion

This Chapter has been particularly concerned with the development of public policy towards basic research and development. There is of course an underlying paradox at the centre of the complex, and stakeholders have different motivations and understandings. At the core of the paradox is the fact that the motivations of researchers and those of the government as a funder can be very different. Researchers may in many instances be concerned primarily with the pursuit and development of knowledge, whereas, in the final analysis, government is concerned about the returns to society. Yet the paradox is compounded by the fact that it is essential that government finances research. The presence of market failures in the form of uncertain outcomes, the so-called free rider phenomenon, and very long pay-back periods, essentially mean that basic research has many of the characteristics of what economists describe as the public good, which essentially make it an unattractive area for private sector investment. Basic research is an uncertain enterprise, it is novel, it is risky and unpredictable.

The requirements for future development include the presence of government as a substantial and consistent investor in R&D. Consistency is absolutely vital. At the centre of the challenge lies the aspiration to successfully complete the transition to an innovation economy. This journey will be complex but, according to Michael Porter, is well within reach for Ireland. According to Porter, Ireland's success in the past bodes well for our ability to meet new challenges. He says that we have identified many of the key steps that need to be taken. Now it is a matter of persistence and implementation. 'Competitiveness is a marathon, not a sprint!'[50].

---

[49] Higher Education Authority, *PRTLI Impact Assessment Volume I* (Dublin: Higher Education Authority, 2004), p. 54.

[50] Michael Porter, lecture to the Irish Management Institute, *Strategy – The Ultimate Competitive Imperative*, Thursday, 9 October 2003.

Ireland's Environment

John Feehan

When last the British Association for the Advancement of Science (BAAS) visited Dublin in 1957, I was eleven, growing up on the edge of a small town in the midlands. I belonged to the last generation of boys for whom looking for birds' nests and collecting their eggs was a culturally important as well as legitimate activity. The emotional and intellectual excitement of bird nesting is now a thing of the past. Recreation took place out of doors, bringing children in constant touch with their real surroundings, rather than in front of a TV or computer screen that *mediates* the world; it was around this time the first television aerials began to appear above the homes of rural Ireland.

Every other field was flowery meadow, and there was in some years a corncrake in every one of them. On summer evenings, the nightjar churred in the pine and willow scrub at the edge of the bog where we cut turf for domestic fuel, and from which you could still hear the corncrakes in the fields beyond. And the small river which threaded its way through this typical corner of rural Ireland teemed with the distinctive brown trout we called croneen. It is a reflection of the reputation Ireland enjoyed as a mecca for anglers back in those days that the editors of the New Naturalist Series turned to a demonstrator in zoology at Trinity College Dublin for their book on the entomology of fishing, a remarkable volume of popular science that brought biology to bear on a sport of great economic importance in a significantly new way. Harris' *The Angler's Entomology* (1952) can be said to mark the apogee of the art of angling, appearing as it did just before a steady decline in the quality of fishing that can be laid at the door of the modern intensification in agriculture.

Today, fifty years on, prolific fields of dull green silage have taken the place of meadow, and they are silent of corncrakes. The palette of forty shades with which Ireland's green image has been painted in the popular imagination has been reduced. Nobody cuts turf by hand any more; the cutover has been planted with lodgepole pine and the nightjar has fled. Each year fewer croneen make their way upstream to spawn in the headwaters of the rivers in the midlands.

What is behind it all?

In 1961, the population of the Republic of Ireland (2.82 million) was the lowest ever recorded, but by 1996 it had risen by 29% to 3.63 million. However, this growth has been concentrated mainly in the cities and major towns. Rural Ireland continues to experience depopulation and a thinning in the fabric of rural society. Population growth has been accompanied by increasing affluence, and these forces of change – affluence and population growth – have brought about substantial change in all sectors of the environment, often causing concerns about an accompanying deterioration in quality. This prosperity, and the accompanying environmental transformation, which Ireland has witnessed over the last half century have been driven and mediated by the injection of resources that resulted from membership of the European Union (EU): but its immediate causes are the expansion in population and an extraordinarily rapid and widespread rise in living standards. The negative aspects of that transformation are accentuated by the low level of environmental awareness. It is sobering that 75.3% of Irish people surveyed (the highest of any country in the EU) claimed to have made no particular effort to inform themselves on environmental issues[1].

Ireland has moved from having the highest rate of economic dependency in the EU in the 1980s to one of the lowest today. Increasing population growth, agricultural intensification and urbanisation have all brought unprecedented pressure to bear on the environment: through increased housing, a burgeoning consumption of goods and services, increased vehicle and energy use, industrial production, and the growth of forestry and tourism.

Air quality

One of the most immediate evidences of that deterioration was the decline of air quality in Irish cities as population rose in the 1960s. At this time, Dublin experienced levels of air pollution comparable to many cities in the United Kingdom and elsewhere, in which bituminous coal was the principal fuel. The introduction of smokeless fuel legislation led to dramatic improvement, and lichenologists in recent decades have recorded with satisfaction the ever-increasing tally of species that records this improvement.

The urban air quality legislation of the 1960s marked the beginning of a vigorous scientific focus on air quality that now looks at air quality not only from the perspective of local health, but in the context of global challenges, especially in relation to greenhouse gases and global warming. Ireland is committed to reducing its emissions of greenhouse gases (carbon dioxide, methane and nitrous oxide) to 13% above 1990 levels in the period 2008–2012, but a thriving industrial economy makes it very difficult to rein emissions in to such levels. The percentage increase still exceeds this limit, and on present trends it could be as much as twice the permitted level by 2012. The main contributor is agriculture, followed by transport and energy.

---

[1] EC (European Commission), *Les Européens et l'Environnement en 1999. Enquête Réalisée dans le Cadre de l'Eurobaromètre 51.1* (Brussels: European Commission, 1999).

Ireland is also failing to meet its international obligations in relation to emissions of nitrogen oxides and sulphur dioxide from industry, transport and power generation, although the new IPC (Integrated Pollution Control) licensing mechanism and other measures are beginning to put an effective break on growth in emissions. And although emissions from smoky fuel have been eliminated from cities, emissions of nitrogen dioxide, fine particulate matter and benzene from traffic – which is many multiples of what it was in the 1960s – have replaced them with a vengeance. Ireland struggles to meet EU standards for these pollutants. On the indoor front, air quality in public places has been dramatically improved by the extension of smoke-free zones to the workplace, where a total ban on smoking was introduced in March 2004, setting a standard which other European countries are likely to adopt.

Water quality

Surface and ground waters are the lifeblood of landscape, and their quality a measure of the extent to which land use is sustainable. This chapter opened with memories of rural Ireland at the time of the last BAAS visit to Dublin and, in a later section, I will point to shifts in the status of certain plants and animals that serve as auguries of change. Blanket weed (*Cladophora*) is another such indicator of environmental deterioration. It was almost absent from Irish streams of the 1950s. Today it is almost ubiquitous, as a result of a greatly enriched supply of nutrients to surface waters, particularly due to the diffuse pollution that has resulted from agricultural intensification. The main threat to water quality is eutrophication, especially in relation to phosphorus (though nitrogen gives rise to concern in certain areas). Since the 1970s, there has been a steady decline in river water quality; about a third of rivers are now slightly to moderately polluted, and twenty-four of the 124 lakes described in the Water Quality Reports are eutrophic to a greater or lesser extent (at the last survey). Strong or very high levels of nutrient pollution were recorded in seventeen of these. There has also been local pollution of groundwater aquifers in places, resulting in contamination of drinking water in some group water supply schemes.

The deterioration in water quality over recent decades has been the object of several pieces of legislation, each focussing on a different aspect. The new Water Framework Directive (WFD) sets out to rationalise and streamline this piecemeal approach with the ambitious aim of restoring all surface waters to satisfactory status by 2010. This is an endeavour which involves the efforts of scientists of many disciplines. In particular, it is an area where the practical application of taxonomy and ecology can be seen especially clearly, because the aquatic fauna and flora are taken as the yardstick of water quality. Since 1973, the routine monitoring of freshwater has been carried out by assessing the status of plant and animal communities, particularly aquatic macroinvertebrates[2]. Efforts have been ongoing to come up with a Europe-wide

---

2 J. Lucey, 'The Use of Macroinvertebrate Methods of Water Quality Assessment in EEC Countries', *Irish Journal of Environmental Sciences*, **3** (1) (1984), pp. 74-76. J. Lucey, J.J. Bowman, K.J. Clabby, P. Cunningham, M. Lehane, M. MacCarthaigh, M.L. McGarrigle & P.F. Toner, *Water Quality in Ireland 1995-1997*, Appendix 1 (1-3-1-10): 'Biological and physico-chemical surveillance and water quality assessment of rivers' (Environmental Protection Agency, 1999).

protocol for the biological monitoring of freshwater, and Irish scientists have played a key role in this development.

The best of scientific knowledge and expertise is being applied in the implementation of the WFD (and indeed other environmental legislation). Our understanding of how our activities can damage the integrity and diversity of our surroundings has grown enormously in recent decades, and we have learned to manage and monitor our impact. However, these skills need to be accompanied by a new level of awareness, respect and caring for the gift of an enriching environment. In this regard, it is worth pondering on the care accorded to holy wells in an earlier Ireland. Science has lifted the veil from the mysterious workings of the natural world, and we can scarcely recover the placebo magic of the past. A modest dose of scientific understanding has cured most people of belief in the medicinal or magical powers of spring water or wells (although the extraordinary success of dozens of local bottled waters in recent years suggests otherwise!). There is the danger that the adoption of a more rational attitude will weaken the fundamental instinct that the continued supply of water is contingent upon our reverence. And yet we know in our own day this is no more than scientific fact: a basic scientific understanding can help farmers maintain their springs and wells in order to safeguard the quality of the water.

Solid waste

Another consequence of our affluence is the generation of waste. More than fifteen million tonnes of non-agricultural solid waste were produced in 1998. Most of this is still disposed of at landfill, an area of considerable debate and conflict at present as suitable landfill sites become harder to find and less acceptable to their host communities. Strict enforcement, with strong penalties, will be required if Ireland is to measure up to the standards set by EU legislation in the area of waste management – waste prevention and minimisation, recycling. But such enforcement needs to be reinforced with in-depth education. There has however been considerable (albeit necessary) progress in the area of waste management. In 1998, nearly a third of solid waste was produced in the manufacturing sector, but waste recovery had increased from 31% in 1995 to 51% in that year. The overall recovery rate from packaging waste was 14.8%, but this is steadily improving due to increasingly stringent legislation.

The problem of litter and unauthorised dumping is a serious one and, although the imposition of a tax on plastic bags in 2002 has been very successful, its impact on the appearance of the countryside is not as effective as might have been hoped. The problem here is a low sense of environmental aesthetics, and it will take a very determined effort to raise the threshold of public awareness in this regard.

Land use change; housing

The rate of house building in Ireland is the highest in Europe relative to population. Urban sprawl and inappropriate rural housing are particularly contentious issues that polarise rural and urban values. New housing developments have proceeded in the almost total absence of sustainable transport provision, not in urban areas only, but in rural areas, where there is an assumption that unlimited car usage is not a sustainable solution to the problems of access such housing presents. Encroachment on rural land by the infrastructure needed to support population and the economy continues unabated, and in several respects without adequate control or effective concern to maintain the integrity of the natural and cultural landscape. The expansion of housing into the countryside has had major environmental impact, especially the one-off type of dwelling that is perhaps more characteristic of Ireland than of most countries with a more developed tradition of nucleated rural settlement. This creates environmental problems in such areas as transport (because workplace, schools and shops etc. are often far away), water and waste management. Rural Renewal Schemes have played an important role in stabilising the rural community, but whether holiday home schemes that have been prominent recipients of their largesse are sustainable in the longer term is open to question.

Energy and transport

The half-century since the BAAS last visited has seen remarkable developments in transport infrastructure, but this has proved unable to keep pace with the growth of vehicular traffic. The number of vehicles increased by more than 50% between 1990 and 1998. Apart from the air pollution consequent on the dramatic increase in car ownership, traffic congestion and noise are major problems, especially in Dublin. Cycle lanes are a small beginning, but there is a long way to go before there is adequate provision of the good quality, efficient public transport that is the only solution.

Nature and biodiversity

Increasing affluence is beginning to bring greater appreciation of non-material values in the environment. In particular, there is a growing awareness that natural diversity, expressed both in wild places and the flora and fauna that inhabit them, enrich living. This is a sea change from an attitude prevalent not many decades ago, well articulated by Sean Lemass in a Dáil speech in 1930. The Protection of Birds Act was passed in that year to put a halt to the capture in great numbers of goldfinches, linnets and skylarks that were caught with bird-lime and exported to England in cages. Lemass claimed that the Protection of Birds Act would bring greater misery to the 300 people who made a living of some sort capturing the birds for export. 'If the economic situation becomes better' he said, 'we can then afford to indulge in luxury legislation of this kind, but we must put the necessities of human beings before those of wild birds'[3].

Since the Convention on Biodiversity drawn up in 1993, following the UN Conference on Environment and Development at Rio de Janeiro, there has been an ever-growing awareness of the importance of biological diversity and the need to

---

[3] J. Feehan, 'Biodiversity and Ireland – Meeting the Challenge of the Convention', pp. 23-28 in F. Convery & J. Feehan (Eds), *Achievement and Challenge: Rio+10 and Ireland* (Dublin: The Environmental Institute, UCD, 2002).

preserve it. Ireland signed the Convention in 1996 but only produced its National Biodiversity Plan in 2002, by which time many other European countries were well-advanced in implementing their plans. Tardy though they have been, the local action plans now in preparation on a county basis provide an unprecedented opportunity to raise public awareness and to devise more effective conservation strategies that will ensure no further habitat loss occurs after 2010, in line with the EU target of halting habitat loss by 2010: an ambitious target that stands in parallel with the determination to return all waters to satisfactory status by then; indeed, the success of the WFD will be reflected in and evaluated by its effects on aquatic flora and fauna.

Ireland's biological diversity is modest by comparison with other regions in Europe for well-known biogeographical reasons. Ireland has few species that are considered important in the broader European conservation perspective: otter, lesser horseshoe bat, roseate tern and corncrake, freshwater crayfish. Of the numerous species of insects listed in Annex 2 of the Habitats Directive, the only one that occurs in Ireland is the marsh fritillary. Few species have actually been lost. The corn bunting no longer occurs in Ireland, however, and we have no way of knowing what invertebrates may have slipped quietly and unnoticed over the threshold of extinction on the island in the face of the forward march of intensive agriculture. Drainage and eutrophication have taken their toll of salmon and trout populations, and brought about the extinction of char from several lakes.

The emphasis tends to be on the loss of those habitats that are rare or absent elsewhere in Europe: raised and blanket bog, turloughs, coastal lagoons, offshore maerl beds, machair and shingle beaches. All habitats of international or national importance are now protected in a constellation of Special Areas of Conservation (SACs), Special Protection Areas (SPAs) and Natural Heritage Areas (NHAs). SACs are protected under the EU Habitats Directive (which arrived too late to save the great peatlands that still extended over vast tracts of Ireland, totally nearly a fifth of the land surface at the time of the last visit of the BAAS to Dublin). SPAs are areas set aside for the protection of birds under the EU Birds Directive, and the NHA network comprises sites of lesser conservation importance.

Some 10% of the area of Ireland is considered to be important for nature conservation. The number of SACs is around 400, covering some 650,000 ha, and there are 109 SPAs covering around 230,000 ha. The NHA network is more extensive: more than a thousand, extending over some 750,000 ha. NHAs will be given statutory protection under the new Wildlife Amendment Act (currently at Committee Stage).

Looking to the future, it is clear that three recent developments will have a profound impact on natural diversity in the decades ahead. The prospective negative impact in terms of production on intensive agriculture of a dramatic reduction in the level of nitrate (under the Nitrate Directive) was used to argue for the retention of a higher level, but this is being firmly rejected by Brussels. Such a reduction is seen to be necessary if the WFD is to meet its target of returning all waters to satisfactory condition by 2010, with all the opportunities for ecological enhancement this implies.

Finally, there is the newly-introduced Single Farm Payment which decouples rural income support from production, and seems likely to lead to a much less intensively managed rural landscape overall. One development it may lead to is a return to the use of more traditional grassland mixes which may prove more productive under less intensive conditions and will promote the enhancement of grassland biodiversity, returning the 39 shades which have been bled from the rainbow of green that remains the most immediate impression Ireland makes on the visitor.

Agriculture[4]

The years since the last visit to Dublin of the BAAS have seen the transformation of Irish society. Ireland became a member of the EEC sixteen years later, in 1973, and the embrace of Irish agriculture by the Common Agricultural Policy (CAP) that followed has transformed the countryside. Productivity soared as Irish agriculture became intensive and farming became fully mechanised; hitherto undreamed-of quantities of cheap fertiliser were applied to farmland to make up for centuries of depletion. More than any other single factor, the improvement in Ireland's agricultural productivity over the last 50 years can be attributed to a dramatic rise in the rate of fertiliser use. When Ireland joined the EEC in 1973, the percentage of overall production from Irish grassland that could be attributed to fertiliser use was 'more representative of subsistence type pastoral farming than an agricultural system which should essentially be operated at a high level of competitive efficiency'[5]. It was calculated that a 470% increase in nitrogen use was needed, a 440% increase in phosphorus and a 540% increase in potassium. These ambitious targets have been met and surpassed long since.

Part of the price paid for this unprecedented rise in agricultural production has been the deterioration in water quality discussed elsewhere, but it has also had a less familiar and less frequently chronicled impact on air quality. A century ago the community of lichens that is dominated by the common orange lichen *Xanthoria parietina* was largely confined to the vicinity of bird roosts, where an abundant natural fertiliser provided the high-nutrient conditions to which the community is adapted. Today, however, the community is almost ubiquitous on trees in farmland, often dramatically so on ash, horse chestnut and hawthorn, as the nutrient-hungry lichens mop up the generous fraction of fertiliser applied to the fields that is carried away in the air.

Xanthoria and the co-citizens of its coprophilic lichen community are informative biological indicators of change. For the observant naturalist, such indicators are everywhere in the living landscape, because all plants and animals adapt to a changing environment to a greater or lesser extent, at times in ways that are obvious, but more usually less so. The changing ways that are currently attracting most attention are those that are consequent on the global warming that has crept up on us in recent decades.

---

4 See also the Chapter 5.
5 T. Walsh, P.F. Ryan & J. Kilroy, 'A Half Century of Fertiliser and Lime Use in Ireland', *Journal of the Society for Statistical and Social Research, Ireland,* **19** (1957), pp. 3-35.

Observing these auguries, one is reminded of the druids of an earlier Ireland, who seem to have been splendid naturalists in their way. Their calling was to study the science and mystery of the world in order to guide their communities through life, and they were trained to read the signs in nature of what was happening in a wider world. Things as trivial as a bird at the tip of a branch, the form of a knot in a tree, were meaningful expressions of nature in this way, and featured in the augury of the druids. So too a modern augurer can read of a changing agricultural world in the yellow blaze of dandelions seen today in many a re-seeded ryegrass pasture in April – in which they were never *intended* to be, but who could foresee they would find conditions here so to their liking! – and where a generation ago cowslips visually dominated a species-diverse sward.

Intensive farming

Agriculture still accounts for 5.2% of GDP in the Republic of Ireland and, although this is only a fraction of what it was in the past, it is still twice the European average. The number of farms today (2000) is 146,000, the average size c. 30ha. Grass-based farming accounts for more than 90% of Irish agricultural enterprise. Although there are increasing numbers of pigs and poultry, they are concentrated almost entirely in very large numbers in a relatively small number of specialised enterprises in a few areas. This scale and concentration give rise to a number of serious environmental problems and challenges, particularly in relation to the disposal of pig slurry. Intensive pig farming has caused some of the most serious pollution for which Irish agriculture has been responsible, of which the case of Lough Sheelin has been one of the more dramatic examples[6]. Much effort is currently being directed towards making the enterprise sustainable, particularly in relation to nutrient management[7]. The number of poultry (around thirty million) is about the same as it was fifty years ago, but almost all are in large production units. Half a century ago, when small flocks of free-range birds were an almost indispensable part of the farmyard scene, they were scattered more or less evenly throughout the island[8].

Many of the changes that accompanied intensification resulted in a deterioration in environmental integrity and diversity. This of course was unintended and largely unforeseen, as is often the case where science is applied to the solution of a problem without adequate evaluation of the context. Over-wintering of livestock in slatted houses has led to increased production of slurry for disposal by land spreading. Silage has largely replaced hay for winter feeding. Both changes can cause eutrophication

---

[6] P. Duggan & T. Champ, 'Lough Sheelin Reviewed', pp. 487-498 in J. Feehan (Ed), *Environment and Development in Ireland* (Dublin: The Environmental Institute, UCD, 1992).

[7] T.P. Curran, W.L. Magette & V.A. Dodd, 'Recent Developments in Minimising the Environmental Impact of Pig Production', pp. 14-17 in F. Convery & J. Feehan (Eds), *Achievement and Challenge: Rio+10 and Ireland* (Dublin: The Environmental Institute, UCD, 2002). W. Magette, T. Curran, G. Provolo, V. Dodd, P. Grace & B. Sheridan, 'Environmental Evaluation of Intensive Animal Production Facilities', pp. 58-72 in F. Convery & J. Feehan (Eds), *Achievement and Challenge: Rio+10 and Ireland* (Dublin: The Environmental Institute, UCD, 2002).

[8] J. Feehan, *Farming in Ireland: History, Heritage and Environment* (Dublin: Faculty of Agriculture, UCD, 2003).

without careful and responsible management. The process of field enlargement in areas of more intensive agriculture has resulted in loss of hedgerows and their resident flora and fauna. The reclamation of land hitherto marginal to agriculture and the adoption of new agricultural practices less supportive of wildlife saw a dramatic retreat in natural diversity.

Impact of changes

It was the change from hay to silage in all likelihood that led to the disappearance of the corncrake. Of greater impact arguably was the wholesale replacement of traditional grassland by clover-ryegrass swards throughout Ireland, which saw a reduction from as many as thirty species of herbs and grasses to half a dozen in most fields, and a consequent contraction in the diversity of the invertebrate food chains they supported.

Again it is worth noting that these impacts were not foreseen at the time of their introduction, although they *could* have been foreseen: and this may be seen as a failure to be *sufficiently* scientific in planning for and managing the environment. A particularly good example of this kind of short-sightedness was the application of headage payments in 1980. This was primarily intended as a social measure to bolster farm income but, in the west of Ireland, while it undoubtedly did succeed in this respect, the environmental impact of sheep headage was disastrous. Long experience has shown that the carrying capacity of blanket bog is around one sheep to three hectares, but the EU headage regime often led to densities as much as ten times this – or even more. In the more vulnerable areas of Connemara and parts of Mayo, Donegal and Kerry, extensive areas of bog were turned to deserts of black slime. This degradation has been halted by the implementation of Commonage Framework Plans, accompanied by substantial compensation payments to upland farmers, who are more aware than anybody that their livelihoods depend upon sustainable farming methods.

It is more than a little interesting that the lowest level of environmental awareness should be found in a country with one of the lowest levels of intensive land management, where nature and an immensely rich cultural palimpsest have survived without any special effort or awareness on our part. We have not yet fully grasped the fact that here in Ireland we are at a turning point in the relationship between man and nature, because from now on we must *consciously* support the maintenance of diversity. We have reached the point where we have so little left that we must not only retain all that we have, but, wherever opportunity allows, we must recover as much as we can of what has been lost. Nature has always looked after itself, but it cannot do so *unaided* any longer; *we* must *allow* Nature the space to grow back.

A beginning has been made in tackling the challenge of restoring integrity and natural diversity to the rural landscape. With the implementation of the EU Environmental Impact Assessment (EIA) directive in 1989–90, it has become standard practice to routinely evaluate the impact of major development on every aspect of the environment. The legislative teeth of EU directives has enabled problems and challenges to be tackled with a sense of purpose that might not otherwise have been present. The reason for this is that, although the level of environmental awareness in Ireland is very much higher than it was half a century ago, it still lags way behind that of other EU countries; membership of environmental organisations in Ireland is only a twelfth of what it is in Germany, and a much smaller fraction of such membership in Great Britain.

While it is scarcely a matter of pride that we stand on the bottom rung of the ladder of environmental sensitivity, it is not by any order of magnitude. We have undergone greater cultural awakenings before in a matter of decades. If the development of a new environmental ethic and aesthetic is seen as the priority it should be, then we can do so again.

Forestry and the recovery of Ireland's woods[9]

At the beginning of the twentieth century, Ireland was the least wooded country in Europe: tree cover had been reduced to 1%. A century later the figure had risen to 9%. However, the type of commercial forestry practiced in Ireland through most of the twentieth century – regimented evergreen monocultures – has had a disastrous impact on scenic landscapes and their natural diversity. Large areas of blanket bog have been planted with coniferous woodland, a land use which would be uneconomic without the incentive payments which encouraged it. The afforestation of blanket bog took little account of the exceptional contribution of these peatlands to the character and quality of heritage landscapes. A new ethos is now at work; such inappropriate afforestation is now at an end and a determined effort (driven by the drive to reach the requirements demanded by the new Irish National Forest Standard) is being made to return some lost ground to wildlife.

One of the challenges in farming today is to recover something of Ireland's lost woodland, not merely in terms of hectares planted or restored, but in terms of the values trees represent in our lives. The hope must be that the care and management of trees can become again a normal part of rural life, as it was for most of our forgotten past. Four-fifths of Ireland's woods today are state forests, and 90% of this is under conifers, almost exclusively Sitka spruce and lodgepole pine. Only since the late 1980s has new planting on farms become at all significant, largely in response to the generosity of farm forestry grants. The new regime presents us with the opportunity and challenge to restore something of the wooded diversity that existed before the stripping of woodland from the everyday farmed landscape which began four and a half centuries ago.

There is currently a great drive to involve farmers and private interests alongside Coillte (The Irish Forestry Board) in the re-afforestation of Ireland. Almost all tree-planting today is in privately-owned forests. The target is to have 17% of land cover in the Republic under forest by 2030 (1.2 million hectares) – 'a transformation of landscape on a scale and at a rate unprecedented in the island's history' in the words of Michael Viney: and an objective which will require the afforestation of a further

---

[9] See also the Chapter 6.

20,000ha each year from now until 2030. Coillte's forests are still largely single-species conifer woods, but the amount of broadleaf planting is increasing. In 1998 only 5% of new plantations were broadleaves, but the target now is to increase broadleaf planting to 30% by 2030. The Heritage Council recommends equal numbers of broadleaved and coniferous trees, citing an EU national average of 60% broadleaves. It may come as a surprise to learn that much of the ash used for making hurleys is imported from the UK and elsewhere; the country's hedgerows and older woods can no longer supply the demand, and the ash woodlands planted under the new schemes will not be ready to harvest for some years.

A new environmental perspective can be seen to influence Coillte and the State Forest Service. This new perspective is driven by the ideas of Sustainable Forest Management (SFM) which is the code of forest protection (known as the Helsinki Process) initiated by Europe's environment ministers in 1993, one of the core objectives of which is the maintenance of biodiversity. Coillte has committed itself to SFM across an estate that includes 15,000ha of SACs, 2,000ha of 'enhancement and restoration forests' and great areas of unplanted hills, peatlands, swamps and lakes. 15% of its lands are to be managed with nature conservation rather than timber as the primary objective. The Forest Service has issued remarkably sound and thorough biodiversity guidelines in its Code of Best Forest Practice, abiding by which is now a condition of forest grant aid.

Another key new initiative targeted on the enhancement of biodiversity is the new Native Woodlands Scheme launched in 2002. Working with Dúchas – The Heritage Service – and expert woodland groups, the Forest Service will give substantial grants for the restoration of 15,000ha of native broadleaf woodland in private hands, and the planting of the same amount of new woodland, primarily for conservation, with selective felling and continuous cover, incorporating 1,000ha of riparian trees in each group of woodlands. A third key initiative is the People's Millennium Forests launched in 2000 and managed by Coillte. This has planted more than a million trees in restoring eight native woodlands to something of their old diversity and creating eight new ones with a mix of native species. Finally, there is the new NeighbourWoods Scheme, which is primarily recreational in its objectives, but with considerable emphasis on the enhancement of biodiversity and the experience of biodiversity by the community.

But, while grants and a twenty-year premium for farmers appear attractive, there is a major economic disincentive to the planting of farmland: it seriously reduces its value as farmland – by more than half when it has been planted with oak. A possible solution to this is to recognise that new woodland enhances the public good: even if the compensation paid for such recognition needs to be balanced by increased access and enjoyment by that public of the woodland's non-use values.

Peatlands

At the time of the last BAAS visit to Dublin in 1957, Bord na Móna had just celebrated its tenth anniversary and had embarked on its Second Development Programme for the large-scale exploitation of Ireland's peatland resources[10]. It is interesting to note the absence of protest when this major onslaught on the only area of true wilderness in the country was launched. This is no more than a reflection of society's values at the time: the paramount environmental value of peatlands was the calorific value of peat as fuel, though with an eye to productive capacity of a new kind when the great bogs came to the end of their productive life, and an area of agricultural land the size of an additional county would be added to the country's land bank. Within Bord na Móna itself, there is a residue of this narrow perspective on peatland valuation, but in the wider society there can be seen the development of a new evaluation of this landform and the development of a new agenda for science in relation to it[11]. Back in the 1950s, the challenge to science in relation to peatland management was narrowly focused on the development of productive capacity in the cutaway, initially along the three productive possibilities of arable, grassland and forestry. It was quickly realised that the production of crops other than grass was not economic on any scale and, although the scientific challenge of transforming suitable cutaway to productive grassland was met successfully, the need for more grassland at a time when Europe is trying to cut production and encourage extensification is questionable. Costly experience has also shown that afforestation is not an easy option for cutaway bog; a new phase of research is currently attempting to discover new planting options[12].

In recent years, there has been a growing appreciation that peatlands are more than stockpiles of sub-fossil fuel awaiting exploitation. In a global context, their importance as carbon reservoirs is enormous; and in Ireland, as in many other countries, ongoing research is currently attempting to evaluate the potential as carbon sinks of the ecosystems that develop on cutaway. The value of the cutaway for the support of biodiversity has become a focus of attention among ecologists in recent years. In the early days of the peatland conservation movement, the focus was entirely on the preservation of intact bogs of importance, and there was little awareness of the ecological potential of cutaway. This has changed, as the remarkable development of biodiversity on industrial cutaway areas such as Turraun in Offaly has demonstrated the potential richness of these areas. A complex of diverse ecosystems also develops on abandoned turbary. It should be possible to link all these nodes and strands of wild land by means of an Econet (as envisaged by the Council of Europe) in a country where wilderness is at such a low ebb.

---

[10] John Feehan & Grace O'Donovan, *The Bogs of Ireland – An Introduction to their Natural, Cultural and Industrial Heritage* (Dublin: The Environmental Institute, UCD, 1996).

[11] H. Joosten & D. Clark, *The Wise Use of Mires and Peatlands* (International Peat Society and the International Mire Conservation Group, 2003).

[12] Florence Renou & E.P. Farrell, 'Reclaiming Peatlands for Forestry: the Irish experience', in J. Stanturf, P. Madsen & L. Breland (Eds), *Restoration of Boreal and Temperate Forests* (2004).

Once harvesting activity ceases – indeed, before it in many cases – natural processes of recolonisation take over, and in time the bog is replaced by a mosaic of evolving ecosystems of great ecological interest that develop on the residual peat[13]. There will be woodland and scrub, dominated by pine, birch and willow. There will be oases and fringes of natural acid grassland, fen, marsh and small areas of bog, with considerable areas of shallow open water and the marginal habitats associated with it. These spontaneously established new ecosystems are *in equilibrium with the changed conditions* which human exploitation of the original bog has brought about. It is uncertain that we could have created this new evolving equilibrium and the accompanying natural diversity ourselves, if we had set about it with the hubris of the modern ecologist who believes that management plans can achieve everything. We often don't understand enough about the ecological processes that are going on.

One of the commonest species in the acid grasslands is devil's-bit scabious – (*Succisa pratensis*), which is the food plant of the marsh fritillary (*Eurodryas aurinia*), one of the few Irish insects which appears in Annex II of the EU Habitats Directive – species for which there is an obligation on national governments to provide protection. Some of the wetter grasslands are little meadows of marsh helleborines (*Epipactis palustris*), with the scarlet and red of early marsh orchids dotted among them. There are newts and green hairstreaks, frogs and frog orchids, not to mention the bewildering diversity of smaller lives that have found a niche in this new ecological mosaic.

All bogs, however disturbed, are places of ecological importance. Indeed, they are nearly always among the richest reservoirs of biodiversity in an area, either because of what they already possess, or because of what they can become. From an ecological management perspective, they are usually best left to themselves, except where intervention is needed to prevent complete takeover by soft rush, bramble or furze, which can happen under certain conditions; these aggressively invasive species often act as ecological bottlenecks in particular areas, inhibiting the development of more biodiverse ecosystems.

A modest amount of intervention is also needed sometimes to facilitate the development of new lakes on cutaway bog, or to establish pathways or other facilities for access. But this should never be on a scale, or use materials, which are out of character with the developing wilderness. Wilderness requires that we keep our hands off and let an ecological equilibrium establish itself that is in tune with the altered conditions. Every time this has happened in relation to cutaway or cutover bog – and it has only happened in spite of us, not because we decided to do it for ecological ends – we have been surprised by the ecological results. It is very much open to question whether we could have achieved these kinds of results in terms of biodiversity if we tried to plan for and manage them.

It is encouraging to note the beginnings of a new awareness of this broader range of peatland functions and values not only among scientists and other professionals

---

[13] T. Egan (Ed), *Lough Boora Parklands, Pre-Feasibility Study by Boora Enterprise Group* (Newbridge: Bord na Móna, 1994).

involved in peatland management, but among the wider public. One indication is a growing interest among the communities of the North Midlands in the notion of developing a wilderness park centred on the web of cutaway that will cover the region when Bord na Móna withdraws from peat production in a very few decades time[14]. This embryonic awareness among the broader community is a local instance of a development that needs to be universal if there is to be environmental sustainability in the long term, namely the *democratisation* of a broader concept of environmental valuation.

Natural history and geology

A century and a half ago, the primary field research into Ireland's geology, ecology, archaeology and landscape history had hardly started. That work has now been completed in its essentials, though much important research remains to be done – particularly urgent in relation to current environmental problems. At the time of the last BAAS visit to Dublin, there had been little attempt to bring all this detailed research together, and to paint an overall picture of the natural history, the geology, landscape evolution and so on. That work of synthesis has also now been completed in its essentials. Work now concentrates on two fronts: on elaborating the finer detail, and on moving up to the finer resolution of the *local* picture.

Today we have a much more detailed understanding of Ireland's natural history than we did fifty years ago. In 1950, the great Robert Lloyd Praeger published the first modern attempt at an overview of the island's flora and fauna[15]. Recently published syntheses by David Cabot and Michael Viney illustrate how much our knowledge has advanced in the last half century[16]. At the same time, much remains to be done and discovered. There is still relatively little known of the distribution of invertebrates, and very few scientists are at work in this area.

Meanwhile, several important developments have been taking place outside the Groves of Academia. The power of those who own the land to implement change in the landscape has accelerated a hundredfold; secondly the educational framework of the community as a whole has changed dramatically; and thirdly we have come to realise the economic value of landscape heritage as a resource in tourism, which has been an area of tremendous growth in recent decades. Tourist numbers are currently more than one and a half times the resident population.

There have been remarkable advances in the field of geology in the last half century. These have resulted in part from the revolutionary re-interpretation the arrival of plate tectonic theory has allowed, and in part from the development of new and more sophisticated exploratory techniques[17]. These advances have led to a much clearer

---

[14] J. Feehan, *Towards a New Wilderness* (Dublin: Department of Environmental Resource Management, UCD, 2004).

[15] Robert Lloyd Praeger, *Natural History of Ireland* (London, 1950), republished by EP Publishing Ltd. 1972.

[16] David Cabot, *Ireland* (London: HarperCollins, The New Naturalist, 1999); Michael Viney, *Ireland, A Smithsonian Natural History* (Belfast: The Blackstaff Press, 2003).

[17] C.H. Holland, *The Geology of Ireland* (Edinburgh: Dunedin Academic Press, 2001).

picture of offshore geology than that which pertained even forty years ago. On earlier maps, the coloured jigsaw of the island's geology ended at the edge of the sea. It now extends offshore, tracking the geology of the ocean floor, and this geographically and stratigraphically wider picture has led to the discovery of important offshore petroleum gas reserves.

Another corner of geology into which much new light has been shed in recent decades is the Irish Tertiary. It was generally assumed fifty years ago that, because Tertiary rocks were almost non-existent in Ireland, we would forever be denied a view of what the landscape of pre-glacial Ireland looked like. The researches of Adrian Phillips in his later years had begun to describe in unexpected detail the geography of an ancient landscape buried beneath the mantle of glacial and glaciofluvial debris, and a new generation of researchers has begun to fill in the colour and detail of this buried geological canvas[18].

These new geological insights have been in terrain hidden from our eyes in one way or another, but significant geological discoveries can still be made even in the most familiar landscapes. No landscape has been more intensively studied than the Burren, yet it is only within the last few years that the remarkable suite of hydrothermal dykes exposed in plane view in the Burren National Park has been discovered and described: frozen exhalations of the unseen magma deep beneath the surface, upon which the Burren limestone is cushioned.

Cultural heritage; the loss of cultural detail and local character fabric

The geologist Grenville Cole, in a metaphor that has shed much illumination on subsequent thinking about Ireland's environmental heritage, described it as Europe's Outpost, the island which is Europe's furthest-flung frontier. It is at the distant edge of the continent, and it took flowers and insects longest to reach it after the Ice Age: but it was also the outpost which waves of innovation originating in Europe took longest to reach and, by the same token, took longest to disappear from. So echoes of older ways of managing the land tend to reverberate in our landscape long after they have died away in most of the heartland of Europe, where they are overridden by later and more productive technologies. Echoes from every phase of the human past survive in the landscape of Ireland, the tangible relics of features associated with earlier people: the places they lived and worshipped in, the memorials they erected to their gods, features associated with their management of the land. And this cultural diversity exists side by side with the corners and fringes where something of Ireland's natural diversity still survives. This in large measure explains why Ireland's environment has come under pressure more recently than in most other western European countries: helped by social and demographic factors certainly. We had far more to lose and, because of rapid mechanisation, have been able to lose it faster.

[18] Adrian Phillips, 'The Pre-Quaternary Evolution of the Irish Landscape', Jackson Lecture, No. 23 in RDS *Occasional Papers in Irish Science and Technology* (Dublin, Royal Dublin Society, 2001), pp. 18.

Landscape features

The concept of *the landscape as cultural palimpsest* follows from this. The European rural landscape is often, and accurately, described as a palimpsest of the human cultural achievement. In the days when vellum was used as the medium for the writing of important documents, it was too valuable simply to throw away after use, so the old message was erased and a new one superimposed. When that became redundant it, in turn, was erased and replaced by a newer inscription, and so on. But although the message of the moment was the obvious inscription, it was always possible to see traces of the earlier ones, and even to read bits of them. Everything we see about us in the landscape constitutes the most recent statement etched there by modern man over the last few centuries. But underneath and in the interstices of the modern inscription, there are features which survive from every earlier phase of the human adventure with landscape, fainter as their age lengthens – relics which give us actual physical contact with the people who walked here before us.

The Irish rural landscape contains an exceptional wealth of landscape features resulting from the work of earlier communities. This is generally attributed to our situation away up at the north-west fringe of the continent, fronting the Atlantic, and to our island situation. But as often as not, much of what survives does so because of *neglect* rather than *care* – though perhaps neglect is perhaps seldom *simply* neglect. Consider for instance, the ringfort which in spite of the destruction of the present century, is one of the commonest archaeological features in the Irish landscape. These circular earthworks are the enclosures of the farmsteads of Gaelic Ireland, the focal points of the landscape throughout the country from late in the Bronze Age right down to the sixteenth century. Yet no recollection of this lost functional aspect seems to have filtered through in the folk tradition of the country; the earthworks were not preserved because their presence can open a window upon a particularly significant phase of a treasured past, or because they are sacred places as surely as places where the bodies of the dead are interred: but because a later folk tradition has invested them with a *new* meaning, giving them over to the people of the under-earth, so that they passed into the care and 'ownership' of other-worldly guardians to function on a different level of meaning, feared because of what might befall those who desecrated them. They functioned as anchors in a familiar landscape, valued because they were familiar.

The real significance of features like these was appreciated in an earlier generation only by an educated and leisured minority that belonged to a different social class, with different values and ambitions, coming from a different place. But the features that cumulatively make up the rural landscape heritage are primarily the heritage of those who have shaped that landscape: the local farming community.

Legal protection

The drive for agricultural intensification that accompanied the early CAP has been the latest wave of economic pressure to further erode the already frayed material heritage of the Irish rural cultural landscape. Earthworks such as ring bank enclosures suffered particularly in this onslaught. Still, it is not that this was something new. The features that constitute the cultural heritage were seldom valued in the past because of what they represented in themselves, because they were relics that brought us directly into contact with our roots and helped define our sense of place. A handful of the more outstanding monuments (and some of lesser note) are designated as National Monuments, but this has afforded minimum protection until now. In recent years, a High Court decision that the passage tomb cemetery monument at Carrowmore in County Sligo included the *context* of the monument was an important extension of interpretation in this regard. But there is the danger that such protective legislation is seen as an imposition on the farmer on whose land a monument is situated, imposing restrictions on what he can or cannot do with it. The law is or may be seen as protecting something that is valued by an educated or articulate minority, but does not belong within the value system of the farmer or his community. There is little acceptance in Ireland of the concept that the individual right to land is not absolute: that certain dimensions of the land are the property of all, part of the *Common Wealth*: the mineral rights, the right to the view, and more particularly that these reserved aspects should include those cultural features or natural survivals which can be considered part of the cultural heritage of all the community.

On the other hand, there is still little understanding or acceptance of this central fact, that the features which constitute the cultural heritage of the rural landscape are more profoundly and immediately the heritage of those in whose care they now are: because almost invariably they are the creation of earlier farming communities, who lived from the resources of this same corner of the earth, and loved and cared for it as those in whose keeping it is today. For those who do own these monuments, an understanding and appreciation of their nature and significance has more to offer in the way of meaning, continuity, rootedness in the past, a sense of place, than it does to the occasional visitor. It has to be said, though, that we are still in a transitional period where many farming people – and some of the organisations which represent them – speak as if the care of these features of the cultural landscape were *simply* a burden imposed upon them by other sectors of the community, for the carrying of which they must be adequately compensated.

It is against the background of considerations such as these that the significance of the measures for countryside management accompanying CAP reform must be assessed. These measures stem from a realisation that the CAP not only led to vast over-production and pollution, but that increased production was won at the price of the further reduction of the natural and material cultural heritage of the rural landscape. Throughout the European Union, measures are now in place to protect, enhance and restore this heritage, which contributes so fundamentally to the essential character of Europe's farmed landscape. The driving force behind it is the growing appreciation of the *value* of the detail of which this heritage is composed, of the fact that it is an important part of the *Common Wealth*. Allied to this is the realisation that many of these features have in themselves become valuable economic assets in the context of the growth in tourism, and especially of rural tourism, and that cumulatively the cultural detail which constitutes the fabric of the rural landscape is a principal expression of local or regional uniqueness. So what is happening is that, as we begin a new millennium, our European value system – with ourselves trailing somewhat towards the rear – has, in the first place, evolved to a point where we have set this new value upon material landscape detail which in the past was taken for granted; and secondly, it has acquired, for the first time, a direct financial equivalence, which is perhaps the surest guarantee of its further survival in the short to medium term. The new environmental management programmes in agriculture reflect this new value system, as does the evolving EIA concept.

Cultural impact

Note that cultural impact is often (perhaps usually) at the expense of natural heritage. That was seldom a consideration for its own sake. It only became heritage with the passage of a certain (arbitrary) period of time, acquiring the venerable look of age: e.g. Georgian houses, canals and railways, mills. And some treasured natural ecosystems survive only because of management; in other words they are cultural artefacts – the grasslands of the Burren, the eskers and turloughs for example. Here natural and cultural intersect so intimately that protection can never be simply a matter of fencing them off in order to protect them. It is essential to understand the interaction that maintains them in the state we value.

To those who identify with one particular place as their *home*, the individual components of the cultural landscape (in particular) have value deeper than any that may be put on them by outside experts. Just as natural heritage is not adequately evaluated by biodiversity indices, but needs to take account of ecological diversity, or the capacity of an area to provide diversity of natural experience; so we need to distinguish the importance of a cultural feature to an archaeologist from its significance for somebody for whom it is a defining element of the fabric of their home or otherwise treasured place.

Perhaps it might be appropriate here to point up a useful distinction between three poles of meaning and value we can attribute to cultural landscape features (such as ringforts). Why should a particular ringfort be preserved? For what reason, from what value perspective, is it part of our material landscape heritage? Because of its archaeological importance certainly: which really means, because of the archaeological information it contains, because of its importance to archaeologists. That is one level, which will be strongly argued for by, say, An Taisce (the National Trust for Ireland). But it may also be important because 2,000 years of being left alone have allowed it to gather to itself a considerably diverse ecology, and you may well have conflict between these two. I think of one ringfort I know which has morels and goldilocks on the bank, and inside is ancient scrub where badgers and long-tailed tits and a score of other birds have their homes. That is a second level, whose main advocates might be BirdWatch Ireland. But there is a distinct third level of meaning and value, albeit enriched by the reflected light from these other two. And that is what it means for those whose home its presence enriches. It is part of the intimate landscape of their experience, where nature and archaeology may be enriched with memory and experience – for people who played there as children, who picnicked there on summer days which a gilded memory illuminates with a degree of sunshine unsupported by the meteorological records, or at least has always diversified and enriched the landscape stage on which a local community in each generation uniquely enacts its short human drama. For the community therefore, a particular feature of the landscape may be more important on this level than for more scientifically quantified reasons. Nevertheless, and in spite of the growing appreciation of their significance and importance, recent legislation and new environmental management programmes have failed to stem the tide of destruction of archaeological monuments and features of cultural value in the rural landscape fabric (an issue discussed elsewhere in this volume in Chapter 5).

A continued role for science

Among the principal challenges in Ireland today are the management of development in ways that maintain environmental quality or restore quality status where there has been significant deterioration, and provide the monitoring protocols needed to ensure a quality environment. One of the most important roles of Irish science is the contribution it makes to environmental management, and research is being pursued in all the areas of concern touched on in earlier pages, especially those governed by international agreements and EU directives. Eight state agencies are involved in this endeavour, along with the universities and other third-level institutions: the Environmental Protection Agency, the Department of Agriculture and Food, Sustainable Energy Ireland, the Health Research Board, COFORD (National Council for Forest Research & Development), National Parks and Wildlife, the Marine Institute, and the Heritage Council.

Ireland depends, and will increasingly depend, on its green environmental image. We are perhaps fortunate that our unprecedented economic surge is coming at a time when we are bound by the restraining harness of EU obligation, which will help steer us along a course where economic progress and material prosperity are achieved without a cost to the environment of this wonderful island of which we are for our short lives the custodians: a cost which will be laid to the account of future generations, and which will diminish the prosperity, happiness and well-being of those who inherit the land.

CHAPTER 5

Building a Knowledge Based Multifunctional Agriculture and Rural Environment

Liam Downey and Gordon Purvis

Executive summary

Having outlined the major drivers of change, a perspective presented of Rural Ireland in the coming decade indicates that:

- There may be no more than 15,000 (and conceivably fewer) full-time commercial farmers, predominantly intensive dairy producers, and something in the region of 25,000–35,000 part-time farmers deriving a significant portion (possibly half or more) of their income mainly from extensive beef production.
- Rural Ireland will become increasingly differentiated into three spatial areas namely: *An Intensive Dairy Area* concentrated in large parts of Munster and South Leinster; *An Extensive Beef Area* mainly in the Border, Midland and Western Region; and *A Marginal Farming Area* especially in the West of Ireland, where abandonment of agriculture will present major environmental and socio-economic problems.

Countries that achieve the optimum balance between, on one hand, profitability in agriculture and food processing and, on the other, society and consumer's increasing quality requirements, will succeed best in the immediate years ahead. To achieve this aim and establish an internationally competitive and sustainable agriculture, Ireland must re-position the sector in the emerging knowledge-driven economy by developing a knowledge-based multifunctional agriculture.

In building a knowledge-based multifunctional agriculture and rural environment, the following central issues are considered in this overview:

- The question – *What is a knowledge-based agriculture?* – within the context of multifunctional agriculture in intensive, extensive and marginal farming areas.

- To illustrate the type of livestock systems required to optimise multifunctional outputs, new indicative models are presented of knowledge-based intensive dairy production, extensive beef production and dry-stock farming in marginal areas.
- Development of a knowledge-based multifunctional agriculture requires a major sea-change in Ireland's agricultural research agenda – some important themes are listed that should constitute the core elements of future research in agriculture.
- To strike the optimum balance between the economic dictates of an internationally competitive agri-food industry allied to a sustainable rural economy, and protection of Ireland's rich heritage of natural and cultural resources, a Rural Environment Research Centre is seen as a national imperative.
- Early consideration needs to be given to the introduction of *Public Goods Initiatives* designed to encourage all farmers, especially intensive producers, to manage the rural landscape and optimise the full Public Goods value of agriculture and its contribution to rural economies.

Introduction

The face of Rural Ireland will be fundamentally changed in the coming decade. With European Union (EU) Enlargement allied to the recent fundamental reforms of the Common Agricultural Policy (CAP, Luxembourg, June 2003) and further changes heralded in the coming decade, attainment of the necessary balance between the economic, social and environmental sustainability of Rural Ireland constitutes a major national challenge.

National and international drivers of change

Among the major drivers that will predominately determine the shape of Rural Ireland in the immediate years ahead, the following are of paramount importance:

- Ongoing reform of the EU CAP allied to EU Enlargement.
- The outcome of negotiations under the World Trade Organisation (WTO), resulting in more liberal world trade and greater globalisation of markets.
- The growing need to strike the optimum balance between the price competitiveness of the agriculture and the food industry, and society's concerns in relation to the environment, food safety and quality, animal diseases and welfare and, to an increasing extent, developments in biotechnology.
- Compliance with EU Directives (Nitrogen Vulnerable Zones, Water Framework, and Strategic Environmental Assessment), and with other International Environmental Agreements (Kyoto Protocol and Gothenburg Protocol).

- Increasing demands on rural space, leading to declining consensus on the location of housing, utilities and infrastructure, as well as public access to rural landscapes, including archaeological and natural heritage resources.
- Projected demographic changes, especially the overall ageing of the population.
- Enlargement of farms allied to inflated land values, and the further intensification of farming systems, with a resultant concentration of agriculture and the food processing industry in the more productive farming regions and the withdrawal of farming from areas with predominantly sub-viable farms.
- The threats and opportunities arising from global climate change that will increasingly influence agriculture, the environment and rural economies.
- The need for knowledge and innovation which will be key determinants of the sustained competitiveness of agriculture, the food industry and rural economics.

Perspective of rural Ireland in the coming decade

Some of the diverse array of complex and dynamic changes that Rural Ireland will experience in the immediate decade ahead are synopsised below:

The agricultural and food processing industries will undergo sustained structural changes and rationalisation. The number of full-time commercial farmers will continue to contract, possibly resulting in no more that 15,000 (and maybe fewer) full-time producers, predominantly dairy farmers (perhaps less than 10,000), together with perhaps 2,000, or less, full-time dry stock producers, a roughly similar number of arable/horticultural producers, and less than 500 pig producers[1,2]. The restructuring of farming will be attended by an increase in farm size, as mentioned above.

It is envisaged that Ireland will have something in the region of 25,000 to 35,000 part-time farmers, deriving a significant portion (possibly half or more) of their income mainly from cattle/sheep production. Many of these will have farm-forestry enterprises. There may be no more than two major dairy processing companies and four (or even fewer) large meat exporting groups, as well as upwards of one hundred small and medium scale food companies producing prepared consumer foods and other high value added products.

These structural changes will be attended by increasing geographical differentiation in farm production and the progressive development of the following three spatial areas in Rural Ireland:

- *Intensive Farming Areas* – The projected numbers of full-time commercial farmers, mainly dairy farmers, and associated food processing companies

---

[1] Foresight Technology Ireland, *Natural Resources* (Dublin: Forfas, 1999).
[2] Liam Downey, 'What will the Agri-Food Industry Look Like in 2015?', in: *Proceedings of the Agri-Food Millennium Conference* (Dublin: Teagasc 1999) pp. 1-11.

will be concentrated predominantly in large parts of Munster and South Leinster, leading to growing conflicts in these regions between economic and environmental sustainability, including safe food production.

– *Extensive Farming Areas* – Most of the projected 25,000–35,000 part-time farmers will be concentrated in the Border, Midlands and Western (BMW) Region where they will be engaged mainly in extensive beef production. A sizeable proportion of full-time commercial beef producers (less than 2000) will also be located in this region.

– *Marginal Farming Areas* – As is already evident in the Burren (County Clare) and increasingly in other counties in the West of Ireland, the withdrawal of agriculture from marginal farming areas will adversely effect the unique natural and cultural environment in upland and wetland areas. This will place in jeopardy the amenity-tourism value of environmentally important rural regions and reduce their opportunity to develop alternative multifunctional land uses. In many such areas, traditional landscapes are being replaced with extensive monocrop forestry or scrub encroachment.

While there will be a sizeable decline in economic activity and population in many areas of marginal and extensive agriculture, other areas will experience significant growth. Interfacial areas between urban and rural areas will experience unprecedented economic and social pressures. Once-off housing will become an increasing environmental and infrastructural concern. Coastal and other high amenity areas will experience population growth. Developments in the marine industry will effect the economic viability of certain coastal regions. There will be a further expansion of population allied to a diversification of the economies within enlarged community catchment areas. In response to energy conservation policies and global climate changes, the production of energy crops may be an important feature of farm forestry enterprises.

European policy developments

The multifunctional European Model of Agriculture[3,4,5] requires the development of a knowledge-based agriculture, with the technological, innovative and business capacities to be internationally competitive and environmentally sustainable, and to support the continued viability of rural economies.

In response to the on-going reform of the CAP, EU enlargement and liberalisation of world trade, allied to the growing society/consumer demands and other drivers of change outlined above, Europe's agriculture and rural regions are undergoing

---

[3] Carmel Cahill, *The Multifunctionality of Agriculture: What does it mean?*, EuroChoises, 2001, **1**(1), pp. 36-40.

[4] Larry Harte & John O'Connell, *How Well Do Agri-Environmental Payments Conform with Multifunctionality?*, *EuroChoices*, 2003, **1**(2), pp. 36-41.

[5] L. Van de Pole, 'The European Model of Agriculture: Rhetoric or Reality? Implications for rural Areas', in *Proceedings of the Agri-Food Millennium Conference* (Dublin: Teagasc, 1999) pp. 1-4.

unprecedented changes. Following the fundamental reform of the CAP, the overall policy framework has been shifted towards rural development, and in particular the development of multifunctional agriculture. This is reflected in the establishment of a *Rural Development Fund* (€1.2 billion per annum) to protect the rural environment, and for the production of market-required food products of consistent quality and assured safety in a manner compatible with animal welfare requirements.

The central thrust of the Declaration formulated at the European Conference on Rural Development (Salzburg, 2003) is attainment of the optimum balance between the dual goals of ensuring the continued economic viability of rural regions and preserving Europe's rich heritage of rural landscapes and cultural diversity. The Declaration draws attention to the importance of agriculture in shaping rural landscapes. It also stresses that *'competitiveness of the farming sector must be a key aim of rural development'* as envisaged in the reform of the CAP. Of paramount importance to the future competitiveness of agriculture is the transition to the knowledge-based economy envisaged in the EU Lisbon Strategy[6]. To ensure the rapid development of a knowledge-based agriculture and other rural enterprises, a sizeable proportion of the Rural Development Fund, referred to above, should be deployed for this purpose. Allied to this, the closer alignment of both the European Research & Innovation Area and National Research Programmes with the development of the multifunctional European Model of Agriculture is essential.

In response to the policy changes and other international developments outlined above, and to ensure the future competitiveness of the sector in knowledge-driven international markets, Ireland must develop a multifunctional knowledge-based agri-food industry. Two inter-related questions arise in contemplating such a strategic development, namely 'What is multifunctional agriculture?' and 'What is knowledge based agriculture?'.

What is multifunctional agriculture?

The concept of **Multifunctional Agriculture** recognises that, in addition to producing commodities, agriculture encompasses other functions, such as maintenance of rural landscapes, protection of the natural and cultural heritage, support of rural economic viability, and enhancement of food security. The Organisation for Economic Cooperation and Development (OECD) perspective of multifunctionality is of an agriculture that *jointly* produces a range of commodity outputs (food and fibre) and also a range of non-commodity outputs, including both positive and negative environmental and social products and services.

Quantification of the relative size of the different dimensions of multifunctional agriculture is necessary to achieve a better understanding of the European Model of Agriculture and its further development. Outlined below is a preliminary perspective

---

6 Patrick Crehan & Liam Downey, *Blueprints for Foresight Actions in Regions: Agriblue – Sustainable Territorial Development of Rural Areas in Europe* (Office for the Official Publications of the European Communities, 2004).

of multifunctional livestock production in Ireland. This is envisaged as comprising the following six dimensions: commodity value, rural viability, environment, food safety, food quality, and animal welfare. The method by which the relative scale of the six dimensions was estimated is described in the Appendix (page 139).

Nationally, the commodity value of multifunctional agriculture is envisaged as accounting for roughly half the gross output value of livestock farming (Figure 1a). Together with rural viability (20%) and the environment (10%), it may account for up to 80% of the total gross output value. The value of food safety is envisaged as being about the same order of magnitude as that of the environment, and it is accordingly assigned a weighting of 10%. The value of each of the other two consumer dimensions of multifunctionality, namely food quality and animal welfare/health, is smaller and each is accordingly allocated a weighting of 5%. However, given that dairy farmers are paid on the basis of the microbial quality and composition of milk, and also taking into account the grading of cattle carcasses at slaughter plants, the weighting attributed to food quality may in reality be somewhat larger than that given to animal welfare/health.

Figure 1. Perspectives of the relative size of the different dimensions of multifunctional livestock production

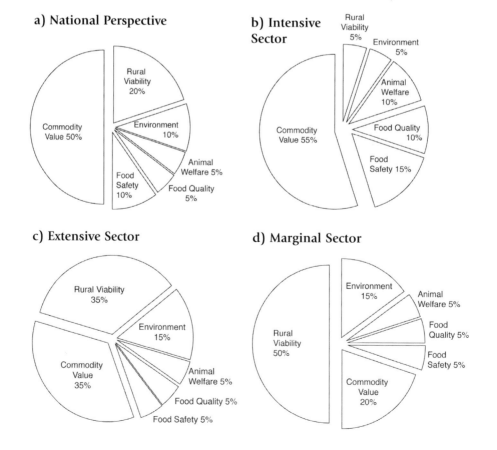

The overall national picture, however, masks major differences in the relative value of these multifunctionality dimensions in the intensive, extensive and marginal farming areas. Dairy farming best reflects the intensive sector in Irish agriculture. Accordingly, the weightings attributable in this intensive sector to the commodity value (55%) and the three consumer dimensions of multi-functionality, namely food safety (15%), food quality (10%) and animal welfare/health (10%), are each envisaged as being somewhat greater than in the national perspective (Figure 1b). These four components of intensive livestock production are seen as accounting for some 90% of the value of the gross output of the sector. The contributions of the environment and rural viability are small (possibly 5% each).

Using cattle rearing as a model for the extensive sector, the weightings attributed to the commodity value (35%), food safety (5%), food quality (5%) and animal welfare/health dimensions (5%), are substantially less relative to intensive dairy farming (Figure 1c). Conversely, as reflected by the proportion of the value of gross output related to direct payments to farmers (in terms of subsidies, headage payments and the Rural Environment Protection Scheme [REPS]), the weightings given to the rural viability (35%) and environmental (15%) dimensions are significantly higher than for dairying. These two components together are seen as accounting for some 50% of the gross multifunctional value of the extensive farming sector.

Marginal farming in Ireland is best represented by hill sheep farming. The commodity value of this sector is relatively low – possibly no more than 20% (Figure 1d). The weightings attributed to the three consumer dimensions of food safety, food quality and animal welfare/health in marginal agriculture each amount to 5% or less of the value of gross output. In reality, it is doubtful if together they account for 15% of the real value of gross output. As reflected by the proportion of the value of gross output related to direct payments to farmers (in terms of subsidies/headage payments and the REPS), rural viability (50%) and the environment (15%) are seen to be the two main components of the value of the gross output of marginal farming – together these account for two thirds or more of the value of the multifunctional output of the sector.

What is knowledge based agriculture?

A new paradigm for competitive agriculture

Throughout the 1970s and 80s, competitiveness in agriculture was largely seen as a one-dimensional requirement for price competitiveness, or profit maximisation. This has lead to an inexorable development of intensive farming systems. Although this strategy has been highly successful in producing cheap food, it has often come at the cost of increased environmental, food safety and quality problems, as well as animal welfare concerns. It also necessitated the introduction of EU intervention and set-a-side policies to deal with production surpluses. Furthermore, the knowledge-base created by this approach has done little to support regional viability in inherently less productive areas where extensive and marginal agriculture are the norm.

As is implicit from the perspectives of multifunctional agriculture outlined above, fundamental changes are now taking place in the conventional understanding of agri-food competitiveness. Today, environmental sustainability is an accepted tenet of agriculture and food processing. In addition to the protection of natural and cultural heritage, maintaining a high quality rural environment is essential from the viewpoint of safe food production. Environmental quality and food safety, combined with other quality-oriented dimensions, including concern for nutritional value and animal welfare, are now central to the longer-term international competitiveness of the agri-food industry. A most challenging additional component is also being added, namely biotechnology. Notwithstanding its potential to improve productivity and combat pest and disease problems, biotechnology will not be readily accepted by society until it has been shown to have no adverse effects but has, on the contrary, demonstrable benefits, especially in terms of food safety and quality.

Countries that achieve an optimum balance between generating profits from the production and processing of food, and at the same time respond to society and consumers' increasing quality requirements and concerns, will succeed best in the immediate years ahead. Attainment of this critical balance will require much closer integration of agronomic, environmental, food safety and economic research and expertise to underpin the development of a knowledge-based agriculture.

Knowledge-based multifunctional agriculture

The perspectives of multifunctional agriculture presented earlier clearly show that, in many rural regions, environmental and socio-economic circumstances mean that the non-commodity outputs of agriculture are now more important than commodity production. A new more flexible approach to the creation and use of knowledge to strategically support agriculture in the intensive, extensive and marginal areas is clearly required. Integration of knowledge from a variety of disciplines is essential in order to ensure that agricultural production systems are developed which optimise the wider economic impact of the sector on rural economies. Such a new paradigm for the support of agriculture would also necessarily result in the development of more 'ecologically-attuned' production systems that address the rapidly growing consumer-related dimensions of agricultural competitiveness. This applies equally well to intensive, extensive and marginal farming systems, and offers a much better prospect of achieving environmental, economic and social sustainability in rural regions. The recent reform of the CAP, with its much greater emphasis on the rural environment, food quality and safety, makes such a goal a realistic possibility. Attainment of this goal will require an integrated knowledge-base to support the development of the multifunctional European Model of Agriculture.

In the past decade, the consumer-oriented aspects of food safety and quality and animal welfare have been seen as the more knowledge intensive. This is reflected in much expanded research programmes being undertaken internationally, and also in Ireland, on these aspects of multifunctionality. The knowledge requirement of the environmental dimension of agriculture has, however, been persistently and grossly underestimated, as is evident from the relatively low level of resources committed to research on the interactions between agriculture and the environment (see 'The future agricultural research agenda' below). Following the relative success of research over the past sixty years and more in achieving higher levels of farm productivity, the commodity dimension of agriculture is now commonly seen as having its knowledge needs more or less provided for, with further support for agronomic research becoming difficult to justify. As outlined above, this view is incorrect, and is incompatible with the development of multifunctional agriculture, optimally adapted to regional agronomic, environment and economic requirements.

To drive the development of a sustainable multifunctional agriculture, Ireland must re-position the agri-food sector in the emerging knowledge-based economy. This will require the development of new models of livestock production designed to optimise the multifunctional outputs of agriculture in the different regions described earlier. Cognisance also needs to be taken of the growing demands for *'healthy foods'* (consistent quality and assured safety), otherwise the longer-term international competitiveness of Irish agriculture may be in question. The development of livestock production systems that optimise these multifunctional outputs, and support the continued viability of rural regions, requires the creation of a co-ordinated knowledge-base of economic, agronomic and environmental expertise. To illustrate the type of livestock systems that may be appropriate, three indicative models are outlined:

Indicative models of knowledge-based multifunctional livestock systems

Intensive dairy production

The grossly seasonal spring-calving and grass-based dairy production system, widely practised in Ireland, is designed to maximise farm incomes. The system has however a number of important cost implications, both for farmers and food processors (Figure 2). The strategy of producing milk by matching the cows' lactation pattern to the grass growth season necessitates greater capital costs in processing plant capacity, storage of products and pollution abatement.

To ensure that the complex array of economic, nutritional and genetic parameters involved are fully understood, early attention needs to be given to establishing the overall costs of producing a tonne of cheddar cheese, butter and skim milk powder, and also a range of higher value added products (including functional foods), using different degrees of seasonal milk production, relative to the more uniform milk production patterns in other European countries. Such an economic analysis should have regard to the various parameters summarised in Figure 2. Arguably two of the more adverse consequences of the seasonal milk production systems relate to *dairy product quality* and *animal nutritional requirements*.

Dairy product quality – The seasonal grass system is not optimal from the viewpoint of driving an internationally competitive dairy processing industry, geared to the manufacture of high added value products of consistent quality and shelf-life. The milk produced exhibits marked seasonal fluctuations in composition and associated processability characteristics. This confers gross seasonal variations on the keeping quality of Irish dairy products. Products manufactured from mid-season milk have keeping qualities comparable to the products manufactured by Ireland's main competitors. Conversely, the inadequate compositional characteristics of milk produced in early spring, and especially late-lactation, more or less preclude the manufacture of a number of export dairy products during these months of the year due to gross non-uniform keeping quality[7].

Animal nutritional requirements – Notwithstanding the greater emphasis given to breeding in recent decades, the expected improvements are not evident in milk production. Quantification of the impact of improved nutritional regimes in conjunction with a labour efficient feed delivery system, recently undertaken in Ireland, UK, France and Germany, revealed sizeable improvements in feed conversion efficiency, annual protein levels and milk yields[8]. Conversely, the fat content of the milk remained relatively unchanged. These improvements involved increased use of farm-grown feeds, with consequential savings in concentrate feed costs. They were attended by higher labour productivity and possibly also reduced animal infertility. The overall improvements in animal performance recorded, indicate that the grass/silage based spring calving system is nutritionally inadequate to deliver on the milk production potential created by the genetic improvements in dairy herds in recent decades.

Figure 2. Cost of seasonal versus uniform milk production

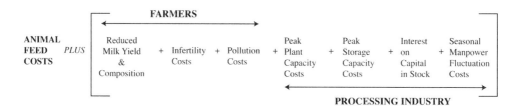

A comprehensive review has recently been published on the reproductive performance in Irish dairy herds[9]. The review concludes that the reproductive needs of a seasonal dairy industry with a compact breeding season may not be compatible with North American Holstein Friesian genetics which originated in an all-year-round-calving dairy industry. The review goes on to point out that strategies are required to improve or halt the decline in reproductive performance, notably the growing infertility

[7] Liam Downey & Michael Brennan, 'The Irish Food Industry – Accelerating Growth for Profit', *Institute of Food Science and Technology Seminar* (Dublin: The Stationary Office, 1976).

[8] Enda Quinn, Charles Purcell, M.P. Vossa, & Liam Downey, 'Quantification of the Impact of TMR Feeding on Dairy & Beef Farms', *RC Dairylink*, (University of Reading, 2004), Edition 1, pp. 16-19.

[9] John F. Mee, 'Temporal Trends in Reproductive Performance in Irish Dairy Herds and Associated Risk Factors', *Irish Veterinary Journal*, 2004, **57**, p. 158.

problem, through the use of feeding systems designed to reduce negative energy balance and maintain body condition. In developing such strategies, attention needs to be given to the more extensive use of farm-grown feeds, including whole crop cereals and maize forage and high protein legume crops, in place of expensive imported feed rations, the quality and purity of which may be less assured.

To address the limitations of the seasonal grass-based milk production system, Ireland needs a new model of dairy production that is designed to produce consistent quality raw materials for the food processing industry, based on the development of low-cost nutritional regimes and labour efficient feed delivery systems that match the animal's nutritional requirements and genetic potential. Attainment of this objective will require a strategic research programme on the interactions between the genetic potential and nutritional requirements of high-yielding cows. Genetics creates the potential, nutrition delivers that potential – the key challenge is to achieve the optimum nutritional-genotype interactions. The dilemma for the agricultural industry in this regard is:

- Whether to modify the current grass-based milk production system, through the adoption of nutritionally balanced feeding regimes designed to match the nutritional requirements and genetic potential of high production cows. An important proposition (Dr M. Rath UCD) in this regard is the need to investigate the economic and environmental feasibility of calving a sizeable proportion of the national dairy herd in October/November. While exploiting grazed grass to the optimum in the second half of the lactation, the animals would be maintained over the winter on nutritional regimes and labour efficient feed delivery systems that meet their nutritional requirements, and maximise milk production without compromising animal fertility.
- Alternatively, the industry could adopt a breed such as the New Zealand Friesian, which is more likely to be better suited to the seasonal spring-calving grass-based system, and could provide the basis for a less intensive production system.

Extensive beef production

As already indicated, it is envisaged that, in the coming decade, there may be something in the region of 25,000 to 35,000 farmers engaged mainly in extensive beef production and concentrated largely in the BMW Region. Full-time commercial suckler beef producers, operating farms of 200 acres or more, are unlikely to exceed 2,000 in number. The sector will comprise predominately part-time farmers with possibly forty suckler cows and supplying stock to large-scale finishers (upwards of 500 cattle) in the Leinster counties.

To provide a good return on investment, both capital and human, and ensure competitiveness in international markets, Ireland's beef industry must be re-positioned in the emerging knowledge economy. This will require the development of a *low-input quality-output model* of extensive beef production, designed to optimise labour productivity in the production of consistent quality beef of assured safety, in a manner that is environmentally sustainable and meets animal welfare requirements. Some important features of the new model would be:

- The production of the animals required by high priced quality markets.
- Efficient use of the best quality breeding stock available.
- Optimum grassland utilisation.
- Cost effective feed delivery systems and nutritional regimes (involving the use of home-grown feeds) that optimise labour productivity and animal performance.
- Compliance with environment requirements, especially the EU Nitrate Directive, involving improved housing facilities, slurry storage capacity and the increased use of lined out-wintering pads.

Farming in marginal areas

Farming plays a pivotal role in maintaining the environmentally fragile upland and wetland landscapes, notably in the West of Ireland and other marginal farming areas in the midlands counties and elsewhere. It is now a well-attested fact that, initially, land drainage and, more recently, overgrazing have caused extensive environmental degradation in a number of those areas. Another most challenging threat is now emerging, namely the withdrawal of agriculture from areas where inherent productivity is low and the traditional farming practices and systems that have for centuries maintained the character of these rural landscapes are progressively being abandoned.

The best known instance of this is the Burren in Co. Clare, where the abandonment of the traditional cattle winterage on the upland limestone pavements is causing the loss of unique botanical diversity and encroachment of archaeological sites. On the Burren limestone, botanical species diversity is optimal under winter grazing at appropriate stocking levels. On poorly grazed sites, species diversity is significantly reduced – on average by 18% – due to competition from rank grasses, litter and mosses, and the gradual encroachment of scrub.

With stocking levels in the Burren areas as a whole now at an all time high, cattle are increasingly concentrated on more productive lowland pastures, where they are causing severe damage. Thus two environmental pressures of growing concern are now simultaneously impacting on the Burren region. These are agricultural abandonment of the upland Burren and micro-intensification of the lowland pastures. Allied to this is the fact that no stocking requirements are attached to the Decoupled/Single Payment System introduced in the recent reform of the CAP. In these circumstances, some farmers will destock, resulting in more widespread under-grazing and scrub encroachment. However, to reduce labour requirements, others will switch from suckler cows to 1–2 year old cattle. Since the latter can graze more intensely, this may to some degree alleviate scrub encroachment on the pavement.

Many other traditional anthropogenic upland and wetland landscapes, especially along the western seaboard, are to varying degrees experiencing similar environmental degradation. This is being caused by changing socio-economic circumstances, including the type of cattle required by markets, and increasingly labour scarcity on farms. The provision of public goods, especially environmental products and services will, in the immediate years ahead, be the primary function of multifunctional agriculture in these marginally productive regions. This will require the development of knowledge-integrated animal husbandry and environmental management systems designed to maintain optimum grazing pressure on under-utilised areas. Some important features of a *new model of conservation grazing* in marginal farming regions include:

- Increased grazing pressure through improved stock access, control and deployment on under-grazed and abandonment areas. The expected shift, already mentioned, from suckler cows to 1–2 year old cattle that can be left longer on winterages will facilitate the strategy of maintaining optimum grazing pressure.
- Cattle deployed in marginal farming regions (currently largely unsuited continental breeds) need to be good foragers that can roam upland areas and eat course grasses and browse scrub vegetation.
- Curtailment of silage, which is environmentally unsustainable, becoming increasingly expensive, and reduces animal grazing, and its replacement with low cost and labour efficient concentrate based feeding systems that stimulate rumen activity and encourage cattle to graze more extensively.

The future agricultural research agenda

The models of livestock production outlined earlier point to the need for a major step-change in Ireland's agricultural research agenda. As previously indicated, the knowledge intensity of the environmental dimension of multifunctional agriculture is habitually underestimated. A better understanding of the complex and diverse interactions between agriculture and the environment is a prerequisite to the development of new models of agricultural production that are economically and environmentally sustainable. To address this requirement there is a pressing need for a *Rural Environment Research Centre* as further detailed below. Among the other important themes that should constitute the core elements of future research in agriculture, the following are of paramount importance:

- Establishment of the optimum nutritional-genotype interactions in dairy and beef production.
- Production of low-cost consistent quality raw materials for the dairy food processing industry.

- Development of integrated agricultural production and food processing systems that match local circumstances and are economically and environmentally sustainable.
- Attainment of the optimum balance between price-competitiveness and society's growing concerns in relation to food safety and quality, the environment and animal welfare.
- Quantification of the costs and benefits of environmental policies, EU Directives, legislation/regulations and agri-environment schemes, and also establishment of the value of public goods associated with agriculture.
- Development of enhanced pest and disease resistance in livestock and cereals and other crops.
- Establishment of national capabilities in agri-food biotechnology.

Research on these themes should be undertaken by consortia of public agencies and private companies, in particular those that have the necessary in-house expertise and technological absorptive capacity to raise the quality and output of dairy and beef production. The potential exists for Ireland to attain an international leadership position in developing the integrated nutritional-engineering solutions required for the production of consumer food products of consistent quality and assured safety. This would reposition Ireland's traditional commodity based agri-food industry in the emerging knowledge-based economy.

The need for a Rural Environment Research Centre

Ireland's environmental research capacity is characterised by fragmentation, lack of critical mass, discontinuity and little overall cohesion. The pockets of high quality research groups in the Universities and Teagasc (The Agriculture and Food Development Authority) individually do not have the capacity to effectively address rural environmental problems of major national importance. Also, with much of the research being undertaken on a short-term contract basis, discontinuity is another adverse feature of the current situation. Allied to this, major gaps and weaknesses exist in such vital capabilities as modelling, hydrology, baseline data, and monitoring protocols, as well as the provision of modern scientific facilities.

If the current inadequate commitment to research in these areas persists, and new environmental measures continue to be introduced without any proper research base, then there is every possibility that the *Rural Environment will become Ireland's new Bovine TB Saga*. Following the undertaking of a limited research programme in the 1990s, it became immediately evident that bovine TB cannot be eradicated in Ireland, but it can be controlled. Unless a comprehensive well-focused environmental research base is put in place, *'one hunch after another'* will be tried to address what has become a growing national concern namely – *'What will Rural Ireland look like in the coming decade(s)?'.*

To strike the optimum balance between the economic dictates of an internationally competitive agri-food industry allied to a sustainable rural economy, and the protection of Ireland's rich heritage of natural and cultural resources, more concerted rural environment research is a national imperative. By building on the nucleus of high quality research and the basic scientific infrastructure in the Universities and Teagasc, this can be most readily provided in a cost-effective manner, through the establishment of a Rural Environment Research Centre. The proposed Centre would be a National Network of Excellence, involving a consortium of the Universities, Teagasc, the Environmental Protection Agency and other relevant organisations. In addition to the intrinsic benefits derived from its own outputs, the scientific and policy-oriented research undertaken by the Centre would act as a strong integrating force in drawing the on-going environmental research conducted by the constituent institutions into a nationally co-ordinated programme, with the focus and capacity to address major national environmental issues. The function, mission and corporate goals of the proposed Centre are outlined below:

Provision of the integrated scientific and policy oriented research base necessary for the effective management, protection and sustainable development of the rural environment would be the primary function of the proposed integrated Rural Environment Research Centre. This is an essential requirement for the further development and proper implementation of environmental policies, EU Directives, legislation and agri-environment schemes designed to accommodate the dynamic range of economic and social pressures that are impacting on Ireland's rural areas. The diverse, complex and fragile processes that underlie the economic and environmental sustainability of rural areas need to be better understood in order to be managed effectively.

The mission of the proposed Centre would be to provide research based understanding of the fundamental chemical, biological, pedological, engineering and socio-economic pressures required to achieve the optimum balance between the economic dictates of the agri-food industry allied to the sustainable rural economy, and the protection of Ireland's rural environment. The integrated scientific and policy oriented research programme of the proposed Centre would include water, air and soil quality, biodiversity, forestry, the rural landscape and environmental economics/legislation. The corporate goals of the Centre in respect of each of these dimensions of environmental research are:

- *Water, Air and Soil Quality*
  To develop the enhanced scientific and engineering knowledge required to protect water, air and soil quality in a cost-effective manner.
- *Biodiversity*
  To develop the scientific understanding of ecological processes that is necessary for the effective management, conservation and economic utilisation of biodiversity and the sustainability of rural ecosystems.

- *Forestry*
  To improve the scientific and technological knowledge required to maximise the ecological, social and economic contributions of sustainably managed forests.
- *Rural Landscape*
  To provide the research capability to guide policy formation in relation to the protection of Ireland's archaeological heritage, and the development of sustainable rural settlement strategies and landscapes.
- *Environment Economics/Legislation*
  To quantify the costs and benefits of environmental policies, EU Directives, legislation/regulations and financial incentives, and establish the value of public goods associated with agriculture and forestry.

Public Goods Incentives

Total expenditure on the REPS since its beginning in 1994 up to October 2003 amounts to €1.3 billion[10]. Over half of this was expended in the less intensive farming counties in the BMW Region. Participation rates in the intensive farming counties (12–17% of farmers) are roughly half that of the western counties (30–35%). Some 40,000 farmers currently participate in REPS. This number is projected to increase to 60,000–70,000 by 2006.

In addition to increasing the family farm incomes of participants by roughly €100 per hectare, REPS has been instrumental in reducing fertiliser usage and protection of habitats. It also may have contributed to arresting the deterioration in water quality. Overall, however, environmental improvements are happening at a slower rate than had been expected, and are not yet evident in terms of biodiversity and archaeological heritage. Clearly, a higher rate of participation not just by the less intensive cattle and sheep producers, but more especially by intensive dairy farmers, would be necessary for REPS to have demonstrably beneficial impacts on the natural and cultural environment. This is not likely to happen. With the restrictions on production intensity in terms of stocking rates and fertiliser usage, participation in REPS will be largely confined to marginal and extensive producers. This will not reduce the prevalence of environmentally insensitive farming and is incompatible with developing the public goods value of multifunctional agriculture.

A conceptual overview of the public goods provision of different intensities of agriculture is illustrated in Figure 3. This Figure, developed in collaboration with Dr J. Finn (Teagasc), compares the levels of public goods provision achievable through: (1) enforcement of regulations (legislation, EU Directives etc.), (2) REPS-type schemes relative to (3) the greater potential that exists and which may be achievable through the introduction of knowledge-based innovative landscape management incentives for all farmers.

---

[10] John Carty, 'Current States and Evaluation of REPS 2', in *Proceeding of the National REPS Conference* (Tullamore: Department of Agriculture & Food, 2003) pp. 1-10.

Figure 3. Conceptual representation of the relative magnitude of non-commodity Public Goods provision achievable in agriculture of different intensities by: 1) enforcement of environmental regulations (light grey), 2) current REPS-type schemes based on obligatory limitation of the farm system (mid grey), 3) potentially available from additional landscape management incentives that do not place limitations on the production system (dark grey).

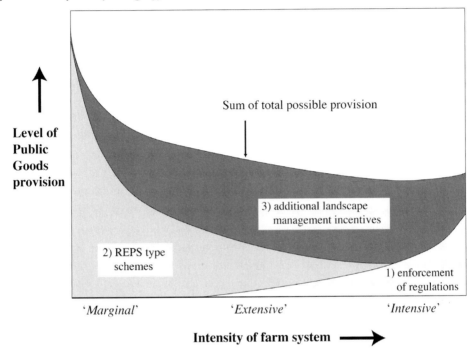

Currently, two different but mutually supportive approaches are being taken to the environmental dimension of multifunctional agriculture. *Firstly,* financial incentives are being provided through REPS to encourage environmentally compatible farming. However, as already explained, the impact of these incentives is largely confined to the marginal and smaller extensive farms. *Secondly,* a growing body of environmental legislation and EU Directives is being put in place to control environmental degradation caused by farming. These impact to a greater degree on intensive farms (Figure 3). While beneficial in reducing the negative externalities of farming by maintaining minimum environmental standards, these measures are not *per se* concerned with developing positive public goods value in agriculture.

Farmers occupy a key position as managers of the rural environment. To capitalise on the full public goods potential of agriculture, and to optimise its contribution to rural economies, additional landscape management incentives are required. In particular, early consideration needs to be given to the introduction of *Public Goods Incentives* designed to encourage all farmers, especially intensive producers, to manage the rural landscape and optimise the level of public goods provision, without penalty to the economic competitiveness of the production system. Instead of subsidising farmers to produce commodities for oversupplied markets, a compelling case can be made for knowledge-based and innovative *Public Goods Payments* for the conservation and management of natural habitats, archaeological sites and field boundaries. These heritage resources are under greatest threat in the most intensive farming areas where competition from other land uses are also greatest and add to the pressures on the natural and cultural landscape.

To maintain biodiversity and the aesthetic appearance of the countryside within intensively farmed landscapes, these incentives could be provided for the protection of natural habitats and the maintenance of field boundaries, located outside the main agricultural production areas. This would minimise the impact on farm productivity and the level of incentives required.

Unlike REPS, the proposed *Public Goods Incentives*, should not have predetermined limitations on farm production. In addition to the conservation of specified heritage sites, payment of the incentives would be conditional on adherence to environmental regulations and Good Farming Practice[11] and the concept of Good Agriculture Condition (GAC). Also, the incentives could be devised so as to address the growing problem of public access to archaeological sites and other amenity areas.

The introduction of agri-environment incentives, along the lines outlined above, would support the further development of multifunctional agriculture. They would be most beneficial, if not essential, for the transition of traditional agriculture to the production of market-required quality food products in a manner compatible with environmental and animal welfare requirements, as envisaged in the recent fundamental reforms of the CAP. Funding for the proposed *Public Good Incentives* could be provided from the Rural Development Fund established under these reforms.

---

[11] Anon., *Good Farming Practice* (Dublin: Department of Agriculture, Food, and Rural Development, 2001).

Appendix 1

Using the Teagasc National Farm Survey results for 2002, estimates of the parameters listed below were derived for three types of livestock farms namely: (1) intensive livestock farms, as reflected by dairy farming, (2) extensive livestock farms as reflected by cattle rearing and (3) marginal livestock farms, as reflected by hill sheep farming.

a) The value of farm gross output.
b) Direct payments to farmers related to farm output. These could be considered to be payments to maintain people in farming and were accordingly used as an index of the proportion of the value of gross output attributable to the value of *rural viability.*
c) Direct payments to farmers for participation in REPS were used to indicate the value to society of environmental goods provided by agricultural activity.
d) Market value of the output was derived by subtracting the sum of (b)+(c) from (a).
e) *Commodity value* was derived by subtracting from (d) above, the sum of the values attributed to each of the three consumer dimensions of multifunctional agriculture – namely *food safety, food quality & animal welfare.*
f) Consumer dimensions. Although subjective, the proportion of the market value of output attributed to each of the three consumer dimensions of multi-functionality is based on a comprehensive understanding of Irish livestock farming and its three main constituent components, namely dairying, cattle rearing and hill-sheep production.

While the individual weightings attributed to food safety, food quality and animal welfare are largely judgmental, the values attributed to these is based on the premise that no one of these components is currently larger than the environmental dimension. Based on direct payments for REPS, this amounts to some 10% of the value of gross output (c above).

It should be noted that the weightings given to the six dimensions of multi-functionality are rounded-off to the nearest 5% and that the smallest dimensions are allocated a weighting of 5%. In the circumstances finer weightings would not be justified.

Acknowledgements

Valuable contributions and advice were received from a number of colleagues in University College Dublin, the National University of Ireland Maynooth, Teagasc, and Richard Keenan & Co. Ltd, in compiling this paper. The contributions received from M. Boland, B. Riordan, M. Downes, L. Harte, S. Regan, T. Shanahan, J. Burke, J. Whiriskey, E. Quinn, J. Giggens, P. Cunningham and others is gratefully acknowledged. The professional assistance of Rhona Bradshaw in preparing this paper for publication is much appreciated.

CHAPTER 6

Forestry in the Twenty-first Century

Edward P. Farrell

The beginnings of modern forestry

When the British Association visited Ireland in the late nineteenth century, the forests of Ireland had been exploited almost to extinction. Today, we have a thriving forest industry. A resource which was lost has been restored. This essay will explore this process of restoration, consider what it means for the country today and how forestry might develop in the twenty-first century.

The native woodlands of Ireland, broadleaved forest of oak (*Quercus spp*), ash (*Fraxinus excelsior* L.) and elm (*Ulmus glabra*, Hudson), were depleted gradually over many centuries. The establishment of the large estates and the building of the great houses in the eighteenth century slowed the process to some extent, as the landlords took a keen interest in both arboriculture and forestry. However, the decline of these estates in the last decades of the nineteenth century led to an acceleration of the rate of deforestation. By 1900, less than 1.5% of the country was under forest.

The Land Acts, which gave ownership of the land to the former tenant farmers, created a new class of small farm owners for whom the land was their sole livelihood. This land had been hard won. In the eyes of the new owners, it was intended for the production of food for their families and for the nation; the famine, after all, was a recent memory and emigration an ever-present reality. These new landowners had little interest in forests, which they associated with the landlords, and they would have no sympathy for any proposal to afforest land which could be considered to have a potential for agriculture. Thus, in the 1920s, the new independent Ireland adopted a rigid policy of prohibiting afforestation on land suitable for agriculture, a policy that was implemented with varying degrees of zeal until the mid-1980s[1].

The new Forest Service (several variations of the name were used at different times, but for simplicity, it will be referred to throughout as the 'Forest Service', its current title), established in 1904, began the process of afforesting land, much of which had been treeless for centuries. Progress was slow until the 1950s, when a vigorous policy of afforestation was adopted – still confined, of course, to land unsuited to agriculture.

---

[1] E.P. Farrell, 'Land Acquisition for Forestry', in J. Blackwell & F.J. Convery (Eds), *Promise and Performance* (Dublin: Resource and Environmental Policy Centre, University College Dublin, 1983), pp. 155-167.

A series of measures, supported by funding from the European Union, led to significant increases in the rate of afforestation in the closing decades of the twentieth century. Restrictions on the planting of agricultural land were relaxed and this move, together with the provision of improved incentives to encourage private planting, led to the afforestation of smaller units, often on land of much higher quality than ever before. Almost 10% of the land area is now under forest and forest based industries have now become an important element of the rural economy.

Irish forestry today

The Irish forest estate is intensively managed, focused on maximizing productivity and return on investment. Market demand for softwoods, suitability of available land, and potential financial return, have resulted in the forest industry being almost totally reliant on coniferous species. Yew (*Taxus bacccata L.*) is the only coniferous forest species native to Ireland. This has meant that all extensive coniferous plantations are comprised of introduced species, mainly from North America. These species can tolerate difficult site conditions and offer a far higher rate of return than native broadleaved species.

A range of species was planted in the past but, as time went on, foresters came to rely heavily on two, Sitka spruce (*Picea sitchensis* Bong. Carr.) and lodgepole pine (*Pinus contorta* L.), often planted in monoculture. This reliance on a small number of introduced species, which is based mainly on economic considerations, is undesirable from an ecological point of view. It reduces biodiversity in plantation forests and it carries the risk of a pathogen or pest attack reaching epidemic proportions. The Forest Service now promotes biodiversity in plantation forests and encourages owners to favour broadleaved species, particularly native species, wherever possible while, in conifer plantations, the use of more than one species is favoured. The afforestation of former agricultural land of higher quality has also led to increased species diversification; in addition, the Forest Service offers greater incentives for the planting of broadleaved species.

For the past two hundred years, the management of forests has been based on the principle of sustained yield. This principle protects against over cutting, ensuring that the harvest does not exceed the growth of the forest as a whole. It can be applied at forest, regional or national scale, and implies that the productive capacity of the soil can be maintained, in perpetuity. The principle of sustained yield is therefore a principle of sustainable development. It is, however, limited in scope, focusing solely on the capacity of the forest to produce timber. Modern society makes increased demands on the forest. The plantation forest is an artificial ecosystem, interacting with the wider environment. The planning, establishment and management of a plantation forest has implications for the environment and can impact, for instance, on water quality, and the concentration of greenhouse gases in the earth's atmosphere. Society sees other values in forests. It expects to be able to use plantation forests for recreation. Forest users require forests that are aesthetically pleasing and they reject large blocks of single species plantations, abrupt forest boundaries and large clearfells. The principle of sustained yield is too narrow to accommodate these multiple functions of the forest, and so it has been superseded by the principle of sustainable forest management. This principle, is better suited to the modern view of the forest.

The criteria upon which the sustainable management of the forests of Europe should be based were agreed at the Ministerial Conference on the Protection of Forests in Europe, in Lisbon, in 1988. Indicators, measures of progress towards sustainable forest management, have been developed at European level and adapted, in many cases, to local conditions: in Ireland, in the National Forest Standard[2]. The emergence of the concept of sustainable forest management has inspired a worldwide movement to force wood producers to establish that their timber has been harvested from forests which have been managed in a sustainable manner. A process of certification has been developed to which major producers have been encouraged to subscribe. There can be no doubting the environmental benefits that have flowed from this movement. In Ireland, the Forest Service has developed environmental guidelines and a code of best forest practice, which have increased environmental awareness of foresters and have resulted in significant improvements in the siting and management of plantation forests. Research on ecosystem processes and the interaction of forests with the environment have contributed to these improvements. As a result, many of the mistakes made in the past, which resulted in a degradation of environmental quality (by acidification, eutrophication, negative impacts on biodiversity and scenic value) will not be repeated, although some existing problems will persist for some time to come. It seems likely that some of the most unsuitable sites afforested in the past, notably some of the blanket peatland forests in the west, will not be reforested, and research is currently underway on the best approach to returning them to their natural condition.

The difficulty with this essentially good movement to promote the sustainable management of forests is that it creates an illusion of sustainability that cannot be scientifically validated. The indicators of sustainable forest management which are used in the certification process set high standards of management and contribute to the protection of the environment. Unfortunately, their relevance to the sustainability of forest ecosystems is limited. Sustainable forest management, while at first glance straightforward, is a difficult concept, clouded by temporal and spatial issues and by the dynamic nature of ecosystems. Should the principles of sustainable forest management be implemented at forest, regional or national level? What is the time horizon within which we assess sustainability – 100 years, 1000 years, infinity?

Fundamentally, what are the natural trends of development of the ecosystem or the soil, and how do they impact on the sustainability of the forest ecosystem? All crop production, including the growing of forests for harvest, generates acidity in the soil (the farmer regularly corrects this acidification by liming the soil). In Ireland, the general direction of soil development, influenced principally by our rainfall levels, is towards acidification, involving a slow, but inevitable, degradation of the soil. This

[2] Anon., *Irish National Forest Standard* (Dublin: Forest Service, 2000)

raises a question as to whether any ecosystem in our climate can be truly sustainable. The problems inherent in the concept of sustainability and its implementation have been well summarized by Bell and Morse who, in 1999, described the quest for sustainability as 'chasing a moving shadow'[3]. They write:

> The situation appears to be that, at the end of the 20th century, a word has been decided upon to conjure up the desirable outcome of social and political endeavours. Scientists and professionals have taken (or been given) the impossible task of achieving definitive measurement of this word. The impossible task was to measure what was never potentially measurable: the immeasurable 'sustainability'.

The long-term nature of the forest enterprise (coniferous forests in Ireland are managed typically on a rotation of about forty five years) demands a consistency of approach and a conservative attitude to management. It may be surprising then to learn that, in this respect, not only has forestry in Ireland experienced enormous change in the past decade, but it is anticipated that the rate of change itself will continue to accelerate in the immediate future. There is widespread recognition that mistakes were made in the past and that decisions on the location of forests were taken with little knowledge or account of their environmental consequences. The large-scale afforestation of the blanket peatlands of the west is a good example. In the 1960s and 1970s, blanket peatland afforestation was seen as a socially desirable exploitation of a neglected resource. Large tracts of naturally treeless peatland, mainly in Galway, Mayo and Donegal, were drained and cultivated using specially adapted machinery. Plantations of Sitka spruce and lodgepole pine, often in mixture, were established. Nutritional difficulties, experienced in the early years, were overcome through research, and a remarkably high level of productivity achieved. However, despite the technical achievement, the economic benefits of the peatland forestry enterprise were always marginal. The inherently wet site conditions continued to cause problems for crop stability. More importantly, the ecological value of these peatlands, in their natural state, came to be recognised. Peatland afforestation continues, but at a much reduced rate and accompanied by a range of environmental restrictions.

The planting of large blocks of coniferous monoculture is more controversial. Forest Service guidelines (which are in effect regulations since grant-aid is dependent on compliance) require diversification in all plantations where site conditions allow. Critics of Irish forestry would go further, some calling for severe restrictions, if not a complete ban, on the use of introduced coniferous species. Fundamentally, this is an issue of sustainability. In Central Europe there is concern that plantation forests of Norway spruce and Scots pine, established in regions far beyond their natural range, may be particularly susceptible to environmental stress factors and consequently may

---

[3] S. Bell & S. Morse, *Sustainability Indicators, Measuring the Immeasurable?* (London: Earthscan, 1999), pp. 175.

be inherently unsustainable[4,5]. This raises the question as to the long-term sustainability of even-aged, coniferous plantations, of one or several species, in Ireland. As yet, there is no definitive answer to this question. Almost certainly, the sustainability of any plantation forest is site-dependent; forests on thin acid soils derived from nutrient-poor rocks are more vulnerable and less likely to be sustainable in the long-term than those on more fertile site types. However, as yet no objective quantitative measures of sustainability have been developed to the point of widespread acceptance. The disturbance effect of afforestation, and perhaps also of reforestation following clearfelling, further complicates the application of objective indicators of sustainability.

In summary, the changes that have taken place in Irish forestry practice will undoubtedly yield ecological benefits far into the future. Our forests will have a higher degree of biodiversity, and the heightened awareness of the need to protect the environment at all phases of the forest cycle has brought about a permanent change in the mindset of foresters.

The future

In 1996, the Government published a strategy document which set ambitious targets for afforestation to the year 2030[6]. This set a target for national forest cover of 17% of the land area. Twenty years ago, virtually all afforestation was carried out by the State. Today, State afforestation has fallen to practically zero, while and the number of private forest owners has increased to 14,000. Undoubtedly, the focus in future planting will continue to be on the private sector; the aim being to take farmers out of agriculture by converting their land to forestry with support from the European Union. The number of part-time farmers in the country is increasing. They hold down full-time, off-farm jobs and run their farms in the evenings and at weekends. While the commitment of these part-time farmers to agriculture is relatively low, their identification with the land and their determination to maintain ownership of it is high. Incentives for afforestation, which covered the cost of forest crop establishment and, in addition, provided an income from the land during the early decades of the life of the plantation, are very attractive. Afforestation grants are weighted to encourage the use of broadleaved species. An annual premium, again higher for broadleaved than for coniferous plantations, provides an income from the land for the first twenty years of the life of the plantation.

---

4 Heinrich Spiecker, Jörg Hansen, Hubert Hasenauer, Emil Klimo, Jens Peter Skovsgaard, Hubert Sterba & Konstantin von Teuffel, 'Glossary of Terms and Definitions Relevant for Norway Spruce Conversion in Europe: An Open Question?', in Heinrich Spiecker, Jörg Hansen, Emil Klimo, Jens Peter Skovsgaard, Hubert Sterba and Konstantin von Teuffel (Eds), *Norway Spruce Conversion – Options and Consequences* (Leiden: Brill, 2004), European Forest Institute Research Report 18, pp. 1-4.

5 Jiři Kulhavý, Torsten Bergerm, Vladimír Čaboun, Axel Gottlein, Blahomil Grunda, Richard Heitz, Petr Kantor, Emil Klimo, Bohumír Lomský, Stanislav Niemtur, Karl-Eugen Rehfuess, Marian Slodičák, Hubert Sterba & Lars Vesterdal, 'Ecological Consequences of Conversion', in Heinrich Spiecker, Jörg Hansen, Emil Klimo, Jens Peter Skovsgaard, Hubert Sterba and Konstantin von Teuffel (Eds), *Norway Spruce Conversion – Options and Consequences* (Leiden: Brill, 2004), European Forest Institute Research Report 18, pp. 165-195.

6 Anon., *Growing for the Future; A Strategic Plan for the Development of the Forestry Sector in Ireland* (Dublin: Forest Service, 1996).

Despite these incentivesis, afforestation targets have not been reached. An alternative scheme to promote more environmentally friendly farming has proved an attractive alternative to some farmers. Confidence in the industry has also been damaged by fluctuating government support for afforestation.

The policy of encouraging small private landowners to convert land to forestry has much to recommend it. It is in accordance with European Union policy to take surplus land out of agriculture. It retains ownership of the land in the hands of the farm families and thus offers support to rural communities. The demand for softwood timber continues to grow and, while the opening up of new, and potentially vast, sources of timber in eastern Europe may give some cause for concern for markets in the long-term, prospects are good for the foreseeable future. There are disadvantages, however. It is much more difficult to impose government policy on a large number of private owners with various degrees of interest and expertise than on a small number of large owners with forest estates managed by professionals and a strong commitment to intensive forest management. The creation of numerous small, isolated forest units with poor road infrastructure will inevitably result in serious difficulties at the harvesting stage as they are of little interest to the operators of modern harvesting equipment. The development of harvesting units adapted to such conditions may contribute to a solution to this problem. A review of harvesting systems for small-scale forestry is currently in progress. Equally, the formation of forestry cooperatives would facilitate more efficient management of the industry as a whole.

The policy of species diversification is likely to be continued. The current approach to species diversification has resulted in a major increase in the use of broadleaved species. The establishment and management of broadleavedf plantations raises new challenges for the forest manager. Compared to conifers, the establishment of these species is difficult, and they require a higher level of maintenance if they are to produce high-quality, commercial timber crops. They require a consistent long-term commitment from their owners if they are to be financially successful. High-quality hardwoods attract large premiums precisely because they are difficult to produce and consequently relatively scarce. However, even with levels of financial support much higher than currently provided, it is doubtful if plantations of oak, which require a much longer rotation than conifers, can yield a positive financial return. Other species, such as ash and sycamore, are grown on shorter rotations, about sixty years, but even this is considerably longer than conventional conifer rotations. Given the many difficulties in achieving a satisfactory financial return from these plantations, and the lack of a forestry tradition amongst farm forest owners, the focus for many is on the short-term income from the annual premiums rather than the long-term return from the forest investment. While these forests will undoubtedly make an important contribution to rural biodiversity, it is unlikely that many will yield an economic return, thus reducing the profitability of the sector as a whole.

Little thought has been given, as yet, to the implications for forest owners, public and private, of the multifunctional approach to forest management. Some aspects of the multifunctional forest are mandatory. These include the implementation of regulations, or guidelines for the protection of water or the promotion of biodiversity. Other aspects, such as the opening of the forests for recreation, are optional, at present. A third category, which may yield a financial return, includes the carbon sequestration potential of the forest.

All growing plants remove carbon dioxide from the atmosphere which they incorporate into their tissues. Human activity, principally the burning of fossil fuels, releases to the atmosphere carbon which had been held in the earth for many millions of years. This is responsible for increases in the concentrations of carbon dioxide and other greenhouse gases in the atmosphere which, it is believed, contributes to climate change. Because trees are long-lived and their woody parts relatively resistant to decomposition, their ability to sequester carbon is greater than that of other forms of vegetation. Plantation forests, therefore, have the potential to mitigate the impact of human activity on atmospheric concentrations of greenhouse gases.

The Kyoto Protocol to the United Nations Framework Convention on Climate Change (UNFCCC), was developed in 1997 with the goal of stabilizing emissions of greenhouse gases. Signatories to the agreement have made commitments to achieve agreed targets for emissions during the first commitment period, 2008–2012. Ireland's emissions are likely to be well above our commitment level. Afforestation, which has been carried out since 1990, can be offset against emissions in order to meet commitments. It will be possible for forest owners to trade carbon credits in the future, although the value of these is as yet unknown.

There are other ways, in addition to carbon sequestration, in which biomass, and in particular forests, can contribute to the mitigation of greenhouse gas emissions. Wood used as a source of energy is considered to be carbon neutral (carbon sequestered during growth is released on combustion); thus, as a replacement for fossil fuels, it directly reduces emissions. Increased use of wood in buildings prolongs the period of sequestration and reduces emissions associated with the production of more energy intensive building products.

The impact of forestry on rural communities will continue to grow. The increase in timber production, from plantations established in the past twenty years, while it will put severe pressures on the rural infrastructure, particularly the road system, will provide significant downstream economic benefits both in in-forest employment and in the servicing of harvesting and transport operations.

Clearfelling is the only method of harvesting employed in mature forests in Ireland. In other words, while thinnings are removed during the rotation, at the final felling all of the remaining trees are harvested. The drastic changes in the ecosystem associated with clearfelling have a number of negative effects. The sudden removal of the tree canopy which, for twenty or thirty years, had intercepted a significant amount of the incoming rain, results in an immediate increase of 40% or more in the quantity of rainfall reaching the ground. Due to the shading effect of the trees, growth of ground vegetation has been limited so that much of this additional rainfall impacts on bare ground, accelerating erosion and leaching of nutrients with a potential for sediment overload and nutrient enrichment of streams in the vicinity. Other systems, some involving partial removal of the trees in individual stands are used in other countries and research is underway to investigate the use of these, so-called 'continuous cover' systems here[7]. These systems are certainly more attractive from an aesthetic standpoint and are probably more desirable ecologically also. It is likely that public pressure will progressively force a reduction in the size of clearfells and may ultimately result in a total ban on clearfelling in certain areas. Alternative systems, however, will be more difficult to manage, possibly resulting in increased incidence of storm damage, particularly if, as predicted, climate change results in a more severe wind climate.

The impact of forests on water yields, although it has received little attention in Ireland, may well become an issue in important municipal catchments in the future. Forests intercept 30–40% of incoming rainfall. As the proportion of semi-mature forests increases, water yields must, inevitably, fall.

Conclusion

The forest industry has become very significant in Ireland. It is important to ensure that it is supported by a sustainable research infrastructure. COFORD (the National Council for Forest Research and Development) was established in 1992. It has funded forest research in a structured, professional manner. There is an urgent need to ensure that it can continue to do so with assured continuity of funding.

When modern forest practice in Ireland is compared with that in Europe, two major differences emerge. In central and eastern Europe, the widespread use of coniferous species on sites to which broadleaved species are naturally adapted is no longer considered sustainable from an ecological, or even from a commercial point of view. This issue has not, as yet, been given serious consideration by the forestry community in Ireland, nor is it seen as an important issue in other countries in western Europe. Nevertheless, it is an issue, which, through research, should be addressed. It highlights the absence, mentioned above, of objective measures of sustainability. At the other end of the rotation, clearfelling is severely restricted in many European countries. While alternatives to clearfelling have been given some consideration in Ireland in recent years and work is in progress to examine their value and practicality, we are still a long way from their application at operational level.

It is clear that forestry has made extraordinary progress in Ireland. A resource which had been lost has been restored. Some may argue about the nature of that restoration, but it is important to understand the long-term nature of the forestry enterprise. One hundred years on, we have created a new forest resource. In the next one hundred years our view of that resource will change as we seek to realise all the goods and services, economic, aesthetic, environmental and recreational, which the forest can yield.

---

[7] Anon., *COFORD Annual Report 2003* (Dublin: COFORD, pp. 136).

CHAPTER 7

Marine Science

Christopher Moriarty

Introduction

The commissioning of the Research Vessel *Celtic Explorer* in April 2003 marked a major development in Irish marine science. Three times the size of any of her predecessors, her operations extend over Ireland's territorial waters, which cover an area equal to ten times the land mass of the island.

The first observations in marine science in Ireland were made in the seventh century by a scholar named Augustine who commented on coast erosion. A thousand years later, the first experimental observations were recorded when fin-clipping of migrating salmon in the Ballinahinch River in Connemara in the seventeenth century confirmed the homing instincts of the species[1]. In the eighteenth century, the Dublin Society published translations of continental work on fisheries and aquaculture[2]. Subsequently, as the Royal Dublin Society, the same organisation employed the naturalist W. Andrews to embark on scientific studies of Irish sea fisheries and, later in the nineteenth century, conducted a series of fisheries-directed surveys. These included hydrological and ecological studies. At the same time, the Royal Irish Academy organised deep-sea exploration.

Sustained systematic studies date to 1900 when the national fisheries service was established, providing permanent employment for W.S. Green, E.W.L. Holt and others who had taken part in the earlier work. The opening of the Fisheries Research Centre in 1978 and the transfer of its operations to the Marine Institute in 1996 were notable recent landmarks in the development of government involvement in the discipline of marine science. Meanwhile, a number of the universities and institutes of technology developed associated courses and research, of which the major achievement was the establishment of the Martin Ryan Marine Science Institute in University College, Galway (now National University of Ireland, Galway), in 1993. The history of marine science in Ireland, together with observations and reports on many aspects of current work, were covered at a symposium held there in 1995[3].

---

[1] Roderic O'Flaherty, *West or H-Iar Connaught* (Galway: Kenny's Bookshop, 1978), pp. 469.
[2] Charles Mollan, *Nostri Plena Laboris* (Dublin: Royal Dublin Society, 1987), pp. 120.
[3] Brendan F. Keegan & Roseanna O'Connor (Eds), *Irish Marine Science 1995* (Galway: Galway University Press, 1996), pp. 626.

This chapter begins with an outline of fisheries science since, over a long period, the development and maintenance of the fishing industry has been the primary driving force behind marine research. The chapter continues with the aquatic environment. Accepted in the past as being of major significance in understanding all aspects of fisheries biology, the environment was considered beyond the control of humankind. Since the mid twentieth century, the effects of pollution and the impact of toxic algal blooms and other natural phenomena have shown that the human influence is of immense importance and demands increasing attention.

The next topic, aquaculture, has a remarkably long history but, largely as a result of scientific and technological advances, has made major developments in recent decades. The discovery of submarine oil and gas fields, together with spectacular improvements in methodologies for submarine surveying and mining, has led to a great increase in studies of the sea bed, in particular to the establishment of a seven-year national seabed survey. These universal topics are followed by a selection of specialised subjects which illustrate some of the variety of approaches made by the scientific community as custodians of the marine environment. The study ends with an outline of the contribution of research vessels – literally and figuratively the flagships of marine research and development.

Fisheries

The fishing industry is unique in its ultimate dependence on the 'hunter-gatherer', a life style which dominated the scene in Ireland for five thousand years, but has been marginal for as long a period again. The essential feature of hunting is that the husbandry of the stocks – in the sense of planting seed or breeding livestock – is beyond the control of the hunter. Fishing takes the problem a step further because the fishers cannot even see the stocks but have to operate in places where their experience tells them the fish should be. Added to this challenge is the unpredictability of conditions at sea. At worst they make fishing one of the most dangerous of all professions. Rough seas, in any case, can inhibit the operation of fishing boats of every size.

Although science, technology and innovation have brought about profound changes in all aspects of the fishing industry, the hunting element remains an integral part of the system. Sonar scanning has made it possible to get a clear vision of the seabed and for an expert almost to 'see' the shoals of fish. But very significant aspects of the size and welfare of the stocks are still the basis of surmise.

Seventy-six species of marine organisms are listed in the official published catch statistics[4]. That is an underestimate of the variety, since some forms, such as the rays, are not identified to species level and others appear under such headings as 'other flatfish'. The results of sea fishing are reported under three headings: demersal, pelagic and shellfish.

These divisions are based partly on the habitat of the fish and partly on the zoological differences between marine organisms. In plain parlance, the term 'fish' applies to almost any form of marine animal, provided it is big enough to be seen

---

[4] Central Statistics Office Website www.cso.ie

without a microscope. To a zoologist, fishes are creatures which breathe under water by means of gills and which have a vertebral column and fins – a definition which excludes whales and dolphins and a considerable variety of edible invertebrates. The term 'finfish' is becoming increasingly popular to avoid confusion.

Demersal fish live on or near the sea bed, pelagic swim in mid-water or close to the surface. The shellfish for the most part live on the sea bed: some on its surface, others burrowing in sediments. To confuse the issue, squid and cuttlefish are shellfish having fins and gills and no evident shells and swim in midwater. The eggs and young of the demersal fish are pelagic and the eggs of the herring, one of the top pelagic species, are demersal. Nature refuses to be accommodated in rigid boxes.

Fishers and fishery owners are at the coal face of the industry: they are the people whose very livelihood depends on their ability to learn about the behaviour of fish and of the nature of the aquatic environment. While they undoubtedly have the intellectual ability, those engaged in the capture and marketing of fish lack the time, training and equipment to discover essential details of the life cycles, food and population biology of the species on which they depend. This third input to fisheries management demands fulltime attention by considerable numbers of specialists. The need for it became widely accepted by administrators towards the end of the nineteenth century, together with recognition of the fact that the fishing industry was not in a position to fund the required research. This led to the universal situation whereby management of marine fisheries is undertaken by state-funded institutions. At the same time, the importance of international co-operation for creatures 'which recognise no national boundaries' was realised and the International Council for the Exploration of the Sea was established in 1902 – with significant Irish involvement from the start.

The goal at that time was to expand the fishery, by applying the scientific method to the discovery of untapped stocks, by improving boat and gear technology and by improving knowledge of the breeding and migratory habits of the fish. The majority of fishing boats were small and powered by sail and the best scientists believed that the stocks of sea fish were inexhaustible. The development first of steam and next of internal combustion led to bigger boats and smaller manpower and the undreamed of probability that particular stocks could be catastrophically depleted. The age of boom and bust had begun.

The ideal of fisheries management is to discover the level of fishing which permits the attainment of the 'maximum sustainable yield'. The obvious aim for the fishing fleet is to catch as much as it can: better technology and more boats are the key. The 1960s saw bigger and better fleets with improved technology. This expansion ignored the fact that the resource was not infinite. Depletion of the stocks is never immediately apparent. Fishing fleets grow, the catch gets bigger and eventually reaches a peak. Turning that peak into a plateau requires ever increasing fishing effort: more boats and more man-hours. But this is now a case of running to keep standing still. By this stage the fishery has gone long past its maximum economic yield. Boats drop out and can't be sold, and the entire industry contracts.

The risk of any single species of fish being hunted to extinction is minimal and, after lean years which decimate communities of human beings, the fish stocks recover and the cycle can begin again. From the perspective of short-term financial gain, this could well be the best way to manage any fishery. But it ignores the factor of human misery and should not be tolerated in contemporary society. Therefore the sustainable yield, a lower catch which can be maintained indefinitely, must be calculated and applied. The work of the first hundred years of population biology and fishery science, culminating in the 1960s, provided the mathematical models for attaining this goal.

The models are being continually improved and the computer allows the development and manipulation of increasingly complex sets of data. In particular, the traditional models were limited in effectiveness because they applied to single species – and no species exists in isolation. What is more, the entire assemblage of fishes depends on the state of the environment. Environmental factors, depending largely on climate change, have to be added to the equation. The complexity of the situation is one of the reasons for occasional failures in predicting the state of a particular stock. More recent developments take the inter-action between species and between species and the environment into account.

Fish lay astronomical numbers of eggs and this means that a small number of spawners can re-establish a depleted population. More importantly, from the management viewpoint, it means that artificial re-stocking is only very rarely a possible solution. While nature can take care of the eventual survival of the species, management is the only means of sustaining the human population which depends on it.

Every fisher is an enthusiast for conservation – but the individual is equally enthusiastic about maximising his catch and income. Determining the ideal – the 'maximum sustainable yield' or the allied 'maximum economic yield' is the task of a small host of workers ranging, in the case of the European Union, from its Council of Ministers, through a series of international committees of experts to the fisheries scientists and administrators in the individual countries to the teams of technicians who gather the statistics and sample the fish. At all levels the work takes place in communication with the most important sector of all – the fishers, both individually and through their official organisations.

Although cod's roe and caviar are highly esteemed, the eggs and young of the majority of fish species have no great attraction for human consumption. Fish need to be allowed to grow and growth to an acceptable market size takes varying numbers of years. The catch of any species usually comprises fish of a range of ages, making year-by-year management a difficult option. The matter is complicated by the fact that little-known factors profoundly influence the survival of eggs and young. Predictions based on the best current information are often upset by some unpredictable increase or decrease in the success of spawning in one season.

Nonetheless, the science of fish stock assessment – determining the size of the stock rather than the quantity caught – plays an essential role in managing the fishery. It is based on collecting samples of each species in question and determining the age and size frequencies. Additional information comes from surveys of the abundance of the eggs and young and, more and more, from acoustic surveys which can identify and quantify a number of the most important species.

This work is the province of the Marine Institute, established in 1991, which took over the research team of the government – in operation since 1900. The observations of the marine scientists are reported to the International Council for the Exploration of the Sea, through a series of species- and region- orientated Working Groups, which pool the data from all relevant national fisheries. Their calculations determine the size of the stock of each species and its age structure. These lead to recommendations on the 'total allowable catch' and on specific needs to reduce effort or to impose such conservation measures as minimum sizes. The International Council reports to the European Commission and the final decisions – most important of all the Annual Irish Quota – are taken by the Council of Ministers.

The practicalities of fish stock assessment

Quantifying the catch of fish is relatively simple. Effective management, however, requires reliable information on the size of the invisible and inaccessible stock. This section describes, first, the techniques used in stock assessment and, second, the international pooling of those results which forms the basis of the management decisions taken by the European Commission.

A number of techniques for estimating fish numbers have become well established and together they provide a good indication as to the current state of a particular stock. The main methods currently in use, all of which are based on annual monitoring, include analysing:

- – the commercial landings
- – the age structure of the stocks
- – the abundance of eggs and young fish
- – racial and migration studies, and
- – acoustic surveys.

Some of these techniques are simple to apply, others are more sophisticated, but all are labour-intensive because large samples are essential. Furthermore, most of these studies have to be carried out annually and will not yield useful data until a time-series of results has been built up. Accurate stock assessment therefore needs a long-term commitment.

Fortunately, the general principles of fish stock monitoring are the same for all species: the goal is to describe a given stock as fully as possible by reference to population structure, in terms of the length, weight and age of the individuals, and the volume of landings taken from the fishery in a particular year. Annual 'fish stock summaries' are then produced which give an overview of the current status of a fishery.

Analysis of the landings is an extension of the routine collection of statistics. Determining the ages of the fish caught requires trained personnel and complex equipment. Ship-based surveys and tagging involve, in addition to the scientists on board, the costs of the boat, while acoustic surveys require in addition specialist workers and expensive equipment.

Since the early 1960s, analysis of the catches of the fishing boats has become the universal and most important stock monitoring tool of all. The study of the prime species, such as salmon, herring, mackerel, cod, whiting, haddock, plaice and sole, is a long-term commitment requiring annual scientific surveys. The research teams work throughout the year making regular visits to the principal ports and fish markets, while samples from the various co-operatives and factories around the coast are delivered to the Marine Institute laboratories for examination.

The commercial landings

Members of teams of port samplers, permanently stationed in the major harbours, measure the lengths of individual fish in large samples from the catch and transmit the data to the Marine Institute month by month. The state fishery officers, deployed around the coast, are charged with implementing management regulations for each fish stock. They work closely with the Marine Institute and provide valuable local information of the current activity and location of both the Irish and foreign fishing fleets.

The age structure of the stocks

The length of a fish is a simple observation, but also one of the most important. Manual recording of length and weight using metre-rule and balance is still used widely. During the 1980s, however, the Fisheries Research Centre in Dublin took part in the development of an integrated, electronic measuring system, comprising a computerised data logger linked to an electronic measuring board and electronic balance.

The data logger at the heart of the system is extremely robust, standing up to heavy usage at fish markets, aboard fishing vessels, and tolerating constant exposure to salt water. The system can be operated effectively by one person and information directly offloaded to the Marine Institute database. This replacement of tedious manual recording has greatly improved the efficiency and cost effectiveness of sampling.

Considerably more fish are measured than are aged for any given stock. However, 'age-length keys' mean that ages may be validly assigned to specimens which have simply been measured with a ruler. Hence the annual age profile of the sample, and the numbers of fish from each age group in the landings, can be estimated. Likewise, the weight of a fish can be calculated from its length. The weight of fish caught is naturally the primary interest of the fishing industry, but length of a specimen can be much more quickly and easily determined and this is the key measurement in the interests of maximising the number of fish sampled.

The age of most of the important 'food fish species' in our latitudes can be determined by counting annual growth rings which are visible on the scales and in the bones. The bone examined in most cases is the otolith, a small calcareous structure found in the skull. Some otoliths, above all those of herring and plaice, are almost transparent and the annual growth rings are easy to count under a microscope. Otoliths from sole and eel have to be burnt and broken before the annual ring structure can be seen. Others, such as those of cod and whiting, are opaque and preparation, let alone interpretation, is a considerable undertaking: these otoliths are sliced using a low speed saw. The thin sections obtained are examined through a microscope. Digitised images are used to an ever increasing degree.

The proportion of fish of a given age within the stock is not constant from year to year. For a variety of reasons – many of them unknown – each species may have good, normal or bad spawning seasons. In a good year, large numbers of young survive long enough to be 'recruited', to grow big enough to be caught by the fishing gear in use.

The abundance of eggs and young fish

Annual surveys are used to determine the success of each spawning season. The results, expressed in terms of 'recruit indices', are used to predict the state of the fishery for several years into the future. Two stages of the fish life history are examined. The eggs and larvae of most of the commercially important fish species drift between the surface and the seabed and can be sampled using fine-meshed plankton nets to determine the numbers per unit area. Such studies are usually internationally operated, with inputs from research vessels of most of the countries which share the fishery for the given stocks. The second stage studied is the 'young fish', those which have grown beyond the plankton stage but are still too small to be caught by commercial fishing gear.

Racial and migration studies

Racial origin is an essential feature of any assessment because the available models are based on single, unmixed stocks. Different herring stocks, for example, are identified by the number of vertebrae. As there is a considerable degree of overlap, hundreds of specimens need to be split open and their vertebrae painstakingly counted to separate out the stocks. Racial differences within stocks of the 'white fish', such as cod, haddock, whiting and the flatfish, are more subtle, and genetic and enzyme analyses are required.

Migration has been studied for over the past hundred years by tagging and releasing fish caught at various stages of their life cycles. A recent example of the results was the discovery that, while some cod migrated from the Irish Sea to the Celtic Sea, none travelled in the opposite direction. The importance of findings such as this lies in defining the area inhabited by particular populations of the species. In this case, they showed that the Irish Sea cod could be treated as a separate entity for management purposes.

Acoustic surveys

Using echo-sounding techniques, acoustic surveys give direct and fishery-independent measurements of the extent of shoals and of the numbers and sizes of fish in them. While the traces provided by the echo-sounders may be interpreted by skilled workers with considerable precision as to species, they have yet to provide investigators with anything approaching the quality of a photographic image. They are making a notable contribution to Irish fish stock assessment but, as with other forms of remote sensing, data from ground-based sampling remain essential.

Stock assessment modelling

Several models can be used to assess stock from the sampling data. The two most popular in the north Atlantic are virtual population analysis and the yield per recruit model. The former gives the numbers of fish at each age in the stock annually (using age frequencies), as well as estimates of natural mortality (losses to predators and other hazards), fishing mortality, and fishing effort levels. It works by examining annual variations in stock biomass, the actual numbers and weight of fish of each age group in the stock. In contrast, the yield per recruit model is used to indicate the long-term catch which could be taken from the stock at varying levels of fishing intensity.

Management

The Stock Book

Summaries of the results of all the stock assessment studies are presented annually in a monumental volume entitled *The Stock Book*[5]. Its purpose is 'to provide the latest scientific advice on commercially exploited fish stocks of interest to Ireland'. The printed version for 2003 ran to 430 pages, with copious illustrations and detailed information on seventy five 'stocks'. Each of the principal species provides material for several chapters. For example, accounts are given of no fewer than six regional populations of herring and of cod, five of whiting, four of plaice, three of sole and of haddock and one or two of most of the others. Each of the seventy five gives a review of the status of the species, including details of the results of the sampling exercises and, most important for the future of the fishery, management advice.

The Stock Book is compiled in the autumn of each year, to be ready in time for the annual reviews of the fisheries and to provide the back-up data that will be used in the negotiations which will lead ultimately to Europe-wide management measures. This is the primary aim of the ongoing stock assessment exercise. Publishing the results in the form of a book – and concurrently on CD and on the Web – makes the information available not only to the negotiators but to a very wide circle of interested parties. Besides the fishers themselves and their representative bodies, the material is of interest to scientists, economists and geographers amongst other professions and its permanent format, both printed and electronic, ensures that it will have a valued place in the archive of national fisheries and marine science.

International assessment

Fish stocks do not recognise the boundaries between nations. The European Commission is the management authority for all the territorial waters of its member states, and engages the International Council for the Exploration of the Sea to provide

---

[5] Anon, *The Stock Book* (Galway: Marine Institute, 2003), pp. 430.

the essential scientific information and advice on which the management plans depend.

In practice, the national scientists bring their stock summaries to the relevant stock assessment working group of the International Council and combine the data so that the population models can be applied to the international fishery. Each working group's results are passed to the Advisory Committee for Fisheries Management, which takes a wider view, including the economic needs of the fisheries, and formulates management advice, including a 'total allowable catch' for the more than seventy stocks fished in the north-eastern Atlantic and the Baltic. The European Commission then takes the final decisions on how to divide the projected catch amongst the member states in the form of annual quotas.

Besides quotas, a number of other measures may be used to control fishing mortality within a particular stock. These include closed areas and closed seasons, minimum landing sizes and minimum mesh sizes, and other regulations on fishing gear. Yet, even after all the scientific assessments have been made and the regulations agreed, problems remain. Most management measures assume that the various fish stocks do not interact and that each fishery targets a single species. This happens in only a handful of cases, such as that of the herring. More often, fishing boats target, and catch, a number of species. In such cases, management measures for one species may be in conflict with those for another.

As an example, the 1993 *Stock Book* reported that cod in the Irish Sea had reached an all-time low level and that drastic measures would be needed to restore the stocks. Whiting and sole were also 'outside safe biological limits'. The ideal would have been complete closure of the cod fishery for a period of seven or eight years. But this could not be achieved without simultaneously closing the fishery for all demersal species. Saving the threatened species, while maintaining the fishery for others, demands a very sophisticated management plan. Similar considerations apply to cod, whiting and hake to the north and northwest of Ireland.

The Irish fishery in the Third Millennium

The total landings of finfish in 2002 weighed 220,000 tonnes for which the fishing fleet was paid €66 million. Shellfish in the capture fishery totalled 61,000 tonnes, value €145 million. The top twelve species by value are shown in Table 1. The top twelve rather than the more usual top ten are given because two of the traditional mainstay species, cod and whiting, would not have appeared otherwise. Most of the species have been long established as front runners in the Irish fishery. Two exceptions are the orange roughy and the horse mackerel. The former is a deep-sea fish whose appearance owes much to scientific exploration. The latter fishery expanded following a sudden natural increase in the stocks which began in 1982.

Table 1. Catch and value of top twelve species landed in Ireland in 2002

	000 tonne	€ million	€/kg
Mackerel	72.0	39.3	0.6
Dublin Bay prawn	7.0	27.1	3.9
Edible crab	10.1	13.2	1.3
Blue mussel	26.5	13.1	0.5
Orange roughy	4.6	13.0	2.8
Horse mackerel	36.5	11.1	0.3
Angler	2.8	9.2	3.3
Megrim	2.8	8.2	3.0
Lobster	0.5	7.6	14.3
Herring	30.8	6.4	0.2
Cod	2.5	5.7	2.3
Whiting	6.6	5.4	0.8

In terms of the national economy, these values represent gross underestimates. The price paid by the dealer to the fisher is a small fraction of the ultimate value of the fish, which requires transportation and processing before it can be consumed. The actual value of a fish lies somewhere between the retail price and the price charged for a portion of it in a restaurant: perhaps somewhere between ten and twenty times the figure for first sale. This places the value of the fishing industry between €2 and €4 billion per annum. Employment in the fishing industry must be measured, not in the numbers of fishers, but in the very much greater numbers employed in the distribution, processing and sales.

The complexity of fish stock assessment and management is daunting. Fishery scientists in Ireland, and in all the other countries which share the north Atlantic fisheries, continuously strive to develop new models and techniques which will lead to more refined and accurate assessments and management of the stocks. The ideal is to operate each fishery at a level which allows the maximum quantity to be harvested, yet leaving sufficient fish to spawn and sustain the stock.

But if the difficulties of stock assessment are enormous, the social problems are even greater. The immediate effects of restricting fishing effort bring hardship to individuals, sometimes even to entire communities. Perhaps the greatest problem facing the fishery scientist – who is, after all, another human being, and one who is constantly in contact with the fishermen themselves – is to convince the industry that the sole aim of management is to ensure, not so much the survival of the fish, as the very existence of profitable fishing.

The marine environment

Studies of hydrography and plankton were well established in Irish coastal waters by the end of the nineteenth century and continued on a considerable scale until the outbreak of war in 1914. Work on the marine environment remained minimal over the next few decades, a notable exception being the study of Lough Hyne, an enclosed sea inlet on the south coast. Research established in the late 1920s by Louis Renouf, Professor of Zoology at University College, Cork[6], is still in progress. The next landmark was the establishment of a Department of Oceanography by University College Galway in 1970. The 1970s then saw a major expansion in environmental studies resulting partly from the need to comply with international agreements and partly from grave problems affecting the developing aquaculture industry.

The basic parameters of the marine environment have been understood since the later decades of the nineteenth century. By that time it had been established that the greater part of the chlorophyll in salt water is contained in the microscopic algae – the phytoplankton. Belonging to a number of species of plants, each individual is invisible or scarcely visible to the human eye. Drifting with the current, in the open water, these algae are the primary source of food and energy for nearly all forms of marine life. Each year, in spring, the algae multiply very rapidly. This phytoplankton bloom is a normal feature of the annual cycle in temperate waters.

The numbers of individual algal cells making up the bloom are kept in check by several factors. Above all, the algae need light to grow and reproduce and therefore are confined to the upper layers of the water. The extent of the bloom also depends on the availability of inorganic nutrients in solution, particularly nitrogen and phosphorous, and these are depleted as the algae increase in numbers.

The upsurge of algae in spring is followed by an explosion in the population of a variety of planktonic animals which feed on the plants. These, the zooplankton, represent many animal groups. In general they are bigger than the phytoplankton and clearly visible to the naked eye. Mostly no more than a few millimetres in length, the group does include creatures as large as jellyfish, the essential characteristic of a planktonic organism being its inability to swim against the current. The majority of the species are creatures which never attain large sizes, but the plankton includes the eggs and young of nearly all the species of finfish and shellfish consumed by humans.

Few of the fish which live in Irish waters feed directly on the phytoplankton. But the zooplankton form the diet of young fish of nearly all species and of the adults of some, herring and basking shark among others. The breeding cycles of most of the fishes lead to the production of young coinciding with the upsurge of zooplankton.

On the sea coast, between the tides and in water shallow enough for sunlight to penetrate, sessile or attached algae grow, better known as seaweeds (*see below*). They need a firm substrate, usually rock – but also man-made objects of concrete, timber or metal – for attachment. Elsewhere the greater part of the sea bed is covered by silt, the 'benthic sediments' or 'benthos'. The surface layers of the benthos teem with animal life, creatures which subsist on the detritus, the rain of organic material that falls from the waters above: a combination of the faeces of plankton and fishes and the dead

---

[6] Dan Minchin, 'An Historical Summary of Scientific Activities', pp. 25-29 in A.A. Myers, C. Little, M.J. Costello & J.C. Partridge, *The Ecology of Lough Hyne* (Dublin: Royal Irish Academy, 1991).

bodies of those individual algae and zooplankton that have not been eaten by larger organisms. The benthic fauna comprise worms and burrowing shellfish and these provide the fodder for the majority of the species targeted by the fishing industry.

Studies of the marine environment are based mainly on regular monitoring. Most of the parameters chosen are directly concerned with the possible effects of pollution on human health or on industry. The principal topics under regular investigation are :

- – Abnormal algal blooms
- – Metals in sediments, shellfish and finfish
- – Pesticide residues in sediments
- – Mercury in the commercial fish catch
- – Nutrients in the water body.

The environmental teams in the Marine Institute and other organisations also investigate irregular occurrences such as oil spills and sudden finfish and shellfish mortality.

Abnormal algal blooms

Besides the regular event in spring, blooms may occur at other, as yet unpredictable, times of the year. One or more of many species of algae may be involved. Some are luminous and account for the wonderful phosphorescence seen from boats at night. Depending on the species involved, the myriads of algae – sometimes millions of individuals per litre of water – can colour the water green, brown, yellow or red, giving rise to the handy, if not very accurate, term 'red tide'.

Such excessive blooms have been recorded over a long time, the earliest in literature being the first plague of Egypt when the Nile, according to the Book of Exodus, turned to blood. The earliest scientific reference to a bloom in Irish waters was an observation at the end of the nineteenth century by an Inspector of Fisheries, W.S. Green, who realised that brown slime on mackerel nets was caused by an excess of planktonic algae.

A prolonged period of calm and bright warm weather can cause a major event. Blooms are also associated with the development of frontal systems in the water body. One frequently occurring case takes place off the southwest coast, where upwelling brings cool, nutrient-rich water to the surface, allowing growth and reproduction of the algae at a greatly increased rate.

The majority of blooms are not associated with any obvious environmental problems, but some cause trouble in several different ways. Certain species are – hedgehog like – invested with spines of silica. These cause severe itching on the very rare occasions when they come close enough to the seaside for swimmers to meet them, and these can also cause damage to the gills of fish, leading to death. Fish kills can also occur, usually in shallow bays, when a dense bloom dies.

The gelatinous coats of species of phytoplankton form the slimy deposits on fishing nets which Green observed a hundred years ago. This reduces the catch and makes for unpleasant conditions, but the fishing fleet can usually move clear of any problem areas.

A number of the species of algae produce toxins. These can be accumulated by the animals which feed on them and transmitted through the food chain. The toxins can affect human health and give rise to a problem which is more subtle and economically more serious than any of the others. It does not require a massive bloom and can manifest itself even when the toxin-producing species are present in low numbers, as few as 100 to 200 cells per litre of water. Filter-feeding shellfish, above all the mussels, suck in the algae and concentrate them in their digestive systems. This causes no apparent ill effects to the shellfish but, since people eat the entire, ungutted mollusc, the toxins enter the human food chain. In Ireland, the most common of the toxins are those associated with diarrhetic shellfish poisoning which causes diarrhoea. Other, more serious, toxins exist which to date have not been detected in shellfish in Ireland. These are involved in amnesiac shellfish poisoning, causing short-term memory loss, and paralytic shellfish poisoning which causes paralysis and sometimes death.

Because of the risk to the industry and to public health, a shellfish toxin and phytoplankton monitoring programme was set up at the Fisheries Research Centre in 1984. Plankton samples for analysis are collected monthly in winter and weekly in summer from fifty or more sites. This work enables an early warning to be given of the presence of any of the few toxin-producing species.

At the same time samples of the shellfish are collected and screened for the presence of the toxins by bioassay. The detection of the toxins at potentially hazardous levels is reported to the local health authorities. They order temporary closure of the shellfish farms and, if necessary, issue a health warning in the district. The monitoring is being accompanied by more basic studies of the distribution of the various species of algae and on the chemistry of the toxins.

Metals in sediments, shellfish and finfish

The ions of many metals are present in normal seawater and are essential to the wellbeing of the entire plant and animal community. Sodium is the major constituent, and the salinity, or sodium chloride content, is the defining feature of salt water. The majority of marine plants and animals are unable to survive in salinities substantially lower than the level of 32 parts per thousand which is typical of all sea water. Freshwater plants and animals, likewise, cannot live in the sea. Estuarine waters, now generally known to marine scientists as 'transitional waters', are inhabited by a relatively small number of plant and animal species which can adapt to major fluctuations in salinity.

In addition to sodium, the metals calcium, potassium, magnesium and iron are essential to most forms of marine life – and rarely pose any hazard to living creatures. Metals such as copper and zinc are present in traces in normal sea water and also play an important role in sustaining life. Others, including cadmium, lead, chromium, nickel, silver, tin and – above all – mercury, make no known positive contribution to the living creatures. All of these are toxic and, at enhanced levels, can cause extremely serious problems both to the marine organisms and to the humans and creatures which consume them. A variety of land-based sources, such as mining, metal industries and sewage can release waste materials which raise the levels of these contaminants to unacceptable heights. Tin, a component of a very efficient anti-fouling paint, was found to pose a serious hazard to molluscs, to such a degree that its use was restricted by law.

Mercury is monitored in shellfish from the major aquaculture areas and in finfish from the main ports. Besides the importance of certifying that the products are safe for human consumption, monitoring the levels in shellfish provides valuable information on the quality of the waters in which they are grown. Besides mercury, regular monitoring of cadmium, chromium, copper, lead, nickel, silver and zinc takes place.

Sediment sampling

The Marine Institute monitors estuarine sediments from Dublin Bay, the Shannon Estuary and Waterford Harbour. In addition to the metals, the levels of chlorinated pesticides, polychlorinated biphenyls and polyaromatic hydrocarbons are determined.

Winter nutrient sampling programme

The levels of nitrogen and phosphorus in coastal and open waters are monitored in winter. This is the season when they are at their maximum as dissolved phosphates and nitrates. From spring to autumn, they are held to a greater extent in the bodies of the planktonic organisms. The bulk of the biomass of these creatures die at the end of the growing season and the nutrient chemicals are returned to solution in the water.

While there is a natural annual cycle of change in the concentration of the nutrients, the levels can be upset by discharge from the land, the principal sources being agriculture, industry and sewage. Imported fertilisers, detergents and even food add to the quantity of nutrients being discharged both to surface waters and to groundwater. Excessive application of fertiliser is one of the most significant sources of nutrient waste and probably the most difficult to control. Sewage and industrial effluents can by treated – though at a cost. The data produced by the monitoring programme indicate where and when control becomes necessary.

Oil spills

Improvements over many decades in controlling transportation and discharge of oil have made spillages something of a rarity. But an oil spillage in coastal waters has a devastating effect on plant and animal communities and on the local tourist and fishing industries. The worst cases are usually immediately and obviously traceable to an identified shipping disaster. A more subtle problem stems from the appearance and movement of an oil slick from an unknown source. The costs of containing an oil slick or, should this fail, of clearing the affected foreshore are high and compensation claims result.

This requires identification of the source, and chemical methods of 'fingerprinting' an oil discharge have been developed and in Ireland are applied by The Marine

Institute team. The approach involves a first stage screening to indicate a possible match between the spill and a suspect source. When this has been established, confirmatory tests are made, based on analysis of particular components in samples from the spill and from the suspect. This confirmatory analysis uses a range of parameters which are not susceptible to the chemical changes which take place as a result of weathering after the oil has been mixed with salt water and exposed to the air.

The 1999 Assessment

The OSPAR Convention 1992 co-ordinates marine environmental and related scientific activities over a very large area, extending from the Arctic Ocean to the Bay of Biscay, going far out into the Atlantic and including the North Sea and the Irish Sea. A target of the OSPAR community was to publish a report on environmental conditions within this area by the year 2000. As a preliminary step, Ireland prepared a comprehensive document[7] of the situation with a cut-off point of July 1998. Published in 1999, this is a comprehensive book combining a broad description of the environment with summaries of data on the parameters outlined in the foregoing paragraphs. The term 'environment' is taken in its widest sense and, besides a survey of the condition of the water and seabed, has chapters on fish and fisheries, birds, marine mammals and all the other major components of marine life.

Aquaculture

Aquaculture in Ireland began not later than the 1840s. In that decade of the Famine, legislation was passed to give some protection to oyster cultivators. The technique was simple, no more than transferring young oysters to specific beds and harvesting them after one or two years. Not long afterwards, in 1852, the country's first commercial salmon hatchery was established in the Galway Fishery. Oyster culture yielded a finished product, ready for market. Salmon culture for the next century was directed largely to the production of early stages of the fish for release in natural waters[8].

The 1950s saw a major step forward in rearing salmon to smolt stage – at which they migrate to sea – and of brown trout and rainbow trout to a size suitable for release into angling waters or for market. Salmon smolt rearing was undertaken by the Electricity Supply Board to replace natural stocks whose life cycle had been disrupted by the Shannon Hydro-electric Scheme.

At the same time, on the Burrishoole River in County Mayo, the Salmon Research Trust, financed jointly by the government and by the Guinness brewery, embarked on a scientific study of salmon breeding which, fifty years later, is still in progress. Originally conceived as a means of explaining aspects of salmon migration, its rearing facilities came to be used in important developments in salmon genetics. Both the Electricity Supply Board and the Salmon Research Trust were, in the 1970s, pioneers in

---

[7] R.G.V. Boelens, D.M. Mahony, A.P. Parsons & A.R. Walsh, *Ireland's Marine and Coastal Areas and Adjacent Seas: An Environmental Assessment* (Dublin: Marine Institute, 1999), pp. 388.

[8] Noel P. Wilkins, *Ponds, Passes and Parcs: Aquaculture in Victorian Ireland* (Dublin: Glendale, 1989), pp. 352.

the commercial cage-farming of salmon which would expand dramatically in the following decades[9].

Beginning in the 1960s, with the support of Bord Iascaigh Mhara and the government Fisheries Division, considerable advances were made in oyster and mussel culture. In 1974 the Shellfish Laboratory of the Department of Zoology, University College, Galway, was opened in Carna and undertook pioneering studies on a number of species. University College, Cork, followed in 1985 with an Aquatic Services Unit and, in 1989, an Aquaculture Development Centre was established there. Scientists in these and other universities, together with the state-funded institutions, have been in the front line of the development of aquaculture and a large proportion of the managers of aquaculture installations are science graduates.

This stands in marked contrast to the development and management of the capture fisheries. The latter, in effect, have developed over centuries. Science and technology have improved their efficiency – in terms of fish caught per individual fisher – beyond all recognition. And application of science, rather than the operation of market forces, offers the only possibility for sustained development. But in aquaculture much of the pioneering has been science-based and will continue to be so. This stems in part from the fact that, until scientific studies had been made on the life cycles, growth, nutrition and health of the relevant marine species, there were few realistic prospects for their successful culture.

The parallel development of widespread interest in aquaculture and increasing scientific knowledge from the 1950s to 1970s led to enthusiastic government support for the industry from the 1980s onwards and to a remarkable degree of success. Output, employment and value of the product have increased rapidly over twenty five years and the rise is expected to continue.

Fin-fish culture and shellfish culture follow different principles. Fin-fish are confined to cages and supplied with imported pelleted fodder. The sea water is simply a medium, obviously essential for the survival of the fish, but not a source of nourishment. The principle behind shellfish culture is of placing the organisms in the best possible natural surroundings and, in cases such as the mussel, giving them additional assistance in the form of structural supports.

Fin-fish culture in Ireland concentrates largely on salmonids: salmon, rainbow trout and Arctic char, by far the greatest component being salmon. The first year of its life cycle takes place in freshwater, after which the young fish are transferred to be grown to market size. In the early years, cages were anchored in sheltered bays. This led in many cases to enrichment of the water, resulting in algal blooms which proved toxic to the salmon. Fortunately cage design was improving, making it possible to operate in open water. This allowed for the dilution of waste products – including the residues of medicinal chemicals – to an environmentally acceptable degree.

Mussels, native oysters, Pacific oysters, clams and scallops were the main shellfish species under production at the beginning of the twenty-first century. Possibilities of

---

[9] D. J. Piggins, 'Thirty Years of Salmon Research', *Royal Dublin Society Occasional Papers in Irish Science and Technology*, 1987, 2, pp. 12.

commercial-scale rearing of other species, such as abalone and purple sea urchins, were under active investigation. All these species feed by filtering organic particles from the water body. While some, such as scallop, clam and sea urchin, can move around to a small extent, mussels and oysters are effectively fixed to one spot for the greater part of their lives. All, however, have a planktonic stage during which their eggs or larvae are transported by the current. The survival of each individual depends on its success in finding a living space in the course of a few critical days at the end of some weeks of larval life. Under natural conditions, the great majority of these larvae never survive to settle and grow.

The general principle of shellfish culture is twofold: first to provide living space for a greater proportion of the young than would normally live, second to locate these in regions where a maximum of planktonic food organisms is available. Shellfish culture, in effect, differs profoundly from fin-fish raising firstly in providing the individual organism with conditions which ensure the maximum degree of comfort and ease of life and, secondly, in being entirely dependent on the supply of local wild food rather than on imports.

According to data from the Central Statistics Office[10], the total quantities of finfish and shellfish produced by aquaculture in 2002 were more than twice the output for 1994. The value of the output in 2002 was €35 million for shellfish and €81 million for finfish.

The greater part of these operations is located on the western seaboard, in more or less remote regions where employment is scarce. They have made a notable contribution in maintaining a permanent workforce. In spite of this success, the concept and practice remain controversial. Partly resulting from this, but mainly because of the necessity to maintain the health of the species involved and to ensure quality both of the product and of the environment in which the sea farms operate, the Marine Institute operates an elaborate permanent monitoring scheme. The Institute claims that its programme is one of the most comprehensive in the world, and in line with international best practice. It covers a remarkable range of studies including: naturally occurring marine toxins or harmful algal blooms, chemical residues, fish health, sea lice levels on finfish farms, water quality, seabed sediment in and around seafood production areas, and levels of fish farm escapees.

Conflict exists in several areas, between traditional followers of the capture fishery, both commercial and recreational and in environmental impact. The scientific monitoring work, by establishing the essential facts, makes a major contribution towards resolving these problems.

Salmon and eel

Salmon and eel are diadromous, spending parts of their life cycles in the sea and parts in inland waters. The typical wild salmon in Ireland breeds in fresh water, grows slowly for two years, migrates to sea in autumn and grows rapidly. The majority return to their

---

[10] Central Statistics Office Website www.cso.ie

natal streams after one winter at sea, a minority stay away for two winters. The eel breeds in warm ocean water in the Sargasso Sea, crosses the Atlantic with the assistance of the Gulf Stream and grows in fresh or estuarine waters. Spawning in most cases marks the end of the salmon's life and in all cases is a final act for the eel. Both qualify for treatment as marine species and at the same time are the only freshwater fish with a tradition of commercial exploitation in Ireland.

The salmon, besides its importance as a food fish and as a pre-eminent sport species, claims an unequalled status as an object of national heritage. Plentiful in rivers and easily caught using unsophisticated gear, the salmon has been such an important part of the diet of Irish people since the arrival of mesolithic hunter-gatherers that it has assumed a mystical significance. Ancient traditions such as the 'salmon of wisdom' testify to its importance. The eel also had been an important item of food since the mesolithic – but it lost its popularity in the course of the nineteenth century. Most of the catch in modern times has been exported. Lough Neagh is one of the biggest and most effectively managed eel fisheries in the world and provides a living for about 400 fishers. Ownership of fishing rights for both species and the need to control the numbers caught have been the basis of much legislation and the operation of a specialised protection service.

Sustained research on the salmon began in the 1930s and is the basis of an elaborate management system developed from the results of seventy years of migration and survival studies. Eel research in Ireland began in the 1960s. Stocks of both species fluctuated during the twentieth century but have declined over recent decades. While there are some indications that exploitation has contributed to the loss of salmon, no direct explanation of the eel situation has yet been advanced. In both cases, factors in the ocean, as yet unquantified, seem to account for the decline.

Controversy, international and national, rages on the ways and means of ensuring the survival of the salmon. Sport fishing for the salmon takes place in fresh water, commercial exploitation in Ireland nowadays is confined to the sea and river estuaries. Angling is an inefficient means of capture and tends to allow the escapement of sufficient spawners. The greater part of the commercial fishery is effected by drift-nets at sea and surrounding 'draft' nets in the estuaries. Although very much more efficient in terms of the numbers caught by each fisher, both gears also allow substantial escapement.

Two arguments advanced by the salmon-angling lobby are that the value of the rod-caught salmon is about ten times that of the commercial fish and that netting is too destructive. The fact that successive governments have refused to ban commercial fishing, in spite of considerable pressure from conservationists, implies that there are reasonable counter-arguments. Briefly, the commercially caught fish should be valued at the price of smoked salmon rather than in terms of first sale. Moreover, good netting seasons coincide with good seasons and vice versa. Ideally, the estuarine draft-net fishery should be advanced in favour of the drift nets. The latter capture salmon indiscriminately from many river-based breeding populations, while the former exploit only the fish from single, more controllable, stocks.

All parties agree that management measures are essential. These now depend on the interpretation of information obtained from a programme of tagging the young fish and counting the adults as they ascend through rivers. Electronic equipment for the latter purpose began to be used in the 1950s. Video-recording was introduced in the 1990s. Tagging of many thousands of young is effected by injecting a binary-coded microscopic steel bar whose presence can be detected magnetically when the adult fish is captured. Fishers are required by law to attach a tag to the carcass of each fish they catch and to return a log-book of their fishing to the authorities. Analysis of all this information provides an accurate assessment of the status of salmon stocks of each river catchment to be made and, from this, quotas for the fishery in the following year. The oceanic factors remain unknown and uncontrollable – but the management scheme maximises the numbers of young salmon which can go to sea.

Seaweeds

The National University of Ireland, Galway, is the main centre for research on seaweed and the southwest, mid-west and northwest coasts account for the annual yield of about 35,000 tonnes[11]. The value of the seaweed industry was approximately €4 million in the 1990s and employment totalled 500 full-time and part-time. Seaweeds were regarded as under-exploited and the numbers engaged in gathering the raw material were declining, with few young people interested in entering the industry. This was explained by increasing affluence and availability of employment in the western regions, making the hardship of the seaweed harvest unattractive to most. The prospects of the introduction of mechanical harvesting, to increase gain and reduce the discomfort, were being investigated. Studies based in Galway take a holistic view of the seaweed industry and, besides working on such basics as growth and distribution of the species, include processing and marketing.

More than 500 species of seaweed have been identified on the Irish coast, but most of the biomass is provided by a much smaller number of species in three groups, the wracks, the kelps and maërl. The wracks are found in the inter-tidal region with four species of *Fucus* and one each of *Pelvetia* and *Ascophyllum* providing the bulk. *Fucus* and *Pelvetia* have a long tradition of use as animal fodder but *Ascophyllum* is the most important economically as a source of important extracts, such as alginates, for the food industry. A survey of *Ascophyllum* on the west coast indicated that at least 130,000 tonnes were available, of which about 34,000 tonnes were actually being harvested. Earlier studies had led to efficient husbandry of the crop, indicating in particular that cutting on a four-year cycle and leaving a stump of 25 cm from each plant would allow for optimal re-growth.

The kelps grow mostly below the low tide level and the stipes or stems of one of the three species of *Laminaria hyperborea* are gathered to be exported for alginate production. In the Far East in particular, the kelps are in high demand as food – but this has not yet led to any great production in Ireland. Estimates are that at least

---

[11] Michael D. Guiry, 'Research and Development of a Sustainable Irish Seaweed Industry', *Royal Dublin Society Occasional Papers in Irish Science and Technology* 1997, 14, pp. 11.

100,000 tonnes of *Laminaria* could be obtained – but information on kelp is seriously limited and much more research is required to ensure rational harvesting.

Consumption of two species of red algae, *Chondrus crispus* and *Mastocarpus stellatus* have a long tradition as a source of food under the names of carrageen or Irish moss. Although carrageen is widely available in health food shops, total production amounts to only about 50 tonnes, one seventh of the estimated sustainable yield. Dulse *Palmaria palmata* is another established food source. Production is about 15 tonnes but the abundance of the species has yet to be established.

Maërl, the calcareous skeletal remains of coralline species, mainly *Phymatolithon calcareum* and *Lithothamnion coralloides,* has the greatest potential for development amongst the red algae. In places the maërl deposits form large beds with potential for commercial harvest. It makes an excellent soil conditioner and also serves as a good filtration agent for water treatment. Brittany produces over 500,000 tonnes – and Ireland about 1,000. Research is directed towards assessing the quantities in existence around the Irish coast, to estimating the sustainable yield and to determining possible environmental impacts of exploitation. The greatest concentration is within Galway Bay and amounts to eight million tonnes.

By comparison with comparable European coastal waters, such as those of Brittany and Cornwall, Irish production of seaweeds is low. The scientific studies have shown the existence of crops that could allow greatly increased exploitation. Work is also in progress on aquaculture of a number of species, including new hybrids, a development which promises to be free from adverse environmental effects. The greatest problem appears to be in recruiting labour to the industry. Development will be of particular interest in being science-led and having a possibility of taking place from the start under controlled conditions based on calculation of sustainable yields.

The Irish National Seabed Survey

Until the end of the twentieth century, much of the information on the seabed around Ireland was based on the Admiralty charts, updated in the most important regions by the UK Hydrographic Office. The basis was one of soundings taken by survey ships which provided an outline of the bathymetry together with a little data on the nature of the seabed, whether of sand, mud or rock. While great improvements, using remote scanning techniques, were introduced in the final quarter of the twentieth century, charts of more than 100 years old remained the sole source of data for some regions.

The year 2000 saw the inauguration of one of the greatest seabed surveys undertaken anywhere in the world, managed by the Geological Survey of Ireland. Planned to run over seven years at a cost of €32 million, it covers the 525,000 square kilometres of Ireland's territorial seabed. As mentioned earlier, the area of the territorial waters is about ten times the size of the island and extends for nearly 1,000 kilometres into the Atlantic Ocean, reaching depths of 4,500 metres.

The basic technique used in the survey is sonar scanning – a system developed in the natural world millions of years ago in the animal kingdom by bats. The principle is to measure the time taken by a pulse of sound to be reflected by the seabed and which is proportional to the depth. Sonar underwent a phase of rapid development during World War II, thanks to its value in detecting submarines. Since then, advances in electronics and the introduction of computers have combined to provide equipment of unprecedented sensitivity – which also operates at speed so that the detailed survey of the immense area involved has become practicable.

The most widely used information resulting from the survey is in the form of detailed bathymetric maps. These have revealed the existence of submarine canyons, valleys and rocky outcrops. On a smaller scale they show up the exact positions of wrecked ships, some of them previously unknown. These details are of immediate practical value both in navigation and in fishing, the nature of the seabed being one of the primary factors in determining the habitat of various species of fish. However sophisticated the equipment, 'ground truth', the sampling and identification of rocks and sediments, continues to be an essential input. So the survey vessels take grab samples as well as amassing data by remote sensing. As a matter of course, they also sample the water column and collect magnetic and gravity data.

Bulletins on the progress of the survey, together with details of the databases available to potential users, are posted on the Seabed Survey website[12]. By the end of the surveying season 2003, eight vessels and one aircraft had been involved in the work. The latest to join in was the research vessel *Celtic Explorer* commissioned for the Marine Institute in April of that year. In addition to its complement of the latest surveying equipment, *Celtic Explorer* had been designed to minimise noise of operation, a feature which adds greatly to the precision of the measurements made by the sonar equipment.

The survey has produced a comprehensive series of bathymetric and geological maps at a scale of 1:250,000, together with digitised data from which astonishing images of the seabed can be generated. The comprehensive results have made a profound contribution to knowledge of the sea, to be used by research workers in many fields. Their value from the economic angle is in indicating to mineral and oil prospectors the best places in which to make the detailed studies which ultimately lead to commercial production.

The seashore

The most accessible sector of the marine environment is the seashore and studies of the littoral fauna and flora have been in progress since the nineteenth century. Cockles and mussels have a long tradition of popularity, as have periwinkles, but scientific studies for the most part have been academic rather than applied. From the point of view of fundamental studies in marine ecology, in the recording of biodiversity and in environmental education at all levels, the seashore is an entity of exceptional importance. Apart from the localised impact of water pollution, the foreshore is the only readily accessible ecosystem in Ireland which has not been significantly altered by human influence.

---

[12] The Irish National Seabed Survey www.gsiseabed.gsi.ie

Periwinkles are of particular interest, having been the basis of a sustained fishery for some nine thousand years, since the arrival of the mesolithic hunter-gatherers. Moreover the fishery, in spite of being pursued on foot and with no gear other than a collecting bag or bucket, gives a substantial return. According to *The Stock Book*, landings in 2002 totalled 1,368 tonnes with a first-sale value of €1.35 million. In view of the virtual absence of investment capital, this is arguably the most profitable of all species harvested in Ireland. Occasional scientific studies have indicated that the stocks are being over-exploited and conservation by minimum size limit and close seasons has been recommended.

Cockles are harvested to some extent by digging at low tide, but the greater proportion of the rapidly expanding fishery is taken by boat. Concern has been raised because of the possibility of a negative impact on populations of birds such as the oystercatcher in conservation areas. As with the periwinkle, scientific knowledge of the species is limited and the position of the stocks is almost unknown.

Baseline studies of the seashore fauna and flora are of great importance in monitoring the state of the marine environment. Among others, an extensive survey was made in Bantry Bay after the oil spillage from the tanker *Betelguese* and around the coast of Wexford, initiated in connection with the abandoned proposal for a nuclear power station at Carnsore. Much university-based work has been done around the shores of Dublin Bay, and Queen's University has maintained a field station at Portaferry at the entrance to Strangford Lough for many years.

Wave energy

According to a consultation document by the Marine Institute and Sustainable Energy Ireland[13], 'the wave climate off the West coast of Ireland is one of the most favourable in the world'. Nobody doubts the desirability of harnessing wave power as a source of clean energy and it has been estimated that half Ireland's requirements could be supplied from it. The problem lies in the detail.

In spite of considerable progress in the theory and in the construction of working models, there is as yet no well-established wave energy industry in the world and the consultation document sought views as to the approach Ireland should take to a development programme. The most challenging and exciting option would be for Ireland to use its foundation of abundance of energy, together with a tradition of excellent research, to become the technology leader in the field. The rewards would be, not only to supply the country with a meaningful input of clean electric power, but also to establish a lucrative industry in the export of expertise and the manufacture and export of equipment. Less ambitious options would be to concentrate simply on the provision of a national resource or, at worst, to see how other nations progress and pay for the applications of their achievements later.

The first option, of taking the lead in research and development, would demand very substantial financing – but would build on projects already receiving state

---

[13] Anon, *Options for the Development of Wave Energy in Ireland: A Public Consultation Document* (Dublin: Marine Institute and Sustainable Energy Ireland, 2002).

funding. These include the deployment of turbine test beds at the Department of Mechanical and Aeronautical Engineering at the University of Limerick and of tank testing facilities at the Hydraulics and Maritime Research Centre at the National University of Ireland, Cork. While working models are very much in existence, the difference between a laboratory tank and the Atlantic coast are significant, and the engineering technology and costs of developing a pilot project at sea are a major hurdle. But the ultimate rewards could be immense.

Research vessels

The first task of the Research Vessel *Celtic Explorer* after her commissioning in April 2003 was to deploy a new weather buoy off the coast of Donegal. She then spent until autumn on the National Seabed Survey (*see above*) and in November embarked on a 45-day groundfish survey of the shelf area in the Irish Sea and off the west coast. In this operation, she was one of a team of three, working with French and Scottish research ships to give a comprehensive view of the abundance and distribution of fish stocks from the Bay of Biscay to the Shetlands. The year's cruises provide a good example of the range of work which a national research vessel undertakes. The *Celtic Explorer* was the second multi-purpose vessel to be commissioned within a short period, following the smaller *Celtic Voyager* (1997). This was the first time in nearly forty years that the Irish government had operated two research vessels and this development made a very clear statement that the marine resource was being taken seriously.

Conclusions

Early in the twentieth century, W.S Green, a founding father of Irish marine science, observed that the people of Ireland – for the greater part of their history – had been so well provided with beef that they had no need to face the dangers of the sea in search of protein[14]. So, in spite of being an island, no great tradition of fishing had ever developed. An upsurge of interest began in the 1950s and was followed by a gradual expansion over the next forty years, a period which included the legal extension of Ireland's territorial waters and culminated in the establishment of the national Marine Institute in 1991.

From the end of the nineteenth century, the government accepted the principle that development of the fishing industry demanded a substantial input from scientists. Improved technology has allowed the Irish fishing fleet to expand and become ever more efficient in terms of engaging fewer people to catch more fish. While entrepreneurs spearhead an expanding fishery, effective management of the stocks to ensure the maintenance of the fishery at its peak level is the province of the fishery scientists. The aquaculture industry is largely science-based, as is the broad field of seabed exploration. Environmental scientists are the front line of the defence of the marine environment, since its early stages of deterioration are visible only to the people engaged in meticulous analysis of the flora, fauna and chemistry of the water.

---

[14] W. S. Green 1902, 'The Sea Fisheries of Ireland', in W. P. Coyne (Ed), *Ireland Industrial and Agricultural* (Dublin, Browne and Nolan, 1902).

The twenty-first century sees undreamed of threats to the environment, together with the development of technology which can increase the success of the fishing industry but, if uncontrolled, could lead to the decimation of stocks and the collapse of fisheries. Seabed exploration promises sources of wealth from minerals and hydrocarbons. The community of marine scientists has developed the means of measuring both potential and risks and the technology to surmount the dangers and achieve rich rewards.

CHAPTER 8

Value in Biomedical Research in Ireland: Past and Future

Dermot Kelleher

"In no way is the vitality of the Medical School more surely gauged than by the quantity and quality of the original work done in its laboratories[1]."

Introduction

The science of medical practice has always been based on the fundamental principles of clinical observation. The initial identification of disease in this high-tech age is still generally accomplished initially largely through the eyes, ears and hands of the practitioner. Although diagnosis is now generally confirmed through the use of advanced technological practices, including multiple modalities of biochemical, immunological and scanning techniques, in areas of medical practise such as psychiatry, diagnosis is almost exclusively based on the ability and skill of the doctor to elicit the cardinal symptoms of disease. In a previous era, Irish physicians made crucial advances in the accurate and scientific description of disease based on physical signs and symptoms, which remain fundamental to medical practice today.

The molecular revolution catalysed by the sequencing of the human genome means that it is now theoretically possible to trace and identify the molecular basis of human disease. Specifically, the identification and annotation of all of the genes within the genome means that we now have some of the tools necessary to put together 'roadmaps' of the progression of pathological events in the course of a disease process. Nonetheless, the utilisation of molecular medicine requires accurate diagnosis and phenotyping of disease, and the application of clinical skills remains essential in order to obtain such a phenotype. It is obviously not possible to link genetic traits with complex diseases if the basis for diagnosis of such diseases is incorrect. Hence, even in technology-based applied medical research, there is a direct linear progression from clinical skill and accurate diagnosis through to our ability to accurately determine the cause and ultimately the molecular basis of disease. The commonly used term, 'from

---

[1] T. Percy Kirkpatrick, *History of the Medical School in Trinity College Dublin* (Dublin: Hanna and Neale 1912), p. 338.

bench to bedside', used to describe translational science, is a direct throwback to the concept of bedside observation developed by the great Irish physicians of the nineteenth century.

The 'Dublin School of Medicine'

In the nineteenth century, the school of physic at Trinity College Dublin (TCD) was fortunate to have on its staff two of the most distinguished physicians in the world in Robert Graves (1796–1853) and William Stokes (1804–1878). These two physicians were responsible for the formal description of a number of medical conditions, including those that bear their names – i.e. Graves disease of the thyroid and Cheyne-Stokes respiration and Stokes-Adams attacks in cardiology. During the time of their pre-eminence in medicine, the Dublin School had a global reputation based on the quality of bedside medical teaching and on the meticulous attention to observation in the identification of patterns of disease. As Graves stated, medical education was based on the principle that 'from the very commencement, the student ought to witness the progress and effects of sickness and ought to persevere in the daily observation of disease during the whole period of his studies'. In 1834, Graves published his lectures in the UK in the form of a textbook of medicine entitled *A System of Clinical Medicine*. This publication was of such import that it was published in the US in 1838. By the time of his death in 1853, he was one of the best known of international physicians, bringing Dublin medicine to global attention and establishing a system of education which has formed the basis of medical teaching throughout the world. Of particular note, international physicians such as James Bovell of Toronto and Palmer Howard of Magill University visited Dublin to interact directly with Graves. The iconic William Osler, a giant of US medicine, studied with these two distinguished physicians and later acknowledged the influence of Graves on his medical career[2]. Hence, a science of medical practice based on principles of strict observation and characterisation was established in the Dublin School, and this forms much of the basis of what we would today call 'phenotyping' in biomedical research.

William Stokes was a second giant of international medicine during the nineteenth century. It is of particular note in his career that he initially worked in Chemistry in the Glasgow laboratory of Professor Thomson and hence achieved a grounding in scientific methodology. He graduated from Edinburgh in 1825 and published a book on the use of the stethoscope prior to his graduation. Stokes' textbook was indicative of the role he was to play in the promotion of observational skills in the science of cardiology. His contributions to the medical literature were legion and included his textbook on diseases of the heart and aorta published in 1854 wherein he described Cheyne-Stokes respiration, a form of respiratory pattern associated with the failing heart. In addition to publishing frequently in the London-based medical journals, Graves and Stokes were the first co-editors of the *Dublin Journal of Medical and Chemical*

---

[2] Davis Coakley, *Irish Masters of Medicine* (Dublin: Town House 1992), pp. 89-98.

Sciences later known as the *Irish Journal of Medical Science*, which had been founded by Robert Kane (1809-1890 – *see page 36*)[3].

Other famous Irish physicians included Dominic Corrigan (1801-1880) who described the clinical signs of aortic valve incompetence, leaving as his legacy the eponym of 'Corrigan's pulse'. In surgery, Abraham Colles (1773-1843) and Edward Bennett (1837-1907) went on to describe the fractures which currently bear their names in textbooks of surgery worldwide. The widespread use of eponyms based on the names of Irish physicians and surgeons leaves us with a 'palimpest' of a vibrant and exciting era in Irish medicine and indeed in Irish medical science.

Loss of impetus

While these names are traditionally associated with the process of observation in medicine, it is clear that their highly focussed clinical skills have formed the basis of much of medical education and practice in the modern age. Significantly, the process of careful observation of disease, coupled to scientific analysis of the phenotype and genotype, remains one of the major principles of excellence in biomedical research. These early clinical scientists promoted a system of learning which is fundamental to current medical research. However, within the twentieth century, much of the impetus arising from the work of these great pioneers of the nineteenth century was lost as Irish medicine became increasingly divergent from the sciences. Certainly there was little evidence of public or state recognition of the principle expounded by Kirkpatrick in the opening statement above[1]. It is likely that research funding for medical research in Ireland suffered by comparison with centres such as Edinburgh following the formation of the Irish state. Research laboratories became separated from the teaching hospital environment and suffered from chronic lack of funding. Progress depended on the considerable efforts of a small number of individuals who continued to produce high quality research despite the overwhelming odds.

It should be noted that the initial development of the sciences took place hand in glove with the development of the medical schools. For example, at TCD, the school of chemistry developed as part of the medical school, and other departments, such as physics, zoology and physiology, emerged and prospered in partnership or as components of the medical school. In University College Dublin (UCD), Professor E.J. Conway (1894-1968) epitomised the principles of the scientific basis of disease in his elegant physiological studies. Notably his extensive research output is clearly of the highest standard, with publications in journals such as *Nature* featuring strongly[4,5]. A particularly intriguing publication was the identification of the enzyme urease in the stomach, in collaboration with Professor Oliver Fitzgerald. The enzyme was of course

---

[3] Gordon Wolstenholme, 'The Victorian Era', pp. 115-146 in Eoin O'Brien & Anne Crookshank, with Gordon Wolstenholme, *A Portrait of Irish Medicine* (Swords: Ward River Press for the Royal College of Surgeons in Ireland, 1984).

[4] E.J. Conway, 'Significance of Various Factors Including Lactic Dehydrogenase on the Active Transport of Sodium Ions in Skeletal Muscle', *Nature*, **198**, 1963, pp. 760-3.

[5] E.J. Conway, 'Critical Energy Barriers in the Excretion of Sodium', *Nature*, **187**, 1960, pp. 394-6.

identified in surgically resected stomachs derived from patients undergoing peptic ulcer surgery. At the time, this observation was not widely regarded as being consistent with other data but, as we now know, it was correct and presaged the identification of the ulcer-inducing organism H pylori as the source of this urease[6]. Interestingly, Professors Colm O'Morain and Conor Keane at TCD were responsible for the studies confirming that failure of eradication of H pylori was associated with recurrent ulceration[7].

Medical science remained a poorly supported entity throughout most of the twentieth century, and the medical schools in Ireland devoted much of their energy towards producing highly skilled medical graduates at low cost. Specifically, the number of academic appointments in Irish Schools of Medicine remained at a minimal level and there was no development of substantial chairs in sub-specialities as there was in most European countries. Hence, while many Irish medical graduates excelled in research careers in other countries, most notably the UK and the US, the career track of 'medical scientist' barely existed within an Irish context. There are still only forty full time equivalents employed in clinical departments in the entire country. Although there has been a significant increase in biomedical funding in recent years, it was only in 2003 that the organisation responsible for regulation of consultant posts in Ireland, Comhairle na hOspideal, took the ground-breaking step of recognising the need for individuals within the health services with research responsibilities. In 2004, the Health Research Board (HRB) announced the provision of grants for Clinician Scientists, designed to encourage the development of a new core expertise in research within the teaching hospitals, and it is likely that two appointments will be made in 2005. While this is a highly welcome development, it represents a faltering first step along a path towards the development of appropriate academic medical structures in Ireland.

Recent changes in Irish Biomedical Research

It is notable that Irish medicine took on a position of international pre-eminence in the nineteenth century based on principles of meticulous observation. As stated above, in the 1950s and 1960s E.J. Conway produced a series of publications in the international literature, many in journals such as *Nature*. However, by the mid 1990s, Irish biomedical science had reached a nadir in terms of international standing, with minimal if any publications in many of the journals of international prestige. For example, in the early 1990s, the publication rate in *The Journal of Biological Chemistry* in Ireland ran at less than one per annum, and publications in *Journal of Immunology* were even less frequent (Figures 1 and 2). Individual researchers continued to make an impact in selected areas, such as the folate pathway research of Weir and Scott and research into respiratory disease from M.X. Fitzgerald's group. Specifically, research performed by Weir and Scott, funded by the National Institutes of Health of the USA

---

[6] E.J. Conway, O. Fitzgerald, K. McGeeney & F. Geoghegan, 'The Location and Origin of Gastric Urease' *Gastroenterology*, **37**, 1959, pp. 449-56.

[7] J.G. Coghlan, D. Gilligan, H. Humphries, D. McKenna, C. Dooley, E. Sweeney, C. Keane, & C. O'Morain, 'Campylobacter Pylori and Recurrence of Duodenal Ulcers – A 12-month Follow-up Study', *Lancet*, **2(8568)**, 1987, pp. 1109-11.

and by the HRB, demonstrated clear evidence that folic acid deficiency during pregnancy was associated with the development of neural tube defects such as spina bifida. This research had a profound effect on public policy in the US, where bread is now supplemented with folic acid. Nonetheless, infrastructural problems meant that the facilities to perform state-of-the-art research in many areas were simply not available in Ireland, and research requiring a high-tech approach frequently depended on international collaborators, thus reducing the net value to Irish science.

Figure 1. Publications in **The Journal of Biological Chemistry** *originating from Irish Laboratories on an annual basis*

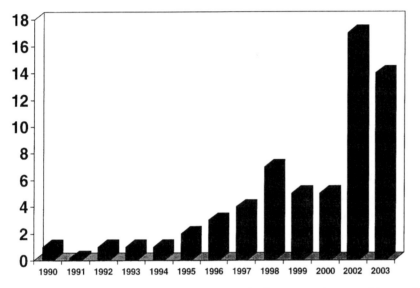

Figure 2. Combined publications in **Journal of Immunology** *and* **Journal of Experimental Medicine** *originating from Irish Laboratories on an annual basis*

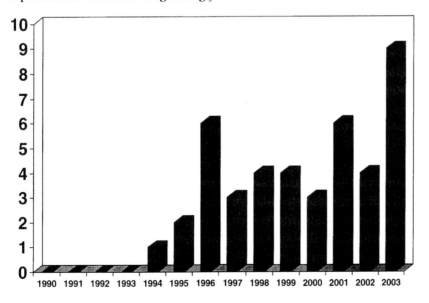

However, in recent years there has been a major change in the research environment. Government funding has increased substantially, with a stepwise increase in funding for research through the HRB followed by a substantial increment in research productivity as seen in Figures 1 and 2. Of particular note is the publication record of Irish biomedical research scientists over the last twenty years. In a journal of high impact in biomedical science, such as *The Journal of Biological Chemistry*, the average number of publications per annum from within the Ireland was, as mentioned above, less than one up until approximately 1995. From 1995 to 2000 there was a exponential rise in the number of publications in this Journal, as seen in Figure 1. By the end of the millennium, Irish publication rates in these journals were comparable to publication rates from Manchester, an area with a catchment of six million population, although clearly lagging behind centres such as Oxford, Cambridge and Edinburgh. This exponential rise largely predates the impact of large increases in funding from the Programme for Research in Third Level Institutions (PRTLI) funded by the Higher Education Authority (HEA) and the large injection provided by Science Foundation Ireland (SFI). Similar changes have been seen in the Irish publication record in the *Journal of Immunology* and the *Journal of Experimental Medicine* (Figure 2). It is unclear what the stimuli have been for this initial growth spurt in productivity. However, it is reasonable to assume that it is at least partially fuelled by the modest increases in funding for the HRB which occurred in the mid-1990s.

During this period, there were a number of additional significant changes in the research environment. The provision of infrastructural grant funding through the HEA's PRTLI came on stream, providing for a substantial expansion in research capacity in Ireland, with a rapid ramping up of technological provision to international standards. This development, which was co-funded by the Department of Education and the Atlantic Philanthropies group, has radically changed the research environment, with the construction of large infrastructural resources such as the Conway Institute (UCD – *see below*), the Institute for Molecular Medicine (TCD), the Clinical Research Centre (Royal College of Surgeons in Ireland) and the Bio-Engineering Centre at the National University of Ireland Galway (NUIG). The provision of physical space, coupled to a major development in technology infrastructure, has resulted in the most radical alteration in research aspirations in biomedical sciences within the state. The focus on research collaboration has been another major feature of this programme. The research collaboration between TCD and UCD which has resulted in the creation of the Dublin Molecular Medicine Centre has been a major step forward both in terms of infrastructural prioritisation between the Dublin Medical Schools and in terms of the development of an integrated post-graduate educational programme. Lastly, SFI is now providing research funding at an unprecedented level for both information technology and biotechnology. It is clear that the benefits of these programmes in terms of scientific output are only beginning to be seen. Of note, two major Centre grants have been made to groups led by clinician scientists – Professor Fergus Shanahan at University College Cork and Professor Tim

O'Brien at NUIG. These programmes support interdisciplinary research in pro-biotic and stem-cell technology respectively at the cutting edge of biomedical science, with major interactions with industry. The full benefits of the enhanced funding should be evident, not only in enhanced publication rates and increased prestige of Irish science, but must ultimately impact economically with the creation of new intellectual property and its exploitation by an indigenous biotechnology industry.

Development of critical mass in publications has also raised the bar for young scientists in terms of their ambition. Before 1995, many young scientists operating within the Irish biomedical sector would have felt that publication in high impact journals was outside their reach. More recently, many such scientists believe that publication in high impact journals is now clearly within their reach and indeed it is an aspiration to which they should aim.

Medical Research, Biotechnology and the Value Chain

Biotechnology is defined as the application of scientific and engineering principles to the processing of materials by biological agents. Within the last thirty years, biotechnology has gone through an expansion phase largely focused on the developments of new technologies for both diagnoses and treatment of disease. These technologies, when applied in research, have also had a major impact in the development of new tools for the study of the molecular basis of disease. It is from our understanding of the biological processes that malfunction in development of disease that new therapeutic targets and therapies are evolving.

Most recently, the results of the human genome project and the ongoing annotation of this process have provided an enormous amount of new information which has yet to be translated into practical benefit in terms of medical biotechnology. The sequencing of many bacterial genomes also provides major opportunities for research. The involvement of Ireland in the medical biotechnology revolution has been limited until recently. There are significant reasons for this. Firstly, although medical biotechnology is a relatively young industry, Ireland has had a limited tradition in the development of critical mass in biology relating to human health within the last century. The infrastructure required to develop biomedical research and biotechnology has simply not existed. Specifically, there has been very limited funding for biotechnological research and virtually no tradition of indigenous chemical and biochemical based pharmaceutical industry. While multi-national pharmaceutical companies have established very large manufacturing facilities in this country (see Chapter 10), this has not significantly impacted on the research and development potential of indigenous academic institutions. Most profoundly, the lack of a tradition in the indigenous chemical industry has left us in a situation in which there has been a serious deficit in the critical mass of both technology and entrepreneurship required to develop indigenous concepts to the point of commercialisation.

However, recent steps taken through both SFI and the PRTLI have started to rectify these deficits, and hence the challenge of the next twenty years will be to establish within this country a vibrant and active medical and biotechnology industry with the potential to provide very significant contributions to the overall wealth of the nation. It should be stressed that the natural history of medical biotechnology internationally is of failure in start-up companies, with the emergence of a small number of successful companies from a pack of start-up ventures. However, the rate of success in new product development is now higher for products developed within the biotech sector than within the conventional pharmaceutical industry. Hence, if Ireland is to succeed strategically in adding value in biomedical sciences, it is essential that a significant number of start-ups emerge so that the one or two major companies will have the potential to emerge within the next ten years. Given the high rate of attrition within the industry, it will be essential that between twenty and forty start-up companies emerge in order to fulfil this goal.

One advantage of the relatively small size of the research infrastructure is the enhanced potential for interdisciplinary research. Such research includes inter-digitating components of biology, physics, chemistry, engineering and medicine, and may represent a key area for rapid development in medical technology. In this regard, the development of the CRANN nanotechnology centre at TCD, funded by SFI, is intended to build bridges in interdisciplinary research between the physical sciences and the health sciences. One example of such inter-disciplinary research is the development of nanowires in physiological solution by the research groups of Yuri Volkov, Yuri G'unko and John Donegan (forthcoming in *Chem Phys Chem*), a process which may provide potential benefits for human health applications. Such collaboration may paradoxically be facilitated in Ireland by the relatively small size of the infrastructure, with maximal benefit provided by enhanced collaboration. There is a pressing need for such interdisciplinary research in Ireland, as such research will move more rapidly up the value chain towards commercial exploitation.

Moving up the value chain in biomedical research – some key principles

In outlining the components required to develop this technology and promote value in biomedical research, this review will initially focus on components which are at the non-technological end of the spectrum, namely tradition, requirements for role models of small to medium biotechnology, and thirdly the business infrastructure required.

1. Tradition

In the early part of the twentieth century, Abraham Flexner undertook a review of the medical schools within the US and succeeded in confirming that a significant portion of these were non-viable and should not be further developed[8]. He identified as a key role for medical schools, not only the education of medical graduates but also the development of scientific knowledge and new understanding of disease, with a natural consequence being the identification of new diagnostic and therapeutic strategies.

Hence, at this time, there was not a great divergence of thought between the views expressed by Flexner and the views of the Irish medical establishment as expressed by Kirkpatrick in the introductory quote. Abraham Flexner's philosophies revolutionised the process of medical education within the US and profoundly altered the concept of what constituted a medical school. He believed that hospitals were essentially part of an academic environment and, as such, should be fully equipped with research laboratories to enable them to achieve their maximum potential. Hence, within this framework, a direct link between the clinical phenotype as identified by practising physicians and the biological composition of the disease process, now largely reflected in the genotype, became possible. Flexner's revolution certainly galvanised the medical community for the development of the US as the powerhouse of medical research that it is to-day[9]. His philosophy was subsequently extended to the UK, which he visited and where his impact was largely seen in the major teaching centres of medical education. Both the US and UK had powerful chemical and pharma-chemical industries, and both were in a position to capitalise on the growing academic medical centre infrastructure. Hence, both the UK and the US in the twentieth century were major players in the development of the bio-pharmaceutical industries.

Within Ireland, however, there was very little development of this tradition, with a few notable exceptions, until relatively recently. Medical schools in the mid-twentieth century were seen entirely appropriately as centres for medical education and for the training of doctors. Sadly, the development of the scientific infrastructure to partner medical education was not seen as a priority, and hence this was particularly epitomised by the fact that Professor Peter Gatenby was the first professional Professor of Medicine in the Republic of Ireland on his appointment in 1968. Nonetheless, the process of medical research was underpinned by a number of giants of their era, who contrived to generate a scientific infrastructure despite the major constraints on both their physical infrastructure for research and on their time in relationship to other duties. Such leaders would have included individuals like E.J. Conway at UCD who has given his name to the hugely successful Conway Institute (*see below*), Professor Oliver FitzGerald at UCD, and Professor Donald Weir at TCD, whose partnership with Professor John Scott, as we have seen, resulted in the understanding of the critical role of folic acid in both maternal health and in the health of populations, which has resulted in major public health changes within the US and Europe. The net effect of the traditions established by these individuals is now becoming apparent, with many academic scientists showing the influence of their mentorship.

In addition to these individuals, there was a small infrastructure for research provided by the HRB, previously known the Medical Research Council of Ireland (MRCI). The MRCI also provided the framework for a stand-alone laboratory within

[8] Abraham Flexner, *Medical Education in the United States and Canada: A Report to the Carnegie Foundation for the Advancement of Teaching; Bulletin No. 4* (New York: Carnegie Foundation for the Advancement of Teaching, 1910).

[9] M.D. Hiatt & C.G. Stockton, 'The Impact of the Flexner Report on the Fate of Medical Schools in North America after 1909', *Journal of American Physicians and Surgeons*, **8**, 2003, pp. 37-41.

TCD which was responsible for the development of a drug, clofazimine, currently used in the treatment of leprosy worldwide. Clofazimine was originally developed to treat tuberculosis but was subsequently found to have greater activity against leprosy. While its strict financial value was limited by virtue of its application in the developing world, it has been of extraordinary benefit in the alleviation of human suffering. Furthermore, the development of clofazimine was an example of what could be achieved at the interface between medicinal chemistry and medicine with a dedicated research team, despite limited resources. It is now time to build on this success and to generate new compounds through innovative approaches, in partnership with medicinal chemistry.

A second step in terms of tradition was the funding by the Wellcome Trust of the Wellcome Centre for Biochemistry at TCD, which provided a purpose-built biochemical laboratory. This, coupled with an imaginative recruiting strategy, led to the development of a central strength in biochemical sciences within that University. In addition, the development of the Genetics Department within Trinity College, largely spearheaded by Professor David McConnell, has resulted in a internationally recognised centre for genetics, staffed by able and committed scientists with significant international reputations (see Chapter 9). A notable success in this department has been the location of the retinitis pigmentosa gene by Professor Pete Humphries's group, a major achievement in international terms[10].

Hence, it is apparent that, in the last twenty years, a serious tradition in biomedical sciences has started to re-emerge, albeit in a rather piecemeal way. However, there is now a need to reunite the scientific disciplines with biomedicine. In an age of rapid development in biomedical science, it is appropriate that tighter integration of medicine with the sciences should be encouraged to prosper. It is in this context that the Conway Institute of Biomedical and Biomolecular Sciences has been developed at UCD under the direction of Professor Hugh Brady and of Dr Andy Robertson. The Conway Institute represents a far-reaching approach to the integration of biomedical research, not only with the biological sciences, but also with physical sciences. Most significantly, in terms of medical biotechnology, the critical technologies of both chemistry and process engineering have been separated from the biomedical sciences. This defect has been remedied to some extent in recent years, a notable example being the synchronous development of chemistry and the biomedical sciences at the PRTLI-funded Conway Institute. Whilst this separation is not a factor which is unique to Ireland, the lack of a tradition in indigenous chemical industry has been a significant deterrent in the terms of developing pharmaceutical biotechnology in this country.

2. *Role models*

It is critically important in the development of indigenous medical biotechnology that there are significant role models for this process. As stated before, the majority of European countries and the US have a tradition in the chemical industry and in

---

[10] P. Humphries, P. Kenna & G.J. Farrar, 'On the Molecular Genetics of Retinitis Pigmentosa', *Science*, **256**, 1992, pp. 804-8.

pharmaceutical chemistry, which has provided significant examples of successful development from small innovation-based companies to major biopharmaceutical entities. There has been little tradition of indigenous chemical industry in Ireland with the exception of major fertiliser companies. In this setting, the stimulus to develop new intellectual property has not been apparent, and hence the incentive to emulate role models in pharmaceuticals has not been available until relatively recently. There are numerous examples of privately based pharmaceutical companies in Europe which have been able to maintain a stable manufacturing base and a capacity for innovation. These have included Jannsen, Servier and Falk, to name but a few. Such companies, which frequently remain in family ownership, have established significant markets and serve firstly as employers of medicinal chemists and secondly as role models for the success of innovation.

What is possibly even more significant in recent years is the deficit in small scale start-up companies in Ireland. Up until recently, there has been limited inducement for researchers to develop intellectual property and to move from 'bench to bedside'. There are very few small biotech companies in this country and these operate in general in rather parlous conditions, being highly vulnerable to changes in the markets and also vulnerable to changes in the philosophy of venture capital companies. The Irish venture capital sector has, by virtue of size and necessity, traditionally adopted a conservative and non-risk-taking approach to funding indigenous industry. While investment in this sector has improved recently, arguably risk has also decreased with the re-emergence of critical mass in world class research in Ireland. Furthermore, while the Industrial Development Authority has been hugely successful in recruiting major pharmaceutical companies to provide employment within this country, it would seem critical that external small to medium research based companies should also be attracted. Such companies could be encouraged by a number of potential incentives in relation to royalties on intellectual property and corporation tax. The attraction of external companies in this sector would provide appropriate role models for the innovative university researcher and would also increase the pool of both business and process expertise in this area in Ireland. However, unless there are significant numbers of such companies established in Ireland within four to five years, then it is unlikely that critical mass can be achieved without recruitment of external industrial expertise within this sector.

3. Business infrastructure

Companies such as Schering Plough, Glaxo Smith Kline, Abbot etc., who are located in Ireland for manufacturing purposes, largely recruit commercial and business expertise based on their understanding and backgrounds in managing existing corporations. There are a very significantly different set of challenges involved in the management and development of small indigenous biomedically-based biotechnology companies, and the critical mass is currently not present in terms of the business expertise required to perform such functions. The challenges for small to medium biotechnology industry include the development and sustenance of new intellectual property, legal protection of intellectual property, the identification of venture capital partners, the successful cultivation of such partners, and the development of strong deals based on mutual recognition of partners' needs. Lastly, the development of strategic partnerships with 'big pharma' is required in order to lead to new developments within the biopharmaceutical sector. Such developments require a new set of skills, not all of which are easily obtainable from the indigenous sector.

Recent developments with recruitments to Ireland of major biopharmaceutical companies, with a biotechnology base, can only help to sustain such developments. However, it should be emphasised that the critical intellectual property that may emerge from such developments will largely lie in the area of process engineering rather than in the basic biotechnology required to establish an indigenous industry.

Hence, it is in this regard that a process in which some, if not all, of the small to medium companies are external companies induced to operate within the Irish sector could provide the business role models for the development of this critical area of the economy.

4. Scientific infrastructure

One of the key problems within Ireland, as stated before, has been the lack of visibility of the development of medical schools as areas of critical mass in biomedical science, with the focus on the developments of new knowledge. Although Irish medical schools are superficially structures along similar lines to their UK counterparts, the staffing of the Irish centres lags seriously behind those of the UK largely in the area of research and development. Specifically, the majority of the Irish medical schools operate on a staffing basis which can be anything from $1/5$ to $1/10$ of their UK counterparts in terms of state funding, and the rate is considerably less favourable when the impact of the charities in supporting academic positions is taken into account. The majority of UK-based departments of medicine have substantial subspeciality departments each staffed with academic teams of professors, senior lecturers, lecturers, technologists etc.[11]. Most of the excess in terms of staffing in the UK *vis a vis* Ireland is devoted to research and development. Nonetheless, it can be said that on a pound-for-pound basis there has been significant value obtained within the Irish sector, particularly in recent years.

5. Human Infrastructure – 'the pipeline'

a. Science Graduates

Irish universities are currently producing approximately 500 high quality graduates *per annum* in the areas related to biotechnology. Unfortunately, there has been some slippage in recent years in the attraction of science as a subject for school leavers, and it is critically important that this slippage is redressed, so that we do have the capacity

---

[11] T. Smith & P. Sime, *A Survey of Clinical Academic Staffing Levels in UK Medical and Dental Schools* (London: Council of Heads of Medical Schools, 2001).

to produce scientists of a high calibre in order to lead the next wave of biotechnology development. Within the training process for Irish scientists, there has been a tradition of spending a number of years abroad at centres of excellence. This tradition has been critically important in maintaining the academic standards within Irish academia and in the biotechnology sector. Hence, exposure to new technologies in international laboratories has been a major factor in driving the Irish academic sector forward. However, at this time, there are a number of significant challenges. Firstly, the increased levels of funding available through many of the funding sources in recent years have led to an increased requirement for high quality graduates. Such quality graduates in research will not necessarily be supplied by the Irish university sector, and recruitment at international level will be necessary in order to prevent any slippage in this process. Secondly, current research programmes do not necessarily provide the skills in entrepreneurship and intellectual property management which are required for new young scientists to enter the biotechnology sector. More recent schemes, such as the HRB PhD Programmes, have specified the requirement for the involvement of PhD students in entrepreneurship programmes, and this is critically important in terms of developing the type of graduate which is required. Lastly, there is a deficit in the creation of long-term career structures in sciences needed in order to maintain the momentum required for sustainable employment in the sciences.

b. Medical Graduates

Irish medical graduates who aim to attain consultants' positions within hospitals in this country have traditionally pursued a period of study either at home or abroad in research subjects, which ordinarily leads to the granting of a graduate degree such as an MD or a PhD, and frequently to very high impact publications. Research degrees are considered to be important criteria for appointment in both academic and non-academic institutions. However, the structures within Irish hospitals (including even the major teaching hospitals) does not permit the facilitation of protected time for research by such highly trained individuals. Hence, there has been a significant waste of a valuable resource in this area in Ireland, with many high quality medical graduates returning to Ireland to take up consultant positions in which there are few or no opportunities for research. More recently, this has been addressed at an early stage by the HRB, which has agreed to fund a number of academic clinician scientist positions. In addition, although the Wellcome Trust Senior Clinical Fellowships schemes do apply to Ireland, there has only been one individual appointed to such schemes at any point. Hence, although we have a significant output of highly trained medical scientists, their utilisation by the research structures within the State has been limited.

This situation may change further with the introduction of recent more formalised training schemes. A feature of the introduction of such schemes, known as Calman schemes in the UK, has been the withdrawal of many of the medical community from research in training, and this has significantly negatively impacted on the UK medical research structures. Hence, within the UK, many universities now find it hard to recruit academic medical staff within several of the medical disciplines. In disciplines such as pathology and surgery there is now a large number of vacant academic posts. In this regard, Ireland has more recently introduced similar training schemes and anecdotally there is a general feeling that their impact has been negative on the ambition and scope of biomedical research by trainees within this country. This, coupled to the fact that there are very few formal academic medical appointments, means that we are probably proceeding towards a serious deficit in this sector. Hence, although we failed to capitalise on the ability to create value through our highly research trained medical community in the past, this failure is likely to be compounded in the short to medium term by a reduction in research activity by medical graduates.

Models for future development of value in biomedical science

The critical aim of all individuals involved in this sector is the development of strength within an indigenous Irish biomedical sector, with ultimate outputs in high quality research and in the creation of national wealth through biotechnology or product development in the devices and software arenas. There have been a number of significant developments in recent years, including provision of SFI funding, and it is clear that it may be several years before we see the economic benefits of such developments. Many of the smaller European countries have also focussed on the development of indigenous medical biotechnology industry. In Denmark and in Sweden, the Medicon valley represents an outstanding example of the effects of well organised and well funded planning in biotechnology within a specific region. The development of a technology region along the Danish and Swedish coastline was a major contributor to the evolution of strengths in these areas within Scandinavia. Such developments were significantly facilitated by the fact that multi-national pharmaceutical companies were already sited in this region, and that the Medicon valley area contained eleven universities, many of which have strong life science departments. Of significant import in this is the fact that twenty-six state-owned hospitals are sited within the Medicon valley, and this is regarded as one of the critical factors required for success. Having started successfully, this community quickly moved to generate a Medicon Valley Academy, which has evolved into a business hub in which there are key collaborations both in terms of research databases, collaborative projects and standard working practices.

Such developments have significant implications for research in Ireland. At this time, biotechnology remains a relatively small sector, and it is critical that research within this sector starts to develop in a integrated way. Certainly, the developments of partnerships at a multinational level with cities and areas within England, Scotland and/or Wales might have significant implications for the development of indigenous biotechnology. A prototype of the development of such a hub in the UK would be the recent siting of the Edinburgh Royal Infirmary outside the city in Frenchtown. This exciting concept involves locating a major academic university hospital on a Greenfield site, with on-site development of very large proportions, including research laboratories, nano-technology laboratories and high quality transgenic facilities. This development is located in a valley in which the Scottish government now proposes to invest several hundred million pounds in the development of indigenous biotechnology companies which are physically associated with this centre of excellence. Clearly, Edinburgh already represents a major hub in biotechnology, containing a number of centres of excellence. However, it is significant that the major research centre is sited on a teaching hospital, and symbolic of the view of the Scottish parliament that this should also be the centre for the biotech industry.

It is unfortunate that Irish biomedical science has undergone such a prolonged period of arrested development. However, recent years have seen Irish output in selected areas, such as immunology, expand to respectable levels by comparison with centres such as Edinburgh or Manchester. It is critical that the concept of medical schools as creators of knowledge and creators of new technological developments is firmly established in this country. In addition, the principles of trans-national geographically based collaboration between Sweden and Denmark has had a major impact in biotechnology. The development of significant trans-national links could have significant implications for this country at this time. The critical mass created by such a development encourages re-location of industry. In the Medicon valley, a new biotechnology company arrives approximately once a month, and it is clear that success breeds success.

Other countries, such as The Netherlands, Belgium and Finland, have also proceeded to start to build on a research base to further develop technology-based industry.

Within Ireland, the development of the PRTLI has played a major role in providing the infrastructure necessary for high quality research and development. It is notable that, prior to PRTLI, the utilisation of high tech approaches in functional genomics and cell biology was extremely remote in terms of the aspirations of research scientists in these areas. The provision of high quality research infrastructure specifically provided by the PRTLI has resulted in an altered level of ambitions by many researchers in the sector. Hence, it is now feasible to take a high tech genomic or proteomic approach to important biological questions and to address issues rapidly through painstaking and limited experimentation. The development of SFI is a second critical component in this section, and provides for approximately €600,000,000 over a five year period for both biotechnology and information technology. A key deficit however remains the ability to recruit and sustain staff within the Irish university sector. Recent years have seen an attrition in the funding available within the university sector, which has made it almost impossible to create new permanent academic positions at senior level, and this is further compounded by the infra-structural problems in academic medicine. We now need to confront these challenges in a realistic way to produce a vibrant and productive new model for biomedical research in Ireland.

CHAPTER 9

Genetics and Biotechnology in Ireland 1950–2005

David McConnell

Introduction

The story of genetics and biotechnology in Ireland 1950–2005 is of course much more complex than can be covered in a short article. However, it is possible to give some idea of what has been achieved and to set that in context, to indicate some of what has been missed, to refer to some of the people who have been responsible, and to give some indication of what may lie ahead. It is a story that ends with a happy if still slightly patchy prospect for Irish science in general. I have written this story with the general reader in mind. If it appears unduly personal, and if it focuses on genetics at the expense of the allied subjects of biochemistry and microbiology, that reflects the information that was to hand and the need for a broader, well-researched review of the development of these related fields in Ireland over this period.

The context is the economic and social revolution that has taken place in Ireland in the period 1960–2000. Until 1960, the Irish economy was based on agriculture and tourism. Today, while these traditional sectors are very important, the economy is based on high technology. In the past, Irish men and women became scientists on the assumption that we would emigrate. Now, we are educated on the assumption that, often after further study abroad, we will have many opportunities to develop our careers in Ireland. We may return to set up well-funded research programmes in universities or research institutes, or to work in industries which are at the forefront of information technology, biotechnology, pharmaceuticals and electronics, or in the sophisticated services which support them. As one measure of our success, Ireland is the main source of about half of the top twenty-five drugs in the world, including Lipitor (Pfizer) and Zocor (Merck) which are the top two on the international market. As another example, Intel Ireland, which produces primarily for the European market, is Intel's largest manufacturing plant outside the USA. And Science Foundation Ireland (SFI) offers research grants which match the best in the world. We have become a relatively highly educated society, now well aware that our prosperity depends on our education.

Irish economic success has been driven by many factors, but the most obvious is the huge inward investment by high technology multinational companies, mostly American, in manufacturing plants and service centres. Irish people now manufacture or support a great range of sophisticated products, but almost all have been invented abroad. Until recently, little industrial research was carried out in Ireland, which was of course disappointing to academic scientists. There were notable examples of companies such as Schering Plough (at its chemical laboratories in Avondale), Elan, Loctite and Iona, which did invest in research and development. But they were unusual.

The Department of Enterprise, Trade and Employment (DETE) and its agency the Industrial Development Agency (IDA) have long recognised the failure to develop strong centres for R&D and have taken some remarkable decisions to rectify the situation. These have been warmly welcomed by the scientific community. Irish economic policy is now aimed at moving up the knowledge ladder. We now intend to move gradually from a knowledge-based economy to a research-based economy.

So, although the industrial development policy has been very successful, it was definitely not built on local science – of course some graduate scientists and engineers were employed by the multinationals, but in production not in R&D. Successive governments failed for thirty years (1970–2000) to institute a sound and consistent science and engineering policy, causing several thousand Irish scientists and engineers to emigrate. The best part of the story concerns the last five years, during which Ireland, through focussing on research, has begun to come of age as a scientific nation; but the reader will have to bear with a rather different story for a quite a while. In the end, we will see that much remains to be done, specially in the funding and organisation of the universities, and the relationship between them and Government.

The leading cause of optimism for scientists and engineers is SFI, set up by the Minister for Enterprise Trade and Employment, Mary Harney, TD, in 2001, on the advice of the Irish Council of Science, Technology and Innovation (ICSTI) and the IDA. SFI now runs a very well financed, internationally peer-reviewed, competitive research programme. The programme is focussed on science and technology, both basic and applied, related to (i) biotechnology and (ii) information and communications technology. Chapter 11 in this volume addresses the latter topic. It will be important to extend this programme to cover other fields of science, and for me the most pressing needs are for chemistry and the earth sciences.

The residual cause for pessimism is the failure over many decades of the Department of Education and Science (DES and its agency the Higher Education Authority – HEA) to pay adequate attention to the importance of research for universities and the role of universities in research. The universities are not well enough resourced in staff or buildings or core running costs, and these weaknesses are now the main impediment to be overcome in the drive by the universities to become internationally competitive research-led institutions. Many departments in science, engineering and medicine have too few staff, the buildings are too old or too small, and the support services are inadequate.

The HEA is the 'statutory planning and development body for higher education and research in Ireland. The HEA has wide advisory powers throughout the whole of the third-level education sector. In addition it is the funding authority for the universities....' To the credit of the HEA, and to successive governments, great strides have been made in third level (higher) education in Ireland. The number of students attending universities has risen dramatically in the last thirty years and now stands at about 75,000. Students, having been exposed to a sound second level education, compete eagerly for places at third level. The opportunities for students to enter third level education, expressed just in terms of places on offer, are now very good indeed. Although there is intense competition to enter certain courses (notably medicine, dentistry, pharmacy, law, human genetics), and good competition to enter many others (including many but not all courses in engineering and science), the fact is that some courses are now under-subscribed. There is now a great opportunity for the emphasis to be switched from quantity to quality.

Courses are generally rigorous. They are provided by well-qualified staff, often with higher degrees from abroad, who have worked hard to create and sustain them, and numbers of wonderful students appear year after year. The courses are monitored by external examiners often from outside Ireland. The result is that Irish university degrees are generally held in high regard abroad. The steady flow of graduates with sound bachelor's degrees has been a major factor in the Irish social and economic revolution. There is however no cause for too much self-satisfaction. Most science, engineering, medical and technical courses are not adequately staffed or otherwise resourced. These courses have been successful to a large degree because of the exceptional contributions made by members of staff. Laboratory courses everywhere are under pressure. As a telling example, it is a great challenge to provide meaningful research projects to final year honours students – in practice these projects, when they are meaningful, rely heavily on research funding and research staff. Too many students are assigned to each member of staff, and HEA funds are not adequate to provide the equipment or the running costs for the projects.

The HEA has not been able to pay as much attention to its remit in research as it has to education. In setting up and expanding these undergraduate programmes, it has been very worrying that the HEA has not been able fully to recognise that the standard of honours degrees cannot be established and maintained unless they are taught in the context of research – that is where the teachers are researchers. This is the best way of ensuring that graduates are encouraged to have accurate, inquisitive, imaginative and independent minds. But teachers cannot be researchers unless they have the time to pursue their research. Student-staff ratios in the universities, now running at 20:1, make it very difficult for staff to maintain strong research programmes. The ratio must be reduced in the research-led departments to less than 10:1 and this of course will mean a massive investment in the core facilities.

The failure to allow for the role of research in undergraduate degrees has been compounded by that fact that the HEA has virtually ignored the need for postgraduate research, until recently. Steps have been taken in recent years, including the Programme for Research at Third Level Institutions (PRTLI), but much remains to be done.

It is clear that there is a deficiency in what has been called 'fourth level education', the education and training of postgraduate students in internationally recognised university research laboratories led by academic staff who have the time and resources to pursue their scholarly interests. What is the relationship to be between the HEA and SFI in developing this fourth level of education in science and technology? This is a common problem – which resources should be provided by the funders of 'education' and which by the funders of 'research'? Actually the dilemma is not too difficult. The university system should be compared to an aircraft carrier. The HEA should provide the ship and its crew (academic staff and support staff) and SFI (and other research agencies) should provide the planes and their crew (the research staff). Perhaps the story of genetics and biotechnology in Ireland over the last fifty years may throw some light on the relationship between education and research.

In consideration of the general reader, I will first say something about the way in which genetics and biotechnology have been developing worldwide, and then show how they have developed in Ireland.

Genetics and Biotechnology – setting the scene, 1900–1970

Genetics is the science of heredity. Biotechnology is the application of the biological sciences to industry and agriculture, and other economic activities. Major discoveries in genetics in the late 1960s and early 1970s gave rise to modern biotechnology. In industry, as examples, it became possible to use purified *genes* (*see below*) to programme living cells to produce valuable materials, especially pharmaceuticals, giving rise to the use of living cells as *factories*. These cell factories, which may be bacteria, yeasts, mammalian cells or plant cells, are of course remarkable because they can *reproduce*. They can be cultured in very large quantities in much the same way as yeasts in making beer, and will produce great quantities of pharmaceuticals. In agriculture, as examples, it became possible to use purified genes to programme crops to be resistant to pests and weed killers. In this section, I shall review the history of genetics for the benefit of the non-geneticist and explain the origins of biotechnology.

In the 1860s, Gregor Mendel, an Augustinian monk working in the monastery in Brno in what is now the Czech Republic, showed that heritable characteristics are transmitted through the germ cells (eggs and sperm or pollen) by units, which we now call *genes*. He showed that genes are found in pairs, one of each pair inherited from the male and one from the female parent. His discoveries lay unnoticed for forty years while Darwin and others struggled unsuccessfully to explain inheritance. Mendel's Laws were re-discovered independently by Correns, von Tschermak and De Vries in 1900, and Sutton and Boveri independently showed that genes are carried on chromosomes. Part of the evidence came from recognising that chromosomes come in pairs and they seemed to replicate (as genes must do) just before a cell divides. Morgan and Sturtevant then found that genes could be arranged as points on lines, called genetic linkage groups, one for each chromosome pair. They began to assign genes to chromosomes and to make *genetic maps* which showed the locations of the genes on the different chromosomes.

No one knew what genes were made of, but the choice lay between protein and DNA, the two main components of chromosomes. In 1944 Avery, McCarty and MacCleod provided beautiful evidence that bacterial genes were made of DNA, but this brilliant piece of work went mostly unnoticed. There was a strong prejudice that genes were made of protein. In any case, bacteria did not seem to be relevant to plants and animals. Avery did not press his evidence as strongly as he might have and was not awarded the Nobel prize he richly deserved. In 1953 Watson and Crick, who were impressed by Avery, and did believe that genes were made of DNA, developed a model for the structure of DNA. They proposed that it was a double helix and, with some other data, this completed the picture. The DNA double helix had qualities which could account for the main properties of genes, especially their capacity to store information, to replicate, and to mutate. Strangely, even this momentous discovery had little immediate impact outside a small group of geneticists. It is now regarded as one of the truly great discoveries of the last century.

In the period 1920–1960, genetics had little or no effect on industry, or indeed on medicine. It hardly mattered to any other science, with the notable exceptions of evolutionary biology and agriculture. In the 1920s, Fisher, Haldane and Sewell Wright combined Darwinism and Mendelism to lay the basis of the modern theory of evolution. The other major impact of genetics, on agriculture, grew directly from the genetical theory of natural selection. Artificial selection of new breeds of farm animals and varieties of plants was just a variant of natural selection (which was of course recognised by Darwin).

Agriculture was revolutionised through the development of powerful methods for plant and animal breeding, and these have added 1% per annum to the productivity of western agriculture from about 1925 onwards. It did not matter to the plant and animal breeders that no one knew what genes were made of; they treated them as units of selection and developed very sophisticated systems for breeding better crops and livestock. Studies of mutagenesis, the process of mutation by which genes are altered, notably by Muller and Auerbach, led to new methods for producing valuable traits in plants, either using radiation or chemicals as mutagenic agents.

The first signs of what is now called biotechnology came from the discovery of antibiotics before and after the Second World War. These were produced during fermentation by fungi, notably *Penicillium* and *Streptomyces*. Genetics contributed to the commercialisation of antibiotics; chemicals and radiation were used to generate mutant strains that produced larger amounts of the antibiotics.

'New' biotechnology emerged from a remarkable series of academic studies in genetics and molecular biology (essentially the molecular analysis of genes and their products) conducted in the period 1944–1970 by microbial geneticists, X-ray crystallographers and nucleic acid biochemists. Most of the work was carried out in the

United States, with major contributions from the United Kingdom and France. The studies were funded by the National Science Foundation (NSF) and the National Institutes of Health (NIH) in the USA, by the Medical Research Council (MRC) in the United Kingdom, and by the Pasteur Institute in France. At the time, some people expected that we would quickly learn more about illness and disease, but there was no expectation that these studies would revolutionise the pharmaceutical industry, agriculture and forensic science, and no one imagined that genetics would create a new technology which would revolutionise most kinds of biological research.

After the rather slow start, more and more geneticists, biochemists and microbiologists, realised the implication of the double helix. The most powerful studies of this period (1953–1970) were focussed on three kinds of macromolecules, DNA and protein, and another, called RNA.

The Watson and Crick double helix showed clearly that DNA could encode huge amounts of information, that this information could replicate and that it could mutate. These were key properties of genes. The structure that they proposed, corresponded closely to the 'aperiodic crystal' discussed by Erwin Schrödinger in his lectures in Trinity College Dublin (TCD or Trinity) in 1945 (later published as *What is Life?*[1]). Crick and others, notably Kornberg at Stanford University, Nirenberg at the NIH, Washington, Khorana at Wisconsin, and Meselson and Stahl at the California Institute of Technology (CalTech), carried out a series of beautiful experiments that led to the formulation of the so-called *Central Dogma* of genetics. This explained the relationship between DNA and protein, including the details of the universal genetic code. The elucidation of the roles of RNA was more tortuous and involved many more people, including Brenner, Jacob, Gilbert, Gros and Watson. By 1964, the main picture was clear.

Genes, made of DNA, are the crucial material of the chromosomes. Each gene carries a specific sequence of information in the subunits of DNA, called bases. There are four bases, called by the symbolic letters, A, C, T and G. A gene is a particular sequence of these units, in bacteria, usually about 1000 units long. A sequence of bases clearly resembles a sentence and, like a sentence, it is of course a piece of information. The question was what could this genetic information be 'telling' the cell at the molecular level.

In the early 1940s, Beadle and Tatum in California had made the extraordinary discovery that each gene coded for a protein. So a gene must carry information that *codes* for a protein. That is, a gene must have molecular information in its sequence that can specify to a cell to make a certain protein.

Proteins like DNA are polymers, made of a sequence of units called amino acids, of which there are twenty different kinds. Each protein is a molecule made of many amino acids joined end to end. The average protein is about three hundred amino acids in length. Some are smaller and some much longer. Function is of course related

---

[1] Erwin Schrödinger, *What is Life? The Physical Aspect of the Living Cell, based on lectures delivered under the auspices of the Dublin Institute for Advanced Studies at Trinity College, Dublin, in February 1943* (Cambridge: Cambridge University Press, 1944), pp. 91.

to structure. A car has a certain structure and therefore can behave as a car. In the case of proteins, we can say that each protein has a specific structure, determined by its amino acid sequence, and this structure causes the protein to carry out a certain function. Some proteins such as enzymes can be regarded as miniature machines, carrying out particular tasks, such as digesting food. Others have structural roles, as in muscle, hair or skin, and others are antibodies or hormones. A nice example is the protein rhodopsin. It is found in the rod cells in the retina, where it absorbs photons of light, turning these signals into electrical pulses that pass to the brain and cause the sensation of sight. There are tens of thousands of different proteins, all with specific structures that allow them to do specific jobs in the body.

Scientists were puzzled for several years about how a gene made of a sequence of four units, A, C, T and G, could encode a protein made of a sequence of twenty different kinds of unit. Some brilliant work showed that the DNA language was expressed in triplets, each group of three bases coding for one amino acid. Altogether there are sixty-four triplets – *codons* – in the genetic code, of which three, TAG, TGA, and TAA code for STOP and are found at the end of each gene. The codon, ATG, codes for the amino acid methionine and signifies START. The other sixty codons code for the other nineteen amino acids. So, for example, AAA codes for the amino acid lysine; GGG codes for glycine; and so forth. Some amino acids are coded for by several codons. For example, phenylalanine is coded for by TTT and TTC.

By the early 1960s, we knew how proteins are made. It turns out that there is an intermediate between gene and protein, called messenger RNA (mRNA). mRNA was the last piece of the jigsaw to be put in place in the grand scheme of the *Central Dogma*. Several lines of evidence had suggested that there had to be an intermediate, notably the evidence (which was disputed at the time) that proteins are not synthesised in the *nucleus*, a membranous bag which contains the chromosomes (and therefore the genes) in the cells of higher organisms. If the genes are in the nucleus, and proteins are made outside it (in the *cytoplasm*) then something must carry the information from the genes to the cytoplasm. This material is mRNA. Each mRNA molecule is a copy of a gene, made by a process called *transcription*. It is a polymer with four subunits called A, C, U and G, where the U corresponds to the T of DNA. The mRNA molecule moves from the gene into the cytoplasm, where it attaches to a very complex molecular machine called the *ribosome* which synthesises the corresponding protein. The ribosome *translates* the sequence of the RNA into the sequence of protein.

Jacob and Monod in 1961 at the Pasteur Institute produced the basic model showing how genes are controlled, so that the right genes are active in the right cell. For example, the rhodopsin gene only works in the rod cells of the retina; in other cells that gene is silent, doing nothing. In other words, the rhodopsin gene is turned on in the rod cells and off in every other cell. The Jacob and Monod model of genetic control was called the *Operon Theory* and contributed significantly to the discovery of mRNA.

Almost all of the genetic and biochemical work which led to the *Central Dogma* was carried out through the study of bacteria and their viruses (bacteriophages) in the twenty years between 1944 and 1964. Bacteria and their viruses were easy to grow, mutants could readily be selected, and three techniques were discovered that allowed genes to be mapped – transformation, conjugation and transduction – and the research did not involve expensive equipment. The extraordinary story is well told for the general reader by Judson in *The Eighth Day of Creation*[2].

One crucial implication of the *Central Dogma*, elucidated mainly by studies in bacteria and their viruses, was that it obviously applied to all organisms, including mammals and plants. The genetic code, which relates the sequence of the bases in a gene to the sequence of amino acids in a protein, was clearly universal (though we now know that there are some slight variations). Apart from anything else, these inferences, which were later shown to be true, provided conclusive evidence that all living creatures were related to each other, and that all were descended from a single common ancestor or small group.

Of more practical interest, it was likely that, if a gene was moved from one organism to another, say from a person to a bacterium, the human gene would probably direct the bacterium to make a human protein. I am not aware of anyone in the 1960s seriously thinking that this kind of experiment was feasible. We quite simply had no idea how to isolate a single gene.

The genetic engineering revolution 1970–1980

By 1970, some distinguished geneticists believed that there was little more of any consequence to be discovered in their subject and some left the field, often to work in neurobiology. In fact, new discoveries have surprised geneticists with wonderful regularity during the last thirty years, and a new technology has appeared. Genetics, the study of heritable variation, has become the most influential of the biological sciences.

While investigating the molecular basis of the main genetic functions (replication, transcription, translation and mutation), a variety of enzymes were identified and characterised. These included DNA ligases, DNA polymerases, reverse transcriptase and restriction enzymes. In or about 1970, it rather suddenly became clear that these enzymes could be used to make new combinations of DNA molecules in the test tube (*in vitro*), that is, new combinations of genes or *recombinant DNA*. It appeared that it should be possible to use this new molecular technology, now called molecular cloning, genetic engineering or genetic manipulation, *to combine genes from different species*. It should be possible to transfer these artificial recombinant DNA molecules into cells and programme the recipient cells to make molecules not found naturally in such cells. For example it should be possible to programme bacteria to make human insulin.

Three discoveries were extraordinarily influential: (i) the discovery of Type II restriction enzymes by Smith and Wilcox, reported in 1970 – these enzymes were the last of the tools needed to make recombinant DNA routinely; (ii) the development of DNA sequencing in the laboratories of Gilbert and Sanger in 1975–1976; (iii) the

---

[2] Horace Freeland Judson, *The Eighth Day of Creation; Makers of the Revolution in Biology* (New York: Simon & Schuster, 1979), pp. 686.

development of the polymerase chain reaction in 1983. Recombinant DNA technology gave birth to the biotechnology industry.

The first genes to be cloned by genetic engineering were some bacterial genes encoding antibiotic-resistance. These genes were cloned by Cohen and Boyer in California in 1974. The genes were chosen for no other reason than experimental feasibility – the antibiotic resistance genes in question were carried on plasmids, small DNA molecules with less than ten genes which could easily be prepared as purified DNA. Also it was easy to *select* cells which carried these genes because they were resistant to the antibiotics. The genes carried on the plasmids coded for proteins that defended the cells against the antibiotics – if a gene encoding resistance to an antibiotic were transferred to a cell, that cell became resistant to the antibiotic and would not be killed (nor would its descendents).

However it was going to be much harder to clone genes from higher organisms, such as human beings, for the simple reason that humans have about ten million times the amount of DNA as a bacterial plasmid. Human DNA molecules are gigantic (they are several centimetres in length) and they carry thousands of genes which we now know are spread very thinly along the DNA; moreover, human genes are organised in a way which means that they need to be processed before they can work in bacteria (this was not known until 1976–1977). Also, there were few if any obvious selection techniques that could be used to identify any particular gene – a gene for insulin does not confer resistance to a bacterial cell.

The development of a technique called cDNA cloning by Mach and Rougeon in Basel, and some clever methods for analysing millions of different recombinant DNA molecules using *nucleic acid hybridisation*, opened up the field. During the 1970s, many human genes of medical interest were cloned and sequenced. These human genes were transferred into bacteria and yeast with the objective of producing the proteins they coded for, in large quantities, suitable for use as drugs and pharmaceuticals.

Much of this work was carried out by small start-up companies, mostly in the USA, financed by venture capital, led by top university scientists and staffed by brilliant young graduates. The US Government investment in the curiosity-driven competitive research programmes of the NSF and NIH from 1945 is the single largest reason for the fact that modern biotechnology was invented in the USA.

The first 'biotech' companies to be founded were Genentech (1976) and Biogen (1978). The most valuable of the early target pharmaceuticals was human insulin. Produced in genetically engineered cells (cell factories), which were grown in huge fermentation vats (by Eli Lilly in the US and NovoNordisk in Europe), genetically engineered human insulin came on the market in the United States and Europe in the early 1980s and quickly replaced pig insulin in the treatment of diabetes. In the 1980s, interferons, growth hormone, interleukins, erythropoietin and a vaccine against hepatitis B, all made in genetically engineered cell factories, followed human insulin onto the market. Many new biotechnology start-up companies were founded, and the multinational pharmaceutical companies began to invest heavily in the new technology. Biotechnology is now one of the main driving forces in the pharmaceutical industry. It is also revolutionising agriculture and has made enormous contributions to forensic science, but these are stories that we cannot go into in this article.

How did genetics and biotechnology fare in Ireland during this extraordinary period?

Genetics in Ireland: George Dawson and microbial genetics 1950–1970

Following independence from the United Kingdom in 1922, experimental science in what is now the Republic of Ireland followed the economy and society into the doldrums. It is not surprising that the essays produced for the 1957 Dublin meeting of the British Association for the Advancement of Science (BAAS) concentrated on describing climate, geology, botany, zoology, fisheries, peat, archaeology and agriculture. *Nothing* is recorded for the *experimental* subjects of physics, chemistry, biochemistry or genetics. In the absence of significant funding from 1922–1957, such subjects were more or less moribund. There were notable exceptions, for example the work of Edward J. Conway, FRS, who was the first holder of the Chair of Biochemistry and Pharmacology at University College Dublin (UCD) (1933–1963), but not enough to hide the weakness of experimental science.

Although scientific plant and animal breeding programmes had been established in Ireland, even in the nineteenth century, and these no doubt were influenced by genetics in the early twentieth century, so far as I can tell, no *fundamental* genetics research of any consequence was carried out in Ireland until George Dawson took up his post as a lecturer in Botany in Trinity College on 1 April 1950.

In 1945, Dawson went up to Cambridge to read botany and genetics, studying under Ronald Fisher, Harry Godwin and David Catcheside. Of these, Catcheside had the greatest influence on Dawson. He had studied at CalTech before the war, and he was familiar with the breakthroughs made in the USA in microbial genetics: the microbial evidence for the one gene-one enzyme hypothesis (Beadle and Tatum, 1941); the discovery that bacterial genes were made of DNA (Avery et al. 1944); the new way of analysing bacterial genes in *E.coli* based on *conjugation* (Lederberg and Tatum, 1946). Catcheside seems to have been one of a very small number of people in Europe who believed that these discoveries were of fundamental importance. In his undergraduate lectures, starting in 1945–1946, which Dawson attended, 'he introduced the ... class to the beginnings of biochemical genetics and, although Watson and Crick were not yet heard of, he gave good reasons for expecting great things from DNA'. When Dawson graduated in 1948, he began his research under Catcheside, just at the time that bacterial genetics was taking off. Catcheside gave him a project on bacterial viruses and it seems that Dawson may have been the first person in Cambridge to work on bacterial genetics. Perhaps not surprisingly he made little progress and never in fact completed his PhD. It has been said that Watson coming to Cambridge in 1952 made people aware of bacterial and bacteriophage genetics. While that is true, there were others who had preceded him, even though to less effect.

Dawson's experiences at Cambridge did not put him off. He brought his interest in bacterial genetics to Dublin in 1950. There he supervised the research of PhD students, including Stuart Glover and Peter Smith-Keary, working mainly on mutation in bacteria. Glover was sent to Cold Spring Harbor, New York, to study briefly with Miroslav Demerec. He picked up new techniques in bacterial genetics, especially transduction, and returned with strains of *Salmonalla typhimurium*. These strains were the main subject of genetics research in Trinity for the next twenty years, some of it funded by grants from the US Army. In the late 1960s, this funding led to erroneous claims by the Trinity Maoist cell that Dawson was carrying out research in biological warfare, and to some, mostly good-natured, confrontations.

It was indeed fortunate that, from the start, genetical research in Ireland focussed on bacterial genetics, the field in which so many great discoveries were to be made in the 1960s, and from which biotechnology was to develop ten to twenty years later. I note here the role of Medical Research Council of Ireland (MRCI) which, with limited funds, supported much of this basic research in Trinity.

As an aside, there is some irony that in the same year, 1950, that Dawson came to Trinity from England, William Hayes FRS, a Trinity graduate who had been educated at St Columba's College in Dublin, left Trinity for London. In the next fifteen years, Hayes was to make several very important contributions to the field of bacterial genetics, and write the most influential textbook in the field *The Genetics of Bacteria and their Viruses*[3]. Unfortunately for Irish genetics, almost all Hayes' work was carried out in London and later in Edinburgh, where he established the Medical Research Council Laboratory for Bacterial Genetics. He became President of the Genetical Society and attended the annual meeting of the Society in Trinity in 1973. Glover went to work with Hayes after completing his PhD in Trinity, and went on to take the Chair of Genetics in Newcastle.

Outside Trinity, in the 1950s, Irish interest in genetics was mainly confined to agriculture, more specifically applied to plant and animal breeding. Dawson made a crucial contact with The Irish Sugar Company, which had started a sugar beet breeding programme. In 1958, he founded the Department of Genetics at Trinity with a grant of £4000 from the Irish Sugar Company, provided through the initiative of the head of the company, General M.J. Costello. The first student to graduate with a degree in Genetics, in 1961, was Adrienne Jessop, who went on to study with Catcheside, who then had the chair at Birmingham, and then to lecture in Pontecorvo's Department of Genetics at the University of Glasgow.

Dawson made other important connections, especially with the new Agricultural Institute (An Foras Taluntais – AFT). The Institute was established by the Government in 1958, with the help of a grant from the Kellogg Foundation. It was headed by Tom Walshe, a dynamic and expansive person. A pattern developed whereby staff of the Institute took and gave courses in the Department. In particular, Patrick Cunningham

---

[3] William Hayes, *The Genetics of Bacteria and their Viruses* (Oxford: Blackwell Scientific Publications, 1964), pp. 740.

(PhD Cornell) and Vincent Connolly (PhD Birmingham) began in the 1960s to give courses to final year students in quantitative genetics and in animal and plant breeding. These continued for more than thirty years and laid much of the intellectual basis for later studies in bioinformatics and molecular evolution.

Smith-Keary, after national service in the United Kingdom, returned to Trinity in 1956, completed his PhD in bacterial genetics, and moved into the new Department of Genetics in 1958. For the next fifteen years, Dawson and Smith-Keary studied patterns of mutation in bacteria and made some strange observations. Dawson recognised that the patterns were somewhat similar to those observed by Barbara McClintock working on maize. She had discovered mobile mutagenic elements, which she called controlling elements. Most geneticists could not understand McClintock, and indeed she was more or less ignored for twenty years. But Dawson recognised the importance of her work and he proposed that Smith-Keary and he were looking at something similar in bacteria, which he called controlling episomes. They may have been looking at what are now called transposons or insertion sequences, and these may even have been carried on plasmids. Their work was noted, rather ascerbically, by Hayes in his textbook. Otherwise, like McClintock's work, it was overlooked for many years until Novick recalled it in a generous review. In 1983, McClintock was awarded a Nobel prize for her work.

The most notable achievement in the Trinity Department in the 'pre-molecular' period was the discovery of external suppressors of frameshift mutations by John Atkins and Shahla Thompson (née Ryasati), reported in the *Journal of Molecular Biology* in 1968. This phenomenon was the first example of non-triplet decoding, now known to play important roles in the read-out of particular sequences of genetic information, notably in retroviruses such as HIV. Although Atkins moved to Cold Spring Harbor and then to Utah, he and Thompson collaborated for many years on the bacterial system. Atkins, the co-editor of *The RNA World*[4], has just returned to Ireland as an SFI professor at University College Cork (UCC).

Cunningham and Connolly set up major cattle breeding and grass breeding programmes at the Agricultural Institute (AFT) in the 1960s. The cattle breeding programme became hugely influential, involving many agricultural co-operative societies and AI (Artificial Insemination) stations and contributing to a steady increase in the genetic merit of the national cattle herd. The plant breeding programme was also highly productive. At the AFT Oak Park Research Centre in Carlow, Vincent Connolly developed varieties of ryegrass which are on the recommended lists in Ireland and Britain, and varieties of white clover that are recommended in Ireland, Britain, France and New Zealand. The potato breeding programme at Oak Park started in the 1960s and, led by Harry Kehoe, produced a series of varieties, notably *Cara*, which is very widely grown in Great Britain, and *Rooster*, which is the biggest crop in Ireland. Other breeding programmes in sheep, barley, sugar beet and wheat were carried on in the Institute, the Sugar Company and in the Department of Agriculture. Taken together,

---

4　Raymond F. Gesteland, Thomas R. Cech & John F. Atkins (Eds), *The RNA World* (New York: Cold Spring Harbor Press, 1993), pp. 630.

these have made a very large contribution to the development of Irish agriculture. As one example, wheat yields in Ireland are now the highest in the world.

Genetics in Ireland: molecular genetics 1970–1980

Graduating from the Department of Genetics in 1966 with a background in chemistry, biochemistry and microbiology, my first interest was in molecular developmental genetics in higher organisms, specifically in genetic control systems. James Bonner at CalTech had just written a delightful book *The Molecular Biology of Development*[5] and typically Peter Smith-Keary had spotted it and bought it for the tiny departmental library. Bonner's book convinced me that we could soon understand the details of genetic control systems in higher organisms such as man, with all that implied for medicine, and I wanted to be part of that enterprise. I was sure that development could be explained by a combination of differential gene expression and the capacity of macromolecules to self organise and interact allostearically with each other and with small molecules (for example hormones). For me, development was not an intellectual mystery, just an experimental puzzle that could be solved by molecular genetics. Dawson, who took a great interest in his students, arranged for me to study with Bonner.

In fact, higher organism molecular genetics turned out to be experimentally a rather immature field in the late 1960s, and expensive too. Realising that this kind of work, rather like nuclear physics, could not readily be pursued in Ireland, where I wanted to base myself, and that it was not likely to reveal very much in the immediate future, my attention turned back to bacterial molecular genetics, specifically to the question 'What is the structure of a *promoter*?' Promoters are genetic control sites first identified by Jacob and Monod through classical genetic analysis.

In 1966, a promoter was expected to be a specific DNA sequence at the start of a gene at which the recently described enzyme RNA polymerase started transcription of the gene; promoters were clearly crucial elements in genetic control systems and were key elements in the Operon Theory. But no one knew the *structure* of a promoter. It was easy to propose that a promoter must have a DNA sequence that distinguished it from other DNA sequences, for example, the DNA sequences of genes. But what was such a sequence, were all promoters the same, or did they differ from one another? If they differed, was there a code for promoters?

At the time I started on this project, no one knew how to isolate a promoter; nor did anyone know how to sequence a promoter. But Bonner was sometimes very open to his students' ideas and agreed to let me strike out on this new track. I devised a molecular strategy for isolating a promoter from the bacteriophage T7 and learned the basic tools of molecular biology in the process. But I did not succeed in isolating, much less sequencing, a T7 promoter, while at CalTech.

Returning to Trinity as a Junior Lecturer in 1970, it appeared I would be the only molecular geneticist in the country. I carried with me photocopies of the two very new

---

[5] James Bonner, *The Molecular Biology of Development* (Oxford: Oxford University Press, 1965), pp. 155.

Smith and Wilcox papers in which they announced the purification and characterisation of the first Type II restriction enzyme, later called *HindII*, from *Haemophilus influenzae* Rd. This was about the same time that Lobban and Kaiser at Stanford and Cohen and Boyer at the University of California at San Francisco were *designing* the first experiments in genetic engineering (which scientists in those early days called recombinant DNA).

The big question for me was how my work in Dublin would be funded. Irish universities, then as now, do not offer 'start-up' grants. I would need a spectrophotometer, an ultracentrifuge, a -80^0C freezer, and so forth, and running costs on a scale that had never been obtained for the research programmes in the Genetics Department. But the omens were quite good.

The Government had adopted Programmes for Economic Expansion in 1958 and 1963 and these had already been quite successful by 1970. New policies were being introduced to modernise both industry and agriculture, to invest in education, to open the Irish market to competition, to attract foreign industrial investment, to reduce our dependence on the UK export market, and to prepare for entry to the Common Market (the European Union). As part of this process, Professor P. Lynch wrote in 1966 that:

> Increased fundamental research as a foundation for future technological changes is most urgently needed. Financial support for fundamental research, which is mostly carried out in the universities, is extraordinarily inadequate....While applied research is necessary, technical development is essential if applied research is to be effective, but without fundamental research, applied research and development would in turn become obsolete[6].

A National Science Council (NSC) to support fundamental research was established and awarded its first grants in 1969. As mentioned, the MRCI also made grants, as did the voluntary Irish Cancer Society.

I made a proposal in 1970 to the MRCI to follow up on the work of Lee Hartwell on the cell division cycle which had greatly impressed me. He had shown in yeast that there was a set of genes (the cell division cycle – *cdc* – genes) which regulated the process of cell division. It seemed obvious to me that other organisms would have *cdc* genes, and it would be important to demonstrate this and to compare them with the yeast system. I proposed to work on *Chlamydomonas* in which cell division could be synchronised by a light dark cycle. I argued, as did Hartwell, Nurse and others, correctly as it turned out, that such studies would help us to understand cancer. It seemed that the MRCI were more likely to fund that sort of work than efforts to isolate and analyse an imaginary genetic element called a promoter. The proposal was rejected by the MRCI.

But the NSC did fund a proposal 'The Isolation of a Gene' also submitted in 1970. As a continuation of my work at CalTech, I proposed to use the newly discovered restriction enzymes to chop T7 DNA into fragments and to isolate and sequence a

---

[6] Patrick Lynch, *Science and Irish Economic Development* (Paris: Organisation for Economic Cooperation and Development, 1966).

fragment carrying a promoter. Funding started in October 1971: Peter Humphries joined my laboratory as my first PhD student and he set out to purify the restriction enzymes, *Hind*II, *Hpa* I and II. We planned to make a restriction map of the early region of T7 phage and to identify fragments that contained the early promoters. Using DNA cellulose chromatography we invented new methods for purifying restriction enzymes and RNA polymerase, and we made reasonable progress on a restriction map of the early region of T7. Unfortunately, T7 was a big molecule and most irritatingly it had evolved (as we later showed) in such a way that T7 DNA was not cut by those restriction enzymes which recognised six base pair sequences. So it was hard to work with. But we were making reasonable progress. We were joined by Patsy Connolly, Thecla Ryan, Peter McWilliam and Garry Mahon and were well on our way to achieve our goals when national science policy was changed.

Following an ill-advised report on Irish science policy by the OECD (Organisation for Economic Cooperation and Development) in 1974[7] – all OECD reports should be treated with caution – the NSC slowly and painfully began to collapse before the promoter project could be completed. The report argued that all university research should be directed at *economic not scientific goals* and the NSC budget faded away. This suited the Government, because the economy was being undermined by expensive employment policies and the oil crisis. Funding for the T7 project, never generous, dried up just as Pribnow and Minkley, in 1973, in Gilbert's laboratory at Harvard, cleverly got the first promoter DNA sequences by sequencing RNA copies. We had been beaten to it. We did get some of the last NSC money, in 1974, for a proposal to isolate oncogenes (genes in which mutations cause or predispose to cancer) from simian adenoviruses, but a big grant proposal to develop these ideas was rejected by the NIH in Washington and this project too collapsed. Irish science was returning to the doldrums just as the recombinant DNA revolution was getting into its stride in the US.

There was nothing for it but to leave again for the US, on the advice of my CalTech colleague, Sally Elgin, this time to the Gilbert laboratory at Harvard, made possible by an Eleanor Roosevelt Fellowship from the International Union Against Cancer. Maxam and Gilbert had just invented the first generally applicable method for DNA sequencing and I used it to sequence the T7 C promoter in 1976–1977. It took about six months to get 400 base pairs of sequence, what could now be achieved in much less than a day. Gilbert was at the time setting up Biogen with colleagues in the United States and Europe, beginning the race with Genentech for the human insulin gene. At one stage, Gilbert and half his staff flew off with their reagents to Charles Weissmann's laboratory in Switzerland to circumvent the US moratorium on genetic engineering.

Genetics and biotechnology: industrial connections 1980–1990

In the mid to late 1970s, the main question for most Irish scientists, whose talents were being wasted and careers crudely interrupted, was whether to stay in, or in some cases

---

[7] OECD, *Reviews of National Science Policy: Ireland* (Paris: Organisation for Economic Cooperation and Development, 1974).

to return to, Ireland. Two things persuaded some of us that there was a future for science in Ireland – the establishment of the National Board for Science and Technology (NBST) in 1978–1979, and the first research grant programmes of the European Union, including the Biomolecular Engineering Programme (BEP), in 1979.

Although both the NBST and BEP programmes were based on seriously defective strategies – the requirement that all research should be applied (which dominates Brussels to this day) – they did offer some hope to molecular geneticists who could devise biotechnology projects that were both interesting *and* applied. There was however a problem – not many industries in Ireland were likely to be interested in biotechnology.

Pfizer had built a very large fermentation plant in Cork in which the fungus *Aspergillus* was used to produce citric acid from molasses. Before the NBST had been set up, a Trinity group comprising a geneticist (myself), a biochemist (Michael McKillen) and a mycologist (Paul Dowding) proposed that Pfizer should collaborate with us to develop methods to genetically engineer *Aspergillus* to produce pharmaceutical proteins (such as insulin). The Pfizer scientists who travelled to Ireland from the main research centre in Sandwich, Kent, to consider this proposal did not seem to be impressed, and it is true that at that time no one had genetically engineered yeast, not to mention *Aspergillus.*

This rebuff recalled the negative reaction of the moribund NSC to an earlier suggestion that I had made that we should approach the cheese industry and clone the gene for rennin, the enzyme that is used to clot milk in cheese production. Rennin was becoming scarce, and it was obvious that the rennin gene should be cloned into *E.coli* or yeast. I was told that the Irish cheese producers would not want to talk with me and, if they did, they would not understand me. The irony is that twenty years later Irish cheese (like most cheese worldwide) was being produced using genetically engineered rennin made by Pfizer in the US and Gist Brocades in the Netherlands.

Although the omens in the late 1970s were not very good, it seemed worth another try to find an industrial partner for an NBST or BEP grant proposal. Two pieces of advice, one from Donal O'Brolchain in the IDA and one from Irish Distillers, pointed to a small enzyme company in Carrigaline, Co. Cork, called Biocon. Founded by a Scottish biochemist, Les Auchincloss, it produced enzymes for the food and drink industry, and had an active research programme managed by Joe Dunne and Owen Ward, both of whom had PhDs. Auchincloss agreed to a series of joint projects, which were later funded by the NBST and by BEP, to genetically engineer *Bacillus* to overproduce industrial enzymes. These were the first serious 'new' biotechnology (i.e. recombinant DNA) projects in Ireland. Conceptually and experimentally, they flowed directly from my interests in genetic control systems going back to lectures from Peter Smith-Keary and the T7 promoter project which I had devised at CalTech. Our first success was the cloning and expression of the alpha–amylase gene from *Bacillus* carried out first by Stephen Ortlepp and extended by Frank Ollington and by Brid Laoide and Eamonn Gormley. Ollington, a graduate of University College Galway (UCG now

National University of Ireland Galway, NUIG) who had taken his PhD with Richard Losick at Harvard, returned to Ireland to set up a genetic engineering laboratory within Biocon. Laoide moved to the Institut Pasteur, working with Agnes Ullmann and later Francois Rougeon, while Gormley, after periods at the Pasteur and in New Zealand, has returned to lead a TB molecular genetics group at the Veterinary College in Dublin, focussing on the development of an oral vaccine for badgers.

Yeast genetics began in Trinity with the work of Bruce Carter. Having studied with Mitchison at Edinburgh and Halvorsen at Brandeis, he joined the Genetics Department in 1974, continuing his research on yeast cell division. With Peter Sudbery, following a suggestion by Paul Nurse, who had found the *wee* mutants of *Schizosaccaromyces pombe*, he isolated a small-size mutant of *Saccharomyces cerevisiae*, which was called *whi* following a bet involving a bottle of whiskey. Carter spent a sabbatical year in the United Kingdom and later moved to become Chief Executive of Zymogenetics in Seattle.

Dr Tom Hardiman, founding Chairman of the NBST, suggested in 1980 that Guinness might be interested in biotechnology, and this led to a very fruitful collaboration in Trinity on studies in *Bacillus* and yeast, led by Barbara Cantwell. The ß–glucanase gene of *Bacillus subtilis* was cloned and expressed in laboratory and brewing yeasts, one of the earliest efforts to apply genetic engineering to brewing. Needless to say, the strains could not be used commercially because of the way the European public came to view genetic engineering. However, the biotechnology and the science prospered. The ß–glucanase clone was commercialised by Biocon, and Noel Murphy sequenced the ß–glucanase gene, the first 'large' sequencing project in Ireland. Murphy moved into the field of trypanosome genetics first in Belgium and then at the International Laboratory for Research on Animal Diseases in Nairobi, Kenya, before returning to Trinity. Geraldine Butler studied the genetics of pyruvate decarboxylase in yeast, collaborating with Hartley's group at Imperial College and Zimmermann at Darmstadt. After working with Denis Thiele in the United States, she joined the Department of Biochemistry, now in the Conway Institute, at UCD, where she has continued her analysis of the ACE2 and SWI5 genes of *Saccharomyces cerevisiae*, and developed new interests in the genus *Candida*. In Trinity, we participated in the European Consortium which initiated the sequencing of the yeast genome, taking part in the sequencing of chromosomes III (McConnell) and II (Wolfe – *see below*).

The *Bacillus* work was developed by Dr Frank Ollington at Biocon (before he went to Genzyme in Boston, where he commissioned the new mammalian cell facility which produces Cerezyme used in the treatment of Gaucher's Disease) and by Kevin Devine and Barbara Dowds at Trinity. Kevin Devine, a graduate of UCD and Trinity, joined the laboratory from University of California at San Diego and, with Stephane Hogan, sequenced and analysed the minimal replicon of the *Bacillus* plasmid pBAA1, which had been discovered in a Biocon production strain. Remarkably, the replication system of pBAA1 was homologous with that of the famous single stranded DNA *E.coli* virus, øX174. ICI (Imperial Chemical Industries) funded the cloning by Dowds of a *Bacillus* gene for alcohol dehydrogenase, and NovoNordisk funded several other industrial enzyme projects. The connection with NovoNordisk developed into a long series of collaborations with Dr Borge Diderichsen, now Vice President of NovoNordisk and President of the European Federation of Biotechnology, on genes for amylases, cellulases and lipases. Diderichsen and I collaborated in an analysis of an industrial lipase gene in *Pseudomonas* carried out by Catherine Buckley and Audrey Hobson, which revealed the role of a 'private' molecular chaperone, required for lipase activity. In the course of this project, Jesper Aamand completed the first *in vitro* synthesis of a gene in Ireland. Cahir O'Kane, a graduate of Cambridge, joined the *Bacillus* group and developed a promoter probe plasmid which he used to isolate a novel genetic control system based on PBSX (phage of *Bacillus subtilis* X). This work was extended by Heather Wood and Gerry McDonnell and led to a patent filed by NovoNordisk. O'Kane went to Basel to work with Walter Gehring on *Drosophila* and developed the enhancer trap, an extension of the promoter probe strategy, moved into neurogenetics, and is now a Reader in Genetics at Cambridge.

The strong research programme in *Bacillus* continues in Trinity, and has been led for many years by Professor Kevin Devine. He has participated in many of the major European *Bacillus* research programmes, notably the sequencing and continuing analysis of the *Bacillus* genome. (During this period Trinity geneticists participated in *Bacillus subtilis*, yeast, *Arabidopsis* and human (bioinformatically) genome projects – *see below*. These projects were a great boost scientifically, and of course we made valuable contacts with many European laboratories.) Devine and Dowds initiated a research project on stress response in *Bacillus* which Devine has developed most elegantly, for example identifying and analysing a series of regulatory systems including YycFG, the only one of the thirty *two component systems* that is essential in *Bacillus subtilis*.

Biocon and the NBST funded an attempt to clone and express rennin, a collaboration between myself in Trinity, Frank Gannon in Galway, and Liam Donnelly at the Agricultural Institute (now Teagasc) Dairy Research Centre in Fermoy in Co. Cork. Chinese students, Yung fu Chen and Lu Qin, participated in the rennin project and these contacts resulted in a contract with China International Trust and Investment Corporation and Beijing Agricultural University to clone and express pig growth hormone (carried out by Dan O'Mahony who later set up the Molecular Biology Laboratory in Elan). Catherine O'Reilly analysed the organisation of *gpt* in *Salmonella typhimuriun* before taking up a postdoctoral fellowship with Heinz Saedler at the Max-Planck-Institut in Cologne, where she cloned Barbara McClintock's famous A1 gene of maize. O'Reilly now lectures at the Waterford Institute of Technology, where she has continued molecular genetic research of industrial systems that she started with ICI in the UK. Throughout all of this work, the laboratory benefited from the knowledge and experience of Terek Schwarz, who later moved to Amersham.

The industrial genetics programmes with Biocon, Guinness, Schering Plough (on the biosynthesis of ephedrine), ICI and NovoNordisk played essential roles in the development of molecular genetics and biotechnology in Trinity in the 1980s, and prepared the way for participation in the 1990s in the yeast and *Bacillus subtilis* genome projects.

Bioinformatics, Molecular Evolution and IdentiGEN

The growing strength of the research and teaching in quantitative genetics and animal breeding in Trinity was acknowledged by the appointment of Patrick Cunningham in 1974 to a personal chair in animal genetics. Further support was provided in 1977 by the creation of a lectureship. This position was later filled by Paul Sharp, who had just received his PhD from Edinburgh, where he had worked with Alan Robertson on quantitative behavioural genetics in Drosophila.

By this time, the methods for sequencing DNA were becoming much more powerful. The first complete genomes had been sequenced, including the bacterial virus øX174 and the bovine mitochondrion, by Fred Sanger's laboratory, the plasmid pBR322 by Gilbert's laboratory, and the bacterial virus T7 by Dunn and Studier. Sharp's research took a new direction when the full T7 DNA sequence of 39,936 base pairs was obtained by Dunn and Studier at Brookhaven National Laboratory, New York; they kindly sent it to me prior to publication. An undergraduate Mark Rogers (later to work with David Sherratt in Glasgow and Stanley Prusiner in San Francisco before returning to a post at UCD), was supervised by Sharp and myself in what turned out to be the first bioinformatics project in Ireland, an analysis of codon usage of T7. We showed, amongst other things, that the codon usage had been subject to selection pressures that had minimised the number of hexanucleotide palindromes which were the targets of bacterial restriction enzymes. Quantitative genetics and molecular genetics had at last converged.

Sharp became an authority on codon usage. He collaborated with Wen-Hsiung Li in Texas, developing his interests in molecular evolution – that is, the way biological molecules have changed during evolution. At Trinity, he began his studies on the evolution of HIV, before taking the Chair in Genetics at Nottingham. His students, Ken Wolfe and Denis Shields, now at the RCSI, and postdoctoral fellow, Des Higgins, who invented CLUSTAL at Trinity, all have significant international reputations in bioinformatics and molecular evolution. CLUSTAL is a computer programme which analyses DNA (or protein) sequences, and is now a standard tool used in molecular evolution.

Wolfe and Sharp had analysed the relative rates of evolution of nuclear, mitochondrial and nuclear DNA, and made several other major contributions to genome evolution. Wolfe moved to Indiana to work with Palmer on the sequencing and analysis of the evolution of the plastid DNA in the non-photosynthetic higher plant *Epifagus virginiana*. He returned to Trinity, and took part in the yeast genome project, contributing to the sequencing of yeast chromosome II. He participated in the first genome-wide analysis of the human genome. He has shown elegantly that the yeast genome has undergone a 'whole genome' duplication. Wolfe has been appointed to an SFI Research Professorship, and is now leading a very strong programme in molecular evolution.

Higgins moved from Trinity to the European Molecular Biology Laboratory (EMBL) in Heidelberg to work on the Nucleotide Sequence Database, later moving with it to Hinxton Hall Cambridge. He moved to University College Cork (UCC) before taking the Chair of Bioinformatics at the Conway Institute, UCD. His paper introducing ClustalW is the most frequently cited paper of all time in Computer Science, and the seventh most quoted paper in Biology/Biochemistry. ClustalW is used to calculate the best match for selected DNA or protein sequences. Higgins has published on many different themes, on various aspects of evolution, showing for example that cetaceans (whales etc.) lie in the Artiodactyla (even-toed herbivores), and that *Plasmodium falciparum* (a human malaria parasite) may have originated in birds.

Dr Colm OhUigin, formerly of the Max-Planck-Institut, Tubingen, where he worked with Klein, and Dr Aoife McLysaght, formerly at the University of California at Irvine, both graduates of Trinity genetics, have also contributed significantly to the development of bioinformatics and molecular evolution in Ireland.

Cunningham's work in the 1960s and 1970s focussed on the theoretical basis of genetic improvement programmes in animals. This research on new methods of selection and crossbreeding, and of computer methods for implementing them, was directed mainly to the Irish cattle population, and was instrumental in the breed changes and selection gains which underpinned the dramatic improvements in efficiency achieved in these years in dairy and beef production. During this period, he began a series of studies on the genetics of thoroughbred horses which have earned wide recognition, one paper with Barry Gaffney being featured on the front cover of the journal *Nature*. Further work, on salmon genetics, with Ashie Norris and Dan Bradley, has pioneered new breeding methods now being used worldwide.

Cunningham became President of the European Association of Animal Production, and later President of the World Association. Following eight years as Deputy Director (Research) he retired from the Agricultural Institute in 1988. He kept a base in Trinity and moved to the Food and Agriculture Organisation (FAO) in Rome as Director of the Animal Production and Health Division. There he supervised the programme for eradication of the new world screwworm from North Africa.

From his experience as a consultant in developing countries, Cunningham had a longstanding interest in cross-breeding European, Indian and African cattle. The gain from cross-breeding is a function of the genetic distance between the parent strains. He reasoned that the rapidly developing methods of DNA analysis could be useful. In 1989, he was awarded an EC grant under the INCO-DC programme, and with Sharp, and PhD students, Ronan Loftus and David MacHugh, set out to measure the genetic distance between thirteen cattle populations using several methods, including comparisons between mitochondrial DNA D loop sequences – another beautiful illustration of convergence of molecular and quantitative genetics. Dr Dan Bradley, a graduate of Cambridge, who had carried out his PhD research on the RP project with Humphries (*see below*), joined the project to supervise the DNA sequencing and molecular analysis. The studies showed that European and Indian cattle had diverged from each other more than 200,000 years ago. This date of divergence implied that domestication (which occurred about 10,000 years ago) must have occurred, not once in the Fertile Crescent, as generally believed, but twice, the second domestication occurring in the Indus valley. Their exploration on the genetic origin of European cattle was featured in *Nature*, and their work with a large team of international collaborators on the origin of African cattle, published in *Science*, was widely recognised as definitive.

In 1996, following the recent bovine spongiform encephalopathy (BSE) crisis, Cunningham, Bradley, Loftus and Meghan founded the biotech company IdentiGEN, which now provides services on traceability to the food industry world-wide. They were the first to recognise the power and utility of DNA traceability for meat products, and the company has been granted a European patent on the process. Recently, the company provided the evidence for a BBC Panorama programme that some European meat processors were adding beef and pork protein to chicken meat.

Bradley has extended his work into the field of genetic anthropology, including studies of ancient DNA, providing some fascinating insights as to the origins of the peoples of Ireland and their domesticated animals. In particular, he has demonstrated a link between the ancient Irish and Basque populations that is evident in the structure of the Y chromosomes found in most Irish men with Irish surnames.

Plant Molecular Genetics

Professor Tony Kavanagh, a graduate of UCD, worked with Bevan and Jefferson at the Plant Breeding Institute Cambridge and invented the hugely important GUS (ß-glucuronidase) reporter gene system. This gene is used as a routine tool in all plant molecular genetics laboratories world-wide. Interestingly, Kavanagh has just invented and patented a new reporter gene system called NAN which has some qualities complementary to those of GUS. He joined the Genetics Department in Trinity in 1987, where he continued his studies on Potato Virus X in a collaboration with Baulcombe (John Innes Centre, Norwich). His work began to diversify through contacts with Vincent Connolly at the Agricultural Institute. Connolly had constructed male sterile varieties of *Lolium perenne* by crossing with *Festuca pratensis*. These male sterile lines would be useful in controlled breeding programmes. The male sterile lines were expected to have a *Lolium* nuclear genome and a *Festuca* cytoplasmic genome. Kavanagh and his student Sophie Kiang showed that the male steriles made by Connolly contained *Lolium* mitochondrial genomes, a rare example of paternal transmission. Kavanagh has subsequently built up a strong plant molecular genetics group. He participated in the *Arabidopsis* Genome Sequencing Project. He has collaborated closely with Harry Kehoe at the Agricultural Institute on constructing virus-resistant potato varieties. Teagasc has recently made new appointments in plant genetics and built new molecular genetics laboratories at Oak Park.

Professor Fergal O'Gara, who had studied the genetics of nitrogen fixation for his PhD with Kieran Dunican at UCG, worked with Ray Valentine and with Helinski in California. He returned to Ireland to take up a lectureship at UCC, where he has built up a strong research programme on the genetics of the interactions between bacteria and plants, notably involving nitrogen fixation and iron assimilation. Much of his research focussed on the fact that nitrogen fixation by the symbiotic bacteria which colonise the root of some plants, notably legumes, depends on a flow of energy (photosynthate) from the plant to the bacteria. He has made many important discoveries on the details of this interaction between the plant and bacteria, for example the role of cyclic AMP, and the importance of dicarboxylic acids and the *dct*A gene.

Starting in 1987, he extended his work into the field of iron assimilation by bacteria in the rhizosphere (the microenvironment around the roots). Some strains of *Pseudomonas* are valuable 'biocontrol' agents because they produce antibiotics that kill or inhibit fungi that are pathogenic for plants. He showed that some Pseudomonds had the capacity to accumulate iron from the soil using iron-binding proteins (siderophores). This work shows the importance of understanding the molecular systems that allow bacteria to colonise the rhizosphere. The antibiotic producers need to be able to accumulate essential nutrients such as iron if they are to thrive in the rhizosphere. He discovered that some Pseudomonads produce an antifungal agent, which he purified and chemically characterised as diacetyl phloroglucinol. He has analysed the genes that are responsible for the biosynthesis of diacetyl phloroglucinol, and shown that these are regulated at the levels of both transcription and translation, at the latter level by a regulatory RNA.

Medical Molecular Genetics, Developmental Genetics and Neurogenetics

Dr Peter Humphries had moved to Pierre Chambon's laboratory in Strasbourg in 1974. He cloned the ovalbumin cDNA, moving to the Beatson Institute in Glasgow just before the discovery that the ovalbumin gene is split. After a period at Queen's University Belfast, he was appointed Lecturer in Molecular Medical Genetics in Trinity. Jane Farrar, a PhD student, David McConnell and Dr Jane Maloney began molecular research on Retinitis Pigmentosa (RP), funded by RP-Ireland Fighting Blindness. Farrar, concentrating first on a group of families which had X-linked RP (XLRP), developed a long and productive collaboration with Humphries on the molecular genetics of blindness. They showed that XLRP in the Irish families was linked to the same RFLP (Restriction Fragment Length Polymorphism) marker first identified by Shomi Bhattacharya. Encouraged by Michael Griffith and Paddy Byrne of RP-Ireland Fighting Blindness (which raised more than £100,000 for the project, a huge sum in those days in the 1980s), Humphries and Farrar obtained significant grants from the British and US RP Societies and later from the Wellcome Trust. They formed a large team (including Peter McWilliam, Paul Kenna, Dan Bradley and Marion Humphries) which was first to map (using RFLPs) an Autosomal Dominant RP (ADRP) locus. They showed that ADRP in a large Irish/British family was caused by a mutation in the gene for rhodopsin. The Humphries-Farrar group has made many significant contributions to the genetics of blindness, and is now concentrating on the development of gene therapies using mouse models. Peter Humphries was appointed to a personal chair in medical molecular genetics in 1991. Dr Farrar was appointed to a Wellcome Senior Lectureship.

In the 1980s, Humphries began an important collaboration with Dr Shaun McCann, Head of the National Bone Marrow Transplantation Unit at St James's Hospital, Dublin, on the molecular genetic analysis of leukaemia. The initial studies were carried out by a PhD student Mark Lawler, now Associate Professor of Experimental Haematology and Oncology at St James's. These studies laid the basis for the development of molecular medicine in the Trinity.

Dr Michael Smurfit, a prominent Irish businessman, made a gift of £750,000 to Trinity in 1989 to establish a chair of medical genetics to mark the 400th anniversary of the foundation of the College. The first holder of the chair was Dr Steven Whitehead, a graduate of Edinburgh and Cambridge, who moved to Dublin from the Harvard Medical School. Working mainly on serum amyloid A proteins, and on homocystinuria with Professor Ian Graham of the Adelaide Hospital, Dublin, he held the chair with distinction before returning to the US in 1998. He was succeeded in 1999 by Dr Seamus Martin, a graduate of National University of Ireland Maynooth (NUIM), who had studied with Green at the University of California at San Diego and had become an international authority on apoptosis (cell death). Martin now holds an SFI Research Professorship. During this period, Dr Michael Gill, who had carried out his MD with Humphries, returned from the Institute of Psychiatry in London to a position in the Department of Psychiatry at Trinity. He set up molecular genetic projects in the Smurfit Institute of Genetics, searching for genes in which mutations predispose to bipolar affective disorders, schizophrenia and Attention Deficit Hyperactivity Disorder (ADHD).

The National Centre for Medical Genetics (NCMG) at Our Lady's Hospital, Crumlin, Dublin, was started in 1994 with Professor Michael Geraghty, Dr Ray Stallings and Dr David Barton as Director, head of the cytogenetics and molecular genetics laboratories respectively. Professor Geraghty returned to Johns Hopkins University in 1996 and was succeeded by Professor Andrew Green in 1997. Dr William Reardon and Dr Sally Lynch were appointed as consultant clinical geneticists in 1999 and 2003 respectively. The NCMG has carried out collaborative research programmes on hereditary breast cancer, amyotrophic lateral sclerosis, male infertility, vesico-ureteric reflux, and childhood neuroblastoma. The NCMG has also developed a fruitful collaboration with Professor Gill of the Departments of Psychiatry and Genetics at TCD into the genetics of autism, participating in a major international autism genome project. The Irish part of the project has been awarded €5 million by the Department of Health and Children.

There is a growing interest in the fields of developmental genetics and neurogenetics in Trinity. Kevin Mitchell, a Trinity genetics graduate, worked with Goodman at Berkeley and Tessier-Lavinge at Stanford on the development of the neural systems of *Drosophila* and the mouse. He has returned to an SFI funded programme in Genetics. Mani Ramaswami, also a developmental neurogeneticist, formerly at the Tata Institute, CalTech and Berkeley, now in Arizona, will shortly take up an SFI professorship in the Department of Zoology. Paula Murphy, who took part in the first *Bacillus* stress response project, and moved into mammalian genetics at Edinburgh, has recently returned to Trinity to the Department of Zoology. A developmental geneticist, funded by SFI, she is collaborating with the Mouse Atlas and Gene Expression Database Project at the Medical Research Council Human Genetics Unit in Edinburgh in an analysis of limb development.

Humphries, Farrar, Gill, Mitchell, Ramaswami and Murphy will contribute significantly to the newly established Trinity College Institute of Neuroscience.

Professor Tommie McCarthy, who had studied at London and at NIH, moved to UCC. Collaborating with Professor James Heffron, he mapped a gene for the ryanodine receptor in which mutations predispose to malignant hypothermia and central core disease. Professor David Croke, who had studied photophysical methods for sequencing DNA at Trinity with McConnell, and with the physicist Professor Dan Bradley FRS, and the photochemist Professor John Kelly, then worked with Claude Helene at the Muséum National d'Histoire Naturelle in Paris. He returned to work at the RCSI, where he has carried out detailed analyses of mutations causing PKU (phenylketonuria) and galactosaemia in the Irish population.

Microbial genetics at UCC, TCD and UCG (NUIG)

The field of microbiology had developed slowly but steadily in Ireland in the 1960s, often associated with clinical microbiology and diagnostics. In the 1970s, several geneticists were appointed at UCC (led by Seamus Condon with strong links to the dairy industry) and at Trinity (led by John Arbuthnott linking with medical microbiology at St James's Hospital) and also at UCG (led by Kieran Dunican). In Cork, in the period 1980–1990, a strong molecular genetics research programme emerged as a collaboration between staff at UCC and Teagasc at Fermoy (later headed by Liam Donnelly). This field was started by Professors Charles Daly and Seamus Condon, and continued by Gerry Fitzgerald, Paul Ross, Catherine Stanton and Colin Hill. They collaborated with many European laboratories, including Venema's at Groningen, in a long and extensive series of studies on lactic acid bacteria, and their viruses and plasmids. Some notable work has been carried on colicins, toxins made by bacteria which kill closely related bacteria. Their programme is widely regarded internationally as one of the most powerful in food microbiology.

In Trinity, Tim Foster, a microbial geneticist, who had studied with Gilbert Howe at Bristol, began to work on transposition, spending a sabbatical year with Nancy Kleckner at MIT in 1977–78. When Arbuthnott was appointed to the Chair, Cyril Smythe, Peter Owen and Greg Atkins joined the staff, and the whole department moved rapidly into the field of molecular biology in the 1980s, mostly working on microbial and viral molecular pathology. On Arbuthnott's move to Nottingham and Strathclyde, Charles Dorman (BSc, UCD; PhD, TCD) at Dundee, where he had worked with Higgins and held a Royal Society University Research Fellowship, returned in 1994 to take up the chair of microbiology at Trinity. His international reputation was established by his studies on the relationship between the tertiary structure of DNA (and DNA protein complexes) and the control of RNA synthesis (transcription; gene expression) in *E.coli.* He is an authority on the relationships between gene regulation and pathogenicity, and on global control networks operating at the level of gross DNA structure. He was awarded the Fleming Medal of the Society for General Microbiology.

In UCG, the main developments in genetics, which were linked to biotechnology, followed the appointment of Dr Frank Gannon. A graduate of UCG, he took his PhD at Leicester before moving to Chambon's laboratory in Strasbourg. At UCG, he set up a biotechnology programme and degree in the microbiology department, and an active research programme in eukaryotic molecular genetics, in particular on estrogen receptors, before being appointed as Director of EMBO.

Other developments in genetics and biotechnology

As the 1990s progressed, cell and molecular biologists, biochemists, pharmacologists and other specialists began to use genetic strategies and genetic engineering. Biological and biomedical departments began to appoint molecular geneticists to staff positions, for example McCarthy and Higgins (now at UCD) to the Biochemistry Department in UCC.

In UCG, James Houghton, in the Department of Microbiology, had set up the Cytogenetics Unit in 1970, carrying out chromosome studies for the Western Health Board. In the 1980s, he also started to provide DNA studies for several inherited disorders. In the Department of Zoology, Noel Wilkins used DNA markers to study the migration of salmon and other problems in marine science. Recently, Noel Lowndes has been appointed to the chair of biochemistry in UCG. Lowndes, a graduate of Trinity, had moved to Scotland to study for his PhD in yeast genetics and then to the Imperial Cancer Research Fund laboratories in London, where he built up a significant reputation for his studies on the genetics of the cell division cycle in yeast. Several new research groups, all influenced by genetics, have been established recently at UCG, for example under Tim O'Brien, Frank Barry, Michael Carty, Ciaran Morrison and Heinz-Peter Nasheuer.

In Trinity, outside the departments of Genetics and Microbiology, the other major centre for cell and molecular biology is the department of Biochemistry, where major programmes in molecular immunology are led by Luke O'Neill and Kingston Mills.

Genetics at Queen's University was for a time organised by a sub-department of Genetics set up in 1964, but biology there has been plagued by a series of re-organisations which took away much of the momentum. Andrew Ferguson has carried out some beautiful work on the evolution of fresh water fish populations in Ireland, especially the salmonids. Michael Hart, who had studied with Hayes at Edinburgh, and Ivor Hickey, worked on phage genetics and cancer respectively. In Medicine, Norman Nevin set up a cytogenetics and genetic counselling unit in the 1970s, and this led to the development of a strong medical genetics service.

In UCD, Eamonn Duke in Zoology, and Jeremy Timmis and Matthew Harmey in Botany, initiated genetical research programmes and caused a number of fine students to choose to study genetics. The main centre for molecular genetics for several years was the laboratory of Finian Martin in Pharmacology, where the prolactin promoter was characterised by Maurice Treacy (now Director of Biotechnology at SFI) and Bill Schuster, and the transcription factor NF I was characterised by Eileen Furlong and Rosemary Kane. Several molecular biologists have been appointed in various departments, including Geraldine Butler, Therese Kinsella, David MacHugh and Mark Rogers, and brought together in the new Conway Institute. The UCD Medical School benefited from the brief tenure of Garret Fitzgerald, before his move to the University of Pennsylvania. He was succeeded by Hugh Brady, who has accelerated the development of the programme in molecular medicine and collaborated with Dermot Kelleher of Trinity and Desmond FitzGerald of the RCSI in setting up the Dublin Molecular Medicine Centre. Brady is now President of UCD.

Institutional developments and Government policy from 1990–2004 *(see also Chapter 3)*

The NBST had been quite successful in promoting biotechnology in the 1980s with its own funds and through active support for Irish applications for European funds. The IDA had been very successful in attracting many pharmaceutical companies to set up production plants in Ireland (Merck, Eli Lilly, Smith Kline etc – *see Chapter 10*). The IDA took an interest in biotechnology and sent a number of missions to the US (I took part in two of these) to explore how Ireland should react. These were to bear fruit in the pioneering decision by Schering Plough to establish its recombinant interferon production plant at Brinny in County Cork, the first recombinant protein plant in Europe.

However, just as biotechnology research was taking off, the NBST, like its predecessor the NSC, fell foul of political lack of vision. It was combined with the Institute for Industrial Research and Standards, with which it had little in common, to form a new organisation called EOLAS (somewhat presumptuously named – Eolas is the Irish for 'knowledge' which is not confined to science and technology), which later became FORBAIRT, before becoming part of Enterprise Ireland. In the process, funding for basic research became capricious and in some years virtually disappeared. Fortunately another government organisation called BioResearch Ireland (BRI) was set up, supposedly to commercialise university biotechnology. Actually very little of this research had reached a stage at which commercialisation was possible. BRI made an important contribution by helping to keep some basic research going on the pretext that it was providing infrastructure; altogether an awkward situation.

BRI wanted to set up its own research centres in each of the universities. This suited some but not all, and bizarrely it became clear that many projects were not being funded solely on the basis of excellence. The result was a confusing mixture of structures, confusing messages both scientifically and politically, conflicting standards and a gradual weakening of local funding for genetics and biotechnology. Some excellent work was done by Barry McSweeney, Jim Ryan and Peter Daly and their colleagues in maintaining contacts with the European Community biotechnology programmes, and these as before helped to prevent a total collapse of genetics in Ireland. The other major positive factor at this time, the 1990s, was the growth in funding from the Wellcome Trust, which was crucial for the work of Humphries, Whitehead, Bradley, Gill and Martin in Trinity.

It was clear that the national biotechnology research situation was most unsatisfactory. Life science research was limited and what did exist was mostly dependent on foreign money, mostly from the EC and Wellcome Trust. But by now, the 1990s, biotechnology had moved into the mainstream of the pharmaceutical industry. The IDA had been hugely successful in attracting multinational pharmaceutical companies to set up manufacturing plants in Ireland – thirteen of the top fifteen pharmaceutical companies had plants in Ireland by 2003, the foreign companies now employ 17,000 people and their exports are worth €33 billion per year (*see Chapter 10*). These multinationals needed to be confident that Ireland could support the burgeoning biotechnology industry.

But all scientists, not just those in the life sciences, and all industries not just the pharmaceutical industry, were concerned about the dearth of research funding in Ireland. Many scientists who had worked hard with successive governments now turned to public debate. The Irish Research Scientists' Association was set up, government policy began to be openly criticised, and critical reports appeared in *Nature* and other influential journals. There was much discussion in government and university circles as to whether the Department of Education or the Department of Industry (both departments changed their names several times in this period) should be responsible for new initiatives. The Government appointed the Science, Technology and Innovation Council (STIAC), and it reported in 1995 with many proposals, but it set modest goals and did not really address the key problem – the weakness of Government funding for science and engineering research in the universities.

The HEA, which had failed to provide for research at the universities, commissioned the CIRCA Report[8]. CIRCA was highly critical of government policy and university performance even in the expurgated version that was eventually published (1996):

> The comparative data are well-known. Public funding for higher education research is among the worst in the OECD....The (university) sector is at the bottom of the OECD league....the situation would seem to be quite untenable.

Yet Richard Taylor, Nobel laureate, noted in his report to CIRCA that:

> I suspect that one could assemble one more first class university in Ireland if only one could repatriate the best people who had gone abroad.

---

[8] *A Comparative International Assessment of the Organisation, Management and Funding of University Research in Ireland and Europe* (CIRCA Group Europe for the Higher Education Authority, 1996), pp. 242.

A report by the Royal Irish Academy (1997) on science research funding and the setting up of the Irish Biotechnology Industry Association (IBIA, chaired by Micheal Comer and run by Matt Moran) by the Irish Business and Employers' Confederation added pressure to the call for decisive action by the Government.

One proposal from STIAC turned out to be crucial, namely to establish The Irish Council for Science, Technology and Innovation (ICSTI) on a statutory basis, and this was taken up by the Government in 1998. There is no doubt that the IDA and its parent body Forfás had been advising the Government that Ireland could no longer rely on the combination of a favourable tax environment (low corporation tax in particular), and a well-educated, young, mobile, inexpensive and flexible workforce for future economic development. It was essential that we should become a research-based economy and that more knowledge should be indigenous and not imported. The Department of Enterprise and Employment (DETE), headed by the Tánaiste (Deputy Prime Minister), Mary Harney, formed a view that Ireland had to develop a strong science and engineering infrastructure. ICSTI was set up to report through Forfás to her Department. The Chairman was Dr Edward Walsh, formerly President of the University of Limerick, and the Vice-Chairman was Dr Brian Sweeney, Chairman of Siemens Ireland.

ICSTI quickly produced comprehensive *Technology Foresight Reports*[9] written by seven panels and covering almost all fields of science and engineering. I chaired the Health and Life Sciences Panel, advised by Michael Comer, formerly of Boehringer Mannheim and then Chairman of the IBIA, Jim Ryan of BioResearch Ireland, and Matt Moran, Director of IBIA. We designed a Biotechnology Programme, based on the idea that Ireland should establish and fund an internationally competitive research programme. This had a large influence on the final *Technology Foresight Report*, which was presented personally to the Cabinet by Walsh and Sweeney in 1999.

The Health and Life Sciences Panel had advised that it was essential that the Government set up a *National Biotechnology Investment Programme* which would cost about IR£75 million per annum. No one had ever talked in numbers like these before. At the time, the total budget for *basic research in all science and engineering* was IR£2 million.

The main proposal of the *Technology Foresight Report* was that Ireland had to establish and fund internationally competitive fundamental research programmes to underpin the development of *biotechnology* and *information and communication technology*. The question was would the government accept this advice and invest massively in relevant but curiosity-led research judged mainly if not solely on excellence.

The Government had already received another report from the highly respected Economic and Social Research Institute (ESRI). In March 1999, it published its report *The National Investment Priorities for the Period 2000–2006*[10]. The Report emphasised the importance of R&D as the 'main engine of growth'. It criticised the low level of public

---

[9] Irish Council for Science, Technology & Innovation, *Technology Foresight Reports* (Dublin: Forfás, 1999).
[10] ESRI, *The National Investment Priorities for the Period 2000–2006 – Policy Research Series Paper No. 33* (Dublin: The Economic and Social Research Institute, 1999).

investment in public good research and proposed that overall expenditure on research in all categories should rise from IR£168 (1999) to IR£250 million (2006), of which IR£10 million was to be allocated to competitive research funding.

This looked like a terrible blow to the universities. There are always difficulties in deciphering just what is included in such figures, but it was clear that the ESRI was not proposing a revolution. The total research budget of Stanford University was about $600 million in the late 1990s. The Smurfit Institute of Genetics, with seven academic members of staff, had a research income of IR£1.5 million in 1999.

Fortunately the Government was prepared to be revolutionary and went even further than the scientific community could have anticipated. *It allocated IR£1.5 billion to research and development for the seven year plan 2000–2006.* IR£560 million was allocated to a new statutory funding body *Science Foundation Ireland* (SFI) to be spent on science and engineering projects related to the two fields, Biotechnology and Information and Communications Technology (ICT). The mandate of SFI was made clear from the beginning by the Tánaiste – it was to fund all research, whether basic or applied, provided the proposals are externally peer reviewed and are related to either of these two fields, biotechnology and ICT.

SFI has been operating for about four years. The Board of SFI, initially chaired by Dr Brian Sweeney, appointed Dr William Harris, formerly of the US National Science Foundation, to be the first Director General. Under the research grant programmes of SFI, candidate principal investigators may apply from any country and proposals are judged solely on excellence by international peer review. Research grants to individuals are typically €200,000-300,000 and may be as high as €1 million per annum for five years. The salaries of SFI professors are paid by SFI and they are relieved from heavy teaching loads. The universities are therefore in a position to appoint replacement staff on contract thereby bringing further talent into the Irish system. In four years 2001–2004, 750 scientists, about half in biotechnology, have been funded by SFI with grants worth in total €317 million. *The SFI programmes are attracting successful applicants from many countries and must now be considered among the best funded in the world.*

To quote Mary Harney, the Tánaiste:

In essence, Ireland has embarked on what amounts to a new direction in industrial policy. This policy aims to generate clusters of world-class technology-based companies, both Irish- and foreign-owned, that work in new knowledge areas in collaboration with university researchers. Together, they will advance scientific knowledge, commercialise research output, create high-level jobs, and build an entrepreneurial environment in which new technology-based businesses will prosper[11].

---

[11] *Chemical and Engineering News*, June 14, 2004, **82**, No. 24 pp. 32-37.

Several centres now have large numbers of well-funded research staff. As just one example, the Smurfit Institute of Genetics now has about 100 research staff funded by external research grants worth more than €4.5 million.

Success brings its own problems. It is somewhat worrying that most research ideas in biotechnology worth funding in Ireland are now being funded or will be soon. Our research capacity in genetics and biotechnology is becoming limited by the availability of top quality principal investigators. This mirrors the development of science in the US which, since 1945, has become more and more dependent on the skills and ideas of immigrant scientists. It is now vital that SFI focuses even more strongly on attracting top class immigrant scientists. This will also help to solve another major problem. The staff student ratio in the universities is 1:20 and getting worse. We need to appoint a large number of top class young research active scientists to the universities using the mechanisms of SFI. It remains to be seen whether the HEA is able to persuade the Department of Education and Science (DES) that it should contribute to the expansion of scientific staff in the universities. Finally, we need to address in a much more sensible way the fact that many university laboratories are either too small or too old to take on further projects.

There has been some progress in building laboratories. Under the seven year National Development Plan, IR£500 million was allocated to the HEA to be spent on the new Programme for Research in Third Level Institutions (PRTLI). This programme emanated from a proposal by the remarkable Irish-American philanthropist, Chuck Feeney, that he would contribute matching funds to selected projects funded by PRTLI. His gifts to Irish universities, mostly for buildings – thereby filling a woeful deficit – are believed to have amounted to more than IR£500 million in the last fifteen years. Many of the PRTLI projects, for example the Conway Institute in UCD, have been focussed on the life sciences and biotechnology. Other Irish and Irish-American philanthropists, including Dr Michael Smurfit, Sir Anthony O'Reilly, Lou and Loretta Glucksman, Martin Naughton, Peter Sutherland and William Vincent have been exceedingly generous in making substantial gifts.

However, the PRTLI was not intended to provide general funds for university staff and facilities. These remain inadequate. Regrettably the policies of the DES (Education) working through the HEA on the one hand, and the DETE (Industry) working through SFI on the other, are not well enough coordinated. The DES has not been prepared *to pay and provide for sufficient core staff* who are the people who should be initiating most of the research proposals to SFI, well funded by the DETE. The Irish universities have gained much more from the latter than the former, and in this we can see the persistent high quality thinking of the IDA.

Conclusion

Those of us who have taken part in Irish science for the last forty to fifty years now have good reason to believe that at long last we have begun to emulate other small northern European nations. In the words of the eminent Irish historian at UCC, Joe Lee, we are now organising our main resource, that is our intelligence, more effectively. There are Irish geneticists and biotechnologists all over the world, and there are many others who are not Irish, who are becoming aware of what is happening in Ireland. If they are up to the challenge, then Ireland is now intent on offering them research environments second to none. The genetics community in Ireland has grown rapidly in the last twenty years, funded at different critical stages by the NSC, European Commission, NBST, BRI, industry, Wellcome Trust, Fighting Blindness and, latterly, by SFI and PRTLI. Irish geneticists are now publishing with some regularity in *Nature*, *Science*, the *Proceedings of the National Academy of Science*, USA, and other leading journals. There is no better sign of the power of Irish biotechnology than the $1.8 billion being invested in the biotechnology campus of Wyeth at Grangecastle in the western suburbs of Dublin, the largest biotechnology project in the world. Wyeth is in the process of recruiting more than 1,000 staff at Grangecastle, most with PhDs or MScs, many of them educated by the Irish research scientists – geneticists, biochemists and microbiologists – who have built up their fields so successfully in the period 1950–2005.

CHAPTER 10

Chemical and Pharmaceutical Sciences

Matt Moran

Introduction

It is not possible to consider the role of Chemistry in Ireland today without outlining the remarkable evolution of this country as it became one of the leading producers of Pharmaceutical and Chemical products in the world today. It is hard to imagine that the industry as we know it today is in fact just over thirty five years old, making it one of the newest such sectors in the modern world. It is worth tracing the history of the sector, as this allows us to place it in context. The following paragraphs explain how the chemical industry has evolved in this country, how it has risen from a very modest beginning to become what it is today – the most valuable sector in the Irish economy.

Post Second World War era

Chemical manufacturing first began to appear in Ireland early in the nineteenth century. In 1823 there were two Alkali plants, seventeen chemical manure plants, eleven plants for sulphate and ammonia, and eleven for the extraction of salts from brine registered under the Alkali Act. However, the growth of the chemical industry in Britain resulted in a rapid decline in the industry in Ireland and, by 1930, only two of the manufacturers listed in 1898 still survived.

The First World War, the Depression in the late 1920s and early 1930s, and the effects of the Second World War resulted in a further depression of the Irish economy, and the period post World War II saw exports low and the imports of essential materials severely reduced. In the period just after the War, when this history starts, Ireland's economy was dominated by food, drink, tobacco and textiles, and there was little evidence of a chemical or pharmaceutical industry. This is clearly illustrated by examining the figures for industrial output from the time. The total output of what was then called the chemicals and drugs industry was just over £1 million: the majority of this was for the home market and consisted of the distribution, preparation and compounding of medicines, soaps, detergents, etc. There was little evidence of any manufacturing or chemical industry *per se*, with the exception of the production of industrial alcohol from potatoes and the manufacture of fertilisers with associated Sulphuric Acid manufacture.

Industrial alcohol production in Ireland

In 1938, a company was established under the Industrial Alcohol Act to manufacture alcohol from potatoes. Five factories were built in fairly remote areas to use up surplus potato crops generated through overproduction or by the presence of disease. These plants were pre-assembled by Skoda in Czechoslovakia and shipped to Ireland for assembly on site at Cooley, Ballina, Carrickmacross, Carndonagh and Labbadish. Petrol companies were obliged by the 1938 Act to blend the alcohol with petrol to make up PAB or petrol alcohol blend, which at the time was considered a premium blend of motor fuel.

In the early days, some of these plants operated without running water or electricity. Plants were operated by DC generators driven by steam, which powered belt driven agitators.

Legislation was passed to change the name of the Industrial Alcohol Company to 'Ceimici Teoranta' and to extend its powers so as to investigate the manufacture of other chemical products. This resulted in starch and glucose being manufactured at some locations. In 1960, the plant at Ballina was the only manufacturer of water white glucose in Europe – one of its major customers was the Foxes Glacier Mint factory in Belfast!

All industry in Ireland was protected by tariff barriers, and this was the environment in which industries were established. Burgess Galvin established a facility in Dublin around 1950, which manufactured putty for the building industry and adhesives for the packaging industry. They then specialised in paints and a range of specialised detergents for the emerging hygiene requirements of the food industry.

One of the largest companies of the time was Gouldings, who operated a number of fertiliser manufacturing plants around the country.

However, it was not until the initiation of the first programme of economic expansion of 1958 that a truly concerted effort was made to establish a substantive manufacturing base in chemicals.

Establishment of Irish refining

In June 1957, a decision was taken to set up an oil refinery in Ireland. Irish Refining Company Limited was established as a consortium of three companies, The Californian Texas Oil Corporation, The Esso Petroleum Company Limited, and Shell Mex and BP Limited. The building of the refinery was justified on the basis of an expanding domestic market, which would consume enough petroleum products to economically justify the amount of capital needed to establish the operation. The refinery, located at Whitegate, Co. Cork, was designed with a capacity of two million tonnes per annum.

This was Ireland's first real exposure to a major petrochemical or chemical installation and the brochure produced at the time refers to fractionating columns as *'strange sea monsters coming ashore'*. It was estimated that, during construction, 500,000 tonnes of rock and earth were moved on to the site for levelling purposes, five miles of road were built for the refinery purposes, seventy five miles of piping were laid above ground and ten miles of piping below ground, and 38,000 tonnes of concrete were used. The annual consumption of electricity would be approximately thirty million units, and the tallest process tower was measured at 265 feet [81 metres] above sea level.

The introduction of the refinery was a very important stage in the development of the Irish industry, especially in the Cork region, as it was from this refinery that many of the skilled people came who went on to work in and help develop what is now such a thriving industry in the Cork area.

1960s

In 1957, Leo Laboratories, the Danish pharmaceutical company, established a facility in Dublin, mainly to supply the UK and home markets. This was followed by the establishment of Loftus Bryan Chemicals Limited by two German entrepreneurs at Rathdrum in Co. Wicklow in 1960–1961. Loftus Bryan manufactured active ingredients for generic medicines at the Co. Wicklow site until it was taken over in January 1981 by the US based Schering Plough Corporation, who renamed the company Avondale Chemical Company, after the nearby birthplace of Charles Stewart Parnell, Rathdrum's most famous son.

In 1963, the Government appointed a Commission of Industrial Organisation, which was charged with the task of examining the difficulties which possible entry into the Common Market might create for existing Irish industry. This Commission produced a detailed report on the Irish chemical industry. The report concluded that, at the time, there essentially was no basic chemical industry apart from four plants manufacturing sulphuric acid for the fertiliser industry. This was attributed to lack of native raw materials and lack of capital available for such investment. What the survey did identify was a secondary chemical industry producing paints, inks, pharmaceuticals, soaps and detergents for the consumer market, employing approximately 2,800 people and generating about £6 million per annum of production. The report noted that, out of the 2,800 employed in the secondary chemical industry, only fifty-two were chemists, reflecting a very low level of development work carried out in the industry at the time. Exports were negligible, and the industry operated in a highly protected home market, providing products nearly exclusively for domestic consumption.

In the same year, Squibb Linson established a pharmaceutical manufacturing plant at Swords, Co. Dublin. 1965 saw the start up of the Nitrigin Eireann Teoranta (NET) plant at Arklow to manufacture calcium ammonium nitrate and ammonium sulphate fertilisers. Plants to manufacture sulphuric acid, ammonia and phosphoric acid as raw materials for fertilisers were also started up at the Arklow site. This allowed the manufacture of Complete Combined Fertiliser (Nitrogen, Phosphorus, Potassium) at the plant.

1979 saw the establishment of a combined ammonia and urea plant at Marino Point at Cork using the natural gas from the Kinsale Field. In the early 1980s, the Arklow plant changed from making Calcium Ammonium Nitrate (CAN) and

Complete Combined Fertiliser (CCF) to just making CAN, which necessitated the shutting down of phosphoric acid, sulphuric acid and CCF plants at the Wicklow site. NET ceased to make ammonia at the Arklow site in 1980. Production at both the Cork and Arklow sites ceased altogether in 2002.

1969 to 1989

The twenty-year period between 1969 and 1989 saw a rapid expansion of the pharmaceutical and chemical industry in Ireland, and it is the investment that took place in this period which is responsible for the strength of the sector in Ireland in the 1990s and on into the twenty-first century. During this period, the Industrial Development Authority of Ireland (IDA) specifically targeted those industries which would benefit most from the type of incentive package that they could offer in terms of grant aid and tax incentives. The type of industry which the IDA needed to attract was one that did not depend greatly on a convenient source of raw materials, or was not too dependent on transportation to get the product to market. This resulted in the IDA identifying fine chemicals and pharmaceuticals as being one of the key sectors for development, along with electronics, information technology and instrumentation. The basic or bulk industry, with its high level of capital investment and recourse to scale, was deemed unsuitable.

The IDA proceeded to aggressively market Ireland as an investment location for these types of industries, one of the prime targets for the IDA executives being the United States of America. The results of the IDA's strategy are plainly evident today. The expansion of the sector has been extraordinary, and a cursory glance at one or two key indicators will clearly demonstrate this. For instance, between 1973 and 2003 exports grew from £79 million to over €35 billion, which represents an impressive growth rate (*see Table 1* – page 227). Ireland is now a net exporter of pharmaceutical and chemical products, the so-called Balance of Payments figure increasing from £110 million in 1982 to over €28 billion in 2003. Currently there are some 220 companies or distribution outlets engaged in pharmaceutical, chemical and associated product manufacture and distribution. In value terms in 2003, the sector was the most important to the Irish economy, counting for some 43% of total exports from this State. At this stage, it should be noted that, during this period of rapid development, Ireland's mainly indigenous fertiliser industry contracted. The availability of cheaper raw materials from the UK heralded the eventual closure of such major manufacturing concerns as Gouldings Fertiliser Company. Cost pressures on what is a commodity based industry, highly susceptible to cyclical fluctuations, have led to closing down of Irish Fertiliser Industries and the ultimate demise of this part of the industry.

Development of Irish PharmaChemical sector

As already mentioned, there was some development of the pharmaceutical and fine chemical companies taking place in the 1960s, but the real inflow of companies began probably in 1969 with the establishment of a citric acid manufacturing plant by Pfizer

Pharmaceuticals Production Corporation in Ringaskiddy. The IDA identified two development areas for the industry in Cork, one at Little Island and the other in Ringaskiddy. In 1972, Pfizers also established a pharmaceutical production facility at their Ringaskiddy site. Pfizers were followed into Ringaskiddy by Penn Chemicals, now Smithkline Beecham Pharmaceuticals, in 1975. Quest Biocon, the Dutch parent company, established its food ingredient plant in Carrigaline in 1976. In the early 1980s, Angus Fine Chemicals developed a chemical synthesis plant, now owned by Hickson PharmaChem, just across the harbour from Pfizer in Ringaskiddy. Major investment in Ringaskiddy culminated with the announcement by Sandoz in 1989 that it was to establish a major pharmaceutical chemical synthesis facility there.

Meanwhile Irish Fher, now Irotec, Henkel, Gaeleo (Pfizer Pharmaceuticals), Mitsui Denman, FMC International, Plaistow, Cara Partners and Janssen Pharmaceuticals were all establishing sites at Little Island, and Eli Lilly, then Elanco, established its facility outside Kinsale in 1981, and Schering Plough took over the Chembiotica antibiotic plant at Innishannon in 1983 to manufacture biotechnology products such as Interferon-A.

Site facilities were being established at Tipperary by Merck Sharp & Dohme in 1976, Sterling Drug (now Smithkline Beecham) in Dungarvan and in Dublin, where Warner Lambert, Organon, Armour Pharmaceuticals, now Reheis, and Loctite, all established facilities. Meanwhile, in the Mid-West in the early 1980s, Syntex, SIFA, PGP, Devcon and Aughinish Alumina all established facilities in or close to the Shannon development area.

1989 to 1997

The 1990s saw a significant slowdown in new investment into the country (with only Helsinn, Organon, Wyeth Medica, and Grelan announcing major greenfield investments during that period). There were a number of reasons why this occurred.

1. Ireland became a victim of its own success with regard to attracting successful pharmaceutical and chemical companies to Ireland. Examination of the league table of the top ten pharmaceutical companies by sales in the world in 1994 revealed that eight of them have plants in Ireland (*See Table 2* – page 228). So it is likely that the IDA simply ran out of obvious targets for investment in Ireland.

2. The world-wide pharmaceutical and chemical industry started to go through a period of dramatic change which was characterised by rationalisation and a process of mergers and acquisitions of the major pharmachem corporations, resulting in a number of plant closures with consequent job losses. In such an environment, new investment becomes more difficult to win. Other locations were now competing aggressively for the companies that Ireland would have competed for back in the 1970s and 1980s. Locations such as Singapore, parts of Europe (Holland,

Belgium and some Eastern European countries), made competition for inwards investment far more difficult.

3. There was relatively little growth of the indigenous industry in Ireland, with some notable exceptions such as Arran Chemicals, Iropharm, Newport Pharmaceuticals, Plaistow and some generic drug companies.

4. There was one theory that the vociferous scaremongering engaged in by some environmental lobby groups caused companies not to consider Ireland as a potential location for investment. This certainly would have been the case with Merrill Dow, who were due to establish a pharmaceutical plant in Killea outside Youghal in east Co. Cork. It is difficult to gauge how much influence the activity of such lobby groups did have, although undoubtedly some of the more high profile activities which took place in the late 1980s did not help Ireland in its attempts to attract further investment to the sector, especially in Cork.

However, all this having been said, the existing sector did continue to grow strongly, and recent surveys carried out by the Irish Pharmaceutical and Chemical Manufacturers Federation (IPCMF) showed employment still continuing to grow at 6% – 7% *per annum*. Examination of the list of new investments announced in 1996 and 1997 (*see Table 3* – page 228) shows ample evidence of continued strong growth in the existing sector. This was particularly encouraging given the difficulties being experienced by the industry globally. It is likely that forward integration into pharmaceutical production will be more characteristic of the sector in the future.

Characteristics of the sector today

Because of the strategy pursued by the IDA in the early 1970s, a quite original pharmachem sector has developed in Ireland. The sector is dominated by fine chemical and pharmaceutical companies, all relatively new, mostly being less than twenty-five years old. This has allowed a high-tech sector with extremely good standards of quality and environmental performance to develop.

Basic chemical production is limited to oil refining, alumina production and the extraction of magnesia from sea water by Premier Periclase.

The high value nature of the sector which produces products not greatly dependent on infrastructural support suits Ireland well. The pharmaceutical and chemical sectors have been identified by Forfás in their document *Shaping Our Future* as important for the future creation of employment and wealth in this country.

The industry is mainly centred in Dublin and Cork, with some other companies scattered around the western seaboards and some midland areas.

Though the industry has had its problems in the past, with a perception that it has caused environmental damage, it is now generally accepted by most of those involved in administration of environmental policy that the sector is committed to environmental protection, and its commitment to waste reduction and clean technology is duly recognised. A report published by the Environmental Protection Agency in 1996 entitled *State of the Environment Report 1996* stated that:

> Sectors with the highest profile in terms of their capacity to inflict environmental damage are also the most conscious of the impact of these issues on their business. Eighty percent of companies surveyed had invested in environmentally friendly technologies and over two-thirds have changed processes to minimise waste.

A survey of the Cork pharmachem industry commissioned by the industry and carried out by Ove Arup and the state agency Forbairt pointed out that the sector has a compliance rate of 99.4% with their environmental licences in the Cork area. It is now accepted by the industry that most of the work needs to be done in communicating their performance to the public rather than actually changing their performance. It seems likely that the Irish PharmaChem industry will continue to be a major contributor to the Irish Economy well into the next century – perhaps the future of the sector is readily encapsulated by a headline that appeared in *The Irish Times* on 4 March 1994 which read '*The Chemical Industry now offers Clean, Green Employment*'.

The industry today

This wave of new investment has allowed Ireland to develop critical mass in the sector. This in turn has led to further investment. Ireland now has sixteen out of the top twenty global pharmaceutical industries operating out of the country.

The most recent figures published by the Central Statistics Office reveal that, in the year 2003, the Pharmachem Sector exported products to a value of over €35.7 billion accounting for some 43% of the national total (*see Table 1*).

Table 1: Exports

1973	€100.31 million
1995	€6.40 billion
1998	€18.03 billion
1999	€21.08 billion
2000	€27.22 billion
2001	€32.25 billion
2002	€39.4 billion
2003	€35.7 billion*

*43% of total exports for Ireland

Source : CSO

The figures indicated in Table 1 clearly track the relentless increase in the value of this sector to this economy.

Table 2: Employment

Year	Numbers Employed	Increase/(Decrease)
1992	15,400	–
1993	16,100	4.5%
1994	17,200	6.8%
1995	18,800	6.0%
1996 (March)	19,700	4.8%
1997	20,900	6.1%
1998	22,700	8.6%
1999	22,200	(2.2%)
2000	23,600	6.3%
2001	24,100	2.1%
2002	24,100	–
2003	24,000	(0.4%)

Source : CSO

Table 2 outlines employment trends, which reveal steady and continual growth. Growth in the sector is set to increase, driven by new Greenfield investment. A summary of some of the recent new investments is set out in Table 3 below:

Table 3

Expansions

	Euro Millions	Employment
Pfizer Ireland	609.47	350
Merck Sharp & Dohme	171.41	50
Organon Ireland	25.39	170
Pfizer Inchera	57.14	150
GlaxoSmithkline Beecham	317.43	100
Wyeth Medica	57.14	170
Elan	209.51	n/a

Greenfield (New Investments)

	Euro millions	Employment
Wyeth BioPharma	1269.74	1300
Bristol-Myers Squibb	380.92	250
Genzyme	317.43	480
Alza	152.37	80
Abbot	406.32	200
Centocor	650	330
Gerard Laboratories	40	380
Altana Pharma	70	150
Taro Pharma	n/a	300
Recordati	28	60

Ireland remains a location of choice for the manufacture of pharmaceutical and chemical products. It is accepted that much of the new investment in this sector will depend on biotechnology, with much of the cutting edge research in pharmaceuticals relying more and more on the knowledge gained through the human genome project. Disciplines such as molecular biology, bioinformatics and proteomics combine with chemistry to deliver novel therapeutics commonly referred to as biopharmaceuticals. It is important that Ireland is seen as location of choice for such investment if it is to maintain the momentum that has driven this sector to date. Cutting edge products attract new investment and allow Irish facilities to keep abreast of state-of-the-art, hence protecting and enhancing existing investment.

The decision by Wyeth BioPharma to construct what will become the largest biomanufacturing plant in the world has sent a very positive message out to the world that Ireland is still on the pharmaceutical map and is ready and willing to embrace the new wave of biotechnology. US-based biotechnology company Genzyme is constructing a pharmaceutical facility in Waterford at present, hence maintaining this wave of new investment. According to IDA Ireland, further investment in the biotech area is being actively sought and is a distinct possibility in the future.

Meanwhile the existing core of companies have maintained investment, and many of these are engaged in significant investment plans to add capacity and upgrade their facilities. Bristol-Myers Squibb is constructing a brand new chemical synthesis plant at Cruiserath in Dublin. Recently, Japanese company Takeda announced that it would construct a pharmaceuticals ingredient plant in Dublin, adding to the pharmaceutical finished products plant that it currently operates in Bray, Co. Wicklow. Pfizer Pharmaceuticals is nearing completion on a series of major investment projects in Cork, where it has expanded its synthesis capacity and constructed a drug products facility.

Future trends

In the post September 11 environment of economic uncertainty, the pharmachem sector seems like a rock of stability in increasingly stormy seas. It has retained its reputation as a solid employer with good long-term prospects for this country.

However, this is a global sector operating out of an open economy which is vulnerable to the vicissitudes of international economic fluctuations. It is key that the sector maintains competitive advantage, especially against locations that also compete for pharmachem investment, such as Singapore or Puerto Rico. It is important that the country retains a low rate of corporation tax and also that it maintains and enhances its skills base. The Government has prioritised investment in R&D. This is welcome; however, it is necessary that, as the R&D infrastructure develops, it does so in close co-operation with science based sectors such as the pharmachem sector. Close liaison between companies and individual institutions will become increasingly important as more companies increase process development at their sites.

The role of Chemistry in the future

Much of the recent debate surrounding the role of chemistry in Ireland today has centred around the study of the subject in Ireland's schools and how readily the science has been accepted by Irish society as a whole. This debate is set against a European backdrop of nervousness by the public as to the intrusion of chemicals into their lives. Much public fear has been reinforced by a fairly consistent campaign of scare-mongering by those opposed to the chemical industry, rather than to the science itself, combined with a reduction in confidence in the ability of regulatory authorities to control industry in general. A recent response by the European Commission to streamline the regulation of chemicals for the better has produced the so-called REACH proposal, which has prompted a vigorous response by the industry in Europe. Though the industry welcomes the principles of consumer and worker protection enshrined in REACH, it views the Commission approach as being heavy handed, producing a set of regulations unlikely to work as set out at present, which will damage the relative competitiveness of the industry in Europe. It is against this backdrop that the role of chemistry in this country is viewed.

The study of Chemistry

The percentage of students sitting chemistry for the Leaving Certificate has fallen substantially since the end of the 1980s (*see Table 4*)

Table 4: Percent of Cohort Sitting Physics and Chemistry in the Leaving Certificate (Higher + Ordinary Level)

	1989	1990	1991	1992	1993	1994	1995	1996	1997
Physics	19.6	19.9	20.0	20.2	19.9	19.2	18.3	16.8	15.6
Chemistry	16.8	16.0	14.9	13.8	13.7	14.3	14.4	13.2	11.8
Physics & Chemistry	3.6	3.5	3.3	3.2	3.1	2.8	2.6	2.4	2.1

Table 4 (continued): Percent of Cohort Sitting Physics and Chemistry in the Leaving Certificate (Higher + Ordinary Level)

	1998	1999	2000	2001	2002	2003	2004
Physics	15.1	14.5	14.1	14.8	15.6	15.7	14.8
Chemistry	11.4	11.1	11.0	11.2	11.7	11.9	13.1
Physics & Chemistry	1.9	2.2	1.7	1.8	1.7	1.7	1.5

Source: Department of Education and Science

The situation has been similar for physics. This indicates a clear problem around the take up of physics and chemistry at second level within our schools system. Inevitably, this causes a knock-on effect into the third level system, causing a reduction in the numbers available to study the physical sciences at third level. This has led to a dramatic reduction in the number of points required to gain entry to these qualifications. This in itself has led to an overall fall-off in the quality of students pursuing third level qualifications in physics, chemistry and related disciplines. Ultimately, this presents a problem for those parts of the economy that depend on the physical sciences – including not only the pharmachem industry but also related industrial sectors such as electronics, the health sector, local authorities, government agencies etc. Though recent figures point towards an arrest in the decline, with a slight recovery being detected between 2000 and 2003, the situation remains serious. The fact the total numbers sitting the Leaving Certificate is declining as the population greys will exacerbate this problem further (*see Table 5*).

Table 5: Numbers Sitting the Leaving Certificate Examinations (Higher + Ordinary Level)

	LC Cohort	Biology		Chemistry		Physics	
		Total	%	Total	%	Total	%
1997	59,053	29,032	49.2	6,970	11.8	9,223	15.6
1998	64,155	30,613	47.7	7,325	11.4	9,659	15.1
1999	62,844	28,750	45.7	6,963	11.1	9,112	14.5
2000	60,737	26,660	43.9	6,711	11.0	8,588	14.1
2001	56,670	24,060	42.5	6,355	11.2	8,411	14.8
2002	55,374	22,024	39.8	6,497	11.7	8,651	15.6
2003	56,237	22,671	40.3	6,698	11.9	8,806	15.7
2004	55,224	24,027	43.5	7,229	13.1	8,152	14.8

Source: Department of Education and Science

The Task Force on Physical Sciences

Recognising the problem of the fall off in the study of the physical sciences, Government established a Task Force on Physical Sciences to study the problem and to provide recommendations as to how it could be addressed. The Task Force was chaired by former President of Dublin City University, Dr Daniel O'Hare. The Task Force comprised forty four members drawn from the educational community, Government, business, professional institutes and a range of other representative bodies. It conducted a total of 1,100 interviews with second and third level students and parents of second and third level students. A wide range of submissions identified 189 different issues, which were considered to be either impacting on, or to having the potential to impact upon, the situation.

In the Foreword to the report, O'Hare said that the problem is real and that, if anything, its extent and importance were understated. He warned of a situation arising whereby much of the money spent by the State to attract overseas industry would go to waste unless the something was done.

The report identified a six point action plan covering the following areas:

1. Planning and Resources for School Science
2. Equity of Access
3. Teaching and Learning of Science
4. School Curriculum and Assessment
5. Promotion of Science and Careers
6. Science Education at Third-Level.

They costed this plan at €178 million in capital investment with an annual recurrent cost of €66 million, based on costs in February 2002.

To date, the Government has been slow to act upon these recommendations in areas that require significant expenditure – such as enhancing laboratory facilities in schools. Nevertheless, a Committee has been established to promote science and engineering to students – Discover Science and Engineering Steering Committee. Chaired by the well known science broadcaster, Leo Enright, this committee will help by supporting a range of initiatives aimed at bringing science to children in schools in a way which will engage their interest. The establishment of this Committee is a welcome development. However, it is critical that Government enhances the work that it can do by investing in the science teaching infrastructure as well.

Industry initiatives

The Pharmachem industry itself views the reduction in numbers of those studying science with some concern. A strong educational system has been one of the primary drivers behind the development of such a strong pharmachem sector in Ireland. With over 50% of those employed in the sector possessing some form of third level qualification, it is not difficult to forecast the impact of a deterioration in this on the further development of the sector. This led the body that represents the industry in Ireland, PharmaChemical Ireland [a business association within The Irish Business and Employers Confederation (IBEC)] to launch an educational strategy which involved the appointment of a full time education officer, Mark Glynn.

The elements of this strategy are to:

- Encourage Government to implement policies which support the provision of skills to the sector
- Help promote science to the public at large
- Support the general knowledge of science throughout the primary curricula
- Increase the awareness of science at junior cycle and increase participation in science subjects at senior cycle
- Increase the number of students studying science at third level
- Increase the retention rates of science graduates in the pharmachem sector.

The industry has organised itself into a set of locally based clusters of companies with a remit to develop close links with schools in their area. This will allow cross-fertilisation between the industry and those schools. It will in turn allow school goers to become aware of the good employment opportunities that are available in the industry.

PharmaChemical Ireland has enhanced its web-site (www.pharmachemicalireland.ie) to provide support materials for teachers and careers guidance councillors. An information resource titled 'Opportunities in the Pharmachem Industry' has been published. This is packed with useful information on the companies themselves. It also outlines which companies run site tours, sponsor school links etc.

PharmaChemical Ireland has targeted the secondary school transition year (between fourth and fifth year) and, in collaboration with Forfás, it has developed a Transition Year Science Programme. The programme is divided into four distinct modules:

- Forensic Science
- Chemical Engineering
- Sports Science
- Cosmetic Chemistry.

Each module is divided into two parts: a careers section and an interactive section. The careers section outlines relevant information for the students – e.g. 'A day in the life ......', career prospects, minimum qualifications required etc. The interactive section has a multitude of experiments that can be conducted on an individual basis or as part of a programme. There will also be the potential to involve public speaking and presentations as part of this programme. It is intended to build a library of lesson plans on science related areas – e.g. astronomy, environmental science etc. These ready-made lesson plans will then be e-mailed on a weekly basis to participating teachers. All these resources will be posted on the website.

Embedding the Pharmachem Sector

The global Pharmachem industry is undergoing change to which the industry in Ireland is seeking to respond. The high cost of development and manufacture of pharmaceutical products is highlighting the need to take new products to market as quickly and efficiently as possible. Typically it takes ten to twelve years to bring a new drug from the laboratory bench to the patient. This can involve the screening of up to six million individual different chemical entities, requiring a total investment of up to one billion US dollars. Despite the increasing investment in R&D by the industry, the output of the R&D has been diminishing in recent years. This is manifest in what is termed the 'pipeline problem'. The number of New Molecular Entities (NMEs) approved by the Food and Drug Administration each year has fallen from 53 in 1996 to 17 in 2002. Similarly the number of New Drug Applications (NDAs) has dropped from 131 to 78 over the same period.

A firm is granted patent protection for a new discovery for twenty years from the date of that discovery: therefore the company is afforded eight to ten years to recover its investment and to generate sufficient income to fund research into the next new product. This whole process is conducted against a backdrop of ever-tightening regulations.

To-day, many of the so-called blockbuster drugs are reaching the end of their patent lives, opening the market up to intensive competition from me-too or generic producers. Given the fact that many of these drugs are manufactured in Ireland, this presents a strategic threat for the industry here. Low tax locations such as Puerto Rico and Singapore compete aggressively for mobile investment based on even lower tax regimes than exist in Ireland. They have enhanced their attractiveness by investing in improving their research base.

In a recent report published by The Irish Council for Science, Technology and Innovation (ICSTI), titled *Embedding the Pharmachem Industry in Ireland*, it is suggested that the industry in Ireland must adapt to the new global environment which the industry now faces. It proposes that the industry in Ireland focus its efforts towards investing in more process development and process optimisation, hence embedding or anchoring the sector more firmly in this country. This report was prepared in consultation with the industry, the research community and relevant Government agencies, so therefore it has support from each of these stakeholders.

This report is in reality proposing a move up the value chain for the industry in Ireland. In turn, this will present a challenge for chemistry in Ireland. Traditionally, the industry in Ireland has offered attractive careers for chemists. However, the vast majority of these would have been related in the main to manufacturing. Now there will be an increasing demand for chemists prepared to work in the area of research to support development in the sector. This in turn will increase the demand for PhD chemists who in the past may have had to look elsewhere for career opportunities.

Role of Research

The centre of gravity for research in the pharmaceutical industry is the US. Spending on R&D in the US totalled €32 billion in 2002, equivalent to 18% of US revenue (domestic sales plus exports); R&D expenditure in Europe was $23 billion. Of the twenty nine NMEs launched in 2002, thirteen originated in the US, eight in Europe, seven in Japan and one elsewhere.

Notwithstanding the tighter budgetary situation, expenditure on R&D in the US increased by 12.3% in 2002; in contrast, expenditure by US firms outside the US *decreased* by 8.9%. US firms currently spend only 18% of their R&D budgets outside the US.

The current balance of global research, where the US expenditure on R&D exceeds that in Europe by 40%, represents a reversal of the situation prevailing at the beginning of the 1990s. In 1990, the European expenditure on R&D exceed that in the US by 50%, and the number of NMEs originating in Europe over the period 1988–1992 was 97, while only 52 originated in the US.

The European Union (EU) Market

The basic statistics relating to the industry in Europe in 2002 were as follows:

- Total Production   €160 billion
- Total R&D expenditure in Europe   €19.8 billion
- Total R&D employment   19,500
- Total Employment   853,000.

The pharmaceutical industry accounts for 15% of business expenditure on R&D in the EU[1].

The relative decline in EU R&D is a key concern for the industry. The problems underlying this phenomenon have been outlined recently by Sir Tom McKillop, President of the European Federation of Pharmaceutical Industries and Associations (EFPIA) and CEO of AstraZeneca[2]. Firstly, the EU has yet to achieve a single market for pharmaceutical products; it still comprises 15 distinct national markets, which clearly has cost implications for the industry. Secondly, there is a lack of consistency between national governments when setting prices; a manifestation of this inconsistency is that *parallel trade* now accounts for 5% (€3.6 billion in 2001) of the EU market for pharmaceuticals. This problem may well become more acute since the recent enlargement of the EU.

EU governments must strike a balance between minimising the cost to consumers and national health care programmes, on the one hand, and supporting innovation on the other.

EC initiatives to address the fragmentation of EU research in general, and medical research in particular, such as the creation of a *European Research Area* and the proposed establishment of a US-style Institute of Health, coupled with the commitment to achieve 3% GERD (Gross Expenditure on Research & Development) by 2010, can only have a positive impact on the sector in Europe, given that the main opportunities for growth lie in innovation and in the development of NMEs. Ireland will be well positioned to benefit from this, given our installed base of global pharmas.

Europe's leaders, recognising the continued erosion of the relative competitiveness of the European Union relative to the USA and Asia, have prioritised investment in R&D. In Barcelona in 2002, EU Heads of State declared that the total spend on R&D in the European Research Area (ERA) will reach 3% of GDP by the year 2010. In Ireland's case, this stands at 1.4% of GNP or €1.36 billion. Government has proposed that this will need to increase to 2.5% of GNP by 2010, totalling some €3.68 billion. Business will be expected to contribute about two thirds of this figure or €2.54 billion. It is inevitable that these trends and developments will impact on Chemistry in Ireland, if not science in general.

[1] European Federation of Pharmaceutical Industries and Associations, www.efpia.org/3_press/20040312.htm
[2] EFPIA, www.efpia.org/3_press/20040210.htm

Industry Response

PharmaChemical Ireland has just prepared its second five year business plan. It has declared a mission and a set of strategic objectives aimed at securing the future of the sector in Ireland. This will profoundly impact the future of chemistry and the physical sciences in this country. It is outlined below:

Mission Statement

PharmaChemical Ireland aims to position Ireland as the most productive, best serviced, added-value location in the world for the sustainable development and manufacture of pharmaceutical and integrated chemical products.

Overall Objectives

- To ensure that the external business environment supports and enhances the relative competitiveness of the pharmaceutical and chemical sectors in Ireland.
- To promote a coherent human relations policy for the industry which makes it the employer of choice.
- To promote science and the study of science based subjects, at all educational levels, in order to ensure that the industry is supplied with a pool of well-educated and motivated young people.
- To maintain the position of the industry as the leading sector in terms of environmental performance by implementing best available techniques in state-of-the-art waste treatment systems, cleaner technology and waste minimisation initiatives.
- To promote and encourage best practice in health and safety within member companies through compliance with regulations, auditing and adoption of codes of practice.
- To promote and support compliance to quality standards in the industry through regular communication and dialogue with regulatory authorities and the establishment of codes of practice and adherence to regulatory requirements.
- To support measures that will further stimulate research and development within the sector resulting in enhanced embedding of the sector in Ireland.
- To promote and build awareness of the industry through a defined communications policy which will be aimed at government, public service, local communities, education and the media.

Conclusion

If one was to cast one's mind back to the early 1960s in Ireland, it would be difficult if not impossible to imagine how central the physical sciences were to become to the economic future of this country. Ireland's economy is dominated by Pharmaceuticals, Healthcare, Chemicals and ICT. Each of these sectors depends on the physical sciences for their future success. Moreover the Irish Government, through Science Foundation Ireland and the Programme for Research in Third Level Institutions, has opened up the option of careers in research.

It is imperative that all of the institutions in this country recognise the vital role that the physical sciences play in this country, and that they receive the level of support that they deserve; otherwise, when we take stock forty years hence, the picture may not be as bright as it is now.

References

1. J.P. O'Donnell, *The Chemical Process Industries in Ireland – Achievements and Prospects* (Chemical Engineering Department, University College Dublin).
2. C. Cathcart, *The Irish Chemical Industry* (Federation of Irish Chemical Industry, 1984).
3. *The World Competitiveness Yearbook,* (International Institute for Management, 1996).
4. *The European Chemical Industry in a Worldwide Perspective* (European Chemical Industry Council, November 1996).
5. Central Statistics Office, various bulletins.
6. Irish Refining Company Ltd, *Brochure on the Occasion of the Opening of Whitegate Refinery,* September 1959.
7. P. Childs, 'The Chemical Industry in Cork', *Chemistry in Action!,* Autumn 1995, pp. 20-27.
8. C. O'Brien, 'Chemistry in Ireland: Avondale Chemical Company', *Chemistry in Action!,* Autumn, 1991, p. 38.
9. *Shaping Our Future, a Strategy for Enterprise in Ireland in the 21st Century* (Forfás, May 1996).
10. G. Van Der Lee, 'The Chemical Industry and National Development', *Paper read to the Association of Higher Civil Servants,* December 1956.
11. W. & H.N. Goulding Ltd, *Dublin Ireland 1856–1956 – a Short History of the Firm.*
12. *Focused on a Health Future, a Report Published by PharmaChemical Ireland* (Irish Business and Employers' Confederation, May 2004).
13. *The Pharmaceutical Industry in Figures* (European Federation of Pharmaceutical Industries and Associations, 2004 Edition), p. 3.

CHAPTER 11

Information and Communications Technology[1]

Henry McLoughlin

Introduction

Information and Communications Technology (ICT) is the name which is now given to one of the fastest growing sectors in the Irish economy. ICT is having a growing effect on the everyday lives of almost all of the citizens of the state. Yet, as recently as 20 years ago, few would have had any contact with such technologies. The sector was a fraction of what it now is and the impact it had on the economy was small. In a few short years, things have changed, and now, as we move into the new millennium, Ireland is rapidly gaining a reputation on the international stage for the quality of its people in this sector and for the innovative products which Irish companies are bringing to the market.

The term ICT is relatively new. Previously the sector was referred to as the IT sector, and before that it was generally referred to as the Computing sector. These name changes aren't just cosmetic, they reflect developments in the underlying technologies and their application, as well as the coming together of sectors that had previously been separate entities. In 2001, an organisation called ICT Ireland was launched to act as a representative group and to bring together a number of existing organisations which were active in the sector. It gives an interesting picture of just how diverse the sector is to look at the list of organisations who joined. In addition to the more traditional players, like the Irish Software Association and the Telecommunications and Internet Federation, we have such players as the Audiovisual Federation, the Irish Cellular Industry Association, and the Music Industry Group. This should give the reader some indication of the breadth of topics covered by ICT.

The impact which the ICT sector is having on the economy is sizeable. In the early 1990s, the number of people employed was less than 20,000, but that had jumped to in excess of 90,000 by 2003. Ireland is the world's largest exporter of software. Almost all of the world's top ICT companies have branches in Ireland. It is estimated that, in exports alone, the ICT sector produces in excess of 30% of all exports. Although the

---

[1] Some other aspects of Information and Communications Technology are discussed in Chapter 12.

presence of foreign multinational companies account for the bulk of the sector, the indigenous companies are now employing around 20,000 people[2].

Ireland is rapidly changing, and we could well be on the way to becoming one of the leading knowledge economies in the world in a few short years. This is a major change from the predominantly agricultural based economy we had fifty years ago.

In this article, I would like to examine some of the reasons why ICT has become such a major force in Ireland. While a major part of the article will focus on the current state of affairs, in order to understand how we got here, it is important to also look at some of the events in the past thirty years and try to show how the technology has evolved and how it has enabled the changes that have taken place. I will look at what I consider to be the key technologies that have powered the ICT revolution.

Having been involved in ICT for nearly thirty years, I have witnessed many technological advances and breakthroughs. I have come to the conclusion that some of the changes give rise to incremental progress but, every now and then, some new development arises which opens the door to a major period of innovation. I will look at a small number of the key technologies and try to indicate just why they assumed such major significance.

I will spend some time describing some of the ways in which our day-to-day lives have been, and continue to be, changed as we integrate the technology into our work and leisure. It can be surprising to see just how fast a new technology changes from being something new and interesting into something that is at the core of how we live and how we conduct business. From time to time, it is worthwhile to pause and look back at how much our lives have changed in such a short time.

I shall finish by describing some of the great challenges that face us. Some of them arise from breakthroughs in the underlying technology, others have been with us for a long time. Some of them are purely technical and others are challenges to society. I shall also argue that ICT has provided significant benefits for Ireland so far and that continuing to support research and development in this area will result in further benefits in the future.

I am writing as a member of a university and I shall emphasise the role that the third level sector has had in getting us to where we are today. As we continue to develop towards a more knowledge based economy, the role of the universities and other third level colleges will become even more important. We must continue to educate and train people, equipping them with the most up-to-date skills and knowledge. We must continue to provide the environment where postgraduates can conduct world class research, and we must continue to actively encourage the spirit of innovation and entrepreneurship which has given us such success to date. I believe that the benefits to Irish society of supporting this sector in its research will continue to provide value for money.

---

[2] http://www.ictireland.ie

The key technologies

The number of technological advances that have taken place in the past forty years which have underpinned the ICT sector would take volumes to describe. However, I believe that there have been a number of key developments that stand out. I shall mention some of them here and show how they had an impact on the ICT sector and on society.

The digital computer

The earliest commercially available computers began to arrive in the late 1950s. These were large machines which are generally referred to as mainframe computers. They were expensive systems and few companies could afford them. Physically they were enormous, often requiring an entire floor of an office to house them. They were sensitive machines and usually the rooms they were in were air-conditioned, had filters to eliminate dust and were entered by means of an air lock. The raw computing power of these machines was minuscule compared with what we have available today on our desktops. Memories of 128K were considered large.

To try to get value for money, companies tried to utilise these machines twenty-four hours a day. The cost of computing was large. They needed to be staffed twenty-four hours a day by operators. The Data Processing departments of companies were large. Most companies developed all of the software in-house, and so needed a team of systems analysts, a team of programmers and computer operators to run the machines, a large secretarial staff to punch the programs onto punch cards, and the management structures that accompanied such a department.

The machines themselves were expensive. Housing them was expensive and, with the quota of staff required to run them, the cost of software was very high. These weren't the sort of machines that small to medium companies could afford. The effect of this was that throughout the 1960s in Ireland, although there were a number of companies that had computers, their impact on business in general and on society was very small.

The companies which owned the machines wanted to maximise their return on investment. Once their basic business software had been written, they found that they had some spare resources. Often their development team had time available. Often their in-house data processing didn't occupy their machine twenty-four hours a day. The natural thing to do was to sell some of their spare capacity. Quite a number of companies did this, writing software for other companies and running that software on their machines. This began to allow other companies to computerise at much lower costs. This was also the birth in Ireland of a number of what were to become leading software houses in the 1970s and 1980s.

During the 1970s, the cost of computing fell. This was due to a combination of the silicon chip and the introduction of mini-computers. The latter were smaller versions of the mainframes and cost significantly less. Mind you, we are still talking in the region of £50,000. The combination of using bureaus and of buying mini-computers meant that more companies were computerising their business systems. The demand for skilled programmers increased, and the third level colleges began to see an increase in students studying for Computer Science degrees.

It is important to note that, at this stage, computerising a business generally amounted to writing software to automate accounting procedures, stock control and purchasing. Quite a number of these systems were custom built. The era of off-the-shelf software packages lay in the future. The result of this was that automating one's business was still an expensive undertaking. Only reasonably sized companies could afford to do so. The impact that computing was having on the man in the street was still small.

The personal computer

Breakthroughs in fabricating integrated circuits gave rise to the development of the micro-computer. The first micro-computers were little more than hobbyist machines. Memory of about 16k, storage on a cassette tape, and little software available, meant that, for many, the machines were looked on as curiosities.

In the early 1980s, IBM who had ignored micro-computers during the 1970s, decided to build their own version. The IBM Personal Computer was launched in 1981, and such was its impact that to this day most micro computers and workstations are still referred to as PCs. A combination of IBM's reputation, together with the availability of some off-the-shelf software packages, caused a revolution in business.

Having a computer that could be purchased for less than €2,000 and which didn't need specialised facilities made them affordable to almost all businesses. But the key was the software. A number of applications appeared on the market. Probably the most famous of them was VisiCalc, which was a spreadsheet developed by Dan Bricklin. This package allowed non-computer specialists to create complex financial models. In the hands of an accountant, you could create an entire accounts package for a company. Within a few years there was hardly a business of any size that didn't have at least one PC.

What occurred now was that, in a few short years, from being the reserve of the few, computers now were in general use in business. The initial success of Microsoft dates from this era. IBM wanted an operating system for their early PCs, and they purchased it from Microsoft. With the IBM name behind it, and some killer applications available, these PCs sold in very large numbers. Each PC came with the Microsoft operating system installed, and thus Microsoft began to grow.

Early versions of Word Processors began to appear. Compared to what we currently have, these were primitive systems but, compared to having a typist type each letter from scratch, they were a major improvement. A secretary could store each letter produced, could store templates for commonly used letters, and gone were the days of correction fluid. You composed the letter and made whatever changes you wanted, and only when it was perfect did you actually print it. Now it wasn't just the accounts department that wanted a computer; the secretarial staff could benefit from having them. Once again this led to increased sales.

With a growing base of PCs installed in industry, the opportunity was there for software houses to produce packaged software. The hardware base was out there. Most of the machines ran the same operating system so, if you could write software for that target market, you could sell it at a low cost and still make money because of the number of sales.

At this time, there were many who predicted that we would soon have computers in the home. This didn't happen for a long time. In hindsight the reasons are clear. Although the price of a PC was within the grasp of most, there simply weren't the applications available that might appeal to the home user. Some games were available, but even these were quite primitive. I recall some sales people advocating the benefits of the home PC by imagining the busy housewife who could store her recipes on the machine. Thankfully we don't have advertising like that anymore.

Computer networking

The ability to create networks of computers and thus exchange data between them was the next key technological advance. The earliest networks date from the late 1960s and were experimental systems developed in the US. Initially, the motivation behind their development was to find a way in which Command and Control for the military could be distributed across a number of computers, which could be linked together in such a way that they would be able to withstand machines going offline or some of the network links being broken. This work gave rise to Arpanet and eventually to what we now call the Internet.

In Ireland, the earliest network was an X25 that linked computers in Trinity College Dublin (TCD) and University College Dublin (UCD). This was built in 1976, and it led to the establishment of the Irish Universities Network in 1979. During the early 1980s this was linked to EURO net, which was a European wide network.

At the same time, we witnessed the development of Local Area Networks (LANs). These were networks of PCs linked together and usually containing a large storage device or server. The idea behind these was that a group of users in an organization could share data stored on the central server. PC to PC communications was also possible, but the main use was to have access to a common file store.

The machines in these networks were linked by dedicated lines. Networking was having an impact in businesses, and to the few that could access the wider networks, such as EURO net and Arpanet, there were benefits. Sometimes, when a technology is deployed, it may be used in ways a bit different from what was originally envisaged. With networking, it began to become apparent that people were using it to communicate *via* e-mail, and early versions of discussion boards. These weren't the sophisticated chat rooms that we have today, but the signs were there that this technology could play a big role in human communication.

The World Wide Web

The biggest breakthrough in enabling technology in the ICT sector to date has been the World Wide Web (WWW). Ten years ago, few outside the academic community in

Ireland knew of its existence. Now it is so popular that few could claim not to have heard of it or to have used it.

It began as a project in CERN (Centre Européen pour la Recherche Nucléaire in Geneva) to find a way in which the many documents that visiting scientists produced there could be indexed and retrieved. It was a marriage of two existing technologies, networking and hypertext. Networking had been developing over the previous decade, while hypertext was an idea dating from the 1940s which had actually been implemented by Apple in a product called HyperCard.

The basic model of the web is simple. A computer can act as a server. That is to say, it can store a set of documents and, upon receiving a request from another machine, *via* the Internet, for a particular document, it can transmit the document to that other machine. It is possible to restrict access to the documents but, in general, the idea is to make them available to all. The documents themselves are marked up in a language called HTML (Hyper Text Markup Language), and this describes how the content of the documents should be displayed.

The machine making the request is called the client machine. Running on the client machine is a piece of software called a browser, which is capable of rendering the HTML document when it receives it. At the client side, all of the interaction takes place through the browser. An HTML document is displayed, and that may have links to other documents. All the user has to do is to click on the link to that document, and a request is sent to the appropriate server to download it.

Although this is a very simple model, it had far-reaching consequences. First of all, the browsers were made available free. So anyone who wanted to use the web simply had to install a copy of a browser and get connected to the internet. At first, the number of web sites was small. But soon they began to increase, as both individuals and companies realised that they could disseminate information freely and cheaply this way. As more information became available, more people wanted to access it.

The level of interest increased. More and more people began to use the web and began to realise that here was a source of a large amount of useful information. Internet Service Providers (ISPs) began to form. These offered access to the internet from home or from the office for the price of a local phone call. An ISP would have a direct link to the Internet and, by dialling into their machine, you could access the web through them.

Finally, there was a reason for people to want a home PC. Since the mid 1990s, sales to the home market have rocketed. At last, a key computing technology was having an impact throughout society. With such a large base of computer users, all connecting to the web, the scene was set for the development of value-added applications to sit on top of this technology. Later on, we shall look at some of the applications which are already having an impact, and we shall then speculate on what developments may occur in the future.

ICT education

Between the late 1950s and the late 1960s, in a number of Irish universities, academics began to take an interest in these new digital computers. In many cases, the interest came from Engineers or Mathematicians and, when Computer Science departments began to be formed and courses began to be given, it was academics from these disciplines who were most involved.

For example, in UCD, a young Physicist, Dr Frank Anderson, persuaded his Department to purchase a computer to analyse data from physics experiments. When the machine arrived, he was put in charge of it and became so fascinated by it that a number of years later he was instrumental in founding the Computer Science Department there. Between then and when he retired in the late 1990s, he worked in that Department, serving as head of Department on a number of occasions. We can imagine that, in many of the other universities, what began as idle curiosity about these machines lead to similar career changes, and gradually Computer Science as an academic discipline in Ireland began to emerge.

The Department in TCD was founded in 1969, that at UCD a few years after that. Our colleagues in Queen's University Belfast (QUB) seized the opportunity even earlier with the first appointment of a lecturer in the area being in 1959, and their Department was officially formed in 1967. By 1990, departments were established in all of the universities on the island; and, in the Regional Technical Colleges (now the Institutes of Technology), similar moves took place.

To start with, these departments delivered service courses to students as part of other degrees such as Engineering, Physics, Commerce and Mathematics. But by the mid 1970s, actual Computer Science degrees began to be established.

At first, student numbers were small. Graduating classes of less than ten people were common. This was due to a combination of the subject being so new and the perception that the job market for graduates was small.

Some of the graduates opted to stay on and pursue postgraduate research degrees. This was a difficult option at the time because the level of support and funding available was very small. However, their persistence paid off, and many of the current staff in Computer Science departments are drawn from this early group of postgraduates.

During the 1980s, there were two developments which I believe were to prove significant for the future. Firstly, most of the universities revamped their undergraduate Computer Science curricula and brought them in line with some of the best in the world. Student numbers steadily increased year by year, and graduating class sizes in excess of forty became the norm.

For many of these students, the opportunities for a career in Ireland were limited, but these were the boom years in the UK and large numbers went there or to the USA to take up jobs in a variety of high tech companies – particularly in the financial services sector. Many were successful, and this caused many foreign companies to turn to Ireland as a source of highly skilled and well-educated graduates.

In turn, this image of Ireland was to be used very successfully by the Industrial Development Authority (IDA) to attract inward investment and to persuade many multinational companies that Ireland was an ideal place to locate their European operations. Not only were there a growing number of Irish gaining experience with some of the world leaders in ICT, but the opportunities were now there for new graduates to work with such companies without having to emigrate.

Ireland was clearly establishing itself as a country which produced high quality graduates and that, coupled with favourable grants and taxation levels, did attract many multinationals. But few of these were willing to carry out their R&D here. This was because we were yet to establish our name for carrying out high quality research. This was to change.

The second development began in the mid 1980s with the start of the European Union (EU) Framework programmes. Their goal was to support co-operative research and development between industry and academia across national boundaries in the EU. These programmes, such as ESPRIT, DELTA, RACE and DRIVE, offered Irish academics, and indeed some industries, access to research funding and research opportunities that were orders of magnitude better than what had been there before.

The opportunities were there to work with some of the leading European companies and research institutions, to gain exposure to state-of-the-art technologies and ideas, and to be at the forefront of ICT research. The Irish representatives on the management boards of these programmes originally worked with the funding agencies, the National Board for Science and Technology and subsequently with EOLAS (Irish for 'knowledge'). They played a major role in identifying potential partners throughout the EU, and their support for Irish researchers was immense.

The support offered by these programmes enabled more and more graduates to stay on as postgraduate researchers. The financial support certainly made this career choice a lot easier than it had been. But, most importantly, the opportunity to work at the leading edge of European ICT research meant that Ireland was developing a pool of world class high-tech researchers.

Some of these subsequently moved on to join the R&D divisions of leading European companies, some stayed in academia, and some saw the opportunities to exploit the research and commercialise the results. By the early 1990s, Ireland was beginning to be seen as a country with highly skilled researchers, as well as highly educated graduates. Now, more and more foreign companies felt comfortable establishing research divisions here.

By the mid 1990s, the third level colleges were producing a steady flow of graduates and trained postgraduate researchers. Many of the graduates over the previous twenty years, who had emigrated, were returning to Ireland as the economy improved. There was an air of confidence that we had the skills and the ability to innovate and that we could compete successfully on the world stage. We had people who knew how ICT was being used in a range of sectors, and we had people who knew what the latest research in ICT was producing. And, added to all this, the World Wide Web was just beginning to have an impact on us.

ICT in our daily lives

One of the things that characterises ICT is its global impact. For companies lucky enough to develop a new technology in this area, the financial benefits can be enormous. However, even those who aren't the innovators can reap benefits as they seize upon the opportunities that the new technology enable. In fact, in a number of cases, it is those who see ways to use the technology rather than its inventors who reap the big rewards.

In this section, I would like to look at a number of the ways in which ICT has had an impact on society in Ireland. In less than thirty years, the way in which we live our lives has been altered quite radically. There have been changes in the way business is conducted, changes in the way we organize our lives, and changes in the way we interact with each other. As change happens, most of us seem to be able to integrate it into our lives and almost forget about it. But, when one looks back over a few years, one can be surprised by how much the rate of technological change has had an effect.

Some of the technologies we will mention were developed in Ireland and are now being used globally. Others have their origin outside Ireland. What I hope to show is just how much of an impact ICT currently has on how we live and, in that way, show why there is potentially tremendous value for us if we continue to support the development of these technologies.

Banking

The way in which we interact with our banks and manage our finances has changed. No longer do we have to spend time queuing in our local bank branch (if we were lucky enough to get there during the opening hours). Instead, almost all account holders have ATM (Automatic Teller Machine) cards.

Originally, these were designed to allow the user to withdraw cash at the bank's own network of ATM machines. Now they offer a range of functionality. One is no longer restricted to using a particular ATM. Different banks share their networks. One isn't even restricted by country. Most ATM cards allow access to your accounts throughout the world and allow withdrawals in the local currency.

ATMs are now being installed in places such as local shops. The range of functionality is such that one can pay bills, top up your credit on your mobile phone, and transfer money between accounts.

More recently, we now are being introduced to Internet banking, where you can access your accounts from your PC whether at home or in the office.

E-commerce

We are currently at the start of a revolution in the way in which we shop. The traditional weekly trip to the supermarket may well become a thing of the past. Most supermarket chains allow you to place your order on-line, arrange payment electronically, and indicate the time and day when you want the goods delivered to your home. For the consumer, the benefits are obvious. You no longer have to schedule a trip to the shops. The retailer can fill the order from a warehouse and may reach a wider customer base without the need for costly additional branches.

Eventually we might see the demise of the physical shop. Already this is happening. Companies such as Amazon allow you to browse through a collection of books larger than any you could hope to find in a high street bookshop. Once again, payment for your order is electronic and your order generally ships within days.

From a retailer's point of view, this model is very attractive. If you don't have to have a costly high street presence, but can operate from a warehouse, then you can dramatically reduce your costs. You no longer have to worry about keeping limited shelf space stocked with goods. Shoplifting becomes a thing of the past. All payments are electronic so you aren't handling cash. Staffing levels may be reduced. But, most importantly, you can now sell to global markets without the need for a physical presence locally.

It is now possible, while sitting at home or in the office, to book flights for a weekend away in another country, book your hotel accommodation, search for particular types of restaurants in your destination city, and actually make a reservation for dinner for when you arrive.

Mobile communications

At the start of the 1990s, it was unusual to know someone who had a mobile phone. Now it is unusual to know someone who hasn't. This technology now pervades society. And the benefits are enormous. Parents can feel more secure when their children go out. Motorists can contact the emergency services if their vehicle breaks down or is involved in an accident. Sales teams can communicate instantly with their home office.

Sometimes a new technology is launched, but the way in which it is used surprises even the manufacturers. This was certainly the case with the mobile phone. While it was primarily sold as a device for making phone calls, it is now more often used as a device for sending text messages.

Companies seeing this are now busy developing other applications which could work with mobile phones. Already we have mini browsers available. Soon we can expect personalised news updates to be sent to us.

Travel

As recently as fifteen years ago Ireland was one of the most expensive places to fly from. In that era, the usual way to book a flight was to visit a travel agent and let it take care of the booking. But all of this is changing.

Low cost airlines were launched which tried to eliminate as many costs as possible. One way to do so was to stop giving travel agents a commission on bookings. Customers had to book directly with the company. It reduced costs, but one still had to maintain a booking office for the customers. But when the web gained popular acceptance, the companies switched to on-line bookings and eliminated the need for a front office. People became free to act as their own travel agents and to book their own flights.

The diminishing role of the travel agent and the growth of low-cost travel has in part been enabled by the use of Internet technology.

Music

Those of us born before 1980 probably spent time in their youth discussing their LP (Long Playing Record) collection. Those born after that time wouldn't know what we were talking about. Since the gramophone was invented by Edison until the late twentieth century, music was recorded as grooves on vinyl disks. This was an analogue storage medium and the disks were easily damaged.

In the 1980s, a revolution began with the introduction of the CD (Compact Disk). This is a smaller disk, it has a large storage capacity, and it stores the music in a digital form. The introduction of the CD quickly led to the demise of the LP. But it also enabled newer developments. A CD records digitally. One didn't have to be limited to music, any digital data could be stored. It soon became common for software to be sold on CD. Such disks became known as CDROMs (Compact Disk Read Only Memory) although they are essentially the same thing.

Digitally recorded music can be transmitted over a network, so it was only a matter of time before we were able to transmit and receive sound files. With the development of recordable CDs, you could copy albums. The opportunities for copyright infringement were certainly there and this was a big concern for the music industry.

However, recently we have seen the launch by Apple computers of an on-line music store. Instead of having to buy an entire album, even if you only wanted one of the songs on it, you can now download and pay for only the particular tracks you want.

The development of the DVD (Digital Video Disk) brought things to yet another level. These have much larger storage capacity than CDs, although they are physically the same size, so now it is possible to store movies on a disk. Just as the CD sounded the death knell for the vinyl record and the cassette, so too the DVD is signalling the demise of the video tape.

Computers in the home

With the advent of the PC in the early 1980s, it was predicted, as already mentioned, that soon there would be computers in the home. For a long time that didn't happen, mainly because few could imagine what exactly they could be used for.

The arrival of the web and cheap access to the internet has changed all that. E-mail is fast replacing physical letters as a way to keep in touch. Families can keep in touch with their loved ones and exchange photos and home movies. Software is available to transmit voice over the internet, which allows people to make long-distance phone calls for the price of the local call for accessing the internet. Video conferencing software is coming as standard on many home computers and, as more and more homes get broadband connections, this is replacing phone calls.

With the vast amount of information which is now available, the communications facilities that can be accessed and the growing availability of inexpensive broadband access to the internet, having a home PC is becoming less of a luxury and more of a necessity.

Electronic publication

ICT is revolutionising publishing. Authors are making copies of their books freely available. Academic journals which once cost a great deal to subscribe to are becoming freely available in electronic form. Small organizations are able to publish newsletters. Businesses can produce brochures and distribute them at a fraction of the previous cost.

On-line training

Few of us will go through our careers nowadays without having to upgrade our skills regularly. However, doing this can be difficult. Traditional training courses take place at specific locations and at specific times. Taking time off to do the training may pose a problem. The cost of attending courses, together with the additional costs of travel and accommodation while training, can be prohibitive.

However, this is changing. WBT (Web Based Training) is a technology that can deliver training over the Internet to an individual or group of students in their own time and at whatever location they choose. This flexibility means that people can integrate their training into their busy schedules.

It is now possible to be doing a course while still at work: to be applying the new skills that you are learning in your work environment and at the same time having access to your individual tutor to ask questions or seek advice. As the training takes place over the Internet, the students and the tutors can be geographically distant and yet still interact as in more traditional settings.

As one example, it is now possible for primary school teachers in Ireland to take courses in how to cater for children with special needs and to do so during term time. We have had instances where a teacher from Cork was sharing experiences with a teacher from Austria while their tutor, who was in Fiji at the time, also contributed to the discussion.

A number of colleges are now allowing students to take courses on-line, and one can foresee a stage when this technology may become the standard way to deliver continuing professional training.

ICT research at third level

Earlier, we mentioned the situation in the 1980s when research funding was scarce. During that period, there were research groups in the colleges, but they were small due to the lack of resources. The availability of funding through the EU Framework programmes went some way to alleviating the problem, but these too had drawbacks. The amount of travel involved, together with the difficulties of managing diverse groups that came from different countries and different backgrounds, lead to an awful lot of paperwork and administrative overload. The need to manage them also meant that very detailed work plans had to be agreed, and the amount of flexibility that researchers had was sometimes constrained.

This is not to say they were a bad thing. They enabled Irish researchers to have more resources available to them than before. And indeed the results of some of these projects have led to successful commercial products. But, ideally, one would wish for more flexibility and freedom to pursue one's research.

In the past decade, there have been a number of major developments in the third level sector. Irish researchers are winning many international awards for their innovative research. This is attracting much international interest both amongst global industries, which see in Ireland a place where true innovation is happening, and amongst the international academic community, many of whom are developing strong ties with Ireland.

When MIT decided to establish a branch of their Media Lab in Europe, they chose to situate it in Dublin. Unfortunately, this is one initiative which didn't work out.

The universities and institutes of technology have become aware of the commercial potential of the research being conducted within the institutions, and almost all of them now have innovation centres whose aim is to assist academics in bringing their results to the market place through campus companies. We are seeing new technologies being transferred to the commercial sector more rapidly than ever.

Within my own university department at UCD, we have seen quite a number of small start-up companies take research results and succeed in carving out niche markets for their products. In recent years WBT Systems and ChangingWorlds have succeeded in establishing themselves as major players in international markets. Between them, they employ well over 100 people. A number of other start-ups are predicted to have similar success.

The list of campus companies at TCD include Broadcom Eireann, Iona Technologies, Baltimore Technologies, Trintech, and Havok. These too began as vehicles to commercialise the results of research at the university, and went on to become market leaders in their sectors. All of the other third level institutions can point to their own commercial successes.

Research funding, which traditionally was scarce, has been increased, thanks to government funding initiatives. This has lead to a significant increase in the number of talented graduates remaining on to do higher degrees and train as researchers. The most important funding initiative is Science Foundation Ireland (SFI).

Through this organisation, in excess of €600 million is being invested in academic research teams during the period 2000–2006. This represents a substantial investment, and is an enormous vote of confidence in Irish researchers. SFI's mission is probably best summed up in the words of its Director General, William Harris, when he says:

> We want to stimulate discovery and innovation and to help magnify the impact
> of good ideas. So we will choose among proposals based upon the assessments
> of scientists, who will consider the quality of the ideas and research record of

the scientist or engineer – that is, the potential of the research to shape other fields and, where possible, to generate technological advances[3].

In fulfilling its mission, SFI has a number of programmes. It seeks to attract world leaders in ICT to move to Ireland to set up research teams. It funds individual Irish researchers to develop their particular fields. It provides significant levels of funding for postgraduate training.

As a result of the recent support for ICT research, we now have a research community in Ireland that is in excess of 1,000 people, and this number is growing. This group contains academic staff, postdoctoral fellows, visiting scientists and postgraduate students. It is clear that, at a number of the institutions, a critical mass of researchers has now been reached, and the research activities are reflecting this.

The level of investment is beyond anything that we have seen previously. But one can hardly say it is a gamble. Irish researchers have shown over the years that they can carry out innovative research in ICT. They have also shown that they have the drive and the spirit of entrepreneurship to bring their results to the marketplace. Many of the leading indigenous ICT companies in Ireland can either trace their origins to research carried out in the academic sector or have amongst their staff people who learned their skills as postgraduate researchers. The value for money is clearly there to be seen, and this came about when the levels of investment in ICT research were much smaller.

These new levels of funding, if they continue or increase, should set the scene for Ireland to become a major player in ICT over the next decade. The benefits to the economy will be very significant. The EU Lisbon strategy, which was adopted in 2000, set as one of its targets that the EU expenditure on R&D would reach the level of 3% of Gross Domestic Product (GDP). Currently we are still below that, but the situation has improved.

The range of research activity

In this section I want to give an overview of some of the research which is currently being undertaken in ICT in Ireland. I must warn the reader that is this far from being an exhaustive list; such is the diversity of the topics being addressed that it would not be possible to list them all. In addition, I plan to describe the areas without always mentioning the institutions where the research is happening. In many cases it is being carried out in more than one institution. For more details of what the individual institutions are doing I would refer the reader to the institutes' web sites, where a wealth of detail is available.

The overriding theme of most if not all of this research is to address the issues of how we can cope with the vast and growing amount of information which is available, and how, from the chaos, we can learn to integrate and manage our information society.

---

[3] http://www.sfi.ie

Security

Probably the greatest worry that people have, and the major reason why they would shy away from doing business on the Internet, is that of security. They may be worried that their credit card details will be stolen and they will end up with bills for services or goods that they didn't order. If we can develop ways in which we either increase security by better encryption methods, or change the models of payment, then we could eliminate this worry, and this would lead to more people shopping on line.

Digital media, be it video, audio or text can be downloaded or copied quickly. There are difficulties in trying to prevent piracy or unauthorised transmission. We need effective means to establish ownership and copyright. Novel methods of hiding digital signatures within the actual media files are being developed. These will give the owners more confidence that they can distribute their material whilst protecting the rights.

Software engineering

With the computing power that is now available to us, we are developing more and more complex systems. Many of these are now being deployed in critical situations. We need to find ways to construct software which will be highly reliable. This issue of software correctness has been with us for over forty years, and remains one of the great outstanding challenges for Computer Science.

The development of large software systems is one of the most intellectually challenging things that we have ever been faced with. Managing this development will require engineering methodologies far beyond what we have today. In the more traditional engineering disciplines, standard components tend to be reused in different designs. This level of reuse is in its early days in software engineering, and determining what are the appropriate components to use and how to use them remains a challenge.

Research into programming language design seeks to produce languages that can make the programming task less complex.

Hardware

At the level of hardware the ongoing challenges remain as to how to produce faster, smaller and more powerful processors. Researchers are looking at novel computer architectures and ways to configure processors to meet specific needs.

Parallel and distributed system

Some programming problems are inherently very difficult to solve in what we would consider a reasonable time. With some this, it is because of the vast amount of data that needs to be processed, with others, the amount of data may not be large but it is the sheer complexity of the problem. Our traditional model of computing is one where a single processor runs the program to solve the problem.

However, in some cases, it may be possible to partition the data or partition the problem itself into a number of separate, yet interlinked parts, and use multiple processors operating in parallel to solve it. The hope is that by doing so you can solve the problem faster. Being able to partition a problem in such a way is a major research challenge. But, with the amount of processing power that is potentially available to use by sharing resources over a network, it is a challenge worth taking up.

Information retrieval

One of the great benefits of the web is that we have vast amounts of information available at our fingertips. But that in itself is a problem. We need to find ways in which we can search this massive resource quickly and retrieve the information that we want. Much of what is published on the web is in the form of text documents. The authors may include some keywords that would identify the content but, in most cases, this doesn't happen. A great challenge here is to find ways to automatically extract semantic information from text documents, and to use this to index the documents.

But the nature of the web is such that, as nobody controls it, there are few controls over what is actually available. With the printed word, we relied upon the reputation of the publisher or magazine to reassure us as to the accuracy and validity of the material we were reading. But when information is published on a web page, we need other methods of determining its legitimacy.

The overriding challenge is to be able to access the information you want as quickly as you can and with as high a level of assurance of its authenticity.

Access to information

On the other side of the coin is the problem of making sure that you don't access material that you don't want. Of great concern is how to protect children from accessing inappropriate material or from being exposed to danger in chat rooms. Here we will encounter challenges that are not just technical, they also raise legal and ethical questions which society must address.

One of the strengths of the web is that it isn't controlled by any organisation or government. Because of that, it can be used to give freedom of expression to people of all countries and all political beliefs. But all freedoms are open to abuse. Libellous or slanderous material can appear on a web site that lies outside the legal jurisdiction of your country, which leaves the victim with little means of legal redress.

Attempting to block access to such material whilst maintaining freedom to access other material is a great challenge. It is a challenge not only to the technologist but also to society. Who defines what is or isn't appropriate material, and what if such definitions vary from country to country?

E-commerce

Earlier we described some of the benefits of e-commerce. But there are problems too. Purchasing a book on Amazon may be simple enough, as all you need to know is the title or the author. A simple search will determine whether it is available and, if so, you can decide to purchase it. But suppose you can't characterise what you want to purchase in such exact terms. Perhaps you want a new PC but aren't quite sure what all of the terms like memory and disk space mean? Suppose you want to purchase some clothing? In traditional shopping, we can interact with the sales assistant and seek assistance in finding what we want to purchase

The open questions in this area address ways in which we can better support the customer. It may be that the system can use information it gleaned from previous customers. It may be that the system presents you with a range of possibilities and tries to work out from your response some idea of what would suit you.

Networking and mobile computing

The cell phones available today are much more sophisticated than those which were available less that ten years ago. The devices now have increased storage and increased processing power. The boundaries between cell phones and mobile computers are being blurred. The majority of the population now have cell phones. Already, most phones allow the user to send and receive e-mail and to perform a limited amount of web browsing. The challenges here are to explore novel ways in which the cell phone network can be used to deliver information to people.

Researchers are looking at ways in which geographic information can be made available on these devices. Public transport timetables, maps to guide you to the nearest bus or train station, tourist information, these are but a few of the services which could be made available.

E-learning

Ireland has been to the forefront in e-learning for quite a while. We have a history of developing computer based learning material. Web based training is now a rapidly growing area worldwide and has its origins in research carried out in Ireland. But there are a number of open challenges. The ultimate goal would be to be able to match the learning material to the learning needs of the individual and to tailor the delivery of that material in such a way as to maximise the learning experience.

Open challenges here include monitoring a student's interaction with the e-learning system, identifying learning difficulties based on their interaction, and devising appropriate remedial strategies.

A.I.

It has long been a dream that some day computers could understand natural language. We would be able to interact with our computer by speaking, and the computer would respond by speaking back at us. Some would question whether it makes any sense at all to say that a computer could understand. But, if we leave that debate to another day, it is clear that having an interface that was driven by speech could have major benefits. We have research groups actively working on both speech recognition and speech generation. If the problems in this area can be solved, then I believe that this would give rise to a key technology and that the opportunities for applying it would be significant.

At another level, a significant topic in this area is to take typed natural language and to try to extract semantic knowledge from it. Such techniques would enable you to extract from and classify some of the huge resources of textual material that are available on the web. Once indexed in this way, search engines could make use of the knowledge

Forensic computing and computer crime

Computer crime is a new phenomenon. It comes in many guises, and lawmakers struggle to update the law to take account of it. As many critical systems, such as air-traffic control, become automated, there are possibilities that computer crime may become more than just white collar crime. Human life could be put at risk.

We need ways in which we can detect attempts to access or change confidential data. We need models to allow us to recreate the sequence of events that lead to some incident, and to do so in a way that will stand up as legal evidence.

Communication on the internet is a two-way process. Once you are connected, you can send messages to other machines, and messages from them can be received. The great danger here is protecting your machine from attack. As we pointed out earlier, most software in use today contains bugs or areas where it is vulnerable.

Unfortunately, there are people who actively seek to exploit these weaknesses and create programs called viruses which are designed to attack computers. They range from ones whose goal is denial of service to those which try to destroy data on machines.

Denial of service means flooding particular machines with unwanted email or requests. Whilst not actually damaging your machine or the data contained in it, these viruses clog the network and make access to your site difficult or impossible for others. How we deal with these issues is once again a major research challenge.

Human-computer interaction

As more and more people use computers in their daily lives, a major challenge is to find ways in which we can interact with these systems in a natural way. Voice input and output enable hands-free interaction. Virtual reality interfaces allow us to move through virtual environments in what seems to be a natural way.

Advances in visualisation can present the results of web searches in ways that are easier to comprehend, rather than just being presented with lists of results.

Advances in Bio-metrics, whereby a user's identity can be authenticated based on their voice or their fingerprint, could lead to increased security and guard against fraud.

But having such personal data stored could be seen as infringement of privacy. So much data about ourselves is stored already that there are major concerns about how it could be used in the future. Nobody wants to have the situation where Big Brother is watching us.

Conclusion

In this article, I have tried to give the reader an overview of ICT. I have been selective as the area is just too broad to cover fully in the space available. I must apologise to readers if at times they felt I was stating the obvious. But this in itself is significant. Such has been the speed with which developments in ICT have been brought from the research lab to the market and integrated into our daily lives that we take them for granted. I know of no other field in science where this happens so fast. It is because of this that I chose to describe the impact of ICT in our daily lives. Here are technologies that didn't exist thirty years ago, and now they are central to our lives.

I spoke of how Computer Science had begun an§d developed in the third level sector over a short time, and my aim here was to show how, even with very limited resources, we have been able to get to the point where Irish researchers are having an impact globally both for their research and for their ability to transfer the research results to the marketplace.

I spoke of some of the key technologies, each of which underpinned the development of others. At each stage, the technologies had an impact on a wider section of the community. We are now at a stage where most businesses are computerised, where a large number of homes have PCs, and where the cost of broadband Internet connectivity is affordable. We can expect that the coming years will deliver increased computing power without any noticeable increase in cost. We can also expect that higher bandwidth will continue to become available in the home. This is a global phenomenon.

What this means is that any breakthrough in the underlying technologies or any application of the technologies which proves useful will have a global market. Furthermore, the technologies of today have already laid the basis for Irish companies to operate globally. E-commerce models similar to those used by Amazon and E-bay can be used by Irish companies, and sales to global markets can be accomplished without the need for a physical presence in those different countries.

Given the track record of Irish researchers in ICT and the significant increases in the levels of support and funding that are now becoming available, I believe that the future is bright and that, in the years to come, we as a society will reap the benefits as we move forward towards being a knowledge based economy.

CHAPTER 12

Irish Contributions to International Science

Fionn Murtagh

Introduction

The university as an institution has evolved to embrace three components: teaching, research, and technology transfer. My review of the current state of Irish science will be mainly focused on research and essentially university research. Axiomatically, research has to be taken in the international dimension.

I approach this survey of Irish science with more than one eye on the future. I shall draw conclusions – some conclusions – based on discussion of the present and recent past. The present in Irish research is still drawing benefit, and inheriting more problematic aspects, from the Celtic Tiger period. Irish economic growth during this period, from approximately 1993 to 2001, averaged 9% per annum, and to date since then has continued to out-trump other national growth rates in Europe. This has had major positive implications for the financing of, and direction of, Irish science. The natural next question is where to next? The economist will have one answer to this question, and the social scientist may have other important considerations to raise. A necessary task though is to root future Irish developments in the evolution of science itself. This will be done primarily from the platform of my expertise in computing and allied mathematical sciences – the new science of information.

Since sustainability of Irish research output, with a base that was strengthened by the Celtic Tiger period of outstanding economic growth, is one objective shared by all, we have to look a little at how the Celtic Tiger period came about. We will also gain from drawing conclusions from high points of Irish science in earlier times. The historian, Eric Hobsbawm, has characterized the twentieth century as the 'Short Century'. The history of that century has a sharp change-point in August 1914, with the beginning of essentially three decades of war in Europe. A turning point marking the end of much that happened in the awful period of war and destruction came around 1989 with the 'fall of the Wall', and the implosion of the Soviet economy. For Hobsbawm therefore, the Short Century was roughly the period 1914 to 1989. Roughly too, this period corresponds to the birth and early period of consolidation of the Irish state, up to the Celtic Tiger period.

The notion of a 'Grand Challenge' has been quite widely used in recent decades. Leading models for past grand challenges have included the Manhattan Project, or John F. Kennedy's project to go to the Moon, or more recently the Human Genome Project. A number of grand challenges in science, mathematics and engineering in Ireland in the Short Century will first be reviewed. I shall point to the international dimension, the driver and enabling role of the State, linkage with Irish universities, and aspects of the science.

In a sense this Chapter is written in a way that is reminiscent to what the wavelet transform in signal processing does to a data stream: it decomposes the data into a background trend component – the DC or direct current component – and the foreground, superimposed, detail signal components – analogous to AC or alternating current components. In discussing the Ireland of the last century, and in presenting a short explanation as to how the Irish Celtic Tiger period came about and its links with science, I shall be describing background phenomena that will help to profile some of the events of importance. I would like to look for long or Kondratieff waves in the Irish economy and in related scientific, technological and cultural expression, but such a study will have to wait for another day.

The Shannon Scheme: a grand challenge at the birth of the new Irish Free State

Ernest Walton was Ireland's one Nobel Prize winner in science (*see page 70*). His first lodgings when he started work at Rutherford's Cavendish Laboratory in Cambridge in 1927 had electric fittings for light only and not for cooking or wireless, and for the light he had to pay extra[1]. The establishment of the Irish Free State in 1922 involved meagre resources, not least for science (non-existent) and engineering. Power networks were available in large population centres, but the new Irish Free State had the lowest *per capita* consumption of electricity in Europe, save only for Portugal.

Thomas McLaughlin, vintage Drogheda 1896, completing a BE in University College Galway in 1922 and PhD in 1923, was influenced by Frank Sharman Rishworth, Professor of Civil Engineering, in unwavering belief in the potential of the River Shannon as a source of hydroelectric power[2]. With an aim of contributing to the new Free State, he took a post with Siemens in London, and then in Berlin. He studied there the design of power plants, manufacture of electrical machinery, and the problems of transmission and distribution of power. All across Europe national electricity networks were being established, targeted at economic regeneration and uplift. Lenin's famous dictum around this time was that 'Communism equals socialism plus electrification'. Hydroelectric power had been pointed to as feasible and desirable

---

[1] B. Cathcart, *The Fly in The Cathedral: How a Small Group of Cambridge Scientists Won the Race to Split the Atom* (London: Viking, 2004).

[2] A. Bielenberg, (Ed), *The Shannon Scheme and the Electrification of the Irish Free State* (Dublin: Lilliput Press, 2002).

in earlier studies in Ireland going back to the mid-nineteenth century. McLaughlin pursued his investigations and received support from Siemens in doing this. Returning to Ireland in December 1923, he availed of close linkage with Government ministers. A Government white paper was produced with backing from Siemens. It was not a one-way flow: in 1924, four private parliamentary bills were debated with the aim of hydroelectric power usage of the Liffey, the river of Dublin. McLaughlin's view of the Shannon as being in the national interest won out. He considered the issue of power management and, in 1927, legislation was introduced for the first semi-state body, the ESB (Electricity Supply Board), of which McLaughlin became the first Managing Director. Semi-state organisations along this model were to play a pivotal role in establishing an industrial base for Ireland in the Short Century.

Power from the Ardnacrusha Shannon site was online from 1927. Standardization was then needed for equipment, electric current, marketing to the consumer, rural (completed in the late 1940s) as well as urban access. McLaughlin was to resign as Managing Director in 1931, as a byproduct of the (necessary) overturn of the engineer in favour of the accountant, but remained as a technical director of the ESB for a further 25 years. Seán Lemass, who was to play a central role in economic policy for many decades, on behalf of the new Fianna Fáil Government in 1932 re-appointed him to the ESB Board. By the 1950s, Lemass ended the protectionism of the earlier decades and initiated the new economic policy that gave rise to the Celtic Tiger period of 1993–2001.

In the words of one commentator regarding the Shannon Scheme, never before was such a national financial risk of such proportions undertaken. Work began in 1925 and at its peak in 1928 employed 5,000 workers. Accommodation was provided for many. One hundred kilometres of railway track was laid. Many freight ships were used, to bring in much specialized earth works equipment. Work was completed in about four years, and the Ardnacrusha plant was opened in July 1929. In construction and later, the Shannon Scheme and the ESB were major sources of employment. The project was a fortuitous event too for Siemens-Schuckertwerke in the post-World War I world. For Siemens, it was the largest foreign contract awarded to a German firm since the construction of the Baghdad railway at the end of the nineteenth century. The total commitment of Siemens was striking. No resources were spared, and indeed financial losses were incurred, through tight Irish accounting.

I have noted how the vision and drive of McLaughlin was a prime mover of the Shannon Scheme, and I have noted also the early influence of University College Galway. The corporate linkage of Siemens was crucial. Other aspects were interesting too, such as the overruling of Department of Finance opposition. There had been no call for tenders. Cosgrave, the prime minister, simply indicated that no other firm had expressed interest. The Shannon Scheme was financed (£5.21 million, by Government Act in 1925) by public loans. Associated with the Free State Government, Éamon de Valera (1916 leader, leader of the loosing side in the Civil War, leader of the Fianna Fáil party, later Taoiseach, and President) initially saw the Shannon Scheme as a white elephant, but later gave it his full support.

Engineering and science, industry and Government were united in the Shannon Scheme project. The same was also manifest in another project of epic proportions started a decade later, which I shall turn to next.

Peat: international scientific influence and Government backing

In the previous section, I have described the origins of the semi-state national electrical power utility in the newly nascent Irish Free State. Now I shall describe the origins of another semi-state, also linked to the power sector. In both, grand challenges were addressed and solved, the State played a crucial role, and international science linkages were instrumental in all of this.

The years from the insurrection (1916 Rebellion) in the midst of the First World War up to the Civil War in 1922–1923 were times of intense disturbance and upheaval in Ireland. Following the Civil War, C.S. (Todd) Andrews, who was to play a pivotal role in many semi-state bodies over the following decades, was encouraged by Denis Coffey, President of University College Dublin, to resume studies in accountancy. In his autobiography[3], Andrews describes himself as a 'typical product of UCD', which in turn was a 'high grade technical school'. McLaughlin, who realised the dream of the Shannon Scheme and the ESB, had been an acquaintance of Andrews in UCD, before McLaughlin went to Galway. In 1930, McLaughlin asked Andrews to take a post in the ESB as an accountant. As we have seen, accountancy had become sorely needed in the ESB. Andrews was Chief Accounts Inspector until 1933, bringing to bear (as he says in his autobiography) IRA (Irish Republican Army) organisational methods.

Turf had long been used as a source of fuel, and interest in reclaiming land for agriculture was also of interest at least since the early nineteenth century. Presentations were made to the RDS (Royal Dublin Society) by Professor Hugh Ryan on peat in 1907/1908. In 1918, Professor Purcell presented to the RDS a study of peat in the Canadian context. A Dáil Éireann (Irish Parliament) Commission in 1920, on this theme, was chaired by Hugh Ryan, and in 1922 he translated a seminal book by Hausding – an employee of the German Patent Office – on peat.

Against this history, and with shifting views by pivotal (post-1932 party of government Fianna Fáil) Government figures Seán Lemass and Frank Aiken, Andrews was asked to drive forward the development of national resources based on peat. He was to stay twenty-five years in what was initially the civil service based Turf Development Board, and later from 1946 the autonomous semi-state body, Bord na Móna. In 1935, missions were carried out to north Germany, and to Russia (Moscow, Leningrad). Close contacts were established, and there were further missions in later years. With German equipment and technical support, development work started in 1936, 'as a crusade rather than a commercial project'.

An Experimental Station was set up in Newbridge, Co. Kildare, in 1946, and the First International Peat Symposium in Dublin in 1954 had 200 delegates. It is interesting that conflict with the ESB was to lead to a solution involving some

---

[3]　C.S. Andrews, *Man of No Property* (Dublin: Lilliput Press, 1982).

industrial and university links. After all, power generation through peat burning was, in some degree, in direct competition with hydroelectric and other sources of the ESB's power. Dependence on the ESB's national grid was to be decreased through briquette production. To fund this, Sir Hugh Beaver, managing director of Guinness's stepped in. Notwithstanding opposition by the Minister for Finance, the Goverment was forced to provide collateral for Guinness's support. Jointly, Bord na Móna and Guinness sponsored a Chair of Industrial Microbiology in UCD.

Irish linkage with early molecular biology, and early computing in Ireland

Once again illustrating active and progressive State involvement, the Dublin Institute for Advanced Studies was established in 1940 by Éamon de Valera, who attended many seminars there.

Erwin Schrödinger was appointed first director of the School of Theoretical Physics in the Dublin Institute for Advanced Studies in 1940, and remained there until 1955. It is interesting to note that the discovery of the double-helix structure of DNA by Crick and Watson in 1953 was linked to lectures given by Schrödinger in February 1943 and published afterwards as a book[4], thus testifying to the mutually supporting roles of different disciplines of science. Figure 1 is interesting from my own point of view too, since some time after Crick and Watson's work I grew up a few streets away from where Schrödinger lived in Clontarf, and may – with a small stretch of the imagination – have observed from a baby's pram Schrödinger cycling past on his way into the Institute. Schrödinger's lectures, under the auspices of the Dublin Institute for Advanced Studies, were delivered in Trinity College Dublin in February 1943. In the book[4], resulting from these lectures, Roger Penrose in the foreword indicates how it 'must surely rank among the most influential of scientific writings in [the twentieth] century', stressing in particular its 'cross-disciplinary sweep'.

Serving on the first Governing Board of the School of Theoretical Physics in the Dublin Institute for Advanced Studies was William McCrea. He contributed to the holding of the British Association annual meeting in 1957 in Dublin. I shall return below to the life and work of another outstanding Irish scientist in the last century – John Bell – who contributed to the Belfast meeting of the British Association in 1987.

McCrea[5] (*see also page 28*) was a distinguished astrophysicist, who became a Fellow of the Royal Society and received a knighthood. He was born in Ranelagh, Dublin, in 1904. He was brought up in England, and obtained a PhD in astrophysics in Cambridge in 1929. There followed academic appointments in Mathematics in Edinburgh and Imperial College London, before he became Professor of Mathematics at Queen's University Belfast in 1936. For interest's sake, Ernest Walton took up his studentship at the Cavendish Laboratory in 1927, and returned to a lecturing post in

---

[4] E. Schrödinger, *What is Life? with Mind and Matter and Autobiographical Sketches* (Cambridge: Cambridge University Press, 1967).

[5] P.S. Florides & P. Dolan, 'Professor William Hunter McCrea, FRS, obituary', *IMS Bulletin*, 1999, **43**, pp. 70-72.

Trinity College Dublin in 1934. In 1944, McCrea moved to Royal Holloway, University of London, and in 1966 to the University of Sussex. He died in 1999.

William McCrea's most important work was in solar physics and in relativity theory. During his time in Queen's University Belfast, Armagh Observatory had been in decline, and Dunsink Observatory, then part of Trinity College Dublin, was practically closed. In the late 1930s, then Taoiseach de Valera was advised by McCrea. As a result, Dunsink Observatory, located in north Dublin city, was reopened as part of the Dublin Institute for Advanced Studies.

Figure 1: The birth of molecular biology – acknowledgement of lectures by Erwin Schrödinger, Director, School of Cosmic Physics, Dublin Institute for Advanced Studies, by Francis Crick, Nobel Prize winner with Watson and Wilkins in 1962 for the discovery of the double helix structure of DNA (courtesy of the DIAS)

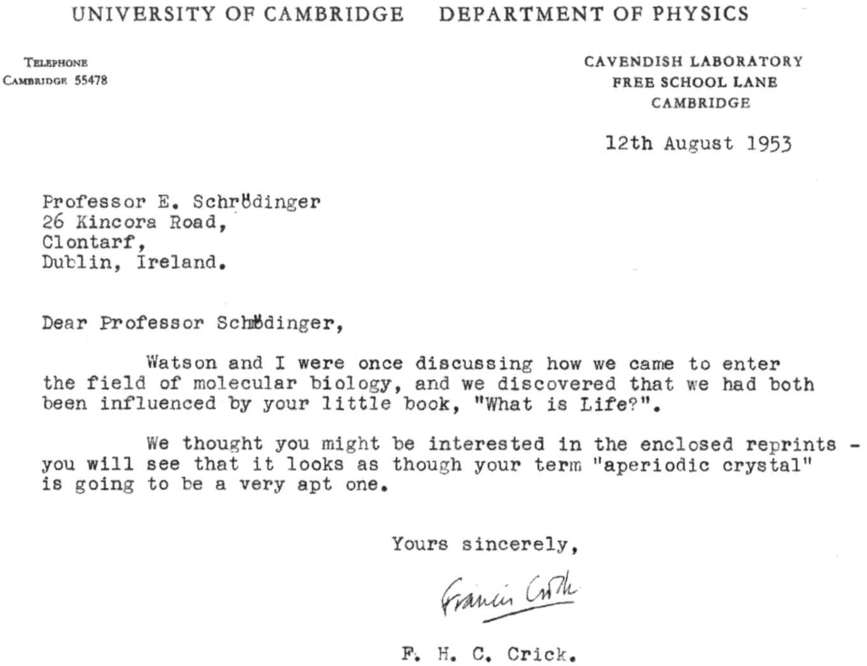

UNIVERSITY OF CAMBRIDGE   DEPARTMENT OF PHYSICS

TELEPHONE
CAMBRIDGE 55478

CAVENDISH LABORATORY
FREE SCHOOL LANE
CAMBRIDGE

12th August 1953

Professor E. Schrödinger
26 Kincora Road,
Clontarf,
Dublin, Ireland.

Dear Professor Schrödinger,

　　　　Watson and I were once discussing how we came to enter the field of molecular biology, and we discovered that we had both been influenced by your little book, "What is Life?".

　　　　We thought you might be interested in the enclosed reprints – you will see that it looks as though your term "aperiodic crystal" is going to be a very apt one.

Yours sincerely,

Francis Crick

F. H. C. Crick.

Interesting reminiscences by R. Johnston[6] include his links with the Dublin Institute for Advanced Studies, which lead on to a description of the early days of computing in Ireland. In 1963, IBM's first realtime commercial systems in Europe were built with Aer Lingus. The first computer science department in Ireland was set up in Queen's University Belfast in 1967. Trinity College Dublin soon followed, in 1969, and John G. Byrne was to lead this until his retirement in 2003. Early work by the faculty in Computer Science in TCD was to run courses for senior civil servants, so that they could become aware of what computerization was all about[7].

---

[6] R.H.W. Johnston, *Century of Endeavour: A Father and Son Overview of the 20th Century* (Academica Press, 2003).

[7] F. Neelamkavil, Professor of Computer Science, Trinity College Dublin, 2004, personal communication.

The Irish Wirtschaftswunder

I have noted that the timeline of the Irish state up to the Celtic Tiger period of economic take-off was very close to the entirety of Hobsbawm's Short Century. While the unrest in Ireland began with the 1916 Easter Rising, this happened against the backdrop of hardly comprehendible slaughter in the trenches of the First World War battlefields.

Garret Fitzgerald, Taoiseach in the 1980s, has raised the interesting economic question[8] as to whether the unrest that gave birth first to the Irish Free State in 1921, and later through constitutional change in 1949 to the Republic of Ireland, was necessary at precisely that time. Some ancillary questions were also raised. Were there particular weaknesses in the ties that bound Ireland and Great Britain around that particular period? And a question that has not been really addressed, and perhaps cannot be easily addressed: how do human and social actors perceive potential social change-points since, after all, such human and social actors do act rightly or wrongly on the basis of a perception or set of perceptions of the framework in which they find themselves. Men make their own history but not in circumstances of their own choosing.

Fitzgerald points to how net inflow of state expenditure in Ireland was, around the 1916 period, soon to change substantially – and hypothetically – to the benefit of Ireland. Later, with the full development of the Welfare State in Britain, it would have been very difficult to countenance a breakaway of a major part of what had been the United Kingdom. In the period of the unrest that gave rise to the independence struggle, there was a divergence in economic interests, in particular from the viewpoint of a largely agricultural Ireland, and a possible need for the industrial protectionism that came about after independence. Such national and state driven economic development became pronounced across most of Europe in the following decades, with the rise of fascist and communist – all protectionist and 'national' – systems.

Fitzgerald's analysis[9] of the Celtic Tiger period from 1993 to 2001 – 'a unique and unrepeatable boom' – is also thought-provoking. Up to 1995 there had been a rapid rise in exports to what is now the European Union (EU). This was in large measure due to US (and Japanese) inward investment to Ireland, with export of goods from the Irish base within the EU mainly in the computer and pharmaceutical sectors. Fitzgerald locates the boom in the ready availability of a highly skilled and honed, young workforce, available precisely when and where needed to take this export-led upturn on the hop, to the level of a boom. In the 1960s, the Irish birth rate had been increasing, unlike elsewhere in Europe, and the educational level of the Irish young was much above the rest of the EU. Other factors complemented this picture: a large, available, skilled female workforce; high unemployment which was skilled and available for absorption into employment; and large numbers of recent (1980s) educated emigrants ready and willing to return to Ireland. Fitzgerald[10] sees the success of Irish inward

---

[8] G. Fitzgerald, *Reflections on the Irish State* (Dublin: Irish Academic Press, 2003).

[9] G. Fitzgerald, 'Anatomy of a unique and unrepeatable boom', *The Irish Times*, 4 Jan. 2003.

[10] G. Fitzgerald, 'Enjoying the dividends of higher education', *The Irish Times*, 31 Jan. 2004.

investment and continuing international linkages, particularly in regard to the US, as being testimony to the solidity and quality of the Irish educational system.

Fitzgerald therefore solidly locates the great Irish economic boom of 1993 to 2001 in human capital. Going further though, he sees all essential factors as neither sustainable nor repeatable, with a falling birth rate, falling numbers in and less attraction towards education, and great decrease in unemployment.

At the time of writing, the jury is still out on whether Ireland's spectacular growth will continue. As the world slowly pulls out of the great recession that started in early 2001, Irish growth rates are above the European average. The educational system is looking a little wobbly, with numbers of students selecting key science and engineering courses on the decrease. High inflation for a period has gone right back to a very small amount. The threatened chaos of strikes in public transport, airport infrastructure, postal services, and health services, have at times been averted and at other times taken place, but soon ended with what appears to be resolution. The bad public transport infrastructure – frankly unpredictable in view of such dramatic growth in the 1993–2001 period – is being addressed slowly but with commendable results.

Will Ireland's above average growth rates continue? This question is important, because it impacts directly on government support for science. In my view, there are other aspects of the current economic situation that should be taken into account, and which should not be discounted. These aspects are the purely scientific and technological ones.

The Irish *Wirtschaftswunder* in later years was closely associated with the dot-com boom. It was, after all, in areas of computing and biosciences that the international economic balloon was most manifest, as companies sought to use their own valuation as a tool to attract, or more often – defensively – to prevent, company take-over. Economic valuation became a means to an end, a marketing ploy related to the financial markets that had become of supreme importance in a world of shareholder value. The 'new economy' was more open to playing such economic games, compared to more traditional sectors, although all were involved in the traditional sectors and the new sectors (Mannesmann and Vodafone, AOL and Time Warner).

If we seek to date the birth of the new economy in the area of computing and information science and technologies, perhaps no better date can be pinpointed than March 1993. This was the month that Marc Andreessen released the Mosaic web browser, the paradigmatic 'killer app' of modern times. Almost overnight, there was take-off of the World-Wide Web, hitherto one of a number of somewhat arcane protocols vying for attention in the sharing of digital information and knowledge (http, WAIS – Wide Area Information System, gopher, ftp and others built on them – archie, Veronica, and similar). The dot-com boom would not have happened were it not for Andreessen's work. And the Irish boom would not have happened without the computer industry. There are linkages here that lead me to the conclusion that one way to prolong Irish growth rates is through innovation in science and in particular in the 'new information science' that underpins all others. Numerically and otherwise the weight of the Irish on planet Earth is not large, so that in the words of an Irish proverb, *An té nach bhfuil láidir, ní foláir dó bheith glic* – someone who is not strong had better be clever. I shall return below to address this point of what is needed now in regard to innovation in key areas of science.

More secular problems for Irish science and technology are thrown up by the international economy. These include science's industrial linkages, Government funding, and the profile of science in the eyes of the young.

In my survey in earlier sections of some grand challenges addressed successfully by the new Irish state, I indicated how industrial linkage, as well as that of Government, were crucial. In Europe generally, though, the private sector is relatively inactive in supporting basic research. It is interesting to note that, in the work of Ireland's one Nobel Prize winner, the Manchester-based company, Metropolitan-Vickers, played quite an important role in the development of Walton's and Cockcroft's equipment, enabled by Cockcroft's previous employment with them.

Based on OECD figures, Ireland does not spend much on R&D[11]: in 2001 the share of the Government budget allocated to indicators defined by the European Commission was 0.77% as opposed to Greece at 0.76%, Portugal at 1.47%, the EU average at 1.99%, Finland at 2.11%, and the Netherlands at 3.25%.

There have been swings of fortune in research funding in Ireland in the past years. The swings of the economy have meant too that student attraction in regard to science, informatics and engineering, has flowed and ebbed.

Scientific cooperation in Europe

In recent decades, a specific area that is important for Irish science is that of linkage with international – mostly on the European level – collaborative research organisations. Such organisations pool resources in order to build expensive research infrastructure. Ireland belongs already to quite a few, and plays its role productively and to the full. Ireland still does not belong to some others, and it is my hope that such lacunae will soon be filled.

In 1954, CERN (Centre Européen pour la Recherche Nucléaire) was established in the field of high energy physics. It straddles the French/Swiss border at Geneva. It is a leader in high energy physics. It also gave birth to the World-Wide Web in that Tim Berners-Lee at CERN developed http (hypertext transfer protocol) around the start of the 1990s. CERN is now playing a leading role at European level in the development of the datagrid, i.e. the federation of massive distributed heterogeneous data collections. Ireland is not a member of CERN, and regrettably is unlikely to become a member soon.

In 1962, the ESO (European Southern Observatory) was established first within CERN and then headquartered at Garching bei München, and over the following decades it built and ran extensive observing facilities in Chile. There are considerable

---

[11] J. Smyth, 'Future of R&D rests on the Government's shoulders', *The Irish Times*, 2 April 2004, 'Business This Week' section, p. 8.

numbers of astronomical observing facilities in the northern hemisphere, and the role of ESO was and is to have a planetary watch and observation activity in the southern hemisphere. I served under Director-Generals of ESO who included Lo Woltjer, Harry van der Laan, and Riccardo Giacconi – the latter getting a Nobel Prize in 2002 for his early work in high energy astronomy. Catherine Cesarsky is the current Director-General. Ireland is not a member of ESO. Astronomy is a field of 'particular national strength' in Ireland. Somewhat paradoxically it is not a field that has priority in any national Irish research plan.

The EMBO (European Molecular Biology Organization) in Heidelberg supports training, and Ireland is a member. The complementary organisation, EMBL (European Molecular Biology Laboratory), also headquartered in Heidelberg, was set up in 1973. Ireland has recently joined EMBL. Particular research strengths of EMBL are gene function research, gene transcription, developmental biology, and bioinformatics.

Ireland also became a member recently of the European Synchrotron Radiation Facility (ESRF), which was established in 1988, and is headquartered in Grenoble. ESRF is involved in pure and applied X-ray photonic research. Applications are in physics, chemistry, materials and the life sciences.

The Georgia Tech appraisal study[12] of research organisations ranked these four inter-governmental, European, research organisations in terms of the full range of potential benefits for Ireland. In terms of highest ranked first, the rank order was: EMBL, ESRF, ESO and CERN. At the time of writing in early 2004, Ireland has now joined the first two on this list.

I shall look briefly at a number of other important organisations at European level, of which Ireland has long held membership.

The more basic science support organisation, the European Science Foundation (ESF), was set up in 1974 and is headquartered in Strasbourg. National member societies of ESF in Ireland are Enterprise Ireland, the Health Research Board, Irish Research Council for Science, Engineering and Technology (IRCSET), the Royal Irish Academy, and the Irish Research Council for Humanities and Social Sciences.

Collaborative European Economic Community – now EU – research policy was initiated with the Joint Research Centres, at locations that included Ispra, Petten, Geel and Karlsruhe. In terms of support for scientists across the European Union, COST (Cooperation in Science and Technology) is the oldest, and still functioning, programme. The first COST Actions were started in 1971. Later, the Framework Programmes came about, beginning in 1983, and these strategic Europe-wide science and technology research and R&D programmes run at approximately four-year intervals. The Seventh Framework Programme is expected to start in 2006. Through membership in the European Union from 1973, Ireland has actively and beneficially been involved in the scientific cooperation embodied in all of these.

---

12 S.E. Cozzens, P. Shapira, J. Krige & A. Porter, *Assessment of Irish Participation in Inter-Governmental Research Organizations*, Final Report (Atlanta: Technology Policy and Assessment Center, Georgia Institute of Technology, Sept. 2001).

Ireland participates in Eureka, a European cooperation facilitator in the area of industrial research and development. Ireland has also long been a member of the European Space Agency, ESA, which, unlike some other European-level research and R&D collaboration organisations, operates the principle of *juste retour*. This means that industrial contracts accruing to a member state are carefully benchmarked against national membership subscription contributions. In the period 1985 to 1999, it is estimated that thirty eight Irish firms participated in ESA activities. Areas of such work included: communications, electronic components, precision engineering, software, and analytical services.

My Hubble Space Telescope (HST) work with ESA included considerable efforts in deconvolution algorithm development and deployment between the launch of HST by the space shuttle *Discovery*, mission STS-31, on 1990/4/25, the discovery of spherical aberration in the 2.4m primary mirror just after launch, and the first refurbishment mission by *Endeavor*, mission STS-61, in December 1993. If information has been lost through faulty telescope mirror construction, there are limits to how far any computational approach can go in undoing the damage. Nonetheless deconvolution played its role in partially correcting the image data, and hence the faulty optics. Such algorithms are in constant use in generating interpretable images from raw medical data, in improving quality of surveillance imagery, and so on.

Science Foundation Ireland (SFI)

In 2000, Science Foundation Ireland was established as a subgroup within Forfás, The National Policy and Advisory Board for Enterprise, Trade, Science, Technology and Innovation. It constituted the 'largest investment in scientific research in [Ireland's] history'[13], with a €646 million budget from the National Development Plan for 2000–2006. Its focus is on two areas, biotechnology and information and communication technologies.

The initial phase of SFI support for research in Ireland came in for considerable criticism by researchers in Irish universities (Stroyan[14], p. 96: points of criticism included funds allocated to physics under the heading of ICT; funds allocated to incoming SFI Principal Investigators rather than those already in the Irish system; and so on). Later SFI funding came to be more oriented towards those already in the Irish research system, and has now included taking over Basic Research funding from Enterprise Ireland. The latter continues to support commercialisation of research.

Computer science in Ireland is characterized by Stroyan[14] as 'not the strongest from a purely scientific perspective', but good on the applied side. There is, this report indicates, 'relatively little fundamental ICT research in Computer Science – industry collaborations and funding … dominate and drive research', which is not in itself a bad thing. The definition of ICT is broad: praise is given to materials research – magnetic

---

[13] Science Foundation Ireland, *Vision and Goals*, 2003.

[14] J. Stroyan et al., *Baseline Assessment of the Public Research System in Ireland in the Areas of Biotechnology and Information and Communication Technologies* (Dublin: SFI and Forfás, Aug. 2002), pp. 118.

materials, optronics – and physics-oriented, and Mathematics Department based, high performance computing. The report notes that Irish computer science is motivated and highly professional, and well linked with European Framework Programmes.

It is also stated that 'An area of Irish strength is scientific computing, which appeared in many forms – sometimes appearing as inter-disciplinary scientific computing, or as parallel computing, or as basic applied mathematics'. It does not appear to have been highlighted here nor elsewhere that this is precisely a key area of importance for Irish membership of European collaborative research organisations – EMBL, but also ESO and CERN. CERN is playing a leading role in datagrid projects, ESO combines virtual observatory and virtual data analysis with optics and photonics, and so on. Given the computing and instrumentation aspects of modern observational astronomy, it was not surprising that Finland's membership of ESO in 2004 involved a substantial contribution in person-years of software development.

SFI's initial phase was to inject fresh blood into the Irish system, essentially through the Principal Investigator programme. It then evolved into greater support for established researchers.

John Bell and the greatest achievement of Irish science in the last century

I have deliberately held my discussion of the life and work of John Bell until I had first sketched out official Irish links with CERN, and also described current mainline Irish policy in regard to scientific research. The career of John Bell (*see also page 71*) illustrates just how important a part an organisation like CERN plays in scientific achievement, and by implication its important role in Irish science. Furthermore, Bell's fundamental contributions to quantum theory, 'the most successful scientific theory of all time'[15], has immediate and direct results in the new science of quantum computing and quantum information theory[16].

Bell lectured to the British Association meeting in Belfast in 1987. We have already seen that another great name of Irish science in the last century, William McCrea, had contributed to the British Association meeting in Dublin in 1957.

Bell ranked far and above all Irish scientists in the twentieth century. I make this claim not just because of his work in physics, considered as the 'queen of the sciences' in the last century: his experimental work was in a direct line of descent from Walton and Cockcrofts's work in 1932 (resulting in their Nobel Prize in 1951), and his productive intervention in quantum theory took up earlier work of Einstein and Bohr. I also claim Bell as the greatest of Irish scientists in recent decades because of his contributions to the queen of the sciences in the current century, *viz.* the information sciences.

John Stewart Bell was born in Belfast in 1928. He entered Physics in Queen's University Belfast, initially as a technician due to his family's poor financial situation, but he went on to graduate in experimental physics in 1948, and mathematical physics

---

[15] A. Whitaker, 'John Bell and the most profound discovery of science', *Physics World*, 1988, 12.

[16] M.A. Nielsen & I.L. Chuang, *Quantum Computation and Quantum Information* (Cambridge: Cambridge University Press, 2000).

in 1949. Bell then moved to the UK Atomic Energy Research Establishment (AERE), Harwell, working in accelerator design, and more particularly modelling the paths of charged particles through accelerator detectors. This led to consultancy for the design of a Proton Synchrotron at CERN. Bell spent a year at Birmingham University, with Rudolf Peierls, and returned to elementary particle physics work at Harwell. His PhD was completed in 1956. In 1960, Bell moved to CERN. His work was directed towards high-energy physics and field theory. His most important contributions were in theory. He provided clarification on the Einstein-Podolsky-Rosen (EPR) paradox[17] which later was to be applied in quantum computing and quantum information theory. Bell's contributions to quantum theory have been characterized as 'the most profound discovery of science' (quoted in Whitaker). In a career that was suddenly cut short, Bell died of a stroke in 1990.

The Institutional Framework: the Irish Universities and Institutes of Technology

There are seven universities in the Republic of Ireland (and two in Northern Ireland), and with these one should consider the Institutes of Technology, of which there are thirteen in the Republic. The organizational frameworks of the universities and institutes of technology differ. I shall express the view here that the lack of close research integration between the two sectors is a great pity, but I shall not go into the reasons for this, beyond noting that there is far greater integration to be found in our European neighbours. We can consider the Fachhochschule in Germany, the Institut Universitaire de Technologie in France, and the 'new university' in the UK, to indicate a few examples of perception which do not countenance sharp divisions.

Ireland does not have national research organisations governed by fixed annual grant allocations in areas such as computing science and engineering, physics and chemistry, along the lines of CNRS in France, CSIC in Spain, CNR in Italy, MPI in Germany, etc. However, university-affiliated organisations have come to play an important regional role, e.g. the National Microelectronics Research Centre (NMRC) in NUI Cork, or the Research Institute for Networks and Communications Engineering (RINCE) in Dublin City University. In addition, the SFI Principal Investigator programme has similarities with the CNRS research affiliation to host institutes.

Irish universities have not really had a good press. Narrating the story of Walton's work on the splitting of the atomic nucleus in 1932 in Rutherford's Cavendish Laboratory in Cambridge, for which he and Cockcroft in late 1951 were awarded the Nobel Prize, Cathcart[1] says that Walton left the 'scientific backwater' of Trinity College Dublin in 1927, and returned to the faculty there in 1934 with 'a heavy teaching load [that] left him almost no time for research'. (It should be noted, though, that TCD had a distinguished scientific history, particularly in the nineteenth century – see chapter 2 in this volume.) Lee[18] is scathing: regarding the National University of Ireland and

[17] P.C.W. Davies & J.R. Brown, *The Ghost in the Atom* (Cambridge: Cambridge University Press, 1986).
[18] J.J. Lee, *Ireland 1912-1985: Politics and Society* (Cambridge: Cambridge University Press, 1989).

Trinity College Dublin, he says that 'it would be difficult to decide which of the two practised the more ambitious neglect [i.e. of building the Irish nation] in the first generation of independence'. Lee talks of 'Irish retardation' in mobilizing the intellectual resources of the country, and points towards the administration of the universities. 'Close examination of the performance of most presidents, provosts, registrars, finance officers and other relevant university officials has yet to be undertaken.' This is not entirely fair. We have seen that very important grand challenges were realised in the Ireland of Hobsbawm's Short Century. Nonetheless it would be useful to have performance ratings openly and regularly published in the national press.

Of greater import is that the university as an institution is changing, and changing fast. Scott[19] points to how the modern university has come about by and large 'alongside the idea of the state'. Universities that predated the state were fundamentally remoulded by the state. Even in the case of Oxford and Cambridge in the UK, Scott points to Royal Commissions in the nineteenth century, driving forward reform. The Humboldtian university, embracing research as well as teaching, was a central part of the modernization strategy of Prussia. The Humboldt ideal rests on three principles: the unity of science; the unity of teaching and research; and the essential paedagogical role of the scientific method. Land grant universities in the US were to promote agriculture. In a thoughtful essay, Scott (Vice-Chancellor of Kingston University) shows how universities have had internationalist agendas but in the national interest. Universities have shown themselves reluctant to engage in the fast-moving trend towards globalization. Current debates about increased fees to be levied on students – in Ireland as elsewhere – are part of this change of perspective on what the university is, and how it relates to other components in society (state, health sector, and so on). However, for Scott the real challenge is not the New Economy but rather the New Culture of globalization.

The principal forms of Scott's New Culture are related to the Knowledge Society brought about by twenty-first century forms of globalization. These forms include 'remorseless acceleration' of information and communication technologies; and the centrality of uncertainty and risk. Scott advances convincing perspectives on what this means for educational content. Research for Scott, however, is perhaps overly linked to the university's role in technology transfer, commercialisation, regional (re)generation, and wealth creation.

Comparative evaluation of research in Ireland is discussed in von Tunzelmann and Krameer Mbula[20]. The focus is on evaluation governance, i.e. structure of evaluation, control and process. A wide range of other countries are contrasted – Flanders (Belgium), France, Switzerland, Denmark, Norway, Sweden, Finland, Taiwan and elsewhere. While Ireland has approached international norms in science, technology and innovation, it is stated, it lags behind OECD (Organisation for Economic

---

[19] P. Scott, 'The impact of globalization on universities', Talk given to the National Conference of University Professors (UK), London, 17 January 2004, 10 pp.

[20] N. von Tunzelmann & E. Kraemer Mbula, *Changes in Research Assessment Practices in Other Countries since 1999*, Final Report (Sussex: SPRU – Science Policy Research Unit, University of Sussex, Feb. 2003).

Cooperation and Development, affiliated to the United Nations) countries in evaluation. Inputs are quite well monitored, it claims, but not outputs nor impacts. From 1997, a quality assessment programme has been implemented in Irish universities, based both on self-assessment and external peer review. This quality assessment programme is called QAQI, Quality Assurance/Quality Improvement. A number of benchmarking studies have been carried out by ICSTI, the Irish Council for Science, Technology and Innovation.

Quantitative comparative evaluation of second-level education has been published in Irish newspapers, and recently *The Sunday Times*, which publishes an Irish edition, has included a league table of third level institutions in Ireland in its annual 'University Guide'[21]. (Rankings of universities and university departments in the UK and Europe have been published in newspapers like the *Guardian*, *The Times*, and in the German weekly *Der Spiegel*.) Such assessments should surely be carried out on a regular basis. Rankings are beneficial for potential graduate students, industrial linkages, international collaborations, and more.

In Europe-wide rankings, Irish university departments have done well. In a comparative ranking of university departments by discipline in *Der Spiegel*, Electrical Engineering in University College Dublin came second overall in Europe. Stroyan et al. point to two world-class departments in Ireland within SFI's biotechnology remit – Genetics, TCD, and Biochemistry, UCC. The 2003 'Academic Ranking of World Universities'[22] from the Institute of Higher Education, Shanghai Jiao Tong University, has been less happy for Irish universities, with none featuring.

It would be also interesting to have an explicit application of the UK's Research Assessment Exercise criteria applied to Irish universities, not least because it would provide quantitative comparative assessment with the two Northern Irish universities. Limited and all as any such quantitative assessment must be, it is widely recognized that it helps in imparting clear goals and objectives to all of those working in the system. It also lends some impetus to the clustering of expertise, and therefore is one way to tackle the disadvantage of lack of critical mass found at times for Irish research. Personnel movements between Irish universities and institutes of technology are rare and far between. (Here I consider the Republic of Ireland only; the situation is quite different in Northern Ireland.)

The form of output of science: the publication system

In previous sections, I have essentially taken a top-down (governance, influence, motivation) perspective, or indeed an external-internal (social) perspective. From now on, I shall turn to a more bottom-up or internal perspective – from the 'coal face' as it were.

My own view is that the changing times we live in offer new grist for the mill of the researchers. The social and institutional changes we are witness to can perhaps be used

---

[21] Ian Coxon (Ed), *The Sunday Times University Guide*, published with the Edition of 12 September 2004.
[22] Institute of Higher Education, Shanghai Jiao Tong University, 'Academic Ranking of World Universities 2003', ed.sjtu.edu.cn

as a weapon to take on one traditional view of research, which is to dig oneself ever deeper into one's specialism. Instead I counterpose Thomas Jefferson's dictum that one should 'Always work on important problems'[23]. As the Editor-in-Chief of one of the world's leading computer science journals, I have from time to time to deal with a submission of impeccable credentials and presentation; but a judgement is not made easy if the author is the sole and unique world expert in this subfield – leading on to the need for a judgement on the importance of the subfield.

Before taking a look at some aspects of international comparisons of Irish productivity in science, mathematics and engineering, it is useful for the general reader to point out that, since about 1665 – for it was in that year that the journals *Journal des Scavants* in France, and the *Philosophical Transactions* in England, began – the yardstick of quality of research has been peer-reviewed journal publication. Unlike our colleagues in the social sciences, the book form of publication is far less relevant, with only the research monograph being of importance in science.

Between different fields, the peer-review journal system can be quite diverse. I shall take the cases of astronomy (say, the European journal, *Astronomy and Astrophysics*) and more methodological areas such as computer science, signal processing, or statistics. I once marvelled at an announcement that referee review of submissions to a journal would be forthcoming within 24 hours: obviously the theme was an observational one – astronomy, in this case. In statistics, or mathematical engineering fields, one could well wait for one year before the first round of referee reports. The *Computer Journal* has first round referee reports generally available within six to seven weeks. In astronomy, generally there is one referee. In computer science and statistics, generally there are three. As Editor-in-Chief, I did once have to handle a submission where there were eighteen referees! Needless to say, decision-making is if anything made more difficult in such a situation. The custodians of research are the referees, and their role is an unpaid one, an unsung one and, nearly always, an anonymous one. Finding referees to match against a given journal submission is not an easy job: a typical rate of acceptance to do the job is one in two. Helping this matching process is how researchers describe their expertise in their own web site – a widespread and near universal practice in North America, Europe, and Australia/New Zealand, but less so in East and South Asia. Clearly, the entire practice of scientific research has changed totally since 1993, following the take-off of the web.

The changes brought about by the web and, more particularly, by content based access (through indexing engines such as Google), have had pronounced beneficial effects on the research system. Access to desired information has become, in many cases, immediate and quite high in precision. Because they are content-indexed, journals are far more useful online rather than on the library shelf. Pricing has become mainly institutional, with regional library consortia negotiating subscription prices for their (library) members. Most journals are now happy for authors to have their

---

[23] A. Jones, Professor, University of Maryland, and US Governmental advisor on computer science, keynote talk at Grand Challenges Conference, Newcastle (GB), March 2004.

published papers additionally on their own web sites. Indeed, the same is happening for books, with the online version raising the interest of the reader to proceed to buy the far more convenient form of bound printed copy.

Europe outperforms the US with 41.3% of the world scientific literature, compared to 31.4%. However, on citation counts, the US is about one-third ahead[24]. A breakdown by field shows that the US and Europe are comparable in the earth sciences, mathematics and agricultural research. But US lead is evidenced in physics and medicine, and more so in chemistry and basic life sciences. In the computer sciences, the lead of the US, with Israel, is large. Among reasons advanced for why Europe lags behind, there is (i) lack of coordination and cooperation; and (ii) lack of critical mass.

The Georgia Tech study[12] of the potential in Irish membership through buy-in to European-level research organisations carried out a scientific productivity analysis in the relevant areas of science. Using the Science Citation Index, firstly authorship (at least one author) was sought where there was a link with the European research organisation. Considered were: CERN, EMBL, ESO and ESRF. Next, the most common keywords associated with articles authored in this way were found. Finally, Irish authorship was determined, based on at least one author being affiliated with an Irish institute. Ireland (based on the last criterion) produces 0.31% of all papers indexed by the Science Citation Index. The total numbers of papers found for CERN, EMBL, ESO and ESRF were, respectively: 111,422; 243,199; 19,368; and 189,937. The percentages of Irish participation in the fields represented by these organisations were, respectively: 0.28%; 0.33%; 0.39%; and 0.23%. Thus in molecular biology, and more so in astronomy, Ireland by this analysis is over par. Cozzens et al.[12] also note that these fields are high impact fields in regard to Irish research output.

Current national science, mathematics and engineering priorities in the international context: the need for grand challenges

What Irish research science needs is one or more grand challenges, set by the research community, and serving to channel and focus not just research funding, but also the endeavours and energy of teams and individuals. The decadal plan in US astronomy has served to focus the community, raising challenges that are achievable, ranking facilities to be built, instrumentation to be developed, and approaches to knowledge discovery. Community cohesion helps to avoid the worst excesses of internal competition in proposal writing that is wasteful of precious time and energy.

I shall focus my comments on the biosciences and on the computing sciences, since they comprise the major focus of Irish national policy in regard to science funding.

The information theoretic and computational underpinnings of the biosciences have been well-described by Kovac[25] (General Manager, IBM Life Sciences): 'The bridges that are linking information scientists and technologists and biologists are

---

[24] CEC, *Communication from the Commission: Europe and Basic Research*, CEC, Brussels, COM (2004), 9 final, 14 Jan. 2004, 14 pp.

[25] C. Kovac, 'Turing Lecture 2003: Computing in the age of the genome', *The Computer Journal*, 2003, 46, pp. 593-597.

growing stronger every day, and forming the basis for unprecedented scientific discovery'. On the horizon is a humane and client-friendly health care system, an 'information-based medicine', where medical treatment is no longer based on global 'best fit' criteria, but instead is customized and indeed optimized for the individual's well-being and propensity to benefit healthwise over time. This is based on understanding of the individual genetic make-up and what results from this. It is backed up by industrial production approaches in medicaid that allow for individual optimisation rather that the traditional ensemble optimisation. The latter is acceptable to the economist, and has brought about inestimable gains through the improvement in public health (keyword: life expectancy) in the past centuries. However the former – 'personalized optimization' – is also economically important.

In most respects, the biosciences have as underpinnings the computer and information sciences. It is information science, after all, that handles real-world phenomena and observables, but additionally human cognition and perception are based on information in its myriad forms. It is these that are fundamental to human thinking, and as such have primacy over all other sciences. Grand challenges have been launched in computer science in the US and in the UK in recent years. Among other areas, in the US, 'Information Systems' and 'Information Assurance' have been selected as areas of grand challenge. In the computer and information sciences, in general, there is less common focus than, for example, in the biosciences. However let me comment a little further on where Irish grand challenges in our social information infrastructure could be best pursued.

Unlike e-science and the Grid in the UK, aiming at the next generation Internet through jointly developed university/industial middleware platforms, there is no highly visible Irish national orientation. There is no national computing institute like INRIA (Institut National de la Recherche en Informatique et Automatique) in France, or the Fraunhofer/GMD in Germany. The 'communications' in ICT is an anachronism from the dot-com days when telecommunications became all the rage for a period. The most striking manifestation of this was the enormous sums expended on buying 3G (third generation telephony) licences. Nicolas Negroponte of MIT's Digital Media Lab went on record at the time to say that 3G licencing amounted to selling off the irreplaceable communications heirloom of near future generations.

Computing science and engineering could be very validly associated with domains other than just communications, for example the neurosciences, cognition and consciousness; or biomedicine. The very success of computer science has at times been something of a problem. It has been held, for example, that the objective of artificial intelligence has not been realised. However, speech-based systems, responsive and interactive user interfaces, trainable learning machines, Bayesian reasoning and inference systems, have all entered the mainstream and thereby have ceased to be 'artificial' in any way.

It is surprising in fact that no-one associates computer science with potential centre stage solutions for the burgeoning problems of the health sector in our society, or the less prominent but also problematic evolution of the education sector. Compared to these social challenges, communications in the narrow sense (mobile telephony for voice and data) is very limited. The European Framework programmes do target social goals. Design by committee though is not a recipe for clarity of resolve, manoeuverability is limited in the extreme, and there is minimal (if any) linkage with national funding frameworks. In association with recent work on Grid technologies, the 'virtual organisation' has been advanced as an expression for e.g. a car producer with engineering offices in Germany and design studios in California. This too represents a potent grand challenge for science in our time.

An institutional framework issue, that is in a sense a grand challenge, is getting the mix right between innovation and intellectual property. US patenting is based on 'first to invent' and not European-style 'first to file'. In the US, up to one year's grace period is allowed the inventor during which publications can be made. In Japan, the period is six months. In Europe, though, there is a ban on any prior publication[26]. I have more sympathy for the US system in that it does not lead to the polarity of open publication versus non-disclosure and/or costly filing that the European 'first to file' system requires.

The Bayh-Dole legislation passed in the US in 1980 provided for university commercial exploitation of federally-funded work. It has frequently been pointed to as an important enabling basis for technology transfer and spinout from university research.

My starting point has been that essential questions of the day have not – so far – been addressed in a way that would serve to stamp self-confident and authoritative direction on Irish research in relevant areas. I have tentatively raised, as one possible grand challenge, the full deployment of computer and information science perspectives on the burgeoning problems of the health sector (including[27] but not restricted to telemedicine, customized and individually optimised treatment, information content and services based on virtual environments and augmented reality, …). It is not my objective to draw conclusions on what form near future grand challenges could take. In this chapter I want essentially to raise the question: Will Irish science stake out a claim to unique, ambitious, challenging objectives, which will differentiate it from others elsewhere and achieve advanced levels of innovation?

My survey of Irish science with its international dimension has taken us through various grand challenges. Some past achievements have been signalled. I have highlighted the constructive and indeed at times creative interlocking of the State, industry and scientific research. In describing current directions, I have pointed to some curious gaps in coverage. Remedying these could well lead to improved social return. Furthermore, linkage with possible grand challenges ensue. Community-inspired grand challenges would serve to provide leadership and to limit wastage in

---

26 J. Adams et al., Working Paper, *Expert Group Report on Role and Strategic Use of IPR (Intellectual Property Rights) in International Research Collaborations*, Final Report, April 2002, European Commission, Directorate General Research, EUR 20230, 61 pp.

27 F. Murtagh, J. Keating, S. Bergin, C. Harper, G. McParland & M. Farid, *The Evolution of Telecom Technologies: Current Trends and Near-Future Implications*, Report (Armagh: Centre for Cross Border Studies, 2002).

innovation, which constitutes *the* most important aspect of the Irish *patrimoine* (cultural heritage) in this period.

Conclusion

In this survey, I have included mention of the contributions by McCrea and Bell to the British Association meetings in Dublin in 1957, and in Belfast in 1987. I have shown how proactive State support has, at times, led to stunning research and engineering accomplishments in Irish science in the past. I have shown too that current Irish research funding is focused towards computing sciences and biosciences. It is in these fields – not exclusively but in some measure with certainty – that we can expect great achievements in the coming years.

I have also noted Irish pre-eminence in scientific computing. It is strange that there is a major lacuna at the core of Irish scientific research: that Ireland still does not play its rightful role in the ESO, and in CERN, the European high energy physics research centre. The career of John Bell, the greatest Irish scientist of the twentieth century, should suffice to show the potential gain for young (and indeed older) Irish scientists. The sciences of the future that underpin all others, including physics and the biosciences, *viz.* the information and computational sciences, are integrally linked to the work of ESO and CERN in such areas as the datagrid and virtual organisations, and quantum computing and quantum information theory. It is to be hoped that this major gap at the core of Irish science will be soon filled.

Index